William Greenwell, George J. Armytage, Cathedral of Durham

The Baptismal, Marriage and Burial Registers

of the Cathedral church of Christ and Blessed Mary the virgin at Durham,

1609-1896

William Greenwell, George J. Armytage, Cathedral of Durham

The Baptismal, Marriage and Burial Registers
of the Cathedral church of Christ and Blessed Mary the virgin at Durham, 1609-1896

ISBN/EAN: 9783337264161

Printed in Europe, USA, Canada, Australia, Japan

Cover: Foto ©Lupo / pixelio.de

More available books at **www.hansebooks.com**

THE
Baptismal, Marriage, and Burial Registers

OF THE

Cathedral Church

of Christ and Blessed Mary the Virgin

AT

Durham,

1609—1896.

TRANSCRIBED AND ANNOTATED BY

EDWARD ARTHUR WHITE, F.S.A., DECEASED,

AND

EDITED FOR THE HARLEIAN SOCIETY BY

GEORGE J. ARMYTAGE, F.S.A.,
HONORARY SECRETARY OF THAT SOCIETY.

LONDON:

1897.

TO

Her Majesty the Queen

THIS VOLUME

IS, BY HER GRACIOUS PERMISSION, RESPECTFULLY

DEDICATED.

Preface.

This Volume contains a complete transcript of the Registers of Durham Cathedral from the first entry on the 23rd of September 1609 to the end of the year 1896. They were transcribed for the Harleian Society as far as the year 1877 by the late Captain EDWARD A. WHITE, F.S.A. (the permission of the Dean and Chapter having been obtained in November 1876), and his leisure time for several years was occupied in annotating the numerous entries.

The publication was, however, deferred from different causes; and ill-health, and eventually the lamented death, of Captain WHITE prevented the completion of the work.

His Sister, Miss ELLA WHITE, however, most kindly handed over the manuscript to the Society, and, by the desire of the Council, I have undertaken the completion of the Work.

The manuscripts contained a complete and accurate transcript of the Register and a book of Notes to the various entries. By the help of Canon GREENWELL, the whole of the proofs of the Register has been compared with the original, and the Members of the Society are deeply indebted to him for the generous assistance he has thus given to the Work.

The Notes have been transcribed from Captain WHITE's manuscripts, except in the cases where he referred to certain pedigrees which he had compiled, in which case the notes thus referred to have been abstracted from the pedigrees by the Editor, and acknowledged accordingly.

A few loose notes by Captain WHITE contain the following remarks, which I think it is desirable to print fully :—

'Where "the College" is mentioned it refers to the enclosure or *collegium* (*i.e.* Collection) of prebendal houses lying at the south side of the Cathedral, which is so termed at Durham, and answers to the "Precincts" or "Close" of other Cathedral towns.

'"Bow Church" refers to St. Mary-le-Bow; locally "Big Bow." St. Mary's refers to St. Mary's in the South Bailey, or, as it is now commonly called, St. Mary-the-Less; and locally, but very wrongly, "Little Bow."

'"Crossgate" refers to St. Margaret's, Crossgate, and Elvet to St. Oswald's, Elvet. These being without the City proper and places of themselves being styled legally Crossgate and Elvet *in the County of Durham*.

'"Baliva" is the Bailey, the long narrow winding street running round the Abbey; "Baliva Boreali" and "Baliva Australi" being the North and South Bailey.

'Colonel Chester's invaluable "Registers of Westminster Abbey"* first prompted me to do the same for my own Cathedral. Then when I compared my Work with his I began to think I had been too ambitious, and my heart frequently failed me. Colonel Chester, however, took much interest in the work, and frequently wrote to cheer me and urge me on.

'I hope it may find some favour with the Members of the Society, and that it will be received in the Cathedral City as a not unwelcome addition to the domestic history of her Citizens.'

The text of the Work is a true transcript of the original, omitting only such constantly occurring phrases, as " were married," etc.

In annotating, Captain WHITE has followed Colonel CHESTER's plan very closely, especially in taking as much pains in elucidating the particulars of persons in humble positions as of those of superior rank.

The following is a table of the Contents of the Registers :—

Vol.	Baptisms.	Marriages.	Burials.
I.	1609—1720	1610—1723	1611—1678
II.	1726—1812	1723—1836	1678—1812
III.	1813—1896	1883—1896	1813—1896

Like most Cathedral Registers, the entries principally relate to the Clergy and the families within the precincts, who were mostly connected with the Cathedral.

* Published by this Society in 1875, as Vol. X.

I do not propose to make special reference to the many distinguished persons who are mentioned in these Registers. Their names are fully set forth in the Index, and considerable biographical notes will be found in the text.

It is interesting to call attention to the Burials in Woollen at page 100. They refer to an Act of 1666 (18 and 19 Car. II., cap. 4), made more stringent by one in 1678 (30 Car. II., cap. 3), for burying in Woollen; the object being to lessen the importation of linen and to encourage the woollen and paper manufactories of the Kingdom. The first Act enacted that after March 25, 1667, no person should be "buried in any shirt, shift, or sheete other than should be made of wooll onely." These Acts, however, fell into disuse long before their final repeal in 1814.*

The entries subsequent to Captain WHITE's manuscript have been transcribed by Canon GREENWELL, and I venture once more to express, on behalf of the Members of the Society, their thanks for this additional assistance to the undertaking.

It now remains only for me to state that in 1891 Captain WHITE obtained the permission of THE QUEEN to dedicate this Work to HER MAJESTY, and that, on renewing the application on the completion of the Work, I have had the honour to receive HER MAJESTY's most gracious continuation of that permission.

GEO. J. ARMYTAGE,

Hon. Secretary,

HARLEIAN SOCIETY.

---

* In a Work entitled " Parish Registers in England," by R. E. Chester Waters (new edition, 1883), the whole matter is set out and adequately discussed.

The Registers of Durham Cathedral.

BAPTISMES.

1609 Sep. 23 William, sonne of Edward Smith.¹
1610 Feb. 28 Robert, sonne of Edward Smith.²
1611 Nov. 24 Ciprian Suddick,³ sonne of Mʳ George Suddick, divinitie lecturer in this Cathedrall Church. Mʳ John Barnes, esquier, Mʳ John Richeson the yonger, gentleman, and Mʳˢ Cooper, witnessies.
1612 May 6 Edward, sonne of Edward Smith.⁴
1615 July 2 James Huchinson,⁵ sonne of Mʳ Richard Huchinson, Organest in this Cathedrall Church.
1621 Mar. 24 Richard,⁶ sonne of Mʳ John Robson, parson of Morpeth, in this Cathedrall Church (upon Sonday). The right wo. Rich. Hunt, Deane of Durham, Doctor Cradock, and Mʳⁱˢ Birket, sueities. This child was yᵉ first that was baptized in yᵉ newe fonte.
1622 May 26 Dorothie,⁷ dau. of Mʳ [*blank*] Midford of [*blank*] (upon Sonday). Mʳ Jo. Cradocke, Mistris Dorothie Cradocke, and Jane Cradocke were souereties.

---

¹, ², ⁴ The father organist of the Cathedral; see his burial 4 Feb. 1611-12.

³ Dr. Suddick, the father, was son of Philip Suddick of Monk Hesleden, co. Pal., gent., and named by him in his will dated 14 Nov. 1623. See the marriage of his niece (?) 8 Nov. 1639. [Richard, son of Philip Suddick, cordwainer, baptized 4 April 1689 at St. Nicholas. There are also several Philip and other Suddicks at St. Oswald's.]

⁵ The father occurs as organist as late as 20 June 1634 in the Treasurer's Accounts, but not so on 30 Sep. following; see (perhaps) his burial 26 July 1666. For the sponsors see Mr. Barnes's burial 19 July 1613; Mr. Richardson's 7 Feb. 1639-40. Mrs. Cooper was second wife of the singingman, whose burial see 18 Nov. 1623.

⁶ See his burial 28 March 1644, and his father's 12 April 1645. The mother was Margaret, dau. of Dr. Cradock, prebendary, whose burial see 30 Dec. 1627. Of the sponsors, see Dr. Hunt's burial 3 Nov. 1638. Mrs. Birkett was wife of the prebendary Dr. Birkhead, whose burial see 27 Nov. 1624. "Yᵉ newe fonte" was not the present unworthy pseudo-Norman one which yet remains, testifying to the terrible series of "improvements" carried out at the commencement of Dr. Waddington's Deanship.

⁷ The father's name John; see the baptism of her sister Anne 30 Nov. 1626, and brother Bulmer 11 May 1623. The mother [probably Anne, baptized 16 Sep. 1599 at Gainford] was dau. of Dr. Cradock, whose burial see 30 Dec. 1627.

1624 Feb. — Johannes,[1] filius M[ri] Johannis Robson, p'bendarii, & rectoris de Morpeth. Johanne Cradock, generoso, et Richardo Cradock, & uxore D[ris] Clerke, sponsoribus.

1622 July 7 Richard,[2] sonne of M[r] James, prebend. M[r] Geo. Walton (for Mister Deane), M[r] Edward James, and M[ris] Ewbanke, suerties.

1623 April 20 Elizabeth,[3] dau. of M[r] Nicholas Heath. M[r] Clarke, M[ris] Smyth, and M[ris] Martyne, suerties.

April 29 Elizabeth, dau. of Jo. Awbrey.[4] Christopher Boucke, Elizabeth Rangall, and [blank].

May 11 Bulmer,[5] sonne of M[r] [blank] Midford. Sir Bartram Bulmer, Knight, Doctor Cradocke, & M[r] John Robson, suerties.

1624 April 1 Harrie,[6] sonne of M[r] Will'm James, prebend. M[r] Ewb., M[r] Clarke, sponsores.

1625 April 20 Anne,[7] dau. of M[r] Will'm James, prebend.

June 21 Marian,[8] dau. of Jo. Awbree.

Nov. 12 Sarah,[9] dau. of M[r] Lyveley.

Feb. 9 John,[10] sonne of Richard Curtious.

Mar. 16 Sarah,[11] dau. of M[r] Fardinando Morecroft.

---

[1] He was admitted at St. Peter's College, Cambridge, same day as his brother Richard (see *ante*), and was the only surviving son at the date of the will of his father, whose burial see 12 April 1645. The sponsors were two sons of the prebendary. [Mrs. (Mildred) Clerke was the wife of Gabriel Clarke, D.D., Archdeacon and Prebendary of Durham. See her burial 14 Nov. 1659, in the Cathedral. MS. Ped. by E. A. W.]

[2] See his burial 15 Sep. 1623. Of the sponsors, Edward James was third son of Richard James, a brother of Bishop James, but who does not appear in Surtees' pedigree, vol. i., 216; Mr. Walton, the Dean's proxy, was Mayor in 1616; Mrs. Ewbanke, wife of the prebendary.

[3] Eldest child; afterwards wife of Archibald Waddell. Her father of Little Eden, co. Pal., Esq. See Surtees' pedigree, i. 38, to which this baptism adds.

[4] John Aubrey and Alice Page were married 17 April 1620 at Darlington. Mr. Boycke or Boucke, a sponsor, was probably Rector of St. Mary's in the South Bailey, although his name has not appeared in the list of rectors; he married there, 9 Nov. 1596, Anne Rothwell, by whom he had nine children, bapt. there and at Billingham, of which he was made vicar 1603, and where both he and his wife are buried. Elizabeth Rangall was widow of John Rangall, buried 6 Jan. 1622-3.

[5] See his sister's baptism 26 May 1622. Sir Bertram Bulmer, a sponsor, was of Tursdale, co. Pal.; he married at Ryton, 13 July 1600, Isabel, oldest dau. of Sir Nich. Tempest of Stella, first Bart., and was buried 6 May 1638, aged 54, at St. Oswald's. Doctor Cradock and Mr. Robson were prebendaries.

[6,7] See their father's burial 21 Jan. 1659-60.

[8] See her sister's baptism 29 April 1623.

[9] Her father, B.D., Vicar of Gainford and of Kelloe 1625—1651, was probably brother to Edward Lively, constable of Durham Castle under Bishop Neile. She married Anthony Richardson, and was living and had a son Ralph 3 March 1650-51, the date of her father's will. The "Bishoprick Garland" says:

"Here lies John Lively, vicar of Kelloe;
He had seven daughters and never a fellow."

[10] See the father's burial 30 June 1670.

[11] She married 20 June 1649, at Merrington, Francis Gaynes (baptized 23 Aug. 1618 at Heighington) of School-Aycliffe, co. Pal., son of Christopher Gaynes of the same place, gent., by his wife Eleanor Hall of Newsham. They had issue Christopher, baptized 16 April 1650; Margaret, 28 Oct. 1651; Frances, 11 June 1654; Anthony, born 9 April 1656; Sarah, 7 July 1659; and Jane, 13 May 1662; all baptized at Heighington.

CATHEDRAL CHURCH AT DURHAM. 3

1626 Nov. 30 Anne,[1] dau. of M[r] John Midford (sonne in law to M[r] Doct. Cradocke).
        Nov. 30 Katherine,[2] dau. of M[r] John Lively.
1627 June 3 Elizabeth,[3] dau. of M[r] William James.
        Feb. 24 George,[4] sonne of M[r] John Cosins, Prebendary. Sir George Toong, M[r] Marmaduke Blaikston, prebendary, godfathers; M[ris] James, godmother.
1628 Sep. 7 Susanna,[5] dau. of Xpofer Cookeson. M[r] Robt. Pleasant, M[ris] Susanna Smart, & M[ris] Eliza Cook, surties.
1629 Aug. 30 Francis,[6] dau. of Xpofer Richardson, tanner.
1631 April 25 Elizabeth,[7] dau. of Toby Brooking (St Mark's day).
        July 16 Richard,[8] sonne of Henry Palmer.
        Sep. 14 Margarett,[9] dau. of M[r] Jo. Geers.
        Oct. 30 Richard,[10] sonne of Mr Elias Smith. Richardo Hunt, Decano Dunelmensis, Augustino Linsel, Decano Lichfeldiæ, Margareta Robson, p'bendarii uxore, sponsorib'.
1632 June 24 Gulielmus,[11] filius M[ri] Gulielmi James, p'bendarii (natus vicesimo die Junii). Guliclmo Shaw, S[tæ] Theologiæ Professore; Johanno Eubanke, generoso ; & Margareta Commin, sponsoribus.
        Oct. 2 Johannes,[12] filius Johannis Geers (natus ultimo die Septembris). Johanne Cosin, SS. Theologiæ Professore, & Johanne Robson, SS. Theologiæ Bacchalaureo, hujus Ecclesiæ prebendariis, & M[ra] Margareta Smyth, sponsoribus.
        Nov. 1 Elizabetha,[13] filia Johannis Wheers. Gabriele Clarke, Sacræ Theologiæ Professore, & Elizabethâ Blaikeston, & Annâ Chapman, generosis, sponsoribus.

[1] See her sister's baptism 26 May 1622.
[2] See her sister's baptism 12 Nov. 1625. She is not mentioned in her father's will.
[3] See her burial 21 Nov. 1628.
[4] He is stated to have died in infancy; his burial occurs neither here nor at Brancepeth, of which the father (who was afterwards Bishop of Durham) was Rector.
[5] The father, a freeman of the Mercers' Company, was Mayor in 1641, and was buried 28 Nov. 1650 at St. Nicholas. Dying intestate, his widow, Frances, was granted administration. A dau., Dorothy, baptized 9 Aug. 1643, and a son, John, buried 3 Dec. 1641, appear in St. Nicholas Registers. Of the sponsors, see Mr. Pleasant's burial 14 May 1635; Mistress Smart would be wife or dau. of Peter Smart, "the turbulent prebendary," who was appointed to the sixth stall in 1609, and afterwards to the fourth. See further of him in Low's "Diocesan History of Durham." (S. P. C. K., 1881.)
[6] The parents, Christopher Richardson and Elizabeth Hopper, were married at St. Mary-le-Bow 1 Nov. 1625. Their other children baptized there are Jane, 18 Oct. 1627; John, 18 Nov. 1632, and buried 7 Aug. 1633 ; Anne, 12 Feb. 1634-5; Christopher, buried 16 Aug. 1638; Margaret, 29 Sep., and buried 28 Nov. 1638; William, 29 Sep. 1639; Mary, 2 Dec. 1641.
[7] See her burial 14 Aug. 1645.   [8] See his burial 7 July 1638.
[9] See her burial 19 Oct. 1631.
[10] See his burial 7 Sep. 1634. Augustin Lindsel, a sponsor, was a protégé of Bishop Neile, who made him a prebendary : he was afterwards successively Bishop of Peterborough and Hereford.
[11] See his burial 3 April 1634.
[12] See his father's burial 4 March 1641-2.
[13] The sponsors were Dr. Clarke, the prebendary ; Elizabeth, wife of Dr. Robert Blakiston, see her burial 18 Oct. 1634; and see Anne Chapman's marriage 19 Feb. 1632-3.

1632 Dec. 23 Thomas,[1] filius Nicolai Raulin. Philippo Ebutts, Thoma Coquo, & Mrs Morecroft, sponsoribus.

Mar. 10 Margareta,[2] filia Johannis Gaydon, hujus ecclesiæ psaltis. Thoma Wright, generoso, et M[ra] Margaretâ Robson et Isabellâ Scisson, sponsoribus.

1633 Mar. 27 Johannes,[3] filius Henrici Palmer, hujus ecclesiæ psaltis. Johanne Cosin, S. Theologiæ Professore; Johanne Heath, armigero; et Elizabethâ, uxore M[ri] Roberti Blaikston, hujus ecclesiæ p'bendarii, sponsoribus. Natus autem erat Johannes Palmer die S[ti] Cuthberti, vicessimo die ejusdem mensis supradicti.

Aug. 15 Margareta,[4] filia M[ri] Jacobi Green, hujus ecclesiæ minoris Canonici. M[ro] Richardo Smelt, ludi literarii didascalo; Margaretâ Coquo; et Gratiâ Smith, sponsoribus.

Feb. 24 Elisabetha[5] Smith, filia Eliæ Smith, artiu' magistri, et hujus ecclesiæ minoris Canonici. Anthonio Maxston, artium magistro, et hujus Ecclesiæ Præbendario; M[ra] Elisabethâ Hunt; et M[ra] Maria Smith, sponsoribus.

1634 May 19 Maria,[6] filia Gulielmi James, p'bendarii. M[ro] Johanne Heath, generoso; M[ra] Jane Plesunst; et M[ra] Margareta Coates, sponsoribus.

1635 May 23 Elizabeth.,[7] filia M[ri] Geeres. M[ro] Nailor et M[ra] Elizabeth Phenicke et Philadelphia Ubanke, sponsoribus.

June 20 Francisca & Johanna,[8] filiæ Thomæ Burwell, Artium M[ri], Epî. Dunelm. Cancellarii. Hujus vitæ amaritudinem tantum gustârunt, et eodem die æternâ fruebantur felicitate.

Jan. 6 Katherina,[9] filia Jacobi Green, hujus Ecclesiæ minoris Canonici.

---

[1] Mary, dau. of Nicholas Rawlin, and Elizabeth, dau. of Nicholas and Barbara Rawlin, were baptized at St. Mary-le-Bow 3 Feb. 1630-31 and 1 June 1640, respectively. Thomas Cooke, a sponsor, husband perhaps to Margaret Cooke, a sponsor on 11 Dec. 1638; Philip Ebutts was married 27 Jan. 1627-8, at St. Mary-the-Less, to Grace, dau. of Dr. Robert Hutton (by his wife Grace Pilkington, whose burial see 23 Nov. 1633), and was buried 28 Dec. 1660 at Houghton-le-Spring; Mrs. Ebutts does not appear in Surtees' pedigree of HUTTON, i., 149.

[2] Also entered at St. Mary-le-Bow, where she was buried 7 Dec. 1634. The father, John Gaydon or Guidon, as in Bow Register, was married there 29 May 1632 to Agnes Hall, widow. There also is recorded the baptism of a son John, 16 Aug. 1635. Thomas Wright, a sponsor, was husband of Jane Hutton, whose burial see 5 Oct. 1635.

[3] See his burial 11 Sep. 1634.

[4] See her father's burial 14 May 1667. Of the sponsors, Richard Smelt occurs as master of the grammar school in 1633; Mrs. Cooke, a dau. of Dr. Morecroft, and wife presumably to Thomas Cooke, a sponsor on 23 Dec. 1632.

[5] See her burial 28 Jan. 1651-2. Her godmother Mrs. Hunt, widow of the Dean, left her £5.

[6] See her father's burial 21 Jan. 1659-60. Of the sponsors, see Mrs. Pleasant's burial 15 March 1676-7.

[7] See her father's burial 4 March 1641-2. Mrs. Naylor, a sponsor, was wife of the prebendary; the burial of "Mrs. Elizabeth Fenwick, widow," occurs 3 Jan. 1667-8 at St. Oswald's, where she was married 31 Jan. 1615-16 to Tristram Fenwick, gent., as Elizabeth Green.

[8] These children are by error called Francis and John in Surtees' (really, Sir C. Sharp's) pedigree of BURWELL, vol. iv., ii., 168. See the marriage of their parents 19 Feb. 1632-3.

[9] See her father's burial 14 May 1667. Of the sponsors, see Mrs. Duncan's burial 12 Jan. 1642-3; Mrs. Comyn, wife of Timothy Comyn, Esq., whose burial see 19 March 1639-40.

CATHEDRAL CHURCH AT DURHAM. 5

     M^{ro} Richardo Newhouse, Doīa Dunkon, et Doīa Cummin, sponsoribus.
1636 May 6 Margareta,[1] filia Eliæ Smith, hujus Ecc. minoris Canonici. Tho'a Burwell, Cancellar; M^{ra} Margareta Heath, et Mrs Elizab'a Smith, sponsoribus.
   July 27 Seth,[2] filius Thomæ Burwell, Cancellarii. Johanne Heath, Henr'o Smith, armigeris, et D'na Hunt, sponsoribus.
1637 Dec. 18 Thomas,[3] sonn of D^{tr} Nailor, prebend. The Right hon^{ble} L^d B^{pp} of Durham and the Right w^{rll} Mr Thomas Burwell, Chancellor, and Mrs Hunt, witnesses.
   Mar. 4 Mathew,[4] filius M^{rl} Geers. M^{ro} Levett, prebendarius (sic) hujus Ecclesiæ, et M^{ro} Tobias Swinborne, et Mrs Cassandra Baddeley, sponsorib'.
   Mar. 15 Dulcebella Smith,[5] filia Eliæ Smith, artium magister (sic), et hujus Ecclesiæ minoris Cannonici. M^{ro} Johan'e Heath; et M^{ra} Nailor, et Mrs Penniman, sponsoribus.
1638 Dec. 11 Margareta,[6] filia M^{ri} Roberti Aisley, generosi. M^{ro} Gulielmo James, p'bend. hujus ecclesiæ; et M^{ro} Morcroft, uxore M^{ri} Ferdinand Morcrofte; et Mrs Margareta Cooke, filia sua, sponsorib'.
1639 Mar. 25 Gulielmus,[7] filius Henrici Palmer, laici cler. hujus ecclesiæ. M^{ri} James et Mr Maxton, prebendarii; et Mrs Duncon, sponsor'.
   Sep. 6 Joseph,[8] sonn of D^{tr} Nailor, prebend. D^{tr} Clarke and Mr Richard Badyley and Mrs Machall, witnesses.
   Oct. 1 Joane,[9] dau. of James Greene, minor Cannon of this church. Mr George Blades, and Mrs Viner, and Mrs Barb. Newhouse the younger being wittnesses.
   Feb. 20 Gulielmus,[10] filius Johannis Geers, hujus Ecclesiæ, psaltis.

---

[1] See her father's burial 9 Dec. 1635.
[2] See the baptism of his sisters 20 June 1635.
[3] The father, Joseph Naylor, D.D., was collated to the second stall 18 Nov. 1636; archdeacon of Northumberland 1632; Rector of Sedgefield 1634; and chaplain to Bishop Morton. He was deprived of his rectory and fled during the rebellion, but returned and died, 1667, at Sedgefield, where he is buried in the church. By his wife Dulcibella, dau. of Richard Baddeley, Esq. (see note to burial of William Bridges 15 Aug. 1634), he had, besides the children here registered, Mary, whose marriage see 25 Oct. 1663, and Dulcibella, Mrs. Morton, whose burial see 22 Sep. 1688.
[4] See his burial 21 Nov. 1638. Of the sponsors, Mrs. Baddeley was second wife of Richard Baddeley, Esq.; see preceding note.
[5] See her burial 18 Dec. 1639.
[6] Eldest child of her parents, whose marriage see 30 Jan. 1637-8.
[7] See the mother's burial 14 April 1638. Of the sponsors, see Prebendary Maxton's marriage 29 June 1637.
[8] See his brother's baptism 18 Dec. 1637. Mrs. Machell is perhaps an error for Machon, which, written phonetically, assumed various forms.
[9] See burial 14 May 1667. Of the sponsors, see Mr. George Blades' burial 29 Nov. 1661.
[10] See his father's burial 4 March 1641-2. Of the sponsors, see Dr. Marley's burial 3 April 1642.

REGISTER OF BAPTISMS IN THE

1640	June 24	Cubto. Marley, sacræ Theologiæ p'fessore, Ever⁸ Gower, Northumbriæ Archidiacano, & Susanna Caldwell, sponsoribus. Sarah,[1] filia Eliæ Smith, hujus Ecc. Minoris Canonici. Guli'o Church, generoso, et Elizabethâ James et Jane Maxton, generosis, sponsoribus.
1641	Dec. —	Elizabetha,[2] filia Henrici Morecroft. Jacobo Peniman; Elizab. James et Anna James, sponsoribus.
	Jan. 10	Susanna,[3] filia Eliæ Smith. Jacobo Peniman, Elizab. Bridges et Anna James, spon'.
1642	Nov. 2	Francisca,[4] filia Pauli Neele, Militis.
	Feb. 10	Henricus,[5] filius Eliæ Smyth, Artium Magistri, et hujus ecclesiæ Minoris Canonici.
1643	July 21	Stuarta,[6] filia Thomæ Thin, Militis. Gualtero Balquancallo, Sacro sanctæ Theologiæ Professore, et hujus Ecclesiæ Decano, et Dominâ Elizabethâ Hammon et Mʳˢ Barbarâ Wren, sponsoribus.
1645	Mar. 1	Marye,[7] dau. of James Greene. Cuthb. Bellamye and Mʳˢ Ann James and Grace Lofthouse being wittnesses.
1646	Aug. 2	Ann,[8] dau. of Mʳ Henrye Morecrofte. Mʳ Dallivall and the lady Ham'ond and Mʳˢ Margarett Morecroft, wittnesses.
1648	June 26	Peregrina,[9] dau. of John Burrow. Ann James, Mʳˢ Copas, and Mʳ Mudd, wittnesses.
1652	Feb. 5	Francis,[10] sonn of Mʳ Francis Foster. Mʳ William James, Mʳ Richard Baddelay, and the Ladye Penniman, wittnesses.

[1] See her father's burial 9 Dec. 1676. Of the sponsors, see marriage of Mr. Church's dau. 30 Nov. 1676 ; Mrs. Maxton was wife of the prebendary, see her marriage 29 June 1637.

[2] The father, Henry Morecroft (probably brother of the Prebendary), and Barbara, dau. of James Hilton of Dyons, gent. (whose burial see 6 July 1638), were married 28 Sep. 1637 at Houghton-le-Spring. See the baptism of her sister Anne 2 Aug. 1646, and the burial of her brother George 28 June 1642. [" Katherne Moorcroft," another child, was baptized 1643 and buried an infant at St. Oswald's]. Of the sponsors, see Lady Pennyman in note to baptism 5 Feb. 1652-3.

[3] See her father's burial 9 Dec. 1676.

[4] [She was the daughter of Sir Paul Neile, Kt., by Elizabeth, daughter of the Rev. Gabriel Clarke, D.D., Archdeacon of Durham. See her burial the next day. MS. Ped by E. A. W.]

[5] See his burial 6 July 1696.

[6] See the marriage of her parents 6 Sep. 1642.

[7] See her burial 8 Nov. 1650.

[8] See her sister's baptism Dec. 1641. Of the sponsors, Mr. Delaval was Thomas Delaval of Hetton, co. Pal., Esq., who mar. at Houghton-le-Spring, 6 May 1645, Elizabeth, widow of Francis James of Hetton, Esq., and was buried 20 Oct. 1663 at St. Mary's ; Lady Hammond, wife of Dean Balcanquall ; Mrs. Morecroft, the Prebendary's wife.

[9] See her burial 25 Oct. 1649. The father probably identical with John Borrow, buried at St. Nicholas 17 Jan. 1684-5, of whom Jacob Bee writes in his Diary under that date, " John Burrow departed this life, and 'twas reported yᵗ he see a coach drawn by 6 swine, all black, and a black maun satt upon the cotch box ; he fell sick upon't and dyed, and of his death severall apparations appeared after." Of the sponsors, Mr. Mudd was the organist.

[10] See his burial 25 Jan. 1653-4. The father, Francis Forster, Esq., of the South Bailey, was a younger son of Thomas Forster of Edderstone, Northumberland, Esq. (see the pedigree in Raine's " Northumberland," to which this adds). The mother was Elizabeth, dau. of Dr. Gabriel Clarke, Prebendary and Archdeacon of Durham, whose burial see 12 May 1662. Besides this child they

CATHEDRAL CHURCH AT DURHAM.   7

1653	July 11	Gabriell,[1] sonn of M[r] Francis Foster. M[r] Mudd, M[r] Grey, and M[rs] Martin, wittnesses.
	Oct. 4	Thomas, son of Robert Gray. D[r] Gray[2] and M[r] John Walton and M[rs] Jane Pleasants, witnesses.
	Jan. 16	An,[3] dau. of M[r] John Farrer. M[r] William James, the ladye Penyman, and M[rs] An Graye beinge wittnesses.
1655	June —	Isabell,[4] dau. of John Durye, sometime Epistoler of this Church. John Nailor, M[rs] Sibby Clerke, — Frizzell, witnesses.
1657	Dec. 8	John,[5] son of M[r] Francis Foster. S[r] John G [*illegible from a blot*] and M[r] Roger Kirbye and M[rs] Hellen Karnabye, witnesses.
	Dec. 14	Jane,[6] dau. of Ezerell Tonge and of Jane his wife, was borne on Thursday the third day of December, and baptized on monday the fowerteenth day of the same moneth in the yeare of our Lord sixteene hundred fiftie and seven, and of the foundation of Durham Colledge the first ["and the last" *has been added in another hand*].
1661	Feb. 27	Margarett,[7] dau. of John Foster, Organist of this Cathedrall Church. M[r] Ambrose Myars and M[rs] Church and Sarah Smith, wittnesses.
1662	April 22	Samuell,[8] son of John Nicholls. M[r] Samuell Davison and M[r] George Barchas and M[rs] Maxton, wittnesses.
	Mar. 17	Susanna,[9] dau. of Samuell Bolton, minor Cannon of this Church. M[r] William Church, M[rs] Susanna Smith, and M[rs] Margarett Tempest, wittnesses.

had Gabriel (whose baptism see next entry), John (whose baptism see 8 Dec. 1657). Two children, Matthew, baptized 12 Dec. 1678, and Frances, baptized 11 July 1680, occur in the Registers of St. Mary's, but query if by the same mother? The father's will is dated 15 July 1681, when he mentions his wife Elizabeth and only two daughters (evidently his coheiresses), viz., Elizabeth (see her marriage 3 Sep. 1685) and Frances. "The Lady Penniman," a sponsor, was wife of Sir James Pennyman of Ormesby, co. York, Knt. and first Bart., and dau. of Stephen Norcliffe, Esq. The baptism of their son Thomas Pennyman, afterwards second Bart., occurs at St. Mary's 29 Aug. 1642, as also that of an elder son James Pennyman 6 April 1637, who was buried there 13 April 1638.

[1] See his brother's baptism, preceding entry.

[2,3] Of the sponsors, Dr. Robert Grey, Prebendary of the eighth stall and Rector of Bishopwearmouth, was half-brother of the first Lord Grey of Warke, and dying 9 July 1704, æt. 94, was buried at Bishopwearmouth; see burial of John Walton's sister-in-law 25 March 1631, and Mrs. Pleasant's burial 15 March 1676-7.

[4] See her burial, where the name is *Drury*, 9 April 1662.

[5] See his burial 22 April 1658.

[6] See her burial 27 June 1660. "The foundation of Durham Colledge" refers to Cromwell's short-lived university, a brief account of which see in Low's "Diocesan History of Durham" (S. P. C. K.), p. 265.

[7] See her father's burial 21 April 1677. Of the sponsors, see Ambrose Myers' burial 18 March 1667-8, and the marriage of Mrs. Church's dau. 30 Nov. 1676.

[8] See the father's burial 6 June 1681. The above Samuel made his will 21 July 1719; by it he leaves his estate at Trimdon to his nephew William Burletson, son of his sister Thomasine, whose marriage see 30 Dec. 1686. Mr. Davison, a sponsor, was the third husband of Elizabeth, Lady Burton, whose burial see 14 Jan. 1699-1700.

[9] See the marriage of the parents 24 June 1662. Mrs. Margaret Tempest, a sponsor, may be the eldest dau. of John Tempest, Esq.; see next entry.

1664 Mar. 29 John,[1] son of John Tempest, Esquir; for bow church.
     June 19 Christopher,[2] son of Christopher Mickleton; for bow church.
     Dec. 21 John,[3] sonn of Samuell Bolton, minor Cannon of this Church.
              Elias Smith, Mr Broughton, Mrs Prudence Charlton, wittnesses,
              Anno 1664.
     Jan. 25 Willia',[4] son of John Foster, Organist of this church. Anthony
              Pearson and Willia' Jordan and Elizabeth Myers, wittnesses.
              The 1 in the new font.
     Jan. 31 George,[5] son of John Spearman. Mr George Barchas and Anthony
              Lodge and Mrs Mary Jackson, wittnesses; bow church parish.
1665 May 15   Elizabeth,[6] dau. of Mr Anthony Lodge. Mr George Barchas,
              Mrs Merrill Sissons, and Mrs Elizabeth Spearman, wittnesses;
              bow church parish.
     Nov. 28 Margarett,[7] dau. of Christopher Stones. Elizabeth Myers, Margarett
              Greene, and Ralph Johnson, wittnesses.
     Dec. 12 William, sonn of Mark Todd.
     Dec. 28 Isabell,[8] dau. of John Miller, bellringer. Isabell Smith, Alexand{r}
              Shawe, and Elizab. Martin, wittness.
     Jan. 25 John,[9] son of George Bullocke. Anthony Lodge and John
              Foster and Elizabeth Kirby, wittnesses.
1666 June 26 Kattern, dau. of John Brass. Kattern Hubbuck, [blank] Rowell,
              et George Kirby, wittnesses; bowe Church.
     Sep. 4   Thomas,[10] son of Mr Nicholaus Conyers. Collonell Tempest,
              Mr Peacocke, and the lady Coale, wittnesses.

---

[1] The father, John Tempest, Esq., of The Isle, Sedgefield, M.P. for the county. The mother, Elizabeth Heath, sole heiress of John Heath, Esq., of Kepyer, Esq. See both their pedigrees in Surtees, vol. iv., part ii.

[2] See his burial 15 April 1718, and pedigree in Surtees, vol. iv., ii., 140, to which these registers make additions.

[3] See the marriage of his parents 24 June 1662. Mrs. *Carleton*, a sponsor, was wife of Dr. Guy Carleton, Rector of Wolsingham (where she was buried—" Laday Carlton, wife to Bishop Carlton "—24 May 1672), afterwards, 1660, Dean of Carlisle, and made same year Prebendary of the twelfth stall at Durham (installed 2 Nov.), which he retained nutil his death; Bishop of Bristol 1671; and translated to Chichester 1678; he died 6 July 1685, and was buried in Chichester Cathedral. The Bishop had issue Hester, aged 15 in 1670, who married George Vane, Esq.; Elizabeth, married at Wolsingham 26 Oct. 1665 to Thomas Swinburne, Esq.; Jane, wife of Robert Curr, Esq.; and Prudence, named in a lease of Wolsingham Park 1676.

[4] See the father's burial 21 April 1677. Of the sponsors, Mr. Pearson was appointed undersheriff 1663; Mrs. Myers was wife of Ambrose, the Cathedral plummer.

[5] Born 28 Jan. 1664-5; eldest child of his father, whose burial see 22 Sep. 1703. See his own burial 4 Feb. 1664-5.

[6] See her father's burial 21 July 1687; she was living 12 Nov. 1683, the date of her grandfather Lodge's will. Of the sponsors, see the burials, 1 April 1690, of Mr. Barkas, and 4 April 1688, of Mrs. Sissons.

[7] See her burial 12 Nov. 1668.

[8] See her burial 8 Jan. 1665-6.

[9] His baptism entered at Bow as 2 Feb., and more probably the correct date. See his mother's burial 12 May 1678.

[10] See his parents' marriage 15 Nov. 1664. Colonel William Tempest, a sponsor, was M.P. for Durham 1678, 80, and 89; Mr. Peacock, probably Simon Peacock of The Bailey and Burnhall,

CATHEDRAL CHURCH AT DURHAM. 9

1666 Nov. 30 Frances,[1] dau. of Mr Anthony Lodge. Colonell Steward and Mrs Mickleton, senior, and Mrs Barchas, wittnesses; bow church parish.

Dec. 7 Elias Turvill,[2] a greek by nation, born in Constantinople, a jew by religion, having beene instructed, and being desirous of Christian Baptisme, on the thirtieth day of november, wch was St Andrewe's day, was presented to the font by Daniell Brevent, dtr in divinitye, and Dennis Greenvill, mr of Arts and Archdeacon of Durham, Prebendaryes of the Church of Durham, godfathers, and by Frances Basiere, wife to Isaac Basiere, dtr in divinitye, godmother; and was in this Cathedrall Church solemnly babtized by the said Isaac Basiere, prebendary of the same church, by the name of Andrew, and afterwards did solemnly receive the confirmation by the hands of the Right Reverend father in God John, Lord Bpp. of Duresme, and on the 2 day of december following did also receive the holy sacrament of the lord's supper at the hands of the above named dtr Basiere.

Jan. 6 Christian,[3] dau. of Arthur Phillips. Mr Lancelott Hilton et Mris Martin, wittnesses; being for bow Church parish.

1667 Mar. 25 Dorityc,[4] dau. to John Miller, bellringer. John Charlton, Dorityc Scruton, and Elizabeth Dorma', wittnesses.

April 30 Elizabetha,[5] filia Johannis Spearman. Joh'e Brown, Dorotheâ Spearman, et Elizabethâ Barkas, sponsoribus.

Sep. 29 Christianus,[6] filius Mri Johannis Foster, hujus Ecclesiæ Organistæ. (festo Sti Michaelis Archangeli).

1668 July 1 Robert Hilton,[7] ye son of Mr Cuthbert Hilton.

Esq.; Lady Cole was Margaret, second wife of Sir Nicholas Cole of Brancepeth, first Bart., and was buried 15 Nov. 1675 at St. Oswald's.

[1] See her father's burial 21 July 1687. Colonel Steward was probably quartered with troops in the city; Mrs. Mickleton probably second wife of Christopher Mickleton of Crookhall, Attorney; Mrs. Barkas, wife of George Barkas, notary, buried 1 April 1690.

[2] The date 7 Dec. appears to refer to nothing in the context. Dr. Brevint, a sponsor, was a native of Jersey, and Fellow of Jesus College, Oxon; Bishop Cosin obtained for him the tenth stall and the Rectory of Brancepeth, both vacated by himself; in 1681 he became Dean of Lincoln, retaining his Durham preferments; he died in 1695. See the burial of Dr. Granville's wife 14 Oct. 1691, and of Mrs. Basire 27 July 1676.

[3] She was perhaps by a third wife (being born several years after the last child baptized at Bow) of the father, whose burial see 30 May 1681.

[4] See her sister's baptism 28 Dec. 1665. Dorothy Scruton, a sponsor; see her marriage 11 Nov. 1669.

[5] Born 25 April 1667. See her marriage 4 July 1687. Of the sponsors, see Mr. Brown's son's baptism 30 June 1670. See SPEARMAN Pedigree, Surtees, i., 95.

[6] See his burial 26 Nov. 1683.

[7] Born 29 June 1668. Is also registered at Bow. He was an Attorney-at-Law, of Bishop's Auckland (where he was buried), and Registrar of the Consistory Court, an office in which he succeeded his mother's brother, Gabriel Newhouse, Aug. 1705. See his son's burial 8 Sep. 1724, and his father's 28 April 1686; also pedigree of HILTON in Longstaffe's " Darlington."

C

10   REGISTER OF BAPTISMS IN THE

1668 Oct. 21   Elizabeth,[1] dau. of Richard Neele, sq[r]. M[rs] Elizabeth Jefferson,
                M[rs] Elizabeth Stapleton, wittnesses.
      Nov. 29   Georgius,[2] filius Nicholai Barwick, Generosi.
      Jan. 26   Franciscus Spearman,[3] filius Johannis Spearman, Atturnati.
1669 Jan. 6   Nicholaus,[4] filius Georgii Bullock.
1670 April 12 Margaretta,[5] filia Richardi Neile, Dunelmensis Subvicecomis (sic).
      June 29   Jana,[6] Nicholai Barwick filia.
      June 29   Dorothea,[7] filia Johannis Spearman.
      June 30   Johannes,[8] Johannis Brown, Atturnati, filius.

[1] [She was buried 17 June 1672, at St. Oswald's. MS. Ped. by E. A. W.] Mrs. Stapylton was wife of the Bishop's Secretary, whose burial see 10 May 1685.

[2] He married at Crossgate, 4 June 1689, Elizabeth Robinson. He was living 1687 at the date of the will of his father, whose burial see 7 Dec. 1687.

[3] Born 21 Jan. See his burial 22 June 1678, and his father's 22 Sep. 1703,

[4] His birth, 1 June, is given in Bow Register. See his mother's burial 12 May 1678.

[5] [Administered to her father 8 April 1693. She afterwards married Stephen Harwood, and died ante 4 Dec. 1696. MS. Ped. by E. A. W.]

[6] See her father's burial 7 Dec. 1687, when she was living.

[7] Born 19 June 1670. See her father's burial 22 Sep. 1703. She married (licence dated 21 July 1690) John Cuthbert, Esq., Serjeant-at-Law, of Gray's Inn, Recorder of Durham and afterwards of Newcastle. In her will, dated 23 April 1731, she mentions her father and mother's and "aunt Crompton's" pictures; she was buried 5 Oct. 1731 in St. Nicholas Church, Newcastle, with her husband. They had the following issue: I. John Cuthbert, whose burial see 16 Oct. 1700. II. William Cuthbert, baptized at St. Mary-le-Bow 23 March 1692-3, Serjeant-at-Law and Recorder of Newcastle, who purchased in 1743 the Witton Castle Estate for about £15,000, and died, aged 54, 28 Aug. 1746, and was buried at St. Nicholas, Newcastle; he married, firstly, 27 Jan. 1721-2 at St. Nicholas, Jane, youngest dau. of John Stevenson, gent., by whom he had a daughter Margaret, married at Kendal, 27 July 1747, to Joseph Reay of Newcastle, merchant (he died 9 Dec. 1785, æt. 69), and left issue; he married, secondly, 29 Dec. 1730 at St. Nicholas, Dorothy (who survived him), dau. and coheir of — Robinson of Black Heddon, gent. (whose other dau. and coheir married the last Clennell of Clennell), and had by her: 1, John Cuthbert, Esq., F.R.S., F.S.A., of Witton Castle, baptized at St. John's, Newcastle, 17 Nov. 1731, and died s.p. at York 15 Dec. 1782, aged 51, and was buried at St. Nicholas, Newcastle; 2, William Cuthbert of London, merchant, baptized 27 Oct. 1732 at St. Nicholas, and died s.p. circa 1766 in the East Indies; 3, Philadelphia, baptized 24 Sep. 1733 at St. Nicholas, and married Ralph Hopper, Esq., Barrister-at-Law, of Bishop-Middleham, co. Pal. (where she was buried 1780), and had issue, with others, a son, John Thomas Hendry Hopper, Esq., who inherited Witton Castle from his uncle John. III. Robert Cuthbert, baptized 12 April 1693 at St. Mary-le-Bow. IV. Richard Cuthbert, baptized at Bow 6 April 1696, B.D, and Fellow of Trinity College, Cambridge, Vicar of Kendal 1733. See his widow's burial 26 June 1767. V. Charles Cuthbert, whose burial see 18 Oct. 1700. VI. John Cuthbert, baptized 24 Feb. 1700-1701, M.D., of Portsmouth, where, according to the newspapers, he died in 1772, leaving a dau. Dorothy, wife of Sir John Carter, Knt., Mayor of Portsmouth. VII. Theophilus Cuthbert, whose burial see 9 Aug. 1703. VIII. Margaret, baptized 27 Dec. 1704 at Bow. IX. George Cuthbert, baptized 4 Jan. 1705-6 at Bow, who was aged nine when named in a Bishop's lease of 26 Oct. 1714. X. Ralph Cuthbert, baptized 3 Feb. 1708-9 at St. Nicholas, Newcastle.

[8] Died an infant apparently. The father, an Attorney-at-Law, living in the North Bailey, died, according to Bee's Diary, 8 July 1684; his will is dated 6 March 1683-4; in it he mentions his uncle Jerrard Brown, his sisters Abigail and Elizabeth Hutchinson, wife Jane, dau. Elizabeth, and dau. Jane, whose marriage see 30 April 1683.* See baptism of a second John 9 Nov. 1675, and another son 18 Feb. 1678-9.

---

* The mother was Jane, dau. of Richard Hutchinson of Framwellgate, who entered his pedigree at Dugdale's Visitation, 1666.

CATHEDRAL CHURCH AT DURHAM. 11

1670	Oct. 27	Barbara,[1] Cuthberti Hilton filia.
	Nov. 29	Maria,[2] Johannis Yape filia.
	Dec. 21	Cuthbert,[3] Johannis Brasse filius.
	Jan. 19	Elizabetha,[4] Tho. Battersbie filia.
	Feb. 6	Maria,[5] Willfredi Clarke filia.
1672	Mar. 28	Frances,[6] filia Richardi Neile, Dunelō Subvicecomis (sic).
	Mar. 28	Johannes,[7] Johannis Spearman filius.
1673	May 6	Anna,[8] Gualfridi Clarke filia.
	July 17	Paul,[9] filius Rich'di Neile, generosi, Dunelm : Subvicecomis (sic).
1675	June 7	Carolus,[10] filius Thomæ Cartwright, Sacræ Theologiæ Professoris, & hujus Ecclesiæ Præbendarii. Isaaco Basire, Sacræ Theologiæ Professore, & Roberto Gray, Sacræ Theologiæ Professore, hujus Ecclesiæ P'bendariis, et D'na Anna Brevint, sponsoribus.
	Aug. 17	Jana,[11] filia Joh'is Yapp.
	Oct. 28	Gilbertus,[12] filius Joh'is Spearman, Gen^{sl}.
	Nov. 8	Richardus,[13] filius Wilfridi Clerke.

[1] Also entered at St. Mary-le-Bow, where she married, 27 Dec. 1694, Geoffrey Shaw of Barnard Castle. See her son's burial 12 Dec. 1746, and her father's 28 April 1686.
[2] See her burial 26 Jan. 1704-5.
[3] Cuthbert Brass and Ann Forster were married 28 Nov. 1699 at St. Oswald's. He appears to have been a joiner, and had a son, another Cuthbert, a singing-man at the Cathedral. They have several children baptized at St. Oswald's.
[4] See the burial of her father, to whom she was sole executrix 6 Nov. 1716.
[5] See the father's burial 16 March 1679-80.
[6] [Administered "de bonis non" to her father 4 Dec. 1696, then wife of John Setton of Durham City. Living in Newcastle 1699. MS. Ped. by E. A. W.]
[7] See the father's burial 22 Sep. 1703. This child was born 21 March. Afterwards of Hetton-le-Hole, co. Pal., Esq., J.P., and was buried at Houghton-le-Spring. By his wife Anne, dau. and coheiress of Robert Bromley of Nesbitt, Esq. (see her sister's burial 26 Jan. 1700-1701), who was buried at Houghton 22 Nov. 1703, he had issue, Elizabeth, whose burial see 22 Feb. 1695-6 ; and (these all baptized at Houghton) 2, John Spearman, 16 Feb. 1690-1, afterwards of Hetton, Esq., who died unmarried ; 3, Isabella, 26 June 1698, and buried 11 Dec. 1767 unmarried ; 4, Dorothy, 18 July 1699 ; 5, Anne, 30 March 1700, and buried 4 June 1766 unmarried ; 6, Phillis, 10 May 1702, who lived in the North Bailey, where she died 16, and was buried 21 Oct. 1792 at Houghton. She died unmarried, and by her will, stating that she was " entirely against leaving the little money for the education of boys and girls, as they want sense to make the proper use of it," she founded a charity for the relief of " servants when they grow old, and not so capable of service. As far as it will go to unmarried women or widows, that will make their lives more comfortable, which I hope it will be doing more good." Five such persons, each receiving £20 a year, have at the present time reason to bless the name of kindly Miss Phillis Spearman. The above dates will be found to add to Surtees' pedigree.
[8] See her father's burial 16 March 1679-80.
[9] [Buried 21 Aug. 1674, at St. Oswald's. MS. Ped. by E. A. W.]
[10] See his mother's burial 6 Jan. 1682-3. The father was installed in the fifth prebend 15 Nov. 1672, and became Dean of Ripon 1675, and Bishop of Chester 1686. See a good Memoir of Dr. Cartwright in Bliss's " Wood's Athenæ." Ann Brevint was wife to the Prebendary, see baptism under 7 Dec. 1666.
[11] See her burial 11 Aug. 1675.
[12] Born 21st. See his marriage 1 Sep. 1701.
[13] See his burial 18 Dec. 1678.

1675 Nov. 9 Joh'es,[1] filius Joh'is Browne, Gen[si].
Dec. 2 Lancelotus,[2] filius Thomæ Lowther, Gen[si].
(———) Joh'es,[3] filius Thomæ Batersby.
Feb. 8 Rob'tus,[4] filius Joh'is Mitford.
1676 Nov. 1 Gulielmus,[5] filius Georgii Bullock.
Nov. — Maria,[6] filia Joh'is Simpson.
Dec. — [blank][7] filius Will'mi Horsman.
Feb. 18 Isaacus,[8] filius Isaaci Basire, Advocati. Dionysio Greenvile, S.T.P., Gilberto Gerrard, Milite, & D'na Vane, viduâ, sponsoribus.
1677 Jan. 1 Margareta,[9] filia Cuthberti Hilton, Gen[i].
1678 May 2 Gulielm[s],[10] filius Gulielmi Stagg.
July 17 Pryscilla,[11] filia Tho. Battersbie, Ludim'g'ri.
Dec. 31 Joh'es,[12] filius Joh'is Bowman.
Jan. 5 Joh'es,[13] filius Nich'ii Fewster, Cl'ici.
Jan. — Margareta,[14] filia W[mi] Snawdon.
Feb. 18 Gerrard[s],[15] filius Joh'is Browne, Gen[si].
1679 July 23 Martha,[16] filia Cuthberti Hilton, gen[sl].
1681 Sep. 25 Robertus,[17] filius Joh'is Dury.
Mar. 9 Anna,[18] filia Johan'is Mickleton, Armig., Bapt. die Martis (viz.)

[1] See his brother's baptism 30 June 1670.
[2] See his marriage 4 June 1698.
[3] See his burial 14 Aug. 1676.
[4] Also registered at St. Mary-le-Bow, where his birth is given 2 and baptism 11 March. See his burial 6 Oct. 1678.
[5] This date is given in Bow Register for the *birth*. See his burial 6 June 1681.
[6] See her burial 15 July 1693.
[7] See the father's burial 17 Jan. 1723-4. This nameless child may be the William Horseman who has a son baptized 12 Dec. 1726, or Timothy Horseman buried 12 April 1694.
[8] See his burial 2 May 1678. The father, Isaac Basire, Esq., Barrister-at-Law, eldest son of Dr. Basire, the Prebendary (whose burial see 14 Oct. 1676), was baptized 22 Nov. 1643 at Egglescliffe, and married, as her fourth husband, 4 July 1672, at Stanhope, "Lady Elizabeth Burton," whose burial see 14 Jan. 1699-1700. This appears to have been their only child. Of the sponsors, Sir Gilbert Gerard, created a Baronet 1666, was husband of Bishop Cosin's eldest dau. Mary. "Domina Vane" was probably Frances, dau. of Sir Thomas Liddell of Ravensworth, second Baronet, and widow of Thomas Vane of Raby Castle, Esq., who was elected M.P. for the county 21 June 1675, but died of small-pox four days afterwards. Mrs. Vane remarried Colonel Sir John Bright of Badsworth, co. York, Bart., the distinguished Parliamentarian, to whom she was third wife.
[9] See her father's burial 28 April 1636. She was living unmarried 1717.
[10] Also entered at Bow. See his father's burial 19 Feb. 1692-3.
[11] See her burial 15 Jan. 1682-3.
[12] See the father's burial 27 Jan. 1695-6.
[13] See his burial 22 Aug. 1681.
[14] See her parents' marriage 1 May 1678.
[15] See his brother's baptism 30 June 1670.
[16] See her burial 26 Nov. 1681.
[17] The father son of Rev. John Drury, Epistoler; see baptism of one sister June 1655, and marriage of another 29 Aug. 1682.
[18] Her baptism is also entered in French in Bow Register, where she is stated to have been born 29 July previous; see her burial 16 July 1710. Of the sponsors, see Mr. Robert Smith's

CATHEDRAL CHURCH AT DURHAM. 13

		9º die Augusti, 1681. M^{ro} Rob. Smith, M^{ra} Anna Bell, et Mrs Eliz. Dobson, sponsoribus.
1682	April 2	[blank]¹ the dau. of Francis Hanby.
	July 11	Gulielmus,² filius Gulielmi Tempest, Armigeri. M^{ro} Rob. Delavall, M^{ro} Sudall, et Doïa Moore, sponsoribus.
	Aug. 22	Dulcibella,³ filia D'ni Joh'is Morton, hujus Eccl'iæ Prebendarii. D^{re} Smith (Decano Carleol), D'nâ Dulcibellâ Naylor, et D'nâ Eliz. Blakiston, sponsoribus.
	Aug. 29	Jacobus,⁴ filius Joh'is Yapp.
	Aug. 31	Johan'es,⁵ filius Nicholai Barwick, Gen.

burial 23 Feb. 1703-4, and Mrs. Ann Bell's burial 6 Dec. 1737; Mrs. Elizabeth Dobson ("widow" in Bow Register) was probably wife of Wheatley Dobson of Durham, mercer, Mayor in 1692, 1693, 1696, and 1697, and in her marriage licence, 1670, she is described as Elizabeth Welbury, spinster. Welbury Dobson, her eldest child, was baptized at St. Nicholas 27 Aug. 1671.

¹ The parents, Francis Hanby, Proctor of the Consistory Court, and Isabella (see her brother's marriage 1 July 1679), dau. of William Brockett, were married 22 Oct. 1667 at St. Oswald's. The birth-dates of their six older children are all recorded together at Bow, although baptized at St. Oswald's. This was Frances, the fifth of eight children, and was born 30 March 1681. Two younger are baptized at Bow, where the mother was buried 31 July 1702, and the father 24 May 1708. The Proctor was perhaps a son of "Mr. William Hanby" (buried 3 May 1693 at St. Mary-le-Bow), who was Undermaster of Grammar School under Elias Smith and Thomas Battersby, and by the latter *amotus ob negligentiam et contumaciam*. Mickleton terms him gentleman. "Mrs. Mary Hanby," buried 13 June 1688 at Bow, was probably his wife. The Hanbys remained in the parish to a later period, and there is a flat tombstone of the family close at St. Oswald's, close under the Vicarage.

² Fourth son of Colonel William Tempest, M.P. for the City (see baptism of Thomas Conyers 4 Sep. 1666), by his wife Elizabeth Sudbury, niece of Dean Sudbury. He was living 1729. See baptism of a sister 29Jan. 1683-4, and the TEMPEST Pedigree in Surtees, vol. iv., part ii., p. 93. Of the sponsors, Mr. Robert Delavall was Mayor 1686, 1687, 1688, 1689, in which last year it is recorded that he, "by reason of many debts and incumbrances and judgements entred against him and his estate, hath withdrawn himself," a course approved by the Bishop. He was eldest child of Thomas Delaval of Hetton, Esq., who occurs as a sponsor 2 Aug. 1646, and was baptized at Houghton-le-Spring, where his birth is given as Sunday, 17 April 1646.

³ Daughter, by his first wife Dulcibella Naylor (whose burial see 22 Sep. 1688), of the Rev. John Morton (Linc. Coll., Oxon. B.A. 1664, M.A. 1667, B.D. 1674, D.D. 1692), installed Prebendary of the seventh stall 16 Oct. 1676, of the sixth stall 29 Nov. id. ann., and of the twelfth 18 July 1685, and collated to the Archdeaconry of Northumberland 5 Oct. following; Rector of Egglescliffe 1672—1711, and Rector of Sedgefield 1711, until his death there 10 Nov. 1722, æt. 78. He lies buried in the chancel of his church, and a tablet lengthily records his virtues. The child Dulcibella, baptized as above, married at Sedgefield 30 Dec. 1713, as second wife, William Davison of Beamish, Esq. (*vide* pedigree in Surtees, ii., 227), and dying 15 Jan. 1737, was buried with her husband at Tanfield. She was ancestress of the present Lord Auckland, Sir William Eden now seventh Baronet of Windlestone, and of the late John Eden (formerly Methold) of Beamish, Esq. Her great-granddaughter, Mary Anne Eden, became the wife of Lord Chancellor Brougham; and her granddaughter, Catherine Eden, married Dr. John Moore, Archbishop of Canterbury (see baptism of their son George 19 Nov. 1770). See the baptisms of her brother, sisters, half-brother, and half-sister hereafter. Of the sponsors, Dr. Thomas Smith was Prebendary of the fourth stall 1661, and of the first 1668; afterwards, 1684, Bishop of Carlisle. Domina Dulcibella Naylor was the maternal grandmother. Domina Elizabeth Blakiston was wife of Henry Blakiston, Esq., whose burial see 15 May 1683. See the burial of Dr. Morton's second wife 12 Feb. 1724-5, and MORTONS in Index.

⁴ See the marriage of his parents 3 Feb. 1667-8.
⁵ See his burial 16 Oct. 1682.

14   REGISTER OF BAPTISMS IN THE

1682 Nov. 29 Jana,[1] filia Joh'is Bowman.
     Jan. 8   Georgius,[2] filius Wil^{mi} Snawdon.
     Jan. 15 Johan'es,[3] filius Andreæ Wilkinson.
     Jan. 17 Georgius,[4] filius Edwardi Carlton.
     Mar. 12 Elizabetha,[5] filia Johan'is Simpson.
1683 June 14 Robertus,[6] filius Joh'is Mickleton, Armigeri, Bapt. die Jovis (viz.) 14to mensis Junii. M^{ro} Rob. Smith, M^{ro} Tho. Blakiston, et M^{ra} Margaretâ Smith, sponsoribus.
     June 20 Maria,[7] filia posthuma Ambrosii Heighington, Gen.
     July 24 Samuell,[8] filius Roberti Adamson, Cl'ici.
     Oct. 30 Georgius,[9] filius D'ni Joh'is Morton, hujus Ecclesiæ Prebendarii.
     Jan. 29 Elizabetha,[10] filia Guliclmi Tempest, Armigeri.
     Jan. 29 Johannes,[11] filius Johannis Taylor.
1684 April 2 Henricus,[12] filius D^{ris} Henrici Bagshaw, Prebendarii nonæ Preb. hujus Eccl., et Rectoris de Houghton in le Spring. Rob. Grey, S.T.P., W^{mo} Tempest, Arm., et D'na Musgrave (Preb. uxore), sponsoribus.

---

[1] See the burial of her father 27 Jan. 1695-6.
[2] See his parents' marriage 1 May 1678, and (probably) his burial 4 Nov. 1730.
[3] See the marriage of his parents 20 Sep. 1682.
[4] See the baptism of another child of Edward Carlton 24 Feb. 1684-5.
[5] See her burial 4 Oct. 1685.
[6] Also registered at St. Mary-le-Bow; the entry is in French, and he is styled "fils ainé," his birth date, 4 June, being recorded. See his burial 20 Aug. 1684. Of the sponsors, Mr. Robert Smith was the second husband of the child's grandmother; Mrs. Margaret Smith was aunt. See Mr. Blakiston's burial 25 March 1711.
[7] She was buried at Crossgate 27 Aug. 1684. The father was a younger son of William Heighington of Durham, gent.,* and was baptized at Crossgate 30 May 1654, where, dying 4th (Bec's Diary), he was buried 5 May 1683. The mother was Catherine, dau. and coheir of Dr. Thomas Musgrave, Prebendary of Durham and Dean of Carlisle; see his burial 30 March 1686. Their marriage licence is dated 26 Sep. 1676. Besides this child, they had William, baptized 12 March 1677-8 at Crossgate, Musgrave, baptized 2 March 1679-80, and Catherine, all mentioned in the will, dated 13 March 1692-3, of their grandfather, William Heighington, who was buried 29 Nov. 1693 at Crossgate. [" Richard Heighington of the North Bayley, cordwyner, and Gartrett Waller of this parish, spinister," married 1 May 1654 at St. Oswald's.]
[8] See his mother's burial 10 Aug. 1684. Observe the burial 9 Aug. 1680 of a Samuel Adamson, who might be the grandfather.
[9] See his burial 22 Jan. 1690-91.
[10] Dau. of Colonel William Tempest, M.P., of Old Durham (whose baptism see 31 Jan. 1653-4), by his wife, Elizabeth Sudbury, niece of Dean Sudbury. She married 26 Feb. 1714-15 at St. Oswald's, Anthony Salvin of Elvet, gent., and died at the birth of her first child, Anthony, who was baptized on the day of his mother's burial at St. Oswald's 25 Feb. 1715-16.
[11] See his burial 20 June 1684.
[12] See his burial 14 Feb. 1684-5. The father, D.D. of Christ Church, Oxon, was instituted Rector of Houghton-le-Spring 13 Dec. 1677, and installed in the ninth Prebend 20 July 1681. He is described on his monument in Houghton Church as son of Edward Bagshaw of Morton

---

* William Heighington, barber, of St. Nicholas, and Frances Heighington of St. Margaret's, married 1 Dec. 1636 at St. Oswald's.

CATHEDRAL CHURCH AT DURHAM. 15

1684 June 12 Robertus,[1] filius Johan'is Wood (Gardiner). Marmaduco Allenson, Gen., Roberto Delavall, gen., et D'nâ Eliz. Kirkby, sponsoribus.
July 6 Brigida,[2] filia Gulielmi Horseman.
Aug. 17 Johan'es,[3] filius Gulielmi Wilson, Gen. Gulielmo Tempest, Joh'e Sudbury, Armigeris; et D'na Elizab. Spearman, sponsoribus.
Oct. 19 Anna,[4] filia Johan'is Morton, hujus Ecclesiæ Prebendarii.
Feb. 24 Martha,[5] filia Edvardi Carleton.
1685 May 18 Cuthbertus,[6] filius Joh'is Bowman.
June 11 F[7] [*blank*] Joh'is Martyn.
June 23 Maria,[8] filia Tho. Butler, Gener.
July 21 Jacobus,[9] filius Joh'is Benson.

Putney in the county of Northampton, Esq. By his wife, Mary Wilshere, who died 10 and was buried 18 Oct. 1703 in Houghton Church, he appears to have had three sons and five daughters, viz., Ralph, whose burial see 7 Jan. 1681-2; Henry, as above; Edward, whose baptism see 21 July 1690; Mary, buried 21 Oct. 1680, and Anne 18 Feb. 1686-7, both in Houghton Church; Prudence, baptized 25 May 1685 at Houghton, her father's executrix and only surviving dau.; and Elizabeth and Sarah, whose baptisms see 15 April 1689 and 22 Dec. 1692 respectively. Dr. Bagshawe in his will, dated 10 Nov. 1708, with a codicil 20 Dec. 1709, mentions his niece Mrs. Dorothy Wilsher and nephew Peter Lancaster, and a silver tankard given to him by Lady Fanshaw.

[1] See baptism of another child 30 Jan. 1686-7. The father, doubtless, was college gardener. Of the sponsors, Marmaduke Allenson of West Rainton, co. Pal., and a mercer of Durham, was Mayor 1684 and 1685. He was baptized 18 July 1630 at Crossgate, the son of Ralph Allenson of Durham, Mayor in 1635, 1642, and 1643 (son of Anthony Allenson of Bishop's Auckland), by his wife Mary, dau. of Archdeacon Blakiston, Prebendary of the seventh stall, which Ralph was buried 29 Jan. 1656-7 at St. Nicholas; Marmaduke Allensen died 19 and was buried 20 Jan. 1689-90 at St. Mary's, leaving a numerous family, and his widow Alice proved his will 25 id. men. See the burial of Mrs. Kirkly, another sponsor, 16 July 1721.

[2] See the father's burial 17 Jan. 1723-4.

[3] See the parents' marriage 18 Dec. 1677. This child probably died young, as he is not mentioned in a Bishop's lease of 1691 with his brother and sisters, viz., Elizabeth, stated to be eldest dau., and then aged 11; Bridget, whose baptism see 15 Dec. 1685; Mary, baptized 13 March 1686-7 at Bow; and Sudbury, youngest child, whose burial see 6 Jan. 1700-1701. [Perhaps of this family was Richard Wilson, gent., who married 13 Dec. 1740, at St. Oswald's, Bridget, then aged about 50, dau. of Colonel William Tempest, M.P., who is a sponsor.] John Sudbury, another sponsor (whose sister Elizabeth married the before-mentioned Colonel Tempest), was nephew of Dean Sudbury, and LL.B. (1682) of Trinity Hall, Cambridge, and was created a Baronet 1685; he married Bridget (she remarried Edward Carteret, Esq., M.P., and had issue), dau. of Sir Thomas Exton, Knt., Judge of the High Court of Admiralty, by whom he had an only dau. Anne; at his death in 1691 the title became extinct. Mrs. Spearman was wife of the Undersheriff, whose burial see 22 Sep. 1703.

[4] See her burial 28 Dec. 1685.

[5] See her brother's baptism 17 Jan. 1682-3.

[6] See the father's burial 27 Jan. 1695-6.

[7] The father perhaps the Minor Canon whose burial see 11 Nov. 1697.

[8] See her marriage 30 March 1709; also the pedigree of BUTLER (to which this date adds), Surtees, iii., 49.

[9] See the father's burial 19 Dec. 1696. This child apparently by a second marriage, for see burial of Isabell Benson 20 June 1682.

1685	Dec. 15	Brigida,[1] filia Gulielmi Wilson.
	Jan. 5	Elizabetha,[2] filia Francisci Hanby.
1686	Sep. 21	Elisabetha,[3] filia Joh'is Benson.
	Dec. 12	Thomas,[4] filius Joh'is Proud (Bow).
	Jan. 20	Johan'es,[5] filius Joh'is Wood, ap'd Bow church.
1688	April 2	Jacobus,[6] filius Michaelis Mickleton.
	April 8	Johan'es,[7] filius Joh'is Proud.
	April 22	Elisabetha,[8] filia Joh'is Morton, Prebendarii.
	April 15	Elisabetha,[9] filia Henr. Bagshaw, S.T.D., Prebendarii.
	Sep. 17	Richardus,[10] filius W'mi Grahme (S.T.P., Decani Carliol, et hujus Ecclesiæ Prebendarii).
1689	Dec. 1	John,[11] son of John Lisle, Minor Canon.
16—	(——)	Anne,[12] daughter of John Proud.
1690	July 21	Edward,[13] son of D'r Bagshaw.
1691	Nov. 4	George,[14] son of William Greggs, Organist.
	Feb. 1	Samuel,[15] son of John Lisle, Min'r Canon.
1692	Sep. 4	Hamond,[16] son of John Clement.
	Sep. 29	Elisabeth,[17] dau. of W'm Horseman.

[1] See her brother's baptism 17 Aug. 1684. She was, doubtless, named Bridget after Lady Sudbury. She probably died an infant, as she is not included in the lease of 1691.

[2] Born, according to Bow Register, 25 Dec. 1685, being fourth dau. and sixth child. See her sister's baptism 2 April 1682.

[3] See the baptism of her brother 21 July 1685.

[4] See the marriage of the parents 17 Jan. 1685-6.

[5] See the baptism of his brother 12 June 1684.

[6] Born 27 March preceding. See his parents' marriage 4 July 1687. He was afterwards a Barrister-at-Law, of Gray's Inn; he married Hannah (baptized 26 Jan. 1685-6 at St. Helen's), fifth dau. of Sir Robert Eden of West Auckland, first Bart., but died s.p., circa 1717, according to Surtees' pedigree, iv., ii., 140, probably in London. His wife was sister to Dr. Eden, whose burial see 6 March 1754. His sponsors were Sir Robert Eden (afterwards his father-in-law), and his grandparents James Mickleton and Mrs. Spearman.

[7] See his (probable) marriage 22 Sep. 1713, and his brother's baptism 12 Dec. 1686.

[8] See her burial 24 May 1697.

[9] Died an infant, and was buried in Houghton-le-Spring Church 26 May 1689. See her brother's baptism 2 April 1684.

[10] Born 30 Aug. preceding; see his burial 23 Dec. 1689.

[11] See his burial 28 June 1690. The father graduated at St. John's College, Cambridge, B.A. 1680; M.A. 1684. See the baptisms of his brothers, Samuel, 1 Feb. 1691-2, and Henry, 31 Aug. 1693. ["Mr. Maurice Lisle, Master of Arts," who has a son John baptized 4 Sep. 1683, and others, at St. Oswald's; and Mrs. Rowe, whose burial see 22 Oct. 1707, were perhaps relations.]

[12] See her brother's baptism 12 Dec. 1686.

[13] He is mentioned on his father's monument as the only surviving son. See his brother Henry's baptism 2 April 1684.

[14] The father, appointed Master of the Song School 19 Feb. 1690-91, and Organist on the death of John Foster 1677, was buried in the churchyard of St. Mary's 16 Oct. 1710, where the inscription on his altar-tomb states that he died 15th in the 48th [?] year of his age, and "was son of Jo. Greggs, gent., of York, a sufferer for K. C. I."

[15] He entered, then aged 17, at St. John's College, Cambridge, 3 May 1709, and graduated B.A. 1712, M.A. 1716, and B.D. 1724. See his brother's baptism 1 Dec. 1689.

[16] See his burial 4 March 1732-3.

[17] See her burial 17 April 1695.

CATHEDRAL CHURCH AT DURHAM. 17

1692	Oct. 4	Frances,[1] dau. of John Proud.
	Dec. 22	Sarah,[2] dau. of D[r] Bagshaw.
1693	May 1	Ositha,[3] dau. of D[r] Morton.
	Aug. 31	Henry,[4] son of M[r] Lisle, Min[r] Can.
1694	June 26	Thomas,[5] son of D[r] Morton.
1696	Oct. 25	John,[6] son of D[r] Smith.
	Oct. 18	John,[7] son of John Clement.
169⁴⁄₇	Aug. 11	Penelop Dobson,[8] dau. of D[r] Dobson.
	Aug. 29	Thomas,[9] son of Tho. Rudd.
	Jan. 26	Mary,[10] dau. of D[r] Smith.
1698	Sep. 22	Eliz.,[11] dau. of D[r] Dobson
	Nov. 24	John,[12] son of Tho. Rudd.
1699	Aug. 9	———,[13] son of D[r] Smith.
170⁰⁄₁	Aug. 16	Dorothy,[14] dau. of D[r] Dobson.
	Mar. 20	John,[15] son of M[r] Nich. Burton, Schoolemaster.
1701	April 29	Joseph,[16] son of John Smith, D.D.

[1] See her brother's baptism 12 Dec. 1686.
[2] She was buried in Houghton-le-Spring Church 18 May 1694. See her brother's baptism 2 April 1684.
[3] Dau. of Dr. Morton by his second wife, whose burial see 12 Feb. 1724-5, and her own burial 23 May 1702. See her half-sister Dulcibella's baptism 22 Aug. 1682.
[4] See his burial 27 Nov. 1693, and his brother's baptism 1 Dec. 1689.
[5] See his burial 28 Jan. 1720-21.
[6] See his burial 24 Nov. 1731.
[7] See his burial Oct. 1696.
[8] The father, the Rev. Henry Dobson of Magdalen College, Oxon (B.A. 1674; M.A. 1677; B.D. 1689; D.D. 1693), was appointed Rector of Boldon 1692, and installed in the sixth Prebend 8 June 1695; he died in London, aged 67, 23 March 1717. See baptisms of other children Sep. 1698, Aug. 1700, and Feb. 1704-5.
[9] The father, M.A. of Trinity College, Cambridge, was at this time Head Master of the Grammar School; he had afterwards (1711—1725, when he became Vicar of Northallerton) the Vicarage of St. Oswald's, where the registers all carefully kept by himself are a specimen of most beautiful and indeed wonderful penmanship, a standing reproach to the often undecipherable writing in our modern registers. See RUDD Pedigree in Surtees, vol. iv., part ii., p. 107, where a full account will be found of both father and son. They are now represented by Wilbraham of Rode, Cheshire. See baptism of another son 24 Nov. 1698.
[10] See her burial 5 Dec. 1698, and her brother's baptism 25 Oct. 1696.
[11] See her burial same day, and her sister's baptism 11 Aug. 1697.
[12] Born 12 Nov. These dates add to Surtees' Pedigree. He died 30 June 1720, and was buried 2 July in St. Oswald's Church, where his M.I. describes him as " optimæ spei juvenis ; in flore ipso ætatis diuturno morbo consumtus et tandem (magno suorum dolore) extinctus." The Vicar invariably spelt his own name *Rud* in the Registers.
[13] His name was William ; see his burial 11 Aug. 1702, and his brother's baptism 25 Oct. 1696.
[14] See her sister's baptism 11 Aug. 1697.
[15] Son of the Rev. Nicholas Burton, M.A. (whose second marriage see 18 May 1704), by his first wife, Anne, who died 10 (M.I.) and was buried 12 Aug. 1703 within the communion rails of St. Mary-le-Bow beside her dau., whose baptism see 30 June 1702.
[16] He graduated B.A. 1721, and M.A. 1725, at Trinity College, Cambridge, and was afterwards presented to the Vicarage of Houghton, Sussex. He is stated in Surtees' Pedigree to have married Elizabeth Woodger, and to have died at Cambridge, 1734, s.p.

D

REGISTER OF BAPTISMS IN THE

1702	June 30	Martha,[1] dau. of M[r] Nich. Burton, Schoolm[r].
1704	Feb. 2	Fitz-Herbert,[2] son of Hen. Dobson, D.D.
1707	Sep. 22	William,[3] son of John Smith, D.D.
171¾	Jan. 25	W[m], son of Eliz. Smith, a Traveller, privately bapt.
1715	Nov. 15	Elizabeth,[4] dau. of Jo. Rymer, Clerk.
1720	Mar. 13	John,[5] son of Jn[o] Waring, was born Feb. y[e] 27th, and baptiz'd March y[e] 13th by y[e] Rever[d] M[r] Rob[t] Lecke, Præcentor.
1726	May 31	Frances, a new-born infant left in the Abby Church and Christned in the Vestry.

(Robt. Pigot, Sacrist, Nov. y[e] 20th, 1726.)

	Dec. 12	Robert,[6] son of William and Mary Horseman.
1729	July 14	Margarett[7] and Mary, daughters of Hammond and Priscilla Clement.
1730	Feb. 2	James,[8] son of y[e] Rev[d] D[r] Thomas Sharp, Arch-Deacon of Northumberland.

---

[1] She was buried 26 May 1703 within the communion rails at St. Mary-le-Bow, of which her father was Rector. She is termed "filia hornotina" on her mother's M.I. See her brother's baptism 20 March 1700-01.

[2] See his sister's baptism 11 Aug. 1697. Dr. Fitz-Herbert Adams was at this time Prebendary of the Tenth Stall; and Colonel William Tempest, M.P., several times before mentioned, had a son, born 1687, named Fitz-Herbert. This name probably came from one source in each instance.

[3] Youngest child. See his burial 24 Nov. 1730, and his brother's baptism 25 Oct. 16

[4] See her burial 7 Oct. 1728.

[5] The father, the Rev. John Waring of St. John's College, Cambridge (B.A. 1709; M.A. 1713), a Minor Canon, was appointed Vicar of Billingham 1715, Sacrist 1719, afterwards Precentor; and, 1721, Rector of St. Mary's in the South Bailey, where he was buried 26 Nov. 1732.* The son baptized as above was probably the John Waring who graduated at St. John's, Cambridge, B.A. 1737, M.A. 1741.

[6] The parents, William Horseman and Mary Smith were married 11 Jan. 1725-6 at St. Mary-le-Bow. The father may have been that nameless child of William Horseman (whose burial see 17 Jan. 1723-4) who was baptized — Dec. 1676.

[7] See the burial of Margaret 21 Sep. 1729.

[8] [The father was the son of Archbishop Sharp, by Elizabeth, youngest dau. of William Palmer of Winthorp, co. Leicester, Esq. He was born 12 Dec. 1693 and baptized 1 Jan. 1693-4 at St. Martin's in the Fields; of Trinity College, Cambridge (B.A. 1712; M.A. 1716; D.D. 1729); Rector of Rothbury, Northumberland, 1720; one of Lord Crewe's Trustees; Archdeacon of Northumberland (collated 27 Feb. 1722-3); Prebendary of the tenth stall in Durham Cathedral (installed 1 Dec. 1732); and Prebendary of York and Southwell; official to the Dean and Chapter of Durham 1755. He died 16 March 1758 and was buried in the Galilee Chapel in Durham Cathedral. The mother was Judith, dau. of the Rev. Sir George Wheler, Knt., Prebendary of Durham, and Rector of Houghton-le-Spring; born 1700; died 2 July (according to M.I.) and buried in the Galilee Chapel in Durham Cathedral, near her father, 9 July 1757; married 19 June 1722 at Houghton-le-Spring (the Rothbury Register gives the date of her death as 1 July). James was the seventh son, of Leadenhall Street, London, ironmonger. He married 3 May 1764 Catherine, dau. of John Lodge of London, who died in 1834, æt. 95. By her he had a dau. Catherine, his sole heiress (who placed the monument in Durham Cathedral),

---

* He married Barbara (baptized 18 Nov. 1694 at Bow), fourth dau. of Peter Burrell, Notary-Public, of the Bailey, and sister of Lady D'Arcy of Navan. See BURRELLS in Index.

CATHEDRAL CHURCH AT DURHAM. 19

1733	Nov. 25	Judith,[1] dau. of y[e] Rev[d] D[r] Thomas Sharp, Prebendary of this Church.
1735	Nov. 21	Granville,[2] son of y[e] Rev[d] D[r] Thomas Sharp, Prebendary of this Church.
1737	April 19	Ann,[3] dau. of y[e] Rev[d] D[r] Thomas Sharp, Prebendary of this Church.
1738	May 6	Frances,[4] dau. of y[e] Rev[d] D[r] Thomas Sharp, Prebendary of this Church.
1740	Sep. 11	Henry,[5] son of Robert Pigot, Sacrist.
1744	May 9	Barbara,[6] dau. of y[e] Rev[d] M[r] James Lesley, Prebendary of this Church.
1745	July 8	Mary Ann,[7] dau. of y[e] Rev[d] D[r] James Lesley, Prebendary of this Church.
	Jan. 27	Wadham,[8] son of y[e] Rev[d] D[r] Wadham Knatchbull, Prebendary of this Church.

and who married at Queen Square Chapel, Bath, on July 30, 1817, the Rev. Andrew Bowlt of Bamborough, who upon his marriage assumed the name and arms of Sharp only. James died 5 Nov. 1783 and was buried at St. Mary Axe, London. MS. Ped. by E. A. W.]

[1] [Sister of the above, died unmarried 20 and buried 25 March 1809 in the Galilee Chapel. MS. Ped. by E. A. W.]

[2] [Brother of the above, the celebrated Philanthropist whose name will ever be connected with the abolition of the slave trade; born 10 Nov. 1735; died 6 July 1813, buried in Fulham Churchyard. M.I. Cenotaph (by Chantrey) was erected to his memory by the African Institution in the Poet's Corner, Westminster Abbey. MS. Ped. by E. A. W.]

[3] [Ann, sister of the above, born 1 April 1737; buried at Durham Cathedral 22 April 1738. MS. Ped. by E. A. W.]

[4] [Frances, sister of the above, born 6 May 1738; died 2 Sep 1799. MS. Ped. by E. A. W.]

[5] The father, the Rev. Robert Pigot, one of the Minor Canons, graduated at Peterhouse, Cambridge (B.A. 1715; M.A. 1719) was inducted Vicar of Northallerton 15 Oct. 1748; died 10 and was buried 14 Jan. 1775, aged 79, in the chancel of Northallerton. By his wife Elizabeth (who died, aged 80, 27 Feb., and was buried with her husband 4 March 1776), the Sacrist appears to have had, besides this child, Robert, born 1 Sep. 1724, and Hollis, born 30 March 1726, both baptized at St. Oswald's, where the latter was buried 9 Jan. 1726-7; Thomas, baptized 27 Jan. 1727-8, and buried 15 Oct. 1730; Richard, baptized 25 Aug. 1730; Edward, baptized 14 May 1731, and buried 13 Dec. id. ann.; Edward-Loyd, baptized 21 Dec. 1733; Charles, baptized 11 Nov. 1735, and buried 2 Jan. following; William, baptized 23 April 1737, and buried 11 June 1738, all at Crossgate.

[6] She died ante 1773. The father (D.D. of Trinity College, Dublin) was Curate of St. Nicholas', Dublin, and Chaplain to Dr. Chandler, Bishop of Durham, whose great-niece he married. He was collated (1741) to the Rectory of Wolsingham, which he resigned for Sedgefield 1747; installed in the eighth prebend of this Cathedral 20 July 1743; in 1755 he exchanged his stall and rectory with Archdeacon Lowth, afterwards Bishop of London, for the Bishopric of Limerick, which had been offered to and declined by the latter, who, however, obtained permission to effect this bargain, which was much more to his own advantage than to the Diocese of Limerick. Bishop Leslie died at Dublin. The mother was Joyce (died 1773), only dau. of Anthony Lyster of Lysterfield, co. Roscommon, Esq., by his first wife Elizabeth, dau. and heiress of Richard Warren, Esq., by his wife Joyce, sister of Bishop Chandler. See next entry.

[7] According to Burke's "Extinct Baronetage" (the Bishop's eldest son received a Baronetcy in 1787) she married Francis Warren Bonham, Esq., although in the "Landed Gentry" ("Bonham of Ballintaggart") she is called Joyce. The "Gent. Mag." says she died ante 1793.

[8] See the burial, 31 Dec. 1760, of his father, of whom he was the eldest child. He died in 1773, aged 27.

1746 Jan. 5 Edward,[1] son of y⁣ᵉ Rev⁣ᵈ D⁣ʳ James Lesley, Prebendary of this Church.
1747 Feb. 8 Elizabeth,[2] dau. of y⁣ᶜ Rev⁣ᵈ D⁣ʳ James Lesley, Prebendary of this Church.
(Samuel Dennis, Sacrist, Nov. 20, 1748.)

1748 Dec. 25 Harriot,[3] dau. of the Rev⁣ⁿᵈ D⁣ʳ Wadham Knatchbull, Prebendary of this Church.
1749 May 18 Richard,[4] son of y⁣ᵉ Rev⁣ᵈ D⁣ʳ James Lesley, Prebendary of this Church.
1750 June 4 John, son of John Ellington and Mary his wife, was rec⁣ᵈ into y⁣ᵉ Church.
Oct. 10 Windham,[5] son of y⁣ᶜ Reverend D⁣ʳ Wadham Knatchbull, Prebendary of this Church.
1752 May 24 Mary, dau. of John Ellington and Mary his wife.
1753 Jan. 18 Catherine,[6] dau. of y⁣ᶜ Rev⁣ᵈ D⁣ʳ Knatchbull, Prebendary of this Church.
Sep. 3 William,[7] son of Jn⁣ᵒ and Eliz. Potts.
1755 Jan. 14 Robert, son of Tho⁣ˢ Clark and Catherine his wife.
1756 Oct. 16 Anne, dau. of Tho⁣ˢ Clark and Catherine his wife.
1760 Oct. 17 Martha,[8] dau. of y⁣ᶜ Rev⁣ᵈ D⁣ʳ Robert Lowth (Prebendary of this Church) and Mary his wife.

---

[1] Eldest son, afterwards of Tarbert House, co. Kerry, and M.P. for Old Leighlin. He was made Hon. M.A. of Wadham College, Oxford, 1769, and created a Baronet of Ireland 1787. He married Anne, dau. of Colonel Cane, R.E., M.P. for Tallagh, and had by her an only child, Catherine Louisa (she died 1851, s.p.), who married in 1807 Lord Douglas Gordon-Hallyburton of Pitcur, M.P. for Forfarshire, only son of Charles, fourth Earl of Aboyne, by his second marriage, and half-brother to Charles, fifth Earl, who succeeded as ninth Marquess of Huntly. At Sir Edward's death the Baronetcy became extinct. See his sister's baptism 9 May 1744.

[2] She died before 1773, as also her sister Joyce. Dr. Leslie had also two other daughters, Catherine-Elizabeth, wife of James Scott, Esq., and Martha, the widow in 1793 of the Rev. James Lowry.

[3] She apparently died young ; she was the elder dau. of her father, whose burial see 31 Dec. 1760.

[4] Afterwards a clergyman, and succeeded, in right of his mother, to her moiety of the Lysterfield estates. (Burke's "Extinct Baronetage.")

[5] Second son of his father, whose burial see 31 Dec. 1760. He married 12 June 1790 his cousin, Catharine-Maria (she died 1807), second dau. of Sir Edward Knatchbull, seventh Baronet, and died, aged 83, in 1833, leaving issue. See Burke's " Baronetage "; also " Landed Gentry."

[6] Youngest child of Dr. Knatchbull, whose burial see 31 Dec. 1760. She married Thomas Knight of Chawton House, Hants, and Godmersham Park, Kent, Esq. (who died 1794, devising his estates to his third-cousin, Edward Austen, Esq., brother of the immortal Jane), but died s.p., 14 Oct. 1812.

[7] The father perhaps identical with John Potts, Surgeon, Mayor of Durham 1787. His arms, Azure, two bars and a bend or, on a copy of Bishop Egerton's Charter, *penes* the Editor.

[8] She died unmarried 12 March 1812, in John Street, Berkeley Square. ("Gent. Mag.") The father was the son of the Rev. William Lowth of St. John's College, Oxford (B.A. 1679; M.A. 1683; B.D. 1688), Prebendary of Winchester, and Rector of Buriton, Hants, "a distinguished figure in the republic of letters," author of " A Vindication of the Divine Authority and Inspiration of The Old and New Testaments " (1692), " Directions for the Profitable Reading

CATHEDRAL CHURCH AT DURHAM. 21

1761 Mar. 6 Isabel, dau. of Thomas Hogg and Anne his wife.
1762 Mar. 26 Robert,[1] son of ye Rev^nd Dr Robert Lowth (Prebendary of this Church) and Mary his wife.
July 28 John, son of Thos Hogg and Anne his wife.
1763 June 30 Margaret,[2] dau. of ye Revd Dr Robert Lowth (Prebendary of this Church) and Mary his wife.
Nov. 17 Thomas,[3] son of Thomas Hogg and Anne his wife.
1764 Jan. 6 Richard Mark,[4] son of Dr Samuel Dickens (Prebendary of this Church and A^ch D^n of D^m) and Margaret his wife.

of the Holy Scripture," "Commentaries on the Prophets," etc., who died 16 May 1732. His yet more distinguished son, Robert, was born either in the Close, Winchester, or at Buriton, 8 Dec. 1710; he was first of Winchester College, Oxford, but afterwards of New College (B.A. 1733; M.A. 1737; D.D. 1754); he was appointed Rector of Overton, Hants (a sinecure), 1736, Archdeacon of Winchester 1750, Chaplain to the Lord-Lieutenant of Ireland 1755; Prebendary of Durham (see note to baptism of Barbara Leslie 9 May 1744 regarding this), and rector of Sedgefield 1755—1777; Bishop of St. David's May 1766, but translated to Oxford July following; and finally translated to London. In Feb. 1768, being then Bishop of Oxford, he writes to the Dean and Chapter that he has "received his Majesty's dispensation from keeping up a statuteable residence in the Church of Durham," and he held his stall *in commendam* until his death 3 Nov. 1787, being buried in Fulham Churchyard. He declined the Archbishopric of Canterbury on the death of Archbishop Cornwallis in 1783. He was a very considerable scholar, and author of "Prelections on Hebrew Poetry," "Life of William of Wykeham," "A Short Introduction to English Grammar," "Translation of Isaiah," etc. Except the above Martha, all his five daughters predeceased him. Mary, the eldest, his favourite child, was born 11 June 1755, and died 5 July 1768, being buried at Cuddesden, Oxford. Although she does not come into these Registers, the Editor cannot refrain from giving the epitaph written by her father:—

"Care, vale, ingenio præstans, pietate pudore,
Et plusquam natæ, nomine cara, vale!
Cara Maria, vale! at veniet felicius ævum,
Quando iterum tecum, sim modo dignus, ero.
Cara, redi, læta tum dicam voce paternos
Eja age in amplexus, cara Maria, redi."

His third dau., Frances, who was baptized at Sedgefield 27 Oct. 1757, died most suddenly 21 July 1783, at a reception by the Bishop at London House, St. James's Square. She was handing a cup of tea to the Bishop of Gloucester when she dropped down dead. The Bishop married in 1752, Mary, dau. and heiress of Lawrence Jackson, Esq., of Christchurch, Hants; she died 14 March 1803, in her 84th year, and was buried in Fulham Churchyard. The Bishop had a strong prejudice against intra-mural burial. See baptisms of three other children in 1762, 1763, and 1765 respectively. See also "The Oxford Sausage," p. 89, and Nichol's "Literary Anecdotes."

[1] He was a clergyman, and of Christ Church, Oxford (B.A. 1783; M.A. 1786); he married Miss Frances Harington, by whom he had issue. See his sister's baptism 17 Oct. 1760.
[2] She died 10 March 1769, in her sixth year, and was buried in Fulham Churchyard. See his sister's baptism 17 Oct. 1760.
[3] He probably died very young. See baptism of another Thomas 23 June 1771.
[4] Afterwards Colonel of the 34th Regiment. See his son's baptism 27 March 1787. The father, Archdeacon Dickens, died 30 Aug. 1791, æt. 73, and was buried at Easington, co. Durham, of which he was Rector. His M.I. there terms Bishop Trevor his "Relation and Patron." The mother, Margaret, was dau. of Dr. Mark Hildesley, Bishop of Sodor and Man, and previously Master of Sherburn Hospital, co. Pal.

1764 Dec. 3   Anne, dau. of Mr Thomas Hogg and Anne his wife.
1765 July 11 Charlotte,¹ dau. of the Revnd Dr Robt Lowth (Prebendary of this Church) and Mary his wife.
1766 Feb. 10 Elizabeth, dau. of Thomas Hogg and Anne his wife.
1767 Mar. 13 William,² son of Mr Thomas Hogg and Anne his wife.
1768 Nov. 16 Jane, dau. of Thos Hogg and Anne his wife.
1769 May   12 Frances-Anne,³ dau. of the Revnd Dr Henry Vane, Prebendary of this Church, and Frances his wife.
1770 Nov. 19 George,⁴ son of ye Revnd Dr John Moor (Prebendary of this Church) and Catherine his wife.
1771 Feb. 28 Henry,⁵ son of Dr Henry Vane, Prebendary of this Church, and Frances his wife.
      June 23 Thomas,⁶ son of Thomas Hogg and Anne his wife.
      Oct. 23 Thomas John,⁷ son of ye Revnd Jonathan and Elizabeth Branfoot his wife.
      Nov. 1   Henry John,⁸ son of Dr Samuel Dickens (Prebendary of this Church) and Margaret his wife.
      Dec. 23 Charles,⁹ son of ye Revd Dr John Moor (Prebendary of this Church) and Catherine his wife.
1772 Oct. 8   Edward,¹⁰ son of Charles Weston (Prebendary of this Church) and Arabella his wife.

(Mr Denson, Sacrist.)

¹ She died 29 May 1768, in her third year, and was buried in Fulham Churchyard. See her sister's baptism 17 Oct. 1766.
² See his burial 13 March 1767, and his sister's baptism 6 March 1761.
³ She married the Right Hon. Michael Angelo Taylor, M.P. for Durham City (son of Sir Robert Taylor, Knt.), who died, aged 77, 16 July 1834. Her father, the Prebendary, married 3 March 1768, at St. Mary's, Frances, dau. and eventual heiress of John Tempest, Esq., M.P. for Old Durham and Sherburn (she died 19 Jan. 1796, aged 51), and by her had, besides this dau., an only son, whose baptism see 28 Feb. 1771. Dr. Vane, who succeeded his father (see his marriage 27 Sep. 1722) in the Long Newton and other estates, was created a Baronet 13 July 1782; he died 7 June 1794, aged 66.
⁴ He was Rector of Wrotham, Kent, and Canon of Canterbury; he married, by special licence, at Lady Finch's, in Hereford Street, London, 11 Oct. 1806 ("Gent. Mag."), Harriet Mary, youngest dau. of Sir Brook Bridges, third Baronet. The father was afterwards Archbishop of Canterbury. The mother was dau. of Sir Robert Eden of West Auckland, third Baronet, and sister to the first Lord Auckland.
⁵ See his sister's baptism 12 May 1769. He assumed the additional name and arms of Tempest, under the will of his mother's brother, John Tempest, Esq., M.P., of Old Durham, Wynyard, and Brancepeth Castle, *ultimus suorum*. He married in 1799, Anne-Katherine (McDonnell), Countess of Antrim in her own right, and by her, who died 1834 (having remarried Edmund Phelps, Esq.), had issue an only child and heiress, Frances Anne Emily Vane-Tempest, second wife of the third Marquess of Londonderry, K.G., and grandmother of the present and sixth Marquess, K.G. Sir Henry Vane-Tempest, who was M.P. for Durham, died 1 Aug. 1831.
⁶ See his burial 14 June 1772, and his sister's baptism 6 March 1761.
⁷ The father son of Rev. John Branfoot, Minor Canon, whose marriage see 31 Jan. 1733-4.
⁸ See his brother's baptism 6 Jan. 1764.
⁹ See his brother's baptism 19 Nov. 1770.
¹⁰ [Eldest son, of Somerby Hall, co. Lincoln, Esq., Deputy-Lieutenant, born 18 Sep. 1772; sometime an Officer in the 11th Light Dragoons, with which regiment he served in Flanders;

CATHEDRAL CHURCH AT DURHAM. 23

1773	Mar. 16	Dorothy, dau. of Thomas Hogg, Treasurer to the College.
	April 27	Stephen, son of Christopher Creed.
1783	Feb. 20	Robert,[1] son of John and Penelope Ann Cracroft (Esqr). He is Captain in the Royal North Lincoln Militia, and she daughter of Mr Weston, Prebendary of this Church.
1787	Mar. 27	Samuel Richard,[2] son of Richard Dickens, Esqr, Ensign in 44th Regiment of Foot, and of Mary his wife, and grandson of Dr Dickens, Prebendary of this Church and Archdeacon of Durham.
1788	July 17	George,[3] son of Richard Dickens, Esqr (now) Captain in the 44th Regiment of Foot, and of Mary his wife, and grandson of Dr Dickens, Prebendary and Archdeacon of Durham.
1790	Dec. 16	James,[4] son of the Revd James Britton, Head-Master of the Grammar School, and Isabella his wife; born Octob^r 25th.
1791	Jan. 24	Elizabeth,[5] dau. of Thomas Gibbon, Junior.

died unmarried 27 Jan. 1844, and was buried at Somerby (in the churchyard). His father, who was born 25 Oct. 1731 in Charles Street, Westminster, was of Christ Church, Oxon (B.A. 23 June 1752; M.A. 18 April 1755); of Somerby Hall; Archdeacon of Wilts 1763; Rector of Therfield, Herts, 1762; installed in the ninth prebend of Durham Cathedral 11 Aug. 1764, and of the sixth (being removed) 2 Aug. 1768. He died 31 Oct. 1801, and was buried in Somerby Church. His mother, the dau. of Henry Delabene, Esq., of York, married 14 May 1771 at St. James's, Piccadilly; she died 30 May 1799, and is buried in Somerby Church. MS. Ped. by E. A. W.]

[1] [The father John Cracroft, Esq., of Hackthorn Hall, co. Lincoln, was High Sheriff of that county in 1797. The mother was born 11 Dec. 1763, and was baptized at St. James's, Piccadilly, 13 Jan. 1764; she married 4 Feb. 1782 at St. Mary-le-Bow, Durham, and died 29 Sep. 1821, and was buried at Hackthorn. MS. Ped. by E. A. W.]

[2] See the baptism, 6 Jan. 1764, of the father, Richard *Mark* Dickens, afterwards Colonel of the 34th Regiment. The mother (married 8 Jan. 1785, at St. James's, Westminster) was Mary, elder dau. of George Hoar of Middleton George, co. Pal., gent., Deputy-Keeper of the Jewels in the Tower (by his wife Frances, dau. of William Sleigh of Stockton-on-Tees), and sister of William Hoar, afterwards Harland, Esq., whose burial see 22 Nov. 1833.

[3] See preceding entry.

[4] Of Christ Church, Oxford, B.A. 1813; M.A. 1815. The parents were married — Jan. 1790, at Brancepeth. The father (to whom a very painful monument is erected between two of the south piers of the Cathedral nave, representing him reclining on one elbow, in an attitude of contemplation, on a sort of mattress) was of Christ Church, Oxon (B.A. 1781; M.A. 1784; B.D. and D.D. 1819), Perpetual Curate of Crossgate 1783, and, on resigning the headmastership, became Vicar of Bossall, co. York, 1809, and of East Acklam, same county, 1819. The mother (born Oct. and baptized 17 Nov. 1763, at St. Nicholas, Durham), was eldest dau. of Henry Mills, Esq., of Willington, co. Durham, J.P., and a banker at Durham, by his wife Elizabeth, eldest child of Robert Fenwick, Esq., of Lemmington, Northumberland.

[5] Afterwards Mrs. Russell Bowlby. Her parents were married 28 Dec. 1788 at St. Oswald's. The father, who died 26 Dec. 1792, aged 27 (tombstone), and was buried at St. Oswald's, was the son of Thomas Gibbon and Grace Chapman ("both of the College"), who were married 3 June 1764 at St. Mary-the-Less. The mother was Elizabeth, elder dau. of . . . . Liddell of South Shields, by his wife Jane, dau. of John Hubback of Coupen, co. Pal., and sister of Barbara Hubback, first wife of Thomas Carlisle, and by him mother of Sir Anthony Carlisle the King's Physician. Elizabeth Liddell's younger brother, George Liddell (born at Durham about Aug. 1771; died 10 April 1851, buried at Sutton, near Hull), was grandfather of George William Liddell of Sutton and Keldy Castle, Yorkshire, Esq., who died at Oxford, 17 Nov. 1888, aged 21. Elizabeth Liddell's younger sister was wife of Stephen Gee, Esq., of Cottingham, Yorks.

1791 April 21 Henry,[1] son of the Revd Charles Egerton (and Catherine Egerton his wife), Rector of Washington.
1792 Mar. 24 Eliza,[2] dau. of the Revd James Britton and Isabella his wife; born February 26th.
April 15 William, illegitimate son of Dorothy Churnside from South Shields, but now in Jail for Debt.
Sep. 21 Ann,[3] dau. of Thomas Gibbon, Junior, Deputy Treasurer.
1794 Feb. 4 Matthew, son of Benjamin and Jane Renwick of Hamsterley, now confined in Durham Jail.
Dec. 25 Thomas, son of Elizabeth Learmouth (illegitimate) of Blackwell, now in Durham Jail.
1795 April 6 Isabella,[4] dau. of the Revd James & Isabella Britton; born Jany 22^d, 1795.
April 25 William,[5] son of Colonel Barrington Price and Lady Maria Price; born March 29. Bapt. by Mr Burgess. Privately before bapt. by Mr Bouyer.
Aug. 24 Jane,[6] dau. of Anthony Mowbray Crofton and of Jane Crofton his wife of Kinnesworth *alias* Kimblesworth, near Durham.

---

[1] Of Lincoln's Inn, Barrister-at-Law; he married Mary (who died 1854), dau. of the Rev. George Sayer, LL.B., Rector of Egglescliffe, but died s.p. The Rev. Charles Egerton, the father, was a natural son of Francis Egerton, Esq., youngest brother of John, Bishop of Durham 1771— 1787. The Bishop was a grandson of John, third Earl of Bridgewater, and his sons, John and Francis (whom his father made a Prebendary), ultimately became seventh and eighth Earls respectively. The mother was dau. of . . . . Leake, a bookseller at Bath; she died 11 July 1801, æt. 35, and was buried at Washington. M.I.

[2] See her brother's baptism 16 Dec. 1790.

[3] See her sister's baptism 24 Jan. 1791.

[4] See her brother's baptism 16 Dec. 1790.

[5] The father was a son of Robert Price of Foxley, Esq., by his wife the Hon. Sarah Barrington, eldest sister of Shute Barrington, Bishop of Durham. The mother, Lady Maria Price (Mary she is called in Burke's "Peerage"), died suddenly, on her 38th birthday, May 1806, at Cerney, Gloucestershire. She was dau. of John, ninth Earl of Strathmore, by his ill-fated Countess, the great heiress of the Bowes family, and so, unhappily, handed down to posterity as the wife afterwards of Andrew Robinson Stoney (Bowes), who assumed her name.

[6] Born at Kimblesworth, near Durham, 22 Jan. She married at Brancepeth, 4 Feb. 1817, William Stoker of Durham, Surgeon, and by him was mother of the late William Stoker, Esq., J.P., M.R.C.S., of Durham. She was the second dau. and child of Anthony Mowbray Crofton, gent., then of Kimblesworth, afterwards of Holywell Hall in Brancepeth parish (son of Richard Crofton by his wife Ann Mowbray of Kimblesworth), by his wife Jane (whom he mar. at Hamsterley 6 Nov. 1792), dau. of James and Dorothy Best of Kayslee, Hamsterley. Anthony Mowbray Crofton died 15 Feb. 1809 and was buried at Witton Gilbert. His wife died 31 Jan. 1821, æt. 57, and was buried at Hamsterley. Besides the children baptized here there was a son Thomas Crofton, born at Kimblesworth 9 Jan. 1798, who married 26 April 1836, at Edenhall, Cumberland, Elizabeth Jane Buston, and left issue; also Ann, born 8 Aug. 1793 at Kimblesworth, and bapt. at Crossgate 18 Oct. following. In the Register her mother is called Dorothy *Basto* Crofton, the only explanation of which is that, as stated above, her maiden name was Best, and that it was a jumble of the clerks. Ann Crofton married, 31 Jan. 1815, John Wood of Kimblesworth, and died at Darlington 26 Nov. 1880, leaving issue.

CATHEDRAL CHURCH AT DURHAM. 25

1796	Aug. 31	Robert,[1] son of D[r] Bathurst, was privatly bapt. December 10th, 1795, by D[r] Bathurst, Prebendary; and publickly bapt. in the Abbey on the 31st day of August 1796 by the Sacrist.
	Nov. 18	John,[2] son of John Nevill, a soldier in Surry Militia.
1797	Aug. 14	Catherine,[3] dau. of the Rev[d] Francis Haggitt, Prebendary of Durham, and Christina his wife; born July 10th.
	Oct. 24	Caroline,[4] dau. of the Rev[d] D[r] and M[rs] Bathurst. D[r] Bathurst is prebendary of this Church.
1798	Jan. 9	Elizabeth,[5] dau. of Anthony Mowbray Crofton and of Jane Crofton his wife, of Kimblesworth, near Durham.

(J. D., Sacrist.)

---

[1] Born 27 Nov. preceding; of Christ Church, Oxon (B.A. 1815; M.A. 1818); married, 1816, Jane, dau. of Rev. Roger Norris; was Rector of Belaugh and Framingham Pigot, co. Norfolk; died 25 Dec. 1828, æt. 32, leaving a widow and eight children. In the first rank of the many eminent men who have held stalls at Durham, the father, Dr. Henry Bathurst (D.C.L., New College, Oxon), was born in London, either in Hereford Street or at his maternal grandfather's house, Westminster, 16 Oct. 1744. He was the second son and third child of Benjamin Bathurst (a younger brother of Allen, first Earl Bathurst) of Lydney, co. Gloucester, Esq., M.P. for Gloucester City and Monmouth Borough, and eventually "Father" of the House of Commons, by his second wife Katherine, only surviving dau. of Dr. Laurence Brodrick, Prebendary of Westminster and Rector of Mixbury. He was Rector of Saperton (which he retained until about 1833), and became Canon of Christ Church, Oxford, 1774, resigning it in March 1795 for the second stall at Durham, where he was installed 20 April following. This same year he refused an Irish bishopric. He was made Bishop of Norwich circa April 1805. In Aug. 1831 Lord Grey offered him the Archbishopric of Dublin, which he declined. He died in his ninety-third year 5 April, and was buried in Malvern Abbey 14 April 1837. He married, 15 Aug. 1780, Grace, sister of Charles Henry, second Lord Castlecoote, and only dau. of Dr. Charles Coote, Dean of Kilfenora, Ireland (by his first wife Grace, dau. of Thomas Tilson, Esq.), whose second wife was Dr. Bathurst's half-sister, Catherine Bathurst. Mrs. Bathurst died 16 April 1823, æt. 67, and was buried in Malvern Abbey with her husband. They had eight sons and three daughters, of whom one son, Charles Henry, died 5 and was buried 7 Dec. 1795 at St. Mary-the-Less, not St. Mary-le-Bow, as the "Memoirs" say. Dr. Bathurst's Life has been (1850) well and readably written by his second dau. Tryphena, Mrs. Thistlethwayte, of Southwick Park, Hants. He was one of the most liberal, high, and yet simple-minded men who have sat on the Episcopal bench, and was a zealous supporter of the Catholic Emancipation Bill, and of reform generally. In searching for his baptism at Mixbury the following baptisms of his brothers and sisters were found, which it may not be amiss to record, viz., Mary, 25 April 1747; Susannah, 2 May 1748; Selina, 29 March 1749; Hester, 4 April 1750; Frances, 29 July 1751; Charles William, 10 May 1753; Robert, 7 Nov. 1754.

[2] The barracks at this time were on the Palace Green, next Bishop Cosin's Library, and the Surrey Militia were quartered there.

[3] She was the only child, and married as first wife, 14 Dec. 1819, at Marylebone, London, the Rev. James Baker, Spiritual Chancellor of the Diocese. The mother was Dr. Haggitt's first wife, and died about Jan. 1811. Dr. Haggitt died in Bruton Street 1826, and was buried at Nuneham Courtenay, of which he was Rector. He was also D.D. and Chaplain in Ordinary to the King. His second wife was Lucy, dau. of William Parry, Esq., of Herefordshire.

[4] She married, 19 July 1820, at Norwich Cathedral, the Rev. Heaton Champion de Crespigny (fourth son of the second Baronet), who died at Ballarat, Australia, 15 Nov. 1858. See her brother's baptism 31 Aug. 1796.

[5] Died young. See her sister's baptism 24 Aug. 1795.

E

1798	Feb. 15	Hannah,[1] dau. of Matthew Woodifield, Dep.y Treasurer, and of Hannah (formerly Gibbon) his wife.
1799	April 18	Elizabeth,[2] dau. of Matthew Woodifield (Dep.y Treasurer) and of Hannah(before Gibbon) his wife.
	Dec. 27	Richard,[3] son of Anthony Mowbray Crofton and of Jane his wife, of Kimblesworth, near Durham.
1800	July 3	Coote,[4] son of the Rev.d D.r and M.rs Bathurst (Prebendary of Durham).
	Aug. 5	Ann,[5] daughter of Matthew Woodifield and of Hannah his wife.
1802	July 1	Matthew and James,[6] twins, sons of Matthew Woodifield and of Hannah his wife.
1803	Mar. 24	Maryann,[7] daughter of the Rev.d James and Isabella Britton.
1804	Jan. 7	Ann, dau. (illegitimate) of Elizabeth Dee, in Durham Jail for Debt.
	Mar. 15	Agnas Wilson,[8] dau. of Richard Wilson, Gentleman, of Lymm in Cheshire, was baptised 15th of March in the Cathedral Church of Durham.
	June 9	Charlotte Belasyse,[9] dau. of the Rev.d George Barrington and Elisabeth his wife. Born March 30th 1804. Privately baptised June 9th 1804 by the said Rev.d George Barrington, Prebendary of Durham (11th stall) and Rector of Sedgefield.
	Sep. 25	Harriot Jane,[10] dau. of the Rev.d James Britton and Isabella his wife, was born July 12th.

---

[1] She died unmarried in the College, æt. 23, 31 March 1821, and was buried 3 April at Crossgate. The parents married by licence at Crossgate 7 May 1797. He was buried 31 Aug. 1824, æt. 67, at Crossgate. She (probably sister to Thomas Gibbon, junior, see baptism of 24 Jan. 1791) died 9 and was buried 12 Jan. 1808, æt. 34, at Crossgate. The Woodifields, Widdifields, or Widdowfields occur in the Weavers' books from an early date. John Widdifield was bound apprentice to his father Matthew for seven years 24 June 1751; Robert Woodifield's eldest son admitted free 1784. Matthew Woodifield, "a very aged man," was buried 4 June 1748 at St. Oswald's, where there are numerous others of the name.

[2] See preceding entry.

[3] Born at Kimblesworth 21 id. men.; died 9 Nov. 1839, and buried at Hamsterley. See his sister's baptism 24 Aug. 1795.

[4] Born 1 Oct. 1799. See his brother's baptism 31 Aug. 1796.

[5] Died unmarried, and buried 27 Feb. 1822, æt. 21, at Crossgate. See her sister's baptism 15 Feb. 1798.

[6] Born day of baptism. James, the younger twin, died 24 and was buried 27 June 1803 at Crossgate. See the burial of Matthew, the elder, 6 April 1857.

[7] See the baptism of her brother 16 Dec. 1790.

[8] Query whether the father was not of the family of Fountayne-Wilson (now Montagu), and thus connected with Prebendary Charles Weston. See Burke's "Landed Gentry."

[9] She married, in 1845, Rev. Henry Burton, Rector of Upton-Cressett, Salop, and died 16 June 1873. The father, nephew of Shute Barrington, Bishop of Durham, youngest son of Major-General the Hon. John Barrington, and grandson of the first Viscount Barrington, was born 16 July 1761; he succeeded to the Peerage in 1813. He married, 1788, Elizabeth, dau. of Robert Adair, Esq., by his wife Lady Caroline Keppel, dau. of the second Earl of Albemarle. He died 1829, and she died 1841. Their other children were all born at Sedgefield, I believe.

[10] See her brother's baptism 16 Dec. 1790.

CATHEDRAL CHURCH AT DURHAM. 27

1805 April 20 Anthony James,[1] son of Anthony Mowbray Crofton and of Jane his wife, of Kimblesworth, near Durham. By J. Deason, Sacrist.
1806 Dec. 17 Phyllis,[2] dau. of Anthony Tyler, the Virger, and Elizabeth his wife. Born October 22nd 1806.
1807 April 16 Francis Daines Barrington,[3] eight [sic] son of the Revd George Barrington (Prebendary) and Elisabeth his wife; born Friday, March 20th 1807.
1808 Oct. 24 Edwin,[4] son of Anthony Tyler, the Virger, and Elizabeth his wife. Born Sepr 19th 1808. N.B.—Mr Anth^y Tyler is the Dean's Virger.
1810 Aug. 31 Susannah Tyler,[5] third dau. and fourth child of Anthony Tyler, the Dean's Virger, by Elizabeth his wife, dau. of William Bates. Born June 25th 1810.
       Dec. 2 Charlotte Cassandra,[6] third dau. of the Revd Henry Phillpotts, Prebendary of the 9th Stall in the Cathedral Church of Durham, and of Deborah Maria his wife. Born September 20th 1810.
1811 Oct. 6 Harriet Sibylla,[7] fourth daughter of the Revd Henry Phillpotts, Prebendary of the 9th Stall in the Cathedral Church of Durham, and of Deborah Maria his wife.
1812 Sep. 24 Agnes Tyler,[8] fourth dau. and fifth child of Anthony Tyler, the Dean's Virger, by Elizabeth his wife, dau. of William Bates. Born Augt 24th 1812.
1813 Mar. 6 Edward Copleston,[9] son of Henry and Deborah Maria Phill-

---

[1] Born 18 id. men. He married at Sunderland, 5 Jan. 1847, Mary Elizabeth Agar, and died (buried at Brancepeth) 29 Aug. 1876, leaving issue. See his sister's baptism 24 Aug. 1795.

[2] Was the second child; she married at St. Mary-the-Less, 22 Oct. 1833, William Caldcleugh, Postmaster of Durham, who dying, æt. 49, 15 Nov. 1854, was buried at Crossgate; she died 23 Sep. 1847, leaving issue, and was buried at Crossgate. See her father's burial 14 July 1849.

[3] See his burial 29 Feb. 1808, and his sister's baptism 9 June 1804.

[4] See his burial 27 Jan. 1871.

[5] Living 1889, unmarried, at Lanchester, co. Durham. See her father's burial 14 July 1849.

[6] So named after her mother's sister, the wife of Sir John Cæsar Hawkins, Bart.; married Benjamin Cherry, Esq., D.L., J.P., of Brickendon Grange, Herts, and had issue. The father (see Burke's "Landed Gentry," "Phillpotts of Porthgwidden"), afterwards so eminent as Bishop of Exeter, held the living of Stanhope, co. Durham, one of the richest in England, which he resigned when appointed to the bishopric of Exeter. He held his canonry till his death. The mother (see "The Landed Gentry," "Surtees of Dinsdale") was bapt. 4 April 1782, at St. John's, Newcastle, and younger dau. of William Surtees, Esq., of Seatonburn, Northumberland, and niece to the wife of Lord Chancellor Eldon. Mrs. Phillpotts very much disliked the rooks, which had their colonies on the beautiful river banks surrounding the Cathedral, and caused their nests to be destroyed. It was a curious circumstance that at her death, though they had been absent for years, they reappeared.

[7] See her burial 21 Feb. 1812 and preceding baptism.

[8] She married at St. Nicholas, 5 Feb. 1850, William Thompson, chemist, of Durham; she died 1 May 1853, and was buried at St. Oswald's. See her father's burial 14 July 1849.

[9] He was third son, Rector of Stoke in Trigishead; married at Exeter Cathedral, 8 Sep. 1840, Georgiana, fourth dau. of Rev. R. F. Hallifax, Rector of Richards Castle, Herefordshire, and granddau. of Samuel, Bishop of St. Asaph. See his sister's baptism 2 Dec. 1810.

REGISTER OF BAPTISMS IN THE

potts; College, Durham; Prebendary of the 9th Stall; By H. Phillpotts.

1814 Jan. 26 George,[1] son of Henry and Deborah Maria Phillpotts; College, Durham; Prebendary of the 9th Stall; By H. Phillpotts.

Dec. 16 William,[2] son of Anthony and Elizabeth Tyler; Porter's Lodge, College, Durham; Porter & Verger; By Jn° Clarke. Born Nov' 3rd 1814.

1815 Sep. 26 Arthur Thomas,[3] son of Henry and Deborah Maria Phillpotts; College, Durham; Prebendary of the 9th Stall; by H. Phillpotts.

1816 July 17 Julia,[4] dau. of Henry and Deborah Maria Phillpotts; College, Durham; Prebendary of the second Stall; by H. Phillpotts. Born June 19th 1816.

1817 Jan. 10 Robert,[5] son of Francis and Caroline Baker; College, Durham; Captain in the Royal Navy; by James Baker.

Nov. 11 Charles,[6] son of Anthony and Elizabeth Tyler; Porter's Lodge, College, Durham; Porter & Verger; by D. Haslewood, Sacrist.

Dec. 12 Caroline Mary Anne,[7] dau. of Francis and Caroline Baker; College, Durham; Captain in the Royal Navy; by James Baker. Born Nov. 17.

1818 Aug. 2 Sibella,[8] dau. of Henry and Deborah Maria Phillpotts; College, Durham; Prebendary of the second Stall; by Thos. Baker, off⁸ Minʳ.

1820 May 15 John Scott,[9] son of Henry and Deborah Maria Phillpotts; College, Durham; Prebendary of the second Stall; by D. Durell, off⁸ Minʳ.

1821 Feb. 9 Amelia Catherine,[10] dau. of Francis and Caroline Baker; College, Durham; Captain in the Royal Navy; by James Baker, off⁸ Minʳ.

---

[1] See preceding entry.

[2] Born 3 Nov. 1814. See his burial 6 Sep. 1825, and his father's 14 July 1849.

[3] Born 23 May id. ann. Second-Lieut. Royal Artillery 21 June 1834; First-Lieut. 10 Jan. 1837; Second-Captain 21 May and Captain 30 Nov. 1845; Lieut.-Colonel 24 Sep. 1855; Brevet-Colonel 24 Sep. 1858; Colonel 9 Feb. 1865; Major-General 6 March 1868; rewarded for distinguished services. See his sister's baptism 2 Dec. 1810.

[4] See preceding entry.

[5] See the father's burial 15 April 1823. The mother, dau. of Dr. Price, Prebendary of Durham, was married to Captain Baker at St. Marylebone, London, 16 Jan. 1816; she re-married at Millbrook, Southampton, 19 April 1825, Thomas Barrington Tristram, Esq., who died s.p.

[6] Born 18 Sep. preceding; married at Marylebone, London, 1 June 1851, Emma, dau. of James Rubridge, coachmaker; died, leaving issue, 30 Sep. 1867, buried at Finchley Cemetery.

[7] She married firstly John C. G. Seymour, Esq., and secondly, 1858, Henry Chaytor, Esq., J.P., D.L., of Witton Castle, co. Durham, fourth son of Sir William Chaytor of Croft, first Bart.; living 1889. See her brother's baptism 10 Jan. 1817.

[8] *Recte* Sybella; married 16 July 1836, at St. Marylebone, London, Rev. Francis Du Boulay, Rector of Lawhitton, Cornwall, and had issue. See her sister's baptism 2 Dec. 1810.

[9] See preceding entry.

[10] See her brother's baptism 10 Jan. 1817.

1822 June 4 Elizabeth Jane,[1] dau. of William Nicholas and Elizabeth Darnell; College, Durham; Prebendary; by W. N. Darnell, off^g Min^r.
1824 Sep. 7 Philip Wheler,[1] son of William Nicholas and Elizabeth Darnell; College, Durham; Prebendary; by W. N. Darnell, offic^g Min^r.
1825 June 3 Thomas Charles,[1] son of William Nicholas and Elizabeth Darnell; College; Prebendary; priv. bapt^d Aug. 9, 1824; received into the Church by W. N. Darnell, offic^g Min^r; born July 25th.
1829 Nov. 12 Jane Grace,[1] dau. of William Nicholas and Elizabeth Darnell; College, Durham; Prebendary; by W. N. Darnell, offic^g Min^r; born Septr 8th.
1831 June 23 Frederick Dawson,[2] son of William Stephen and Jane Charlotte Mary Gilly; College, Durham; Prebendary; by G. Townsend, offic^g Min^r; born & privately baptized Feby 6, 1831.
1832 Mar. 12 Anne,[3] dau. of Edward Chaloner and Sophia Ogle; Sutton Benger, Wiltshire, but now resident in the College; Clerk; by Edward Sneyd, offic^g Min^r.
1844 Jan. 28 Alice Anne,[4] dau. of William Stephen and Jane Charlotte Mary Gilly; College, Durham; D.D., Prebendary of Durham Cath^l; by William Stephen Gilly; born J^y 26th; received into the Church by the Dean of Durham, March 5th.
April 4 Charlotte Georgiana Mary,[5] dau. of Henry, Viscount Chelsea, and Mary Sarah; College, Durham; Gentleman; Rec^d into the Church by Gerald Valerian Wellesley, D.D., Canon of Durham Cathedral; priv^y bapt. Feb. 20th 1844; born Novr 27th 1843.

[1] The father was the Rev. William Nicholas Darnell, B.D.; he was baptized 16 April 1776, at All Saints, Newcastle; of Christ Church College, Oxford (B.A. 1796, M.A. 1800); Rector of St. Mary-le-Bow, Durham (June 1809); Vicar of Stockton-on-Tees; Prebendary of Durham (Jan. 1816); Rector of Stanhope, succeeding Bishop Phillpotts; died there and was buried at Durham Cathedral 24 June 1865, æt. 89. The mother was the eldest dau. of the Rev. William Bowe, M.A., of Scorton, co. York; married 15 June 1815; buried at the Cathedral 7 April 1864, æt. 76. [MS. Ped. by E. A. W.]

[2] The father, William Stephen Gilly, was born 28 Jan. 1789 and baptized the same day at Hawkedon; of Catharine College, Cambridge (B.A. 1812, M.A. 1817, D.D. 1833); Rector of North Fambridge, Essex, 1817; Prebendary of Durham 1825; P.C. of Crossgate, Durham, 1828 (circa); Vicar of Northam, Northumberland, 1831, where he died 10 Sep. 1855 and is buried. The mother, who was the second wife, was the only dau. of Colonel Samuel Thomas Colberg, 90th and 58th Regiments; born Nov. 1804 at St. Helier's, Jersey; married at All Saints, Langham Place, London, 12 Dec. 1825. Frederick Dawson Gilly was the eldest son of the second marriage, born 6 Feb. 1831; died at Portage la Prairie, Manitoba, 24 March 1880, s.p.

[3] Born at Kirkley Hall 19 Jan. preceding. Called Annie-Charlotte in the "Landed Gentry," which see. The father, third son of the Rev. John Savile Ogle, D.D., a Prebendary, of Kirkley Hall, Northumberland (in which estate this Edward Challoner succeeded him), by his wife (married at Southampton 14 Oct. 1794) Catherine Hannah, dau. of Edward Sneyd, Esq., of Dublin.

[4] See note above ([2]) as to parents. She married at Manewden, Essex, 27 Aug. 1878, George Holmes Blakesley, Barrister-at-Law, son of the Very Rev. Joseph Williams Blakesley, B.D., Dean of Lincoln.

[5] See her parents' marriage 13 July 1836. She married at St. Paul's, Knightsbridge, 14 July 1874, Rev. Maynard Wodehouse Currie, who died 1887.

1845 Nov. 30 Charles Pudsey,[1] son of William Stephen and Jane Charlotte Mary Gilly; College, Durham; Canon of Durham Cathedral; by William Stephen Gilly.
1846 Sep. 16 Frederick John,[2] son of John and Maria Thomas; College, Durham; Clerk; by J. B. Chester.
1847 Feb. 10 Bertram Savile,[3] son of Arthur and Caroline Amelia Ogle; College, Durham; Officer in the Army; by The Very Rev[d] George Waddington, Dean of Durham. Born Dec[r] 24th 1846.
1849 Jan. 1 George Charlton Leugers Barnard,[4] son of George Fyler and Georgina Townsend; College, Durham; Vicar of Brantingham; by George Townsend, D.D., Canon of Durham. Born July 18th 1848.
1850 Sep. 10 Lucy Elizabeth,[5] dau. of William and Frances Darnell; College, Durham; Minister of Bamburgh; by H. Exeter.

---

[1] See note ([2]) p. 29, as to parents.
[2] Born 5 Aug. preceding; died unmarried 28 Dec. 1876, and buried in Addington Churchyard, Croydon. The father, the Rev. John Thomas, D.C.L., Trinity College, Oxon (Exhibitions at Wadham 1828 and 1829; Craven Scholar 1829; Scholar of Trinity 1830; Latin Verse Prize 1832; Vinerian Scholar 1834), was Fellow and Tutor of Durham University; Canon of Canterbury 1862. He is son of Thomas Thomas, Esq., of Cefncethin, Carmarthenshire, D.L. and J.P., and was born 23 Sep. 1810; living 1878. The mother was Maria, youngest dau. of John Bird Sumner, Prebendary of Durham and Bishop of Chester, and afterwards (1848—1862) Archbishop of Canterbury, by his wife Marianne, dau. of Captain George Robertson, R.N.; she was married 6 June 1842 at St. George's, Hanover Square, by her uncle the Bishop of Winchester; she died 1 Feb. 1862, and was buried in Addington Churchyard.
[3] Eldest son, born 24 Dec. 1846; of Alveston House, Gloucestershire, and Hill House, Steeple Aston, co. Oxford, J.P., Barrister-at-Law; married, 1885, Edith, elder dau. and coheiress of Arthur Edward Somerset, Esq., son of Lord Arthur Somerset, son of Henry, fifth Duke of Beaufort, K.G. The father, Major in the Army (late 9th Regiment), was seventh son of the Prebendary (see baptism of 12 March 1832), and died 28 Dec. 1878. The mother (married 10 Sep. 1844) was fifth dau. of Vice-Admiral William Lechmere of Hill House aforesaid, co. Oxford, died 21 May 1880.
[4] Eldest son and second child, a Paymaster R.N.; living unmarried 1877. The father (son of Rev. George Townsend, D.D., Prebendary, whose burial see 28 Nov. 1857) was born 12 May and bapt. 7 July 1814 at Littleport, Isle of Ely; of Trinity College, Cambridge, M.A. and D.C.L. by the Archbishop of Canterbury 1876; Vicar of Leominster 1857—1862, and Incumbent of St. Michael's, Covent Garden, 1862. He married at St. Maurice's, York, 1 May 1845, Georgina (living 1877), second dau. of John Ditmas of Walkington Manor, co. York, Esq., formerly an Officer 27th Regiment, a colour of which he carried at Waterloo. Their other children are 1, Georgina-Elizabeth-Frances, born 30 Nov. 1846, and baptized 2 Feb. 1847 at Camberwell, Surrey; 3, James-Frederick, born 9 Feb. and baptized 12 May 1850 at Ellorker, co. York, who married 27 Sep. 1877, at St. Sampson's, York, Henrietta-Marian, eldest dau. of Captain William-Frederick-Lowrie, Governor of York Castle, and formerly 63rd Regiment; 4, Charlotte-Constance-Spenser, born 26 Sep. and baptized 7 Oct. 1852 at Brantingham, co. York; 5, Charles-John-Henry-Fyler, born 12 and baptized 26 Oct. 1854 at Belfry Church, York; 6, Mabel-Surtees, born 30 Jan. and baptized 25 March 1856 at Ellerker; 7, Stephen-Chapman, born Oct. and baptized 26 Dec. 1859.
[5] The father was the Rev. William Darnell, born 19 Nov. 1816 at Stockton Vicarage; of Christ Church, Oxford (B.A. 1838, M.A. 1843); Vicar of Bamburgh, Northumberland; J.P. The mother was the eldest dau. of the Ven. Charles Thorp, D.D., Archdeacon and Prebendary of Durham, and Rector of Ryton; married at Ryton 2 Jan. 1844. [MS. Ped. by E. A. W.]

CATHEDRAL CHURCH AT DURHAM. 31

1853 Jan. 6 Mary Christine,[1] dau. of Edward and Elizabeth Greatorex; The Grove, Durham; Minor Canon and Sacrist of Durham; by Edw[d] Greatorex, Sacrist.

Nov. 30 Edward Harcourt,[2] son of Edward and Elizabeth Greatorex; The Grove, Durham; Minor Canon and Sacrist of Durham; by Edw[d] Greatorex, Sacrist.

1854 Feb. 8 Henry Edmonds,[3] son of Henry and Elizabeth Margaret Anne Holden; Bellasis, Durham; Head Master of the Durham Grammar School; by Edw[d] Greatorex, Sacrist. Born Dec. 17th 1853.

1855 July 25 Elizabeth Antonia,[4] dau. of Edward and Elizabeth Greatorex; The Grove, Durham; Minor Canon and Sacrist of Durham; received into the Church by Edw[d] Greatorex, Sacrist; privately baptized July 16th.

1856 Oct. 20 Louisa Maria,[5] dau. of John George and Frederica Louisa Edwards; Pittington Vicarage; Vicar of Pittington; received into the Church by Edw[d] Greatorex, Sacrist; privately baptized in Scotland Sept. 8th.

1858 Jan. 25 Annie Maude,[6] dau. of Edward and Elizabeth Greatorex; The Grove, Durham; Minor Canon and Sacrist of Durham; by Edw[d] Greatorex, Sacrist.

1859 Oct. 8 Cecilia,[7] dau. of Edward and Elizabeth Greatorex; The Grove, Durham; Minor Canon and Sacrist of Durham; by Edw[d] Greatorex, Sacrist.

1860 Feb. 17 Beatrice Blandina,[8] dau. of Henry and Georgiana Bailey Holden;

[1] Living unmarried 1889. The father (living 1889) of Pembroke College, Oxon (B.A. 1845; M.A. 1848), Minor Canon and successively Sacrist, Librarian, and Precentor of the Cathedral, 1862—1872, and afterwards Rector of Croxdale, was born 1823 at Burton-on-Trent, the youngest son of Thomas Greatorex, Esq. (see the burial of his widow 30 July 1868), who was born in 1758. [It is remarkable that a man, born in the reign of George II., should have a son taking his degree in 1845.] The mother (married 8 July 1851, at St. Mary-the-Less) was the third dau., by his second wife, of the Venerable Charles Thorp, Archdeacon of Durham and Rector of Ryton-on-Tyne; she died 1888, and is buried at Croxdale.

[2] In Holy Orders; living 1896 unmarried. See preceding entry.

[3] The father was born 7 July 1814, baptized at St. Martin's; of Balliol College, Oxford; matriculated 30 Nov. 1832 (B.A. 1837, M.A. 1839, B.D. and D.D. 1857); Hon. Canon of Durham 1867; Head Master of Uppingham Grammar School 1845—1853, of Durham Cathedral School 1853—1882; Rector of South Luffenham, Rutland, in 1881. The mother, who was the first wife, was Elizabeth Margaret Anne Edmonds. [MS. Ped. by E. A. W.]

[4] Living unmarried 1896. See her sister's baptism 6 Jan. 1853.

[5] Born 26 Aug. preceding; living unmarried 1876. The father (Trinity College, Cambridge), son of Canon Edwards (whose burial see 8 April 1862), was born 27 May 1822, and baptized at Warboys, Hunts; he became Vicar of Pittington 1854, and is buried there, dying 16 Oct. 1862. The mother was dau. of Thomas Octavius Powles, Esq., of London (son, by his second wife, of John Diston Powles, who had a grant of arms), and was married at Hackney 31 Aug. 1854; living at Bury St. Edmunds 1876.

[6] Living unmarried 1896. See her sister's baptism 6 Jan. 1853.

[7] Living unmarried 1896. See last entry.

[8] See note above ([3]) as to the father. The mother was the second wife Georgiana Bailey Aldham. [MS. Ped. by E. A. W.]

REGISTER OF BAPTISMS IN THE

		Bellasis, Durham; Head Master of the Durham Grammar School; by Edwd Greatorex, Sacrist.
1861	June 24	Rose,[1] dau. of Henry and Georgiana Bailey Holden; Bellasis, Durham; Head Master of the Durham Grammar School; by Edwd Greatorex, Sacrist.
1862	Mar. 25	Constance Mary,[2] dau. of Edward and Elizabeth Greatorex; The Grove, Durham; Minor Canon and Sacrist of Durham; by Edwd Greatorex, Sacrist.
	Aug. 11	Florence Tovey,[3] dau. of Henry and Georgiana Bailey Holden; Bellasis, Durham; Head Master of the Durham Grammar School; by Edwd Greatorex, Sacrist.
1863	Sep. 19	Josephine Fanny,[3] dau. of Henry and Georgiana Bailey Holden; Bellasis, Durham; Head Master of the Durham Grammar School; by J. C. Lowe, Sacrist.
1864	May 15	Charles Thorp,[4] son of Edward and Elizabeth Greatorex; The Grove, Durham; Minor Canon and Precentor of Durham; by J. C. Lowe, Sacrist. Whitsunday.
1865	Mar. 18	Vere,[5] daughter of Henry and Georgiana Bailey Holden; Bellasis, Durham; Head Master of the Durham Grammar School; by J. C. Lowe, Sacrist.
1866	May 14	Georgiana,[6] daughter of Henry and Georgiana Bailey Holden; Bellasis, Durham; Head Master of the Durham Grammar School; by J. C. Lowe, Sacrist.
1867	July 29	Margaret,[7] daughter of Benjamin Charles and Margaret Caffin; South St.; Second Master of the Durham Grammar School; by J. C. Lowe, Sacrist.
	Oct. 5	Hyla,[8] son of Henry and Georgiana Bailey Holden; Bellasis, Durham; Head Master of the Durham Grammar School; by J. C. Lowe, Sacrist; born Sep. 14.
	Nov. 7	Hilda Diana,[9] daughter of Henry Evelyn and Caroline Howley Turner Oakeley; Bishop Cosin's Hall, Durham; H.M. Inspector of Schools; by J. C. Lowe, Sacrist.

---

[1] See note ([8]) p. 31.
[2] Living unmarried 1889. See her sister's baptism 6 Jan. 1853.
[3] See her sister's baptism 17 Feb. 1860.
[4] A chrisom child. See his burial 3 Dec. 1865.
[5] See her burial 23 Aug. 1865, and her sister's baptism 17 Feb. 1860.
[6] See her sister's baptism 17 Feb. 1860.
[7] Eldest child. The father (died 1895) appointed Second Master of the Grammar School 1862, and Vicar of Northallerton Jan. 1877; he is son of William Caffin of Blackheath, Kent, by Bethia, dau. of George Crawford, Lieut. R.A., and is brother of the late Admiral Sir James Crawford Caffin, K.C.B.
[8] See her sister's baptism 17 Feb. 1860.
[9] Born 12 Oct. preceding. The father, born 1833, Her Majesty's Senior Inspector of Schools, formerly Fellow and Senior Mathematical Lecturer of Jesus College, Cambridge, is third son of the Rev. Sir Herbert Oakeley, third Bart., Prebendary of St. Paul's. The mother (married 6 Sep. 1862) dau. of William Hallows Belli, Esq., Bengal Civil Service, by his wife, a sister of Dr. William Howley, Archbishop of Canterbury.

CATHEDRAL CHURCH AT DURHAM.   33

1869 Feb. 20 Rachel Belasyse,[1] daughter of Henry and Georgiana Bailey Holden; Bellasis, Durham; Head Master of the Durham Grammar School; by J. C. Lowe, Sacrist.
1870 Jan.   6 Ernest Gregory,[2] son of Benjamin Charles and Margaret Catlin; South St.; Second Master of the Durham Grammar School; by Edward Greatorex, Precentor.
     July 13 Rosamond,[3] daughter of Joseph and Rosamond Waite; University College; Master of University College; by Thos. Saunders Evans, Canon of Cath. Durh.
1871 Feb.   9 Sophia Louisa,[4] dau. of John and Georgiana Lambton Chambers; South Bailey, Durham; Head Master, Sandbach Gram. Sch., Cheshire; by J. C. Lowe, Sacrist.
     Aug. 16 Marie Louise,[5] dau. of Louis Bernard and Eléonore de Karp; South Bailey, Durham; Professor of Modern Languages, Durham University; by J. C. Lowe, Sacrist.
     Aug. 30 Arthur,[6] son of Joseph and Rosamond Waite; University College; Master of University College; by George Bland, Archdeacon of Northumberland.
1872 Oct. 25 Henry, son of Robert and Rebecca Jon; College; gardener to Archdeacon Prest; by J. C. Lowe, Sacrist.
1874 May 13 Norman,[7] son of William Henry and Frances Henrietta Robertson; South St.; Minor Canon and Sacrist of D^m Cath¹; by W. H. Robertson, Sacrist.

[1] See her sister's baptism 17 Feb. 1860.
[2] See his sister's baptism 29 July 1867.
[3] Born 15 June preceding; died at Norham and was buried there. The father (see his brother's burial 7 Feb. 1848) born 1824; formerly Fellow and Tutor and afterwards Master of University College, Durham, which he resigned on becoming Vicar of Norham Jan. 1873; is Hon. D.D. of his University; living 1896. The mother (married at St. Mary-le-Bow 7 Sep. 1869), born 1851, is elder dau. of Rev. Thomas Saunders Evans, Canon of Durham and Professor of Greek in that University.
[4] The father (M.A. St. John's College, Cambridge) then Mathematical Master at the Grammar School. The mother, who was married at St. Mary the Less 31 Dec. 1885, was the dau. of Thomas Marsden, Procter of Durham. See his burial 3 July 1857.
[5] Born 2 July preceding. The father, a teacher of foreign languages in Durham, born 14 June 1824, son of Maurice de Karp of Lille, France, by his wife Augusta de Félice; he died 26 April 1876, and is buried at Bournemouth. The mother Eleanora, dau. of Dr. J. G. Baiter, of Zurich, Switzerland, by his wife Susanna Drummond, was married at St. John's, Notting Hill, Middlesex, 12 July 1870; living at Zurich 1877.
[6] Living 1889. See his sister's baptism 13 July 1870.
[7] Born 20 April preceding; living 1889. The father, born at Buxton, Derbyshire, 14 Feb. 1840, was son of William Henry Robertson, Esq., M.D., F.R.C.P., J.P., of Buxton, by his wife Eliza, dau. of John Slater Gill, of Chesterfield, same county; of Christ Church, Oxon (B.A. 1863; M.A. 1866); successively Curate of Thorpe Mandeville and Houghton-le-Spring; Minor Canon of Durham Sep. 1866 and Sacrist 20 Nov. 1872, and also Sub-Librarian; he died 2 Aug. 1885 at Buxton, and is buried at the Cathedral Cemetery, Durham. The mother Frances Henrietta, second dau. of the late Rev. Francis Jones, M.A., Oriel College, Oxon, and Vicar of Moreton Pinkney, Northamptonshire, by his wife Mary Anne Georgiana (living 1896 at Durham), dau of Lieut.-Colonel Peter Taylor Roberton, of Tiverton, Devon, by his wife Mary, dau. of Vice-Admiral Sir William Parker, first Bart., of the Harburn family.

F

1875	June 28	Marion Adela,[1] dau. of Henry Evelyn and Caroline Howley Turner Oakeley; North Bailey; H.M. Inspector of Schools; by W. H. Robertson, Sacrist.
1876	Sep. 19	Eleanor Mary,[2] dau. of William Lyall and Mary Gertrude Holland; The College; late Vicar of S[t] Peter's, Auckland; by H. B. Tristram, Canon.
1877	Jan. 20	Hilda,[3] dau. of William Henry and Frances Henrietta Robertson; South St.; Minor Canon and Sacrist of Durham Cathedral; by W. H. Robertson, Sacrist.
1878	Aug. 31	Archibald Harvey, son of William Henry Robertson and Frances Henrietta his wife.
1879	April 6	Gerald Edward,[4] son of Gerald Rivers Maltby, Gentleman, and Hercy Eliza Cecilia his wife.
1880	Aug. 15	Allan Aylmer, son of John George Wilson, Gentleman, and Anne Louisa his wife.
1883	April 22	James Arthur, son of James Hinson, Coachman, and Isabella his wife.
1885	Mar. 19	Dorothy Kate Gwyllyam, dau. of Henry William Watkins, Archdeacon of Durham, and Kate Mary Margaret his wife.
	Nov. 28	Mary Elizabeth, dau. of Samuel Blackwell Guest Williams, Clerk in Holy Orders, Second Master of the Grammar School, and Catherine his wife. (Born at Cornhill on Tweed Rectory Sep. 11, 1885.)
1886	Oct. 18	Helen Margaret Gwyllyam, dau. of Henry William Watkins, Archdeacon of Durham, and Kate Mary Margaret his wife.
	Dec. 10	Warren Kirkham, son of Samuel Blackwell Guest Williams and Catherine his wife. (Born at Durham Nov. 11, 1886.)
1888	Feb. 20	Alyn Arthur, son of Samuel Blackwell Guest Williams and Catherine his wife. (Born in Durham Jan. 22, 1888.)
1889	Sep. 19	Wynne Austin, son of Samuel Blackwell Guest Williams and Catherine his wife. (Born in Durham Aug. 10, 1889.)
1891	Aug. 17	Edmund Nelson May, son of George William Anson Firth, Sacrist of Durham Cathedral, and Louisa Caroline his wife. (Born July 10, 1891.)
1893	Feb. 5	Geoffrey Leonard, son of Percy John Heawood, M.A. Oxon, Mathematical Lecturer in the University of Durham, and Christiana his wife. (Born at Durham Jan. 5, 1893.)
	April 4	Richard Howard, son of Samuel Blackwell Guest Williams, and Catherine his wife. (Born at Durham Feb. 27, 1893.)

---

[1] Born 4 June 1875. See her sister's baptism 7 Nov. 1867.

[2] The father, M.A., sometime British Chaplain at Riga; now Vicar of Cornhill, Northumberland. The mother eldest dau. of Henry Baker Tristram, LL.D., F.R.S. (Lincoln College, Oxford, B.A. 1844; M.A. 1846); Canon of Durham; the eminent naturalist and author, by his wife Frances-Eliza Bowlby. She was married at Greatham, co. Durham, 1 Nov. 1872.

[3] Born 22 Dec. preceding; living 1889. See her brother's baptism 13 May 1874.

[4] Gerald Rivers Maltby was son of Rev. Henry Maltby, Rector of Egglescliffe and Canon of Durham, who was son of Edward Maltby, Bishop of Durham.

1894 Oct. 24 Christian Florence,[1] dau. of John Henry Eden, Lieut.-Colonel H.M. Army, and Florence his wife.
1895 July 31 Sybil Frances Eleanor, dau. of Edward Jepson, Doctor in Medicine and Mayor of Durham, and Jessie Maria his wife.
All Saints' Day (Nov. 1) Gwendolen Edith Gwyllyam, dau. of Henry William Watkins, Archdeacon of Durham, and Kate Mary Margaret his wife.

---

[1] John Henry Eden was son of Rev. John Patrick Eden, Rector of Sedgfield and Hon. Canon of Durham, who was grandson of Sir Robert Eden, Bart.

MARIAGES.

1610 Feb. 3 Alice Sugar maried to Matthew Blunt, of Newcastle.
1623 Feb. 3 Jo. Johnson, of Newcastle, and Barbaire Reedshaw, of Gaitshed.
1625 Oct. 9 Tho. Tyler, lay singing man of this church, and Anne Sheffeild, widow.
   Jan. 28 Mr. Robert Eden and M^{rls} [blank] Millet.
1630 June 10 Henricus Smith,[1] armiger, uxorem duxit Elizabetham Chapman.
1631 Jan. 22 Johannes Wright uxorem duxit Saram Dodsworth.
   Feb. 7 Anthonius Thompson,[2] regrarius Dunelmensis, uxorem duxit Aliciam Goodayre.
1632 Feb. 14 Johannes Vasius,[3] generosus, uxorem duxit Franciscam, filiam M^{ri} Fardinandi Morecroft, hujus Cathedralis ecclesiæ p^ebendarii.
   Feb. 19 Thomas Burrell,[4] Artiu' magister, Episcopi Dunelmensis vicarius in spiritualibus & cancellarius, uxorem duxit Annam Chapman, Decani Dunelmensis priuignam.
1637 June 29 Anthonius Maxson,[5] ecclesiâ Cathedralis dunelmē'ss, uxorem duxit Jane fetherstenhailgh, viduā'.
   Jan. 30 Robertus Aisley,[6] generosus, uxore' duxit Joanna', filiam m^{ri}

---

[1] He of West Herrington, co. Pal., Esq., Counsellor-at-Law; was aged 6 in 1615, when his father (whose burial see 17 Dec. 1631) entered his pedigree at St. George's Visitation. She dau. of Mrs. Hunt, the Dean's wife, by her first husband Seth Chapman, of Edmundsbury, gent., and is mentioned in her mother's will 16 May 1645. Their dau. Philadelphia married William Cooper, gent., of Scarborough, and had a dau. and coheiress Mary, wife of Dr. John Smith, the Prebendary. See baptism of 25 Oct. 1696.

[2] He son of Mr. Thompson, of Crossgate, and baptized there. See the marriage of his granddau., Mary Church, 30 Nov. 1676.

[3] ["Mrs. Joan: wiffe of m^r John Vasey, gen.," buried 2 Nov. 1631, St. Oswald's.]

[4] He (recte Burwell), LL.D. and Chancellor of the diocese, was aged 63 in 1666; buried at St. Margaret's, Westminster, 25 March 1673, æt. 70. She the dau. by her first husband, Seth Chapman, of Edmundsbury, gent., of Mrs. Hunt, wife of Dr. Richard Hunt, the Dean (whose burial see 3 Nov. 1638). See her burial 28 March 1640, and the baptisms of two children 20 June 1639.

[5] He Rector of Middleton Teesdale and Wolsingham; he married firstly, 10 May 1617, Anne (baptized 21 Jan. 1597-8 at Ryton), dau. of Ambrose Dudley, of Chopwell, co. Pal., Esq., by his wife Isabel, dau. of Richard Grenville, of Wootton, Bucks. She was buried at St. Andrew's, Auckland, 6 Jan. 1678-9.

[6] He was of Coves-houses, near Stanhope, co. Pal., gent.; she (second wife) dau. of the Rev. Ferdinand Morecroft, Prebendary. See the baptism of their dau. 11 Dec. 1638.

Ferdinandi Moorecroft, hujus Cathedralis ecclesiæ prebendarii.
1639 Nov. 28 Jacobus Moorecroft,[1] clericus, uxorem duxit Franciscam Suddicke.
1641 Oct. 23 Jacobus Foster ux. duxit Jana' Hall ; per lic. pet.
Oct. 28 Matthæus Hall uxore' duxit Isabella' Smith.
1642 Sep. 6 Thomas Thynne,[2] Miles, uxorem duxit Stewartam, vena^{lis} viri Gualteri Ballcanquall, hujus ecclesiæ decani, filiam.
1654 April 20 John Walton,[3] Alderman, and Marye James.
1662 June 24 Samuell Bolton,[4] minor Cannon of this church, and Sarah daughter of m^r Elias Smith, minor can'on of the same; it being midsomer day.
1663 Oct. 15 Thomas Davison[5] and Mary Nailor.
1664 July 9 Willia' Metcalfe et An Robson, of the parish of Bronspeth. Eli. Smith.
July 27 Robert Dand et Alce Embleton, of the parish of Shilbottle. Eli. Smith.
Aug. 16 Richard Wrench, prebend of this church, and An Baddelay.
Sep. 6 John Harison, of Elwick parish, et Ann Patteson. Eli. Smith.
Sep. 12 Rowland Kell et Mary Hubbocke, de Billingha'.
Oct. 27 Mr. Thomas Bellay, of the parish of all Saints in Newcastle, and Jane Burton, of the parish of Catherick in Yorkshire. Eli. Smith.

---

[1] He Vicar of Heighington, co. Pal.; she dau. and heir of Michael Suddick, of Monk-Hesilden, yeoman. She re-married the Rev. Gilbert Wildbore, Vicar of Heighington.

[2] Sir Thomas Thynne was youngest son of Sir Thomas Thynne, of Longleat, Wilts, Knt. (ancestor of the present Marquess of Bath), by his first wife Maria, dau. of George Touchet, eighteenth Lord Audley. Stuarta Balcanquall was dau. and coheir of Dean Walter Balcanquall. See the baptism of their first child 21 July 1643. Sir Thomas and Stuarta (who was first wife) were parents also of Thomas Thynne, who eventually succeeded to Longleat, and is so well known to posterity as "Tom of Ten Thousand." In a list published *circa* 1655 Dean Balcanquall (his name was spelt in many different ways), then deceased, appears as having compounded for his estate for Dame Elizabeth Hammond his late wife. Lady Hammond was dau. of Anthony Aucher, of Bishopsbourne, Esq. (by Margaret, dau. of Edwin Sandys, Archbishop of York), and widow of Sir William Hammond, of St. Alban's Court, Kent, Knt., and was married at Bishopsbourne 21 Sep. 1624 to Dr. Balcanquall, who became Dean of Durham in 1639. He was of Pembroke Hall, Cambridge. In 1640 he, with the rest of the Cathedral clergy, fled before the invading army of the Scottish Insurgents, the Bishop himself retiring to Yorkshire. The Dean died 25 Dec. 1645, and was buried at Chirk, co. Denbigh. [The Durham baptismal registers afford numerous evidences of this incursion of "Scotishemen," and many of the "baise-begotten" children of that time are, rightly or wrongly, assigned to both officers and men.]

[3] He a mercer, son of Hugh Walton, draper, several times Mayor of Durham, and in 1615, when he had a grant of arms from St. George; she dau. of William James, the Prebendary, whose burial see 21 Jan. 1659-60.

[4] He died June 1681. [Robert Bolton occurs as *hypodidasculus* 1595—1600.] She died 1691. See her father's burial 9 Dec. 1676; see the baptisms of their children 17 March 1662-3 and 21 Dec. 1664.

[5] He Vicar of Norton, co. Pal.; she dau. of the Rev. Joseph Naylor, Prebendary. See the baptism of her brother 18 Dec. 1637.

1664	Nov. 15	Mr. Nicholaus Conyers[1] et Margarett Tempest, widdow.
	Jan. 2	John Fowler et An Hall, of the parish of Gainforth; with licence.
1665	May 16	Christopher Stoddert,[2] de Hellen Aukland, et Frances Heron.
	Feb. 9	Ottiwell Ryder and Elizabeth Gouerneger, of St Andrew Aukland; having a licence.
1666	April 25	Willia' Wood, of the parish of Gisbrough, et Elizabeth Dowthwaite, of the parish of all Sts in Newcastle.
	May 14	William Sands and Margarett Portesse, the one in the parish of Darlington, the other of Smeeton.
	May 22	John Litster, of Hart parish, and An Walker, of Sedgfield parish.
	June 11	Willia' Agar et An Crawforth, being both of the parish of B{pp} weremouth; wth Licence.
	Sep. 4	Thomas Fowler and Isabell Bracke, both of Merington parish.
	Oct. 13	Willia' Smith, de Billinga', et An Boyce, of Hart; wth Licence.
	Nov. 27	John Thompson et An Emerson, both of the parish of Stanhope; with licence. Dr Basiere.
	Nov. 29	Thomas Stoddert et Jane Jurdison, both of Easington parish; with licence.
1667	April 27	Thomas Knaggs, de Whitworth, uxorem duxit Isabellam Iley.
	May 4	Christopherus Ward, de Sockburn, uxorem duxit Catherina' Lazenby.
	May 6	Joh'is Harison uxorem duxit Margaretam Ainsley.
	May 25	Joh'is Huntley uxorem duxit Dorotheam Wilson.
	May 28	Carolus Middleton, de Gateshead, uxorem duxit Annam Jurdison.
	May 28	Richardus Todde, de Novocastro, uxorem duxit Barbariam Middleton.
	June 5	Georgius Kipling,[3] hujus Eccl'æ virgifer, uxore' duxit Alicia' Spenceley.
	July 10	Thomas Greenwell[4] uxorem duxit Janam Ayre, de Wolsingha', viduam.
	Sep. 21	Nicholaus Barwick,[5] Generosus, uxorem duxit Hellenen Green.
	Oct. 5	Nicholaus Farrow uxorem duxit Mariam Farrow, viduam.
	Jan. 5	Thomas Lowther and Margaret White.
	Feb. 3	John Yappe[6] and Ellenor Hilton.
1668	April 11	Will' Oliver and Jane Sidwick; wth a Licence.

[1] Mary, their eldest child, was baptized at St. Mary's 10 July 1665.

[2] He was son of Christopher Stothard, and baptized at St. Helen's Auckland. The eldest child of this marriage, Margaret, was baptized there 18 March 1665-6, and Frances and Barbara afterwards.

[3] See his burial 26 July 1670. She dau. of John Spenceley, chandler, was baptized 6 April 1643 at St. Nicholas.

[4] Also entered in Wolsingham Register. The Greenwells, a numerous clan, were seated at Greenwell in Wolsingham parish from the twelfth century. The first volume of the register is missing.

[5] See his burial 7 Dec. 1687.

[6] See his burial 2 Dec. 1691, and hers 4 Aug. 1718.

1668	April 14	George Dunn and Merriell Pattison.
	Sep. 8	Gulielmus Taylor uxorem duxit Margaretam Williamson, viduam.
	Sep. 28	Johannes Burnet uxorem duxit Mariam Bell.
	Jan. 14	Johannes Jeckell uxorem duxit Elizabetham Wood, viduam.
1669	May 20	Johannes Gray uxorem duxit Elizabetham Hopper.
	May 22	Henry Nateby and Mary Key.
	June 19	Matthæus Brewer uxorem duxit Annam Shawter.
	July 2	Thomas Watson uxorem duxit Isabellam Em'erson.
	July 17	Robertus Wilson uxorem duxit Annam Thomson.
	July 24	Henricus Arrowsmith uxorem duxit Mariam Kirtley.
	July 27	Josephus Rosden uxorem duxit Isabellam Murton, vidua'.
	Aug. 2	Johannes Harrison uxorem duxit Elizabetham Smith.
	Aug. 7	Johannes Sparke uxorem duxit Annam Allinson.
	Sep. 25	Christopherus Paxton uxorem duxit Janam Reed.
	Sep. 27	Gulielmus Anderson uxorem duxit Annam Johnson.
	Oct. 2	Antonius Harrison uxorem duxit Mariam Suretyes.
	Oct. 9	Gulielmus Paxton[1] uxorem duxit Barbariam Taylor.
	Oct. 11	Thomas Chapman uxorem duxit Margaretam Maddison.
	Oct. 28	Georgius Johnson uxorem duxit Dorotheam Bradford.
	Nov. 3	Johannes Davison uxorem duxit Elizabetham Arrowsmith.
	Nov. 11	Johannes Midford[2] uxorem duxit Dorotheam Scruton.
	Nov. 14	Gulielmus Wright uxorem duxit Elizabetham Langstaffe.
	Dec. 11	Anthonius Ayre, Katherinam Garfoote de Woolsinga' duxit uxore'.
	Dec. 16	Michael Welsh uxorem duxit Annam Moore.
	Dec. 29	Thomas Westgarth uxorem duxit Saram Meggison.
	Dec. 29	Christopher Messenger uxorem duxit Elizabetha' Story.
	Jan. 25	Robertus Melbanke uxorem duxit Ellenoram Harrison.
	Feb. 7	Robertus Lambe[3] uxorem duxit Franciscam Airson.
	Feb. 8	Johan'es Shepheardson uxorem duxit Elizabetham Smith.
	Feb. 13	Jacobus Harrison uxorem duxit Elizabetham Cooper.
	Feb. 18	Johannes Mudspeth uxorem duxit Annam Currye.
	Mar. 10	Johannes Gargrave uxorem duxit Franciscam White.
1670	April 6	Nicolaus Kendall uxorem duxit Annam Raine.
	April 17	Johannes Simpson uxorem duxit Aliciam Peverell.
	April 21	Gulielmus Kitching uxorem duxit Elizabetham Savage.
	April 23	Gulielmus Mason uxorem duxit Janam Dunn.
	May	Gulielmus Darneton uxorem duxit Susannam Bainbridge.
	May 23	Christopherus Bell uxore' duxit Annam Mickleton.[4]

[1] He a mercer. Baptisms of their children occur at St. Nicholas.

[2] Also recorded in Bow Register. See his burial 4 Oct. 1704, and hers 18 Feb. 1684-5.

[3] He the son of John Lamb, of Durham, was baptized 14 June 1642, was a tobacconist and Alderman (chosen 10 April 1704) ; free of the Weavers' Company. He died 2nd and was buried 3rd June 1705 in St. Nicholas Church. Will dated 28 April 1705. His wife the dau. of Alderman John Airson, of Durham ; she was haptized 21 June 1646; buried 12 Feb. 1685-6. [MS. Ped. by E. A. W.]

[4] She was dau. of Christopher Mickleton, of Durham, Attorney-at-Law (whose burial see 29 Aug. 1669), by his second wife Anne Dodshon. See her burial 6 Dec. 1737.

REGISTER OF MARRIAGES IN THE

1670 May 26 Christoph. Hawdon duxit Janam Gilpin.
June 1 Georgius Nicholson, Elizabetham Harrison uxore' duxit.
June 13 Gulielmus Chipchase uxorem duxit Janam Wheathey.
June 20 David Ells[1] uxorem duxit Margaretam Willson.
July 21 Robertus Peverell uxorem duxit Ellenoram Shaw.
July 22 Simonus Pattison uxorem duxit Annam Buttler.
July 23 Georgius Johnson uxorem duxit Janam Lackenby.
Sep. 14 Johannes Day uxorem duxit Elizabetham Makins.
Sep. 28 Gulielmus Watson uxorem duxit Elizabetham Sheraton.
Nov. 3 Johannes Dent uxorem duxit Margaretam Bainbridge.
Nov. 5 Jerimiah Hobson uxorem duxit Annam Reed.
Dec. 7 Nathaniel Robinson uxorem duxit Franciscam Clayton.
Jan. 19 Petrus Taylor uxorem duxit Janam Mason.
Feb. 4 Radulphus Moon uxorem duxit Franciscam Harperley.
Feb. 1 Gulielmus Johnson duxit Margeriam Raddon.
Feb. 25 Richardus Wilson uxorem duxit Janam Elstob.
1671 April 28 Richardus Heighley uxorem Thomasinam Parkins duxit.
June 6 Gulielmus Peverell duxit Annam Oliver.
June 16 Richardus Coultman, Annam Blithman, viduam, duxit.
June 28 Joseph Williamstone, Margaretam Bromwell uxore' duxit.
July 27 Johannes Wright uxorem duxit Aliciam Sampson.
June 21 Jacobus Snawdon, Magdalena' Horsman duxit.
Aug. 11 Johannes Harrison uxorem duxit Mariam Lynn.
Aug. 19 Richardus Arrundell[2] uxorem duxit Margeriam Smurthwaite.
Sep. 26 Gulielmus Johnson uxorem duxit Trotham Lambe.
Sep. 29 Gulielmus Doeshon, Margaretam Renton uxorem duxit.
Sep. 29 Lancelotus Maughan, Annam Mowbrey duxit.
Sep. 29 Henricus Wheldon duxit Elizabetham Hutchison.
Oct. 13 Richardus Marshall uxorem duxit Mariam Adamson.
Oct. 13 Richardus Hawdon duxit Annam Dunne.
Oct. 18 Michaell Burnop uxorem duxit Mariam Atkin.
Oct. 24 Robertus Swaineston, Eden Fowler duxit.
Oct. 30 Randulphus Adamson uxorem duxit Isabellam Hutchinson.
Oct. 30 Georgius Emmerson uxorem duxit Janam Russells.
Nov. 11 Gulielmus Allenson duxit Janam Shafto.
1673 May 6 Radulphus Middleton uxorem duxit Hannam Bateman.
May 26 Thomas Grim uxorem duxit Isabellam Dossy, paro. de Wearemouth ep.
April 30 Anth. Johnson uxorem duxit Marg'tam Watson.
1674 May 27 Edvardus Kirkby,[3] Eccli'æ Cathedralis Dunelm. Minor Cauonicus, uxorem duxit Eliz. Thompson.
June 20 Joh'es Pickering uxorem duxit Bridgetta' Carr.
Nov. 24 Will'us Munday uxorem duxit Jana' Pallacer.

---

[1] See his burial 2 Oct. 1681. This was his second marriage.
[2] The name of Arundell frequently occurs in St. Nicholas Registers. [" Christopher Arundell & Alice Bullmer " were married 11 May 1641 at St. Oswald's.]
[3] See his burial 19 March 1608-9.

1675	April 7	Rich'us Roberts, hujus Eccli'æ Minor Canonicus, duxit Mirriama' Hester.
	July 1	Jacob Maire uxorem duxit Marg'tam Maxwell.
	Aug. 3	Georgius Pearte uxorem duxit Annam Brack.
	Jan. 5	Rich'us Richardson uxore' duxit Dorothea' Hall.
	Mar. 2	Thomas Harperly uxorem duxit Mariam Davison.
	Nov. 4	Johannes Milner,[1] hujus Eccli'æ Minor Canonicus, uxorem duxit Joannam Stones, viduam.
1676	Mar. 27	Michael Hodshon uxorem duxit Anna' Thompson.
	April 1	Joh'es Collin uxorem duxit Annam Boasman.
	April 8	Franciscus Catterick uxore' duxit Anna' Harrison.
	May 23	Tho. Hixon uxorem duxit Marg'tam Atkinson.
	June 17	Henricus Clerke uxorem duxit Joannam Lodge.
	June 26	Josephus Bitleston uxore' duxit Marg'tam Swinburne, vid'.
	July 4	Christopher Deanham uxore' duxit Janam Bainbridge.
	July 15	Joh'es Tweddell uxorem duxit Margaretam Smith.
	July 15	Rich'us Nicholson uxorem duxit Mariam Fowler, vidua'.
	July 21	Samuel Duxbury uxorem duxit Mariam Maddison.
	Aug. 14	Baldwynus Pitt,[2] Ar., uxorem duxit Alicia' Johnson.
	Sep. 11	Rich'us Waugh uxore' duxit Anna' Hutchinson.
	Sep. 12	Joh'es Barker uxorem duxit Franciscam Hutton, viduam.
	Oct. 7	Joh'es Chilton uxorem duxit Margaretam Hett.
	Nov. 30	Thomas Bowser uxorem duxit Mariam Church.[3]
	Nov. 30	Henricus Shawe uxorem duxit Ciciliam Harrison, vidua'.
	Jan. 11	Gulielmus Atkinson uxorem duxit Saram Shaw.
	Mar. 6	Thomas Tueker uxorem duxit Annam Wilson, viduam.
1677	April 3	Gulielm's Agar[4] uxorem duxit Janam Reed.
	April 19	Gulielm's Jurdison uxorem duxit Elizabetham Johnson.
	April 21	Joh'es Mitchell uxorem duxit Annam Hutton.
	May 1	Lancelotus Shawter uxorem duxit Mariam Lodge.
	May 2	Gulielmus Croft uxorem duxit Eliz. Bishoprick, viduam.
	June 5	Edvard's Harrison uxorem duxit Maria' Crawforth, sp'.
	July 14	Rob'tus Clayton uxorem duxit Franciscam Paxton.
	Aug. 7	Thomas Ward uxorem duxit Annam Atkinson.
	Aug. 17	Gulielm's Aire uxorem duxit Aliciam Chaimbers, viduam.
	Aug. 28	Joh'es Sanderson uxorem duxit Ellenora' Blarton, vidua'.
	Aug. 29	Gulielm's Stagg[5] uxorem duxit Alicia' Scurfeild, vid.
	Oct. 18	Anthonius Watson uxorem duxit Mariam Watson, vid.
	Nov. 19	Georgius Hills uxorem duxit Margeria' Hutton, vid.
	Nov. 29	Alexander Shaw uxorem duxit Ellenora' Foster,[6] vid.

[1] See his burial 5 June 1705. She was probably widow of Mr. Christopher Stones, who has a dau. baptized 28 Nov. 1665.
[2] Marriage licence dated 10 Aug.; he described as of the Middle Temple and she as spinster.
[3] She was dau. of William Church, gent., Under Sheriff of the county, by his wife Margaret, dau. of Anthony Thompson, of Crossgate, gent
[4] See (perhaps) his previous marriage 11 June 1666.
[5] See his burial 19 Feb. 1692-3.
[6] She was widow of John Forster, organist, whose burial see 21 April 1677.

1677	Dec. 18	Gulielm⁸ Wilson,¹ Adv⁸, uxorem duxit M⁸ᵐ Maria' Allenson.
	Jan. 31	Joh'es Pallacer uxorem duxit Marg'tam Forrest.
	Feb. 2	Gulielm⁸ Conyers uxorem duxit Saram Watson, vid.
	Feb. 12	Samuel Rawling uxorem duxit Martham Dale.
	Feb. 12	Michael Burnopp uxorem duxit Elizabetham Coulson.
	Feb. 21	Joh'es Toe uxorem duxit Mariam Snawdon, vid.
	Mar. 21	Rich'us Apleby uxorem duxit Rebeccam Welsh.
1678	Mar. 27	Gulielm⁸ Gibson uxorem duxit Annam Lightfoot.
	April 9	Thomas Stainsby uxorem duxit Janam Tyndall, vid.
	April 18	Thomas Rawling uxorem duxit Magdalenam Forster.
	April 23	Joh'es Burrell uxorem duxit Ciciliam Crawforth.
	April 25	Joh'es Jeffreyson uxorem duxit Jennettam Dobson.
	April 28	Joh'es Lamb uxorem duxit Mariam Rutlidge.
	May 1	Gulielm⁸ Snawdon² uxorem duxit Barbara' Wilson.
	July 18	Leonard⁸ Robinson uxorem duxit Maria' Robinson.
	July 24	Timotheus Hickerongill uxore' duxit Anna' Robson.
	Aug. 10	Rob'tus Hutchinson uxorem duxit Alicia' Ranson, vid.
	Aug. 26	Rob'tus Webster uxorem duxit Marg'tam Wood.
	Sep. 28	Gulielm⁸ Marley uxorem duxit Eliz. Iveson.
	Oct. 22	Gulielm⁸ Skurrey uxorem duxit Barbara' Cosins, vidua'.
	Oct. 22	Joh'es Bownas uxorem duxit Isabella Watson.
	Oct. 26	Gulielm's Wharram uxorem duxit Ellenora' Todd.
	Oct. 28	Rich'us Paxton uxorem duxit Catherina' Forster.
	Dec. 28	Rich'us Pollett uxorem duxit Francisa' Peirson.
	Feb. 3	Thomas Brumley uxore' duxit Anna' Gordon, vidua'.
	Feb. 8	Joh'es Geldert uxore' duxit Annam Hilton.³
	Feb. 11	Joh'es Todd uxorem duxit Jana' Stewart.
	Feb. 26	Rad'us Rookby uxorem duxit Susanna' Jackson, vidua'.
1679	April 10	Gulielm⁸ Emerson uxorem duxit Margaretam Smelt, vidua'.
	May 3	Rich'us Wilson uxorem duxit Maria Raw.
	May 7	Rich'us Porter uxorem duxit Marg'tam Parkinson.
	June 10	Rad'us Foreman uxorem duxit Maria' Pickering.
	June 30	Gulielm⁸ Brockett⁴ uxorem duxit Eliz. Coulson.
	July 29	Parcivallus Wheldell uxorem duxit Emmettam Bartram.
	July 30	Gulielm⁸ Marley uxorem duxit Elizabetham Kirkby.
	Aug. 6	Rob'tus Clerke uxorem duxit Marg'tam Maire.
	Aug. 9	Martinus Forster uxore' duxit Maria' Steadman.
	Aug. 12	Stephanus Peart uxorem duxit Marg'tam Lee, vidua'.

---

[1] See his burial 7 Dec. 1690.
[2] See his burial 15 Oct. 1692.
[3] See her second marriage 23 Dec. 1699.
[4] Also entered at St. Mary-le-Bow, where the date is 1 July. He was a plumber, perhaps to the Cathedral, and son of William Brockett, of St. Oswald's (buried there 1688), yeoman and bailiff, where he is registered as born 25 Aug. 1655 and buried 1705; she "inkeeper in South Baily, bury'd near her husband" 25 July 1724. Their children are baptized at Bow, St. Nicholas, and St. Oswald's. One dau., "Mʳˢ Elizabeth Brocket of yᵉ South Baily," married (as second wife) 5 Sep. 1702, at St. Oswald's, Mr. Patrick Ross, schoolmaster, who lies buried at St. Oswald's, under an altar-tomb, with a lengthy Latin inscription.

CATHEDRAL CHURCH AT DURHAM. 13

1679 Aug. 19 Joh'es Robinson uxorem duxit Hannam Croft.
   Aug. 30 Anthonius Sharpe uxorem duxit Annam Hall, vidua'.
   Sep. 20 Cuthbertus Thompson uxorem duxit Eliz. Emerson.
   Sep. 27 Rob'tus Welfoot uxorem duxit Franciscam Bee.
   Oct. 22 Georgius Bullock[1] uxorem duxit Marg'tam Waistell.
   Oct. 25 Joh'es Phillipson uxorem duxit Janam Richardson.
   Nov. 13 Gulielm' Hume uxorem duxit Janam Raw.
   Dec. 1 Georgius Shepherd uxorem duxit Agnetem Young, vidua'.
   Dec. 30 Joh'es Peirson uxore' duxit Eliz. Emerson.
   Jan. 29 Georgius Emerson uxorem duxit Anna' Adamson.
   Sep. 4[2] Milo Eubank uxorem duxit Aliciam Fletcher.
1680 April 8 Gulielm' Elstobb uxorem duxit Janam Spark.
   May 1 Thomas Fairbarnes uxorem duxit Anna' Gallowly.
   May 13 Gulielm' Thompson uxorem duxit Lucie Ord.
   May 31 Thomas Harrison uxorem duxit Ellenora' Trotter.
   June 5 Joshua Sanderson uxorem duxit Francisca' Ward.
   June 10 Georgius Robinson uxorem duxit Marg'tam Loanesdall.
   July 24 Gulielm' Skinner[3] uxorem duxit Mariam Fulthorp, vid.
   July 28 Mattheus Downes uxorem duxit Eliz. Drizedell.
   Aug. 13 Joh'es Sanderson uxorem duxit Mariam Wells.
   Aug. 16 Joh'es Simpson uxorem duxit Jana' Brackenbury,[4] vid.
   Sep. 9 Jacobus Wales uxorem duxit Marg'tam Gibson.
   Oct. 2 Rad'us Ironside[5] uxorem duxit Ursula' Hogg.
   Oct. 11 Rich'us Hull uxorem duxit Catherina' Wilkinson.
   Nov. 15 Carolus Hedly uxorem duxit Marg'tam Marley, vid.
   Nov. 20 Thomas Butler[6] uxorem duxit Mariam Foster, vid.

[1] See his burial 2 Aug. 1699 ; she was the second wife.
[2] In same hand but paler ink, and evidently omitted and written in afterwards.
[3] He was undoubtedly nephew to Dr. Cosin, Bishop of Durham, although considerable research by Charles Jackson, Esq., F.S.A., of Doncaster, has not been successful in establishing the marriage of a sister (Mary) of the Bishop with a Skinner, shewn by Surtees (vol. i., cxiv.), who, however, is also wrong in giving the Bishop two sisters married to . . . . Norfolk and . . . . Daniel. The Bishop, writing about Hull, in an unpublished letter, 12 Feb. 1669-70, to his Secretary, Miles Stapylton, mentions " my nephew Mr. Skinner, an alderman of that towne." This William Skinner was sworn a Free Burgess of Hull 3 Sep. and fined 8 Oct. 1657 ; elected Alderman 16 Oct. 1662, and Mayor 25 Sep. 1664 ; died at Peckham, Surrey, 19 and buried at Holy Trinity, Hull, 28 Sep. 1680, æt. 53. M.I. Will dated 13 Sep. 1680, and proved at York 30 March 1682. He married thrice, and all his wives are buried at Hull. The above, the third wife, was dau. of Peter Smith, of London, and widow of Timothy Fulthorp, of London, and Tunstall, co. Pal. ; she died 5 and was buried 9 Oct. 1719.
[4] She widow of William Bowser, of Auckland. By this husband she had (at least) a dau. Elizabeth, born 28 March 1682, and another Anne, born 22 Feb. 1684-5, who married Michael Pemberton, of Bainbridge Holme, co. Pal., gent., and had a dau. Mary, living 1725.
[5] He was baptized at Houghton 1650, and died 1729 (see Ped. of IRONSIDE, Surtees, vol. i.) ; he is ancestor of the present Henry-George-Outram Bax-Ironside, of Houghton-le-Spring, Esq. (see " Landed Gentry "). She dau. and coheir of Christopher Hogg, gent., by his wife Eleanor, dau. and coheir of Michael Reed, of The Cragg, Northumberland, gent.
[6] He of Old Acres, co. Pal., Esq. ; he was buried 28 Oct. 1712 at St. Oswald's, the register of which states " he dyed in a public-house here." His son Hylton was baptized and buried at St. Oswald's.

1680	Feb. 12	Gulielmus Morrison uxorem duxit Anna' Jackson.
1681	May 23	Georgius Robinson uxorem duxit Janam Hudd.
	May 24	Joh'es Chipchase uxorem duxit Annam Corner, vid.
	May 24	Joh'es Fetherston uxorem duxit Janam Vipont.[1]
	July 27	Thomas Nicholson[2] uxorem duxit Maria' Chipchase, vid.
	Aug. 11	Joh'es Lem'an uxorem duxit Isabellam Sowerby, vid.
	Oct. 9	Thomas Crosby uxorem duxit Elizabetha' Myres.
	Oct. 11	Cuthbertus Philipson uxorem duxit Marg'tam Miller.
	Oct. 22	Georgius Robinson uxorem duxit Mariam Tindall.
	Dec. 20	Thomas Smith uxorem duxit Margareta' Mickleton.
	Jan. 18	Jacob Colson uxorem duxit Annam Hauxly, vidua'.
1682	May 9	Edvardus Furbank uxore' duxit Maria' Westmorland.
	May 13	Thomas Hall uxorem duxit Annam Brough.
	May 29	Thomas Parkinson uxorem duxit Elisabetham Speare.
	Aug. 12	Johan'es Adamson uxorem duxit Dorotheam Kirtly.
	Aug. 29	Johan'es Taylor uxorem duxit Jocosam[3] Dury.
	Sep. 20	Andreas Wilkinson uxorem duxit Annam Burdess.
	Oct. 27	Johan'es Kirkham uxorem duxit Elianoram Stokeld.
	Feb. 17	Thomas Burletson[4] uxorem duxit Dorotheam Lackenby.
	Feb. 19	Thomas Palmer uxorem duxit Annam Mason.
1683	April 30	David Dixon[5] uxorem duxit Janam Browne.
	May 8	Thomas Davison uxorem duxit Marg'tam Darbyshire.
	Aug. 18	Thomas Hutchinson uxorem duxit Annam Askew.
	Jan. 29	Oliverus Kearsly uxorem duxit Francisca' Hobman.
1684	May 1	Johan'es Shaclock uxorem duxit Francisca' Harrison.
	July 12	Gilbertus Potts uxorem duxit Janam Thompson.
	Oct. 29	Jacobus Harle uxorem duxit Rachel Atkinson.
	Jan. 12	Thomas Jopling uxorem duxit Anna' Shipley.
	Feb. 18	Richardus Pilkington uxorem duxit Isabellam Hall.
	Feb. 19	Gulielmus Boutflower[6] uxorem duxit Elisabetham Hutton.
1685	April 18	Henricus Hutchinson uxorem duxit Anna' Guy.

---

[1] A Thomas or William Vipont occurs in Mickleton's MSS. as Under Master of the Grammar School about 1630.

[2] See his burial 9 Nov. 1707.

[3] "Jocosam" has been written over "Joyce." See her burial 26 Jan. 1709-10, and the baptism of their child 29 Jan. 1683-4.

[4] See the baptism of their first child 15 Jan. 1682-3.

[5] He was an Attorney-at-Law; married secondly 24 June 1721, at St. Oswald's, "M" Elizabeth Steele," dau. of Ralph Steele, baptized 5 Dec. 1693, at St. Oswald's (she was buried there 26 Dec. 1734), and he was buried there also 12 May 1728. She was dau. of John Brown, gent., Attorney, and died 19, buried 21 Dec. 1718, at St. Oswald's. See her brother's baptism 30 June 1670.

[6] He merchant of Newcastle (Sheriff 1701), and son and executor of Thomas Boutflower, of Appleby, Westmorland, who was buried at Whittonstall 5 Jan. 1683-4; he was buried at St. Nicholas, Newcastle, 26 May 1712, and is ancestor of the present Venerable Samuel Peach Boutflower, Archdeacon of Carlisle. She, the second wife, was buried with her own people at Bishop Middleham 22 April 1688. As will thus be seen, Surtees is incorrect in making her re-marry.

1685	Sep. 3	Carolus Montagu¹ (Armig⁾) uxorem duxit Elisab. Foster.
	Nov. 26	Edvardus Elstob uxorem duxit Aliciam Rippon.
	Dec. 29	Johan'es Midleton uxorem duxit Anna' Harrison.
	Jan. 17	Johan'es Proud² uxorem duxit Marg'tam Shacklock.
1686	Dec. 30	Bryanus Burletson uxorem duxit Thomasina' Nichols.³
1687	July 4	Michael Mickleton uxorem duxit Elisabetham Spearman.⁴
	Feb. 2	Josephus Hall uxorem duxit Franciscam Gibson.
	Feb. 2	Robertus Allenson uxorem duxit Annam Wilson, vid.
1688	July 14	Thomas Liddell uxorem duxit Elizabetham Robinson.
	July 25	Wrightington Taylor uxorem duxit Rutham Turner.
	Mar. 18	Johannes Eldridge⁵ uxorem duxit Margareta' Lowther.
1689	April 15	Xpoferus Wyvill⁶ (Decan⁸ Rippon.) ux'em duxit Margareta' Markendale, vid.
	Oct. 1	Gulielmus Applegarth uxorem duxit Anna' Heckles, vid.
	Oct. 29	Jacobus Peirson uxorem duxit Ellenoram Wilkinson.
	Nov. 5	Gulielmus Thompson uxorem [duxit] Ellenoram Gray, spin⁾.
1690	Jan. 5	Laurentius Sayre ux. duxit Catharinam Burdon.
	Jan. 24	Nicolaus Hornesby ux. duxit Elisabetham Humble.
1691	June 2	Joh'nes Stockdell u. d. Margaretam Crawford.
	Jan. 7	Joh'nes Smith⁷ u. d. Mariam Cooper.

¹ He was a younger son of the Hon. George Montagu (by his wife Elizabeth, dau. of Sir Anthony Irby, Knt.), who was son, by his third wife, of Henry, first Earl of Manchester. He was returned as Member for Maldon, and afterwards for Westminster, and became a very eminent Statesman *temp.* William III.; while Chancellor of the Exchequer he projected and issued in 1695 the great re-coinage of silver; he was created, by recommendation of the Commons, in 1700, Baron Halifax, and advanced to an earldom 1714. He married secondly, in Feb. 1688, Anne, Countess-dowager of Manchester, widow of his nephew, and dau. of Sir Christopher Yelverton, of East Manhuit, first Bart., but died s.p. She, first wife, dau. and coheiress of Francis Forster, of the South Bailey, Esq. See baptism of her brother 11 July 1653.

² See baptisms of their children. She was buried at St. Mary-le-Bow 3 May 1711.

³ She dau. of John Nicholls, whose burial see 6 June 1681. See also her brother's baptism 22 April 1662.

⁴ See her baptism 30 April 1667, her burial 14 Nov. 1704, and her father's burial 22 Sep. 1703.

⁵ See his burial 24 Feb. 1697-8.

⁶ He, D.D., was third son of Sir Christopher Wyvill, of Burton Constable, co. York, third Bart., by Ursula, dau. of Conyers Darcy, first Earl of Holderness; he died *circa* 1710. She was widow of Evers Markendale, of Old Park, co. Pal. (buried 28 March 1686), and dau. of John Brabant, of Page Bank, gent. (whose only child she was in 1686), by Jane, dau. of Richard Best, of Middleton, Ebor, whom he married 31 March 1646, at Witton-le-Wear; she was baptized at Brancepeth 12 Oct. 1652.

⁷ The father was of St. John's College, Cambridge (B.A. 1680, M.A. 1684, D.D. 1696); he was baptized 10 Nov. 1659 at Lowther, Westmorland, the eldest son of the Rev. William Smith, M.A., Rector of that parish, by his wife Elizabeth, dau. of Giles Wetherell, Esq., Mayor of Stockton, by his wife Anne, sister of Sir George Marwood, of Little Busby, Yorks, first Bart.; he was appointed Minor Canon *circa* 1683, and Sacrist 20 Nov. 1689. The only instance of a Minor Canon becoming a Prebendary of Durham, he received from Bishop Crew, to whom he was Chaplain, the seventh stall (collated 25, installed 26 Sep.) in 1695, having shortly before been

1691 Feb.   3   Richardus Wall u. d. Mariam Richardson.
1692 April 30 Thomas Fairbarnes u. d. Mariam Jopling.
      Oct. 22 Henricus Clerk u. d. Annam Fairbarnes.
1693 Sep.   5   Johannes White ux. d. Isabellam Raisbeck.
      Nov. 25 Thomas Coplin ux. d. Annam Ricaby.
1695 Nov. 12 Robertus Spencelay ux. dux. Isabellam Perkins.
1696 Feb. 11 Robertus Thompson[1] uxorem duxit Margar^{tam} Richardson.
1697 Dec   2 Radulp. Wilkinson uxor. duxit Dorotheam Hilton.[2]
      Jan. 26 Tho. Talbot, de Stockton, uxor. duxit Ellenoram Howell.
      Mar.   2 Rich. Carnaby, de Corbridge, uxor. duxit Hannah Gibson, de Bywell St Andrew.
      Mar.   5 Georg. Liddel uxor. duxit Ann Easterby, de Hesleden Monachor^m.
1698 June   4 Lancelot Lowther,[3] of South Bailey, uxor. duxit Jane Smith, de Lamesley.
      Aug.   5 John Mason, de Heighington, ux. d. Jane Lodge.
      Aug. 20 Dan. Smallpage ux. d. Ruth Ord, paroch. de Sedgfield.
      Aug. 25 Hugh Watson,[4] de Allandale, Dioc. Ebor, u. d. Hester Hall, de Stanhope.
      Sep.   5 Geo. Smithson, de Gateshead, ux. d. Deborah Heighington, ead. paroc.
1699 May   31 John Hudspeth, de paroch. S^{ti} Johannis, Nov. Cast., ux. dux. Ellen. Lackenby, ejusdem parochiæ.
      July 19 Joseph Dixon[5] & Ann Waugh, serv^{ts} together att ye Deanry.
      July 31 Thomas Dodds[6] & Mary Young, of St Oswald's.

preferred to the rectory of Gateshead; he was presented to the rectory of Bishopwearmouth in 1704, and dying 30 July 1715, æt. 56, he was buried in the chapel of his college at Cambridge. He had a grant of arms. She was Mary, dau. and coheiress of William Cooper, of Scarborough, co. York, gent., by his wife Philadelphia Smith (the marriage of whose parents see 10 June 1630), and had, besides the above John, and an elder son George Smith, of Burnhall, co. Pal., Esq. (M.I. St. Oswald's), afterwards in orders of the Non-juring Church and Titular Bishop of Durham, the following, whose baptisms see—Mary, 26 Jan. 1697-8; William, 9 Aug. 1699; Joseph, 29 April 1701; and a second William 22 Sep. 1707. Surtees says (Pedigree iv., part ii., p. 98, to which the foregoing dates add), "Dr. Smith enjoyed the deserved reputation of an elegant scholar and a sound divine, and his fame rests securely on the magnificent edition of Bede's 'Historic Works,' which he had completed for the press with the most devoted labour and industry."

[1] This marriage is also entered in Register 2, among the baptisms, as follows: "Robert Thompson, of Brawnspeth, and Margaret Richardson, of ye College in Durham, were married Feb. ye xith Ann. Dom. 1696."

[2] She was baptized 1651 at Heighington, the dau., by his second wife Dorothy Wright, of Lancelot Hilton, of Durham and Hilton in Staindropshire, Attorney-at-Law, whose burial see 29 May 1685. See her burial 16 Dec. 1708.

[3] See (presumably) his baptism 2 Dec. 1675, and his burial 13 Dec. 1706. Lancelot, son of Thomas Lowther, was bound apprentice 7 April 1690, and admitted free of Mercers' Company 2 Sep. 1701.

[4] Jane, their eldest child, baptized at Stanhope 18 Sep. 1699. He then of West Allen.

[5] See his burial 24 Feb. 1707-8.

[6] "Hylda, dau. of Tho. Dodds, born ye 5th Nov^{br}, but no notice given (tho' desired) till ye 4th of March" [1703]. St. Oswald's.

1699	Aug.	6	Joseph Williamson,[1] of Bishop Wearmouth, & Mary Williamson, of St Hellen Awkland.
	Sep.	9	Bryan Atkinson & Susan Thompson, of ye parish of Bpp. Wearmouth.
	Nov.	9	Abra. Phillips & Ann Claypeth, Cap'^{ne} Se'tre Hildæ.
	Dec.	23	Mr. Richard Baddeley[2] & Ann Geldart, wid., of ye parish of St Mary le bow, N. Bailey.
	Feb.	12	Mr. Rob. Burnet,[3] Phys., & Mrs. Frances Richardson, both of St Mary le bow parish.
	Feb.	13	Tho. Taylor & Mary Yapp, both of Bow parish.
	Mar.	16	George Pickering & Isabel Fairbarns, both of Witton-Gilbert.
1700	April	23	William Smith & Isabel Pattison, both of ye Parish of Elwick.
	April	28	Abra. Yap[4] & Ann Battersby.
	July	15	Thomas Bateman & Mary Dear, serv^{ts} in ye Castle.
	July	23	Nathaniel, Lord Crew,[5] and M^{dm} Dorothy Forster.
	Aug.	8	William Apedail, of Bpp. Awkland, & Ann Brack, of Merrington.

[1] Four children, at least, of "Mr. Joseph Williamson" are baptized at St. Helen's Auckland, the first 3 Oct. 1700.

[2] See his burial 16 Jan. 1713-14.

[3] He buried 18 March 1706-7, and she 27 Nov. 1702, at St. Mary-le-Bow, where their (probably) only child Thomas was baptized 17 Nov. 1700, and buried inf.

[4] See his burial 23 Dec. 1728. She second wife; see her burial 17 Oct. 1732.

[5] This great prelate, who filled the Palatinate throne of Durham for nearly forty-seven years, was born at Stene, Northants, 31 Jan. 1633-4, a few hours before the death of his grandfather, Sir Thomas Crew, Serjeant-at-Law, Speaker of the House of Commons in two Parliaments, and "of proverbial abilities." Sir Thomas, younger brother of Sir Randolph Crew, of Crew in Cheshire, Lord Chief Justice of the King's Bench, married Temperance, dau. and coheiress of Reginald Bray, of Stene. Their eldest son John Crewe, M.P. for Northants, a shrewd, clever man, took an active part against Charles I. He was, nevertheless, greatly instrumental in the restoration of the second Charles, and was by him created Baron Crew, 1661. He died in 1679, having married Jemima, dau. and coheir of Edward Waldegrave, Esq., of Lawford, Essex, by whom he was father of a fifth son, Nathaniel. Nathaniel Crew or Crewe was entered a Commoner of Lincoln College, Oxford, Sep. 1652, but did not take Orders until 1665, when he was ordained Priest and Deacon the same day by the Bishop of Winchester. After that he became, in rapid succession, Chaplain to the Royal Household, a Lenten Preacher, D.D., Deputy-Clerk of the Closet, Rector of Lincoln College, Clerk of the Closet, Dean and Precentor of Chichester 1669, consecrated Bishop of Oxford 2 July 1671, translated to Durham 1674, after the see had been vacant nearly three years, and 9 June 1675 he entered into his new bishopric with great pomp. This last preferment was due to the interest of the Duke of York, whose marriage ceremony with Mary d'Este he had performed. On the accession of James II. he was made Dean of the Chapel Royal and a Privy Councillor. In 1697 he succeeded his brother as third Lord Crewe. He married firstly, 21 Dec. 1691, Penelope, dau. of Sir Philip Frowde, Knt., and widow of Sir Hugh Tynte; she died 9 March 1699-1700, and was buried at Stene; he died 18 Sep. 1721, æt. 88, and was buried in his chapel at Stene 30th Sep. He left no issue, and the peerage became extinct. The "Gentleman's Magazine" for 1801 pronounces that the Baron-Bishop "in his private character was hospitable, generous, and charitable; in his public a rigid high-churchman and a favourer of popery," and in this latter respect he was, no doubt, a harsh, stern man. However, he will always be remembered gratefully by posterity for the munificent charities he founded. Thomas Forster, Esq., of Bambrough and Blanchland in Northumberland, the Bishop's brother-in-law, forfeited his estates in the rising of 1715, and these his lordship bought, and by his will vested in trustees, who still administer them for various charitable purposes which he laid down.

1700	Oct. 23	Ralph Hodgshon & Jane Garthwaite, of Winston parish.
	Jan. 7	John Snawdon & Susanna Deemster, both of yᵉ Parish of Jarrow.
	Feb. 13	Rob. Johnson & Isbel Ferraby, of yᵉ Parish of Bpp. Wearmouth.
	Mar. 4	Michael Rawling & Eliz. Thompson, both of Easington Parish. Shrove Tuesday.
1701	May 31	Anthony Wilde,[1] of Bpp. Wearmouth, & Dorothy Robinson, of Houghton in le Spring. Saturd.
	June 24	Thomas Wake, a Borer, & Ellenor Miller, spinster, parochiæ de Gateshead, Dunelm.
	Aug. 10	Tho. Horseley[2] & Barbara Walton, of Woolsingham Parish. Sunday.
	Sep. 1	Mʳ Gilbert Spearman[3] & Mʳˢ Marg. Pierson.
	Sep. 22	Jo. Andrew & Mary Middleton, both of Sᵗ Nicholas Parish in Durham.
	Sep. 23	Jo. Watson[4] & Mary Emerson, both of Stanhop in Weardaile.
	Dec. 11	Mʳ Rob. Spearman[5] & Mʳˢ Han. Webster.
1702	July 18	William Richmond & Barbara Thompson, both of Easington Parish.

Abra. Yapp, Sacrist of the Cathedral Church of Durham.

	Aug. 1	Mʳ Cristopher Hunter, de Stockton, & Mʳˢ Eliz. Elrington, of Shotley, both in yᵉ County of Durham.
	Sep. 5	Joseph Alderson, of Readmarshal Parish, & Jane Walton, of Preston in yᵉ chappelry of Stockton.

Dorothy Forster was only dau. of Sir William Forster, of Bambrough Castle; she died, aged 42, in 1715, and was buried by the Bishop's first wife in Stone Chapel. It is a tradition that Lord Crewe had offered to make her his wife before his first marriage. Her life is vividly, if fancifully, pictured in one of the most delightful works of fiction, bearing her name, by Mr. Walter Besant.

[1] [Mary his dau. and coheir married, 1731, William Ironside, Esq., of Houghton-le-Spring.]

[2] Also entered in Wolsingham Register, where their children are baptized. She was buried there 28 March 1712, and he 28 July 1713.

[3] He was tried at Durham Assizes, 10 Aug. 1693, for drinking the toast "Here is King James, his prosperitie; here is the confusion of King William." She his second wife; she was baptized at Bishop Middleham 26 June 1679, and was younger dau. and sole heiress (a brother and sister, older, baptized at Startforth, dying young) of Robert Pearson or Pierson, Esq., of Startforth and Forcet, co. York, and of Bishop Middleham jure uxoris [son of Robert Pearson, gent., of Startforth, buried there 8 Sep. 1673?], by his second wife the Hon. Mary Cockayne, dau. of Charles, first Viscount Cullen, in the Peerage of Ireland, by his wife Lady Mary O'Brien, eldest dau. and coheir of Henry, fifth Earl of Thomond. Mrs. Spearman was buried at Bishop Middleham 12 May 1731; her mother the Hon. Mrs. Pierson 23 May 1682; and her father 2 Oct. 1702.

[4] Their eldest child, "Ann, dau. of John Watson of Thimbleby in Stanhope," baptized there 30 June 1702.

[5] Of Old Acres, co. Pal.; see his burial 20 Oct. 1728. She dau. and heiress of William Webster, of Stockton-on-Tees, merchant. In right of this marriage her son Robert Spearman, of Old Acres, Esq., quartered for WEBSTER, Sable, a bend wavy, and in sinister chief a mullet of six points argent. She was, apparently, not related to another merchant family of Webster, settled at Stockton a little later, who bore different arms. See "Landed Gentry," "Webster of Pallion."

1702	Oct. 27	Mr. John Durant & M[rs] Isabella Taylour, widow, both of S[t] John's in Newcastle.
	Oct. 27	John Robson & Ann Nelson, both of the Parish of S[t] Andrew-Auckland.
	Jan. 2	Edward Crosby[1] & Eliz. Arrowsmith, both of Whitwell House in y[e] County of Durham, were married by vertue of a licence.
	Jan. 26	Mr. Humph. March & Mrs. Ann Elstob, both of little S[t] Marie's Parish, in y[e] South Bailey in Durham.
	Feb. 17	Jo. Tiplady and Jane Wilson, both of y[e] chappelry of Stockton.
1703	April 24	Geo. Carlisle & Margery Short were married in the Cathedral by vertue of a licence.
	May 20	John Heslopp & Ann Hunter, of Lanchester Parish.
		(Abra. Yapp, Sacrist.)
	May 22	James Wilsby & Hannah Johnson, both servants to Mad. Grey in y[e] College.
	June 5	Anthony Johnson & Marg. Barker, both of Stranton parish.
	June 6	Tho. Browne, of S[t] Nich. Parish, and Ellinor Hauxley, of South Bailey in Durham.
	Aug 7	David Shethum, of Gateshead, and Eliz. Roxby, of y[e] Parish of Lanchester; by vertue of a Licence.
	Oct. 12	Tho. Wood, of Merrington, & Elizabeth Whitfeild, of Pittington; by vertue of a license.
	Dec. 21	Ralph Johnson, of Branspeth parish, & Mary Friend.
	Dec. 21	Roger Wilson, merchant in S[t] Nich. Parish in Newcastle, & Ann Middleton, of Barfoot in y[e] county of York.
	Sep. 9	Aurelius Headlam,[2] of S[t] Nicholas parish in New Castle, & Mary Marlay, of All Saints.
	Feb. 19	John Clark & Ann Pallaster, both of Witt. Gilbert.
	Feb. 28	John Gibbon, of Hamsterly, & Ann Thompson, of Bpp. Wearmouth.
1704	Mar. 25	Mr. John Willcocks & Eliz. Wall.
	April 29	John Hopper & Eliz. Kirkley, of Lanchester parish.
	May 18	Mr. Nich. Burton[3] & (" my " *erased*) Lady Fenwick.

[1] See possibly his second marriage 10 Jan. 1718-19.

[2] Probably related to George Hedlam, of Newcastle, who by his will 1738, and codicil 1744, names his wife Ann, ex'or; daus. Ann and Hannah; sons George, Ralph, and William; late father George Hedlam (will 1725); late sister Phœbe, wife to Thomas Vasie, of London, merchant, deceased, who left three children, Mary, Phœbe, and *Aurelia*.

[3] He Head Master of the Grammar School, and son of Archdeacon Burton, who is buried in York Minster; of Christ Church College, Oxford, B.A. 1695, M.A. 1698; Rector of St. Mary-le-Bow 1703—1705, and Lecturer at the Cathedral; he was buried at Bow, within the Communion rails (which he gave) 1 July 1713. His first wife Martha was buried there (M.I.) 12 Aug. 1703, with her dau. Martha, whose baptism see 30 June 1702 (see also baptism of a son 20 March 1700-1701). Lady Fenwick, second wife, was previously widow of Sir Robert Fenwick, of Bywell, Northumberland, Knt., sister of Sir Richard Graham, first Viscount Preston, and dau. of Sir George Graham, of Esk and Netherby, second Bart., by his wife Lady Mary Johnstone, dau. of the first Earl of Hartfell (grandfather of the first Marquess of Annandale), by his wife Lady Margaret Douglas, dau. of the first Earl of Douglas and ninth Lord Drumlanrig, by his wife Lady Isabel Kerr, dau. of Mark, first Earl of Lothian, by his wife Margaret, dau. of Sir

1704	June 8	John Waistell & Alice Garthwaite, of Bernard Castle.
	June 22	William Robson, of Simondburn, & Eliz. Todd, of ye Chappelry of Hayden.
	Aug. 12	Cuth. Newton, of Bywell St Peter .... Marg. Pattison, of Tanfield in ye parish of Lanchesr.
	Aug. 22	Rob. Armstrong, de Hexham, ... Sarah Teasdaile, of ye North-Bailey in Durham.
	Sep. 18	Will. Marley & Mary Richardson, of Staindrop.
	Jan. 2	Michael Brabant,[1] Apothecary, in ye Parish of St Nicholas, & Jane Hutchinson, in ye North bailey.
	Jan. 13	Thom. Bownas, of Aikcliff, & Mary Reid, of Sedgfield.
1705	April 28	George Welfoote, of Heighington, and Jane Catherick, of Darlington.
	May 5	John Stephenson, of ye parish of Aickliffe, Ann Arrowsmith, of ye Chappelry of Trimdon.
1706	April 4	Rich. Man and Mary Lupton, both of Gateshead.
	April 27	Giles Rain,[2] of Dalton parish, and Mary Greenside.
	May 14	George Carlisle, of Readmarshall, & Marg. Story, of Sedgfield.
	June 11	Will. Wilson, parochiæ de Wearmouth, & Mary Lamb.
	July 28	Robert Fells, of ye parish of St Andrew Auckland, and Jane Gargett, serv^t, in St Oswald's parish.
	Aug. 8	Robert Wilkinson & Suzanna Watson, both of Morpeth in ye Diocesse of Durham.
	Sep. 9	Rob. Marshall & Alice Richardson, both of St Nich. parish, Durham.
	Sep. 12	Christopher Selby and Rebecca Wilson, both of Aickliffe.
	Sep. 30	Mr. George Bowes[3] & Ann Machon, wid.

John Maxwell, Lord Herries of Terregles. She was sister also of Dr. Graham, Prebendary, the baptism of whose son see 17 Sep. 1689. Lady Fenwick was buried at St. Mary-le-Bow 3 Nov. 1744.

[1] He was Mayor of Durham 1712, 1714, 1718, 1725. The name was generally corrupted into Brabin, and is so spelt at St. Oswald's, where this marriage is also recorded. She was the only surviving dau. of John Hutchinson, Esq., of Framwellgate, Alderman and Mayor of Durham, a man of considerable local importance, the marriage of whose grandson (and Mrs. Brabin's nephew) see 20 April 1732.

[2] Son of John Raine, of Cassop, co. Pal., gent.; admitted (by servitude) free of Mercers' Company 16 Nov. 1705; Alderman of Durham 1715, and Mayor 1720, 1727. He appears to have been thrice married. This was his first wife, and she was perhaps buried at Dalton-le-Dale. He married secondly, 5 April 1708, at St. Oswald's, "Mrs. Elizabeth Stokeld" (baptized 27 March 1687), dau. of Mr. John Stokeld, vintner, who was buried there 18 Feb. 1727-8; John Stokeld and Eliz. Sympson, both this parish, married 27 April 1684; and thirdly, 29 Oct. 1728 (being then described as " of Hart "), at St. Mary's, Alice Johnson, of Monk-Hesilden, co. Pal. He was buried 20 Dec. 1738 at St. Oswald's, where he has children buried.

[3] He D.C.L., Solicitor-General to the Bishop of Durham, and Recorder of Durham 5 Feb. 1706-7; son of Thomas Bowes, of Streatlam Castle, co. Pal., Esq., by his wife Anne, dau. and coheir of Anthony Maxton, Prebendary of Durham, and younger brother of Dr. John Bowes, Prebendary, whose burial see 16 Jan. 1721-2. Mr. Bowes was buried at St. Mary-le-Bow, dying 14 May 1724, æt. 65, s.p. She Ann dau. of Anthony Salvin, of Sunderland Bridge, co. Pal., Esq. (a younger son of Gerard Salvin, of Croxdale, Esq., see ped., Surtees, part iv., vol. ii.), and widow of Gilbert Machon, of Lichfield and Durham, Esq., to whom she was married 3 May 1696, at St. Oswald's. See her burial 13 Nov. 1715.

1706	Jan. 28	William Snowden & Sarah Fox, of Wearmouth.
1707	April 15	James Barras, of St Nich., Durham, and Eliz. Newton, of ye parish of Ryton in ye county of Durham.
	April 20	Will. Wright & Marg. Walker, both of St Andrew Auckland.
	April 23	Will. Browne,[1] of St Giles's, and Eliz. Hickson, of St Oswald's in Durham.
	May 1	John Logan & Marg. Byerly, both of St Margaret's, Durham.
	Aug. 7	John Pemberton, of Bp. Wearmouth, & Thomasin Shadforth, of ye North baily in Durham.
	Jan. 25	John Spark, of Bp. Wearmouth, & Eliz. Paxton, spinster, of ye same parish.
	Jan. 29	Robert Hixon, of St Oswald's, Durham, and Ellinor Lever, of St Mary le Bow in Durham.
	Mar. 8	Math. Morrow & Jane Gibbon, in ye parish of Darlington.
1708	May 29	Will. Mowbray[2] & Eliz. Gibson, in ye parish of Chester.
	June 18	Robt Douglas & Mary Gilkin, both of ye parish of St Nicholas in Newcastle.
	July 6	John Dawson, of Haughton, & Jane Swalwell, of Lanchester.
	July 13	James Richardson, of St Nich., & Jane Chipchase.
	July 18	Lancelot Garret, of St Nich., Newcastle, and Eliz. Hodshon, of all S^{ts}, Newcastle.
	July 29	John Bell & Mary Fetherston, both serv^{ts} in ye Deanry.
	Aug. 16	Mat. Prat & Jane Nicholson, both of St Nich., Newcastle.
	Aug. 19	Will. Clayton, of Richmond in ye County of York, & Eliz. Maugham, of y^r chapelry of St Giles's, Durham, in ye County of Durham.
	Sep. 4	Robert Lindsley, of ye College in Durham, serv^t, and Isabel Hudson, of St Nicholas in Durham.
	Nov. 1	Mr. Will. Turner,[3] of ye College, & Mrs Marg. Butler, of St Mary Le Bow, Durham. Fest. Omn. Sanct.
	Nov. 18	Lamerick Tuart & Dorothy Cork, both of ye parish of Heighington in ye Dioc. of Durh.
	Nov. 29	Tho. Humble & Alice Lawson, of Ryton, Count. Durh., ye one Fourscore years of age at least, ye Woman ab^t 18.
	Dec. 30	Math. Lowthian & Marg. Shadforth, both of Elvet.
	Jan. 29	Tho. Liddel & Jane Fenwick, both of Chester in ye Street.

[1] Also entered at St. Oswald's, where she is called Hixon.

[2] Their child Elizabeth born and baptized 6 Jan. 1708-9 at St. Oswald's, when he is described as yeoman, and later as of Old Durham.

[3] He, William Parthericke Turner, was son of Rev. William Turner, Mus. Doc., Vicar-Choral of St. Paul's, and Lay-Vicar of Westminster Abbey, where he was buried 16 Jan. 1739-40; he married secondly, 17 April 1718, at St. Mary-le-Bow, Elizabeth Wall, and had by her, who was buried 25 July 1730 at St. Mary's, a son John, baptized there 26 Dec. 1719. Margaret Butler (baptized 4 March 1687-8) was second dau. of Thomas Butler, of Old Acres, Esq. (whose marriage see 20 Nov. 1680), and was first wife to Mr. Turner, by whom she had a son, whose burial see 20 Aug. 1713, and another William, bapt. and buried 1710 at St. Mary's. See her burial 6 June 1713, and her sister's marriage 30 March 1709. [Mrs. Theophila Turner buried 31 Oct. 1730 at St. Mary's.]

1708 Feb. 23 Ambrose Procter, of Riton in ye County of Durham, & Jane Erington, of ye parish of Chester.
1709 Mar. 30 Captain Butler[1] & Mrs Mary Butler.
April 30 Robt Story, of Easeington parish, & Doroth. Robinson, of ye parish of Houghton in le Spring.
May 6 Mr. Tho. Ogle & Sarah Knewstob, of ye parish of Felton.
July 1 Anthony Todd and Isabel Dent, both serv^{ts} in ye College in Durh^m.
Sep. 16 Ezekiel Thompson, of ye parish of Heddon, & Sarah Watson, of ye parish of Allendale.
Sep. 27 Tho. Dawson, of ye parish of Bp. Wearmouth, and Eliz. Sanderson, of Monk Wearmouth.
Sep. 27 John Rippon, of Aickliffe, and Eliz. Rippon, of St Andrew Awkland, both in this County.
Oct. 6 James Fynney,[2] D.D., Prebendary of Durham, & Jane Newhouse, Relict of ye late Register Newhouse.
Nov. 26 Robt Hutchinson, of Kelloe, and Ann Duckett, of Merington parish.
Feb. 16 Mr. Peter Burrell & Mrs. Mary Wilson.
1710 April 18 Mr. Thomas Hanby,[3] of St Nich. in Newcastle upon Tine, and Mrs. Dorothy Watson, spinst^r, of ye parish of B^p Wearmouth.
May 2 John Johnson & Ann Sheppard, both of ye Parish of All S^{ts}, Newcastle.
May 29 Robt Nicholson, of ye parish of Tinmouth, and Marg. Wallass, of ye chapelry of St John's in Newcastle.
May 30 John Garth & Ann Crow, both of Jarroe Parish.
Aug. 6 Will. Stephenson and Doroth. Todd, of St Hellen Awkland.
Aug. 7 Tho. Wainwright, of Newburne, and Ann Blakiston,[4] of St Oswald's in Durham.
Aug. 27 Hen. Story, of Witt. Gilbert, & Eliz. Jopling, of Brancepeth.
Oct. 13 James Bell & Isabel Bambrough, of Wearmouth.
Nov. 27 Hauxley Surtees,[5] of ye Parish of Ryton, and Ann Watson, spinst^r, of Chester in le Street.
Dec. 2 Robert Sober & Mary Shaftoe, de Pettington.
Dec. 19 William Watson, of Bp. Wearmouth, and Mary Busby,[6] of Brauspeth parish.
Feb. 23 John Stawart & Jane Wake, of ye Par. of Whitburn.

[1] He James, an Irishman, no relation, and bearing different arms, as appears by the M.I. at St. Mary's. She eldest dau. of Thomas Butler, of Old Acres, Esq., whose marriage see 20 Nov. 1680. See her baptism 23 June 1685.
[2] See his burial 13 March 1726-7. She widow of Mr. Newhouse, Registrar to the Dean and Chapter; re-married Anthony Emerson.
[3] He perhaps son (baptized 9 Aug. 1670 at St. Oswald's) of Mr. Francis Hanby, Proctor, the baptism of whose child see 2 April 1682.
[4] She was dau. of Rev. Francis Blakeston, M.A., Vicar of Whickham, co. Pal., and was baptized 20 May 1688 at St. Oswald's, where she was buried as a widow 7 July 1734.
[5] He a younger son of Robert Surtees, of Ryton, gent., by his marriage with Catherine, younger dau. and coheir of John Hauxley, of Crawcrook, gent.
[6] She probably granddau. of William Busby, of Cassop, and his wife Mary, dau. of Rev. John Lively (see note to baptism 12 Nov. 1625).

1710	Feb. 13	Rob[t] Harrison, of y[e] parish of S[t] Nich., and Eliz. Rowell, of S[t] Margaret's, Durham—memo[m], forgot to be registr[d] in its proper place.
	Mar. 20	Tho. Palmerly & Ann Mason, of Houghton le Spring.
1711	April 10	Gerrard Sidgewick & Eliz. Adamson, both of Bp. Wearmouth.
	July 3	Tho. Busby[1] and Eliz. Fawdon, both of Brancepeth parish.
	Oct. 6	Rich. Henderson, of Kelloe, & Isab. Forster, of Witt[n] Gilbert.
	Nov. 17	Rob[t] Smith & Barbara Lindsley, both of Bp. Wearmouth.
	Nov. 24	Tho. Grundy, of y[e] Parish of Brancepeth, & Ellen[r] Ranson, of y[e] parish of Houghton in le Spring.
	Nov. 24	Rowland Wilkinson & Jane Parker, both of Lanchester in y[e] Diocesse of Durham.

Robert Lecke, Sacrist.

	Feb. 2	Robert Adamson[2] & Dorothy Paxton, both of the Parish of S[t] Nicholas in Durham; by vertue of a Licence.
	Feb. 6	W[m] Barkas & Anne Walton, both of the Parish of Houghton in the spring; by Vertue of a Licence.
	Feb. 14	W[m] Green, of Houghton in the Spring, & Margarett Harle, of the Parish of Sedgfield; by Licence.
1712	Mar. 25	Rich. Huntley & Jane Burletson, both of y[e] Parish of Pittington in y[e] Diocesse of Durham.
	April 19	John Potter & Elizabeth Palmer, both of y[e] Parish of Houghton in y[e] Diocesse of Durham.
	Oct. 3	Thomas Stevenson & Elizabeth Slater, both of the Parish of Aukland S[t] Andrew.
	Nov. 16	James Clark & Frances Allen, both of the Parish of Darlington.
	Nov. 26	Joseph Paterson & Margaret Kay, both of the Parish of Gateshead.
	Dec. 16	Robert Readshaw, of the Parish of Shotley, & Jane Cockerell, of S[t] Nicholas in Durham.
	Feb. 14	Valentine Allison & Elizabeth Snawdon, both of the Parish of Easington.
	Feb. 26	Edward Willis & Elizabeth Hull, both of the Parish of Lanchester.
	Mar. 7	W[m] Hugall & Mary Watson, both of the Parish of Houghton in the Spring.

---

[1] See note to marriage of (probably) his sister 19 Dec. 1710.

[2] He was only surviving son of Ralph Adamson, Attorney-at-Law, of Durham, by his wife Elizabeth (married 17 March 1673 at South Shields), dau. and coheir of William Blythman, of Westoe, gent., and was buried at St. Mary's, his will being dated 7 March 1732-3. She widow of Thomas Paxton, gent., of Claypeth, Durham (who was buried at St. Oswald's only 9th Dec. preceding), and dau. (baptized 2 Nov. 1686 at St. Oswald's) of John Martin, of New Elvet, gent. Their only son William Blythman Adamson (baptized 17 May 1715) sold his Westoe property to Robert Green, of South Shields, gent. Mary, the other dau. and coheir of the William Blythman mentioned above, married Henry Eden, of Shincliffe, Esq., M.D., and had, with other issue, a dau. Jane, second wife of Cuthbert Adamson, gent. and Feltmaker, of Durham, and had a son (which has caused some confusion), also Blythman Adamson, who is ancestor of the late Rev. Edward Hussey Adamson, Vicar of Heworth, and Lieut.-Colonel William Adamson, of Cullercoats, Northumberland. It is not known what, if any, relationship existed between these two families of Durham Adamsons.

1712 Mar. 20 Thomas Carr, of Heighington, & Elizabeth Andrew, of the Parish of Easington.
1713 April 18 John Hall, of the Parish of Tinemouth, & Elizabeth Jopling, of the Parish of Woolsingham.
May 2 Ralph Sheild & Mary Dowson, both of the Parish of St Andrew Aukland.
May 2 Wm Rowell & Mary Heard, both of the Parish of Sedgfeild.
May 4 Francis Wood, of the Parish of Stockton, & Eliz. Merley, of the Parish of Branspeth.
July 2 Godfrey Phillipson & Sarah Nattress, both of the Parish of Stanhope in Weardale.
July 17 Thomas Bailes, of the Parish of Romaldkirk, & Dinah Heslopp, of the Parish of Gainford.
July 18 John Clark & Mary Haswell, both of the Parish of Pittington.
Aug. 1 Jeremiah Langstaffe, of the Parish of Rumoldkirk in the Diocesse of York, & Anne Morresbye, of the Chappelry of St John in Newcastle.
Aug. 1 Henry Langstaffe, of the Parish of St Hellen in Aukland, & Eliz. Sedgwick, of the Parish of Staindropp.
Aug. 3 George Hutton, of Staindropp, & Catherine Robinson, of Easington.
Aug. 10 John Pattison & Margaret Reed, both of the Parish of St Hill in the Diocesse of Durham.
Sep. 10 Thomas Wilkinson, of All Saints Parish in Newcastle, & Margaret Hudson, of Houghton in le Spring.
Sep. 19 Wm Hopper,[1] of the Chappelry of Aukland St Hellen, & Jane Richardson, of the Parish of Hamsterley.
Sep. 22 John Proud,[2] of Bear Park in the Parish of Witton Gilbert, & Catherine Watts, of the College in Durham.
Oct. 21 Mr. Nich. Fenwick, of the Chappelry of All S^{ts} in Newcastle, & Eliz. Barker, of the North Bayley in Durham.
Oct. 31 Thomas Pearson, of Aukland St Andrew, & Elizab. Joby, of the Parish of Hart.
Nov. 13 John Hutchinson & Mary Arrowsmith, both of the Parish of St Andrew Aukland.
Nov. 16 Jacob Dunn & Anne Hutchinson, both of the Parish of Billingham in the Diocesse of Durham.
Jan. 9 John Richardson & Anne Smith, both of the Parish of Branspeth.
Jan. 22 John Hudspeth, of the Parish of St Johnleys in the Diocesse of York, & Isabell Coulson, of the Parish of Pittington in the Diocesse of Durham.
Feb. 7 Tho. Browne & Anne Newton, both of the Parish of Long Newton.

---

[1] He of Evenwood. She buried 30 Oct. 1721 at St. Helen's, where their eldest child Margaret was baptized 18 Sep. 1714.

[2] See (presumably) his baptism 8 April 1688. He buried 23 Feb. 1745-6; and she 9 May 1760 at St. Mary-le-Bow, where they had a son buried 1722.

1713	Feb. 8	Robt Coxon & Dorothy Man, both of the Parish of Chester in the Street.
	Feb. 8	Wm Walton, of Sedgfeild, & Isabell Harding, of the Parish of Castle-Eden.
1714	April 16	Peter Snaith & Isabell Downes, both of the Parish of Norton.
	May 1	Edward Shipley[1] & Mary Bell, both of the Parish of Aikcliffe.
	May 1	Wm Gregson[2] & Hannah Thompson, both of the Parish of Easington.
	May 8	Wm Wanlesse & Jane Bell, both of the Parish of Kellowe.
	May 18	Waistell Pinkney & Mary Stubbs, both of the Parish of Gateshead.
	July 31	John Dawson & Elizabeth Swinsed, both of the Parish of Bp. Wearmouth.
	Aug. 1	John Young, of Aukland St Andrew, & Lucye Bownas, of the Parish of Aykcliffe.
	Aug. 24	Mr Delaval Beaumont[3] & Mrs Eliz. Wilson, both of the Parish of Bp. Wearmouth.
	Sep. 21	Robt Young, of the Parish of Houghton, & Mary Artus (this name has been either Aytus and altered afterwards to Artus, or *vice versâ*, which I cannot confidently say), of the North Baylye in Durham.
	Oct. 12	Joseph Parkin & Eleanor Dickinson, both of the Parish of St Nicholas in Durham.
	Oct. 16	Peter Stone & Mary Fewster, both of ye Parish of Witton Gilbert.
	Oct. 20	Robt Byers, of Bp. Wearmouth, & Dorothy Paxton, of the Parish of Easington.
	Oct. 23	Wm Atkin & Elizabeth Richardson, both of ye Parish of Easington.
	Nov. 27	Thomas Hall & Sarah Palmer, of the Parish of Jarrow.
	Dec. 11	James Croft & Mary Richardson, both of the Parish of Witton on the Wear.
	Jan. 3	Wm Harebottle & Jane Man, both of the Parish of Chester.
	Jan. 4	Thomas Trotter, of St Nicholas's Parish in Durham, & Hannah Thornton,[4] of St Oswald's in the same.
	Jan. 24	Geo. Raw, of Bernard Castle, & Margaret Smart, of Staindropp.
	Feb. 10	Matthew Henderson, of Bp. wearmouth, & Mary Jackson, of Chester.
	Feb. 24	Garret Starkin, of All Sts in Newcastle, & Mary Sidgwick, of Bp. Wearmouth.

---

[1] Possibly "Edward, son of Michael Shipley, draper and taylor," baptized 23 Dec. 1688 at St. Nicholas, Durham.

[2] He probably identical with William (baptized 16 March 1685-6 at Dalton-le-Dale), son of George Gregson, of Murton (born 28 Oct. 1657, Dalton Register), a younger son of Thomas Gregson, of Murton and Dalton (ancestor of Gregson of Murton and Burdon, see "Landed Gentry"), who married, 15 Feb. 1684-5, Deborah Burton or Buston, at Dalton. See a marriage 3 Dec. 1719.

[3] He son of Hammond Beaumont, Esq., and baptized 12 Dec. 1683 at St. Mary's.

[4] She probably (although her baptism is not at St. Oswald's) a dau. of Roger Thornton, yeoman, of Elvet parish, by his second wife Margaret Harrison, whom he married 1 Nov. 1692.

1714 Mar. 24 John Smith & Isabell Russel, both of the Parish of Hurworth.
1715 April 29 Christopher Waistell, of the Parish of Maskin in the Diocesse of York, & Sarah Heslop, of the Parish of Middleton St George in the Diocesse of Durham.
     May 4 Thomas Peverley & Anne Ushaw, of the Parish of Aukland St Andrew.
     May 11 John Gill & Anne Archer, both of the Parish of Branspeth.
     May 28 Joseph Martin[1] & Ellinor Smith, both of the South Bayley in Durham.
     May 28 Richard Burdon & Anne Burdon, both of the Parish of Witton.
     July 16 Geo. Wall & Mary Hull, both of the Parish of Branspeth.
     July 31 John Wilson, of ye Parish of Aukland St Andrew, & Jane James, of ye Parish of Woolsingham.
     Aug. 6 Robt Filmoor & Joan Dipper, both of the Parish of St Nicholas in Newcastle.
     Aug. 20 John Wilson, of ye Parish of Rumbold-Kirk in ye Diocesse of York, & Alice Dobbison, of ye Parish of Hamsterley in ye Diocesse of Durham.
     Aug. 20 Richard Smith & Anne Cole, both of ye Parish of Grindon.
     Aug. 22 Robt Reay & Anne Thompson, both of the Parish of Merrington.
     Sep. 19 Henry Stainesby & Anne Davison, both of the Parish of All Saints in Newcastle.
     Oct. 19 Geo. Cowlin, of the Parish of Aickliffe, & Anne Wennington, of ye Par. of Heighington.
     Oct. 29 John Johnson & Frances Pattison, both of the Parish of Branspeth.
     Nov. 22 Samuel Burne & Elizabeth Nicholson, both of the Parish of Whitworth.
     Dec. 15 James Martindill & Isabell Dixon, both of ye Parish of Hartlepool.
     Dec. 16 George Dale,[2] of ye Parish of St Nicholas in Durham, & Hannah Sowerby, of the Par. of Sedgefeild.
     Dec. 27 Captain Cuthbert Morland[3] & Mrs Margaret Lamb, Wid., both of the parish of St Oswald in Durham.

---

[1] They had two children, John and Anne, baptized at St. Mary's, and she was buried there 30 Nov. 1731. She was dau. of Richard Smith, of Ramside, near Durham, gent., by his wife Eleanor, oldest dau. and coheir of George Crosyer, of Newbiggen, co. Pal., gent., whose youngest dau. and coheir Jane married Edward Surtees, of Mainsforth, gent., and was great-grandmother of the immortal Robert, the Historian. The tombstone of Richard Smith, thereon stated to have died 22 May 1689, æt. 44, with his arms—On a chevron, between three bezants, as many crosses patée fitchée; impaling CROSYER, On a fess, between three crosses-crosslet placed salterwise, as many martlets—was standing in St. Giles's Churchyard before the recent enlargement and restoration—that usual destruction of all old surroundings.

[2] He, an Alderman of Durham and Mayor, was buried at St. Oswald's 30 May 1739.

[3] He ("Mr Cuthbert Morland, Captain of a Foot Company") buried 5 May 1720 at St. Oswald's.

1715	Feb. 1	Tho. Wright, of ye Parish of St Andrew, & Eliz. Dale, of ye Chappelry of All S^{ts}, both in Newcastle.
	Feb. 6	Edward Clark & Eliz. Dobson, both of the Parish of Whickham.
	Feb. 17	Francis How, of ye Par. of Lamesley, & Cath. Dobson, of All Saints in Newcastle.
	Feb. 28	Wm Aire & Jane Weems, both of ye Parish of St Giles in Durham.
1716	Mar. 23	Tho. Garfoot, of ye Parish of Aicliffe, & Elizabeth Alderson, of ye Par. of Bishopton.
	April 14	Geo. Hodshon, of ye Par. of Gainford, & Catherine Gibbin, of Aukland St Andrew.
	April 23	Wm Lee, of Gateshead, & Anne Lee, of ye Par. of Darlington.
	April 27	Wm Stephenson & Margaret Pinkney, both of ye Par. of Middleton in Teasdale.
	May 1	Wm Ridley & Catherine Belwood, both of the Parish of Norton.
	July 10	Henry Carter & Anne Lee, both of ye Parish of Gateshead.
	Aug. 7	George Spencer & Margaret Swainston, both of ye Parish of Gainford.
	Sep. 25	John Trear, of ye Par. of St Nicholas in Durham, & Anne Mensforth, of ye Par. of St Mary Le Bow.
	Oct. 18	Ralph Goodchild & Anne Johnson, of the Parish of Bishop-Wearmouth.
	Oct. 18	Benjamin Blaklock, of ye Par. of Eggscliff, & Mary Walker, of Bishop-Wearmouth.

John Powell, Sacrist.

	Dec. 4	George Smirk, of ye Parish of Wearemouth, & Joanna Reed, of ye Parish of Houghton le Spring, Dioc. Durham.
	Dec. 13	John Bailes & Margaret Lodge, both of ye Parish of Staindropp, Di. Dur.
	Dec. 18	George West, of ye Parish of Gateshead, & Margaret Olliver, of ye Parish of Hamsterly, Dioc. of Durham.
	Jan. 5	John Markup, of ye Parish of Winston, & Ann Renny, of ye Parish of Gateshead, Dioc. Durham.
	Jan. 8	Jeremiah Dikes & Isabel Dodds, of ye Parish of All Saints in Newcastle upon Tyne, Dioc. of Durham.
	Jan. 20	Mr William Owen & Mrs Mary Winshipp,[1] both of ye Parish of Chester in ye Street (Di. D.).
	Feb. 26	Anthony Harrison & Jane Cartington, both of ye Parish of Conscliffe (Di. Du.).
1717	April 22	Roger Wilson & Elizabeth Anderson, both of ye Par. of St Nicholas in Newcastle upon Tine, Dioc. Durham.
	April 23	Mr John Paxton, of ye Parish of Wearmouth, & Mrs Barbara Middleton, of ye Parish of Little St Mary in ye South Baily (Dio. Dur.); per Mr Leek.

[1] She dau. of William Winship, of Whitehill, gent., and baptized 27 Feb. 1693-4 at Chester-le-Street.

1717 May 26 Thomas Robinson, of ye Chappelrie of St John, & Jane Humble, of ye Par. of St Nicholas in Newcastle upon Tine, Dioc. Dur.
May 30 William Roantree, of ye Parish of Bishopton, & Jane Wilson, of ye Parish of Aickliffe, Dioc. Durham.
June 8 George Thompson & Frances Leighton, both of ye Parish of Easeington, Dioc. Durh.
July 1 William Robinson & Elizabeth Watson, both of ye Parish of St Nicholas in Newcastle upon Tine, Dioc. Dur.
July 8 John Lamb & Jane Colling, of ye Parish of Grindon, Dioc. Dur.
July 14 Stephen Holland & Dorothy Nesham, of Darlington Par., Dioc. Dur.
July 16 John Mills, of Richmond, Dioc. York, & Ann Halliburton, of St Nicholas in Newcastle upon Tine, Dioc. Dur.
July 20 Thomas Wilkinson & Alice Fawdon, of Brancepeth Par., Dioc. Dur.
Aug. 8 Thomas Ramsay, of Monkwearmouth Par., & Ann Liddle, of ye Parish of Wearmouth, Dioc. Durham.
Aug. 15 Joseph Brownbridge & Mary Johnson, of ye Chappelrie of St Margaret in Durham, Dioc. Dur.
Aug. 29 Jonathan Newton of Barnard Castle, & Margaret Douthwaite, of ye Parish of Winston, Dioc. Dur.
Sep. 26 Jonathan Carlisle & Ann Race, both of All Saints Parish in Newcastle upon Tine, Dioc. Dur.
Nov. 14 Robert Earle, of Winston Parish, & Ann Wyckliffe, of ye Chappelrie of Whorlton, Dioc. Dur.
Nov. 17 John Tarn, of ye Parish of Allton, Dioc. Dur., & Alice Teasdaile, of Knarsdaile, Dioc. York.
Nov. 28 William Nedby & Mary Beadnell, of Norton Par., Dio. Dur.
Dec. 17 Mr. Thomas Wilkinson,[1] of Xgate Chappelrie, & Mrs Mary Fetherston, of ye Parish of St Mary Le Bow in Durha', Dioc. Dur.
Dec. 24 Nicholas Palmer & Catharine Finch, of ye Parish of Little St Mary in ye South Baily in Durham, Dioc. Dur.
Dec. 27 Cuthbert Lee & Isabel Gibson,[2] both in Stanhope Parish in Weardaile, Dioc. Durh.

---

[1] He Thomas Wilkinson was the second son of William Wilkinson, of the City of Durham, merchant, who made a large fortune in trade, by Margaret Taylor. He was baptized at Crossgate 7 Jan. 1667-8; of the City of Durham, Barrister-at-Law; admitted free of the Mercers' Company 8 July 1702. Died on the 15th, and was buried in a lead coffin within the Communion rails of St. Mary-le-Bow Church, Durham, 20 Feb. 1733-4. M.I. Will dated 26 March 1733 and proved 9 Aug. 1734 at Durham. He wainscotted the chancel of St. Mary-le-Bow in 1731. His wife was the dau. and heiress of William Fetherstonhalgh, of Brancepeth and Stanley, by his wife Elizabeth, dau. and coheir of William Aubone, Esq., Alderman and Mayor (1684) of Newcastle-on-Tyne. She married secondly, as second wife, Sir William Williamson, fourth Bart., High Sheriff for twenty successive years of the Palatinate. She died on the 17th and was buried in Brancepeth Church on the 20th April 1752, aged 63. [MS. Ped. by E. A. W.]

[2] [? Isabel, dau. of John Gibson, of Wearhead, baptized 13 Jan. 1683-4 at Stanhope.] John, their eldest child, baptized 24 Jan. 1718-19 at Stanhope; others.

1717 Dec. 27 Thomas Watson[1] & Mary Nattress, both in Stanhope Parish in Weardaile, Dioc. Dur.
Jan. 2 Simon Meek, of Gateshead Parish, & Ann Ewbanck, of ye Par. of St Nicholas in Newcastle upon Tine, Dioc. Dur.
Feb. 3 William Lawson & Jane Warcup, of ye Par. of Patrick Brunton, Dioc. York.
Feb. 12 John Morgan[2] & Isabel Emerson, of Stanhope Parish in Weardaile, Dioc. Dur.
Feb. 22 Parcival Yarrow & Isabel Burne, of Lamesly Parish, Dioc. Dur.
Feb. 24 John Jefferson, of Sedgefeild Parish, & Elianor Thompson, of ye Parish of Monk-Hesledon, Dioc. Durha'.
Mar. 20 William Gallaly, of Lauchester Parish, & Isabel Cook, of ye Parish of Witton Gilbert, Dioc. Durham.
Mar. 20 Thomas Jon & Susanna Hodgshon, of Woolsingham Parish, Dioc. Dur.
1718 April 8 John Gibson & Mary Young, of Bishopton Parish, Dioc. Dur.
April 12 George Robinson & Jane Watson, of Wearemouth Parish, Dioc. Dur.
April 14 David Revely, of St Nicholas Parish in Newcastle upon Tine, & Mary Stevenson, of Whickham, Dioc. Dur.
April 24 Richard Ingram, of Elwick Par., & Ann Arrowsmith, of Easeington Parish, Dioc. Durham.
May 1 David Smith, of Houghton le Spring, & Alice Johnson, of Easeington Parish, Dioc. Durham.
May 8 Joseph Gibson, of Stockton Par., & Jane Ord, of Elmdon Par., Dio. D.
May 10 Jacob Wray & Ann Ward, of Lauchester Par., Dioc. Dur.
May 13 Jonathan Wooler[3] & Isabel Forster, of Woolsingham Par., Dioc. Dur.
June 3 Mr. Cuthbert Hilton, of St Andrew Par. Awkland, & Mrs. Jane Hodghson, of ye Par. of Witton on ye Wear, Dioc. Dur.
June 21 Joseph Woodmas & Elizabeth Shaffeild, of St Nicholas Par., Durha'.
June 28 Henry Wilson, of Houghton Par., & Margaret Humble, of Chester Par., Dio. Dur.
July 11 Robert Proud, of Yarum Par. (York Dioc.), & Cicilia Morgan, of St Margaret's Chappelrie in Durham (Dioc. Durha').
July 15 Joseph Wheelright & Jane Latimer, of All Saints Chappelrie (Newcastle upon Tine), Dioc. Dur.

---

[1] Their eldest child Mary baptized 22 Oct. 1718 at Stanhope.
[2] Their eldest child, "John Pilkiuton, son of Mr. John Morgan of Langlee," baptized 10 Dec. 1718 at Stanhope. Later he is described in the Register as of New Park.
[3] He (probably eldest) son of "Mr." Anthony Wooler (buried 8 April 1736) by his wife Elizabeth (buried 8 Dec. 1728) was baptized 14 Oct. 1683, and buried 22 Oct. 1762. She (baptized 28 Oct. 1691) was dau. of John Forster, gent., and buried 8 May 1783, æt. 92. All these dates from Wolsingham Register. The descendants of this marriage still reside at that place, in a fine old mansion called Whitfield House, formerly the property of Robert Whitfield of Whitfield in Northumberland, Esq., whose marriage see 2 June 1730.

1718 July 29 Mr. James Sayer, of Stockton Par., & M⁽ʳˢ⁾ Thomasine Middleton, of S⁽ᵗ⁾ Nicholas Parish in Durham, Dioc. Dur.
Aug. 4 George Simpson & Dorothy Wheatley, of S⁽ᵗ⁾ Margaret's Chappelric in Durha', Dioc. Dur.
Aug. 19 Michael Thompson & Ann Gibson, of Stanhope Parish, Dioc. Dur.
Aug. 19 Ralph Gelson,[1] of S⁽ᵗ⁾ Nicholas Par., Dur., & Rebbecca Rowel, of S⁽ᵗ⁾ Margaret Chapp. in Durha', Dioc. Dur.
Oct. 23 Richard Harrison, of Cleasby (York Dioc.), & Margaret Duel, of Aickliffe Par., Dioc. Dur.
Oct. 27 Peter Maugham, of Eglescliffe Par., & Elizabeth Lyn, of Sedgefeild Par., Dioc. Dur.
Nov. 1 Edward Seamer & Ann Wheatly, both of y⁽ᵉ⁾ Parish of Whickham, Dioc. Durha'.
Nov. 11 Thomas Lay & Isabel Lindsly, of S⁽ᵗ⁾ Mary-Le-Bow Par. in Durha', Dioc. Durham.
Nov. 19 Thomas Scott, of Merrington Parish, & Mary Sparke, of Sedgefeild Parish, Dioc. Dur.
Nov. 24 Jonathan Hanby & Mary Robinson, of Barnardcastle Chapp., Dioc. Durham.
Nov. 24 Thomas Armstrong, of Heighinton Par., & Elizabeth Hutchinson, of Grundon Par., Dioc. Dur.
Nov. 26 Joseph Forster & Mary Wilson, of All Saints in Newcastle upon Tine, Dioc. Durham.
Dec. 7 Robert Spoor & Margaret Smith, of All Saints in Newcastle upon Tine, Dioc. Dur.
Jan. 10 Edward Crosby[2] & Ann Pruddus, of Brancepeth Parish, Dioc. Durham.
Jan. 26 Thomas Brass, of Richmond Par. (Yorkshire), & Ann Sowerby, of Sedgfeild, Dioc. Dur.
Jan. 29 William Coates & Ann Peareth, of Monk-Hasleden Parish, Dioc. Dur.
Feb. 3 Rob⁽ᵗ⁾ Huntly & Jane Dent, of Wearmouth Parish, Dioc. Dur.
Feb. 26 John Scott & Mary Burdon, of y⁽ᶜ⁾ Parish of Houghton le Spring, Dioc. Dur.
Mar. 3 John Mason & Mary Speck, of y⁽ᵉ⁾ Parish of Heighington, Dioc. Dur.
Mar. 12 John Catcheside, of Jarroe Par., & Dorothy Brack, of Washington Par., Dioc. Dur.
1719 Mar. 28 Thomas Greenwell & Eliz. Stobbert, of y⁽ᶜ⁾ Par. of Chester in y⁽ᵉ⁾ Street, D. D.

---

[1] He son (several children before him) of Ralph Gelson, and baptized 14 March 1692-3 at St. Nicholas. He is called cousin and "house dyer," and made her ex'or, by Isabel, widow of William Adamson, of Durham, in her will dated 3 Feb. 1730-31. The eldest child of this marriage, Ralph Gelson, was baptized at Crossgate 15 May 1719, and was afterwards a Minor Canon of Durham and Vicar of Merrington.

[2] See, possibly, his previous marriage 2 Jan. 1702-3.

CATHEDRAL CHURCH AT DURHAM. 61

1719 May 19 James Maitland & Anne Raw, both of ye Par. of Ovingham in the County of Northumb., Dioc. Dur.
     May 24 Geo. Emmerson & Anne Stot, both of the Parish of Woolsingham, Dioc. Dur.
     May 24 Robert Cunningham, of ye Chapelry of St John, & Elizabeth Beachman, of All Saints in Newcastle, Dioc. Durh.
     May 25 Robt Swainston & Mary Allan, both of Barnard-Castle, Dioc. Durh.
     May 31 Wm Taylor, of the Par. of Pittington, & Anne Craggs, of the Par. of Chester, Dioc. Dur.
     June 11 Wm Byers & Mary Anderson, both of the Parish of Houghton le Spring.
     June 11 Ralph Conyers[1] & Jane Blakiston, both of the Parish of Chester, Dio. Dur.
     June 19 John Burton & Elisabeth Dobson, both of ye Parish of Wearmouth, Dioc. Dur.
     July 27 Aaron Law & Elisabeth Wild, both of the Parish of Bish^p Wearmouth, Dioc. Dur.
     July 31 Will. Davison & Ann Sureties, both of the Parish of St Nichol. in Durham.
     Aug. 6 Tho. Chapman, of Brough, Dioc. Carl., and Marg^t Jacques, of ye Parish of All Saints in Newcastle, Dioc. Durh.
     Aug. 15 George Bell & Mary Wearmouth, both of ye Parish of All Saints in Newcastle, Dioc. Durham.
     Aug. 23 Fletcher Partis,[2] of St Nicholas in Newcastle, & Ann Bromely, of Bish^p Wearmouth, Dioc. Dur.
     Aug. 25 Tho. Wilkinson, of ye Parish of Hurworth, & Frances Loysclure, of ye Parish of Heighington, Dioc. Dur.
     Sep. 3 Tho. Partis & Ann Peacock, both of ye Parish of Sunderland, Dioc. Durham.
     Sep. 7 James Sheppard & Jane Drum'er, both of ye Parish of Dalton, Dioc. Durham. .
     Sep. 10 Mr. Jo. Wilkinson,[3] of ye chapelry of St Margaret's, & Jane Smith, of ye Parish of St Oswald's, Dioc. Dur.

[1] He was baptized at Chester-le-Street 20 June 1697, and succeeded his second-cousin Sir Baldwyn Conyers as fifth Baronet in 1731, and died 1767. She dau. of Ralph Blakiston, gent., grandson of Sir William Blakiston, of Gibside, Knt., and his wife Jane Lambton, of Lambton. Blakiston, Nicholas, and Thomas, sixth, seventh, and ninth (and last) Baronets were the sons of this marriage. With the unfortunate history of Sir Thomas, the last heir male of this ancient line, all North-countrymen are acquainted. Suffice it to say here that he died in 1810, shortly after his removal, too late, from Chester-le-Street Workhouse. See Burke's "Vicissitudes of Families."
[2] He of Talentire, Northumberland, Esq. She buried 26 April 1763 at St. Nicholas, Newcastle.
[3] He was the third son of William Wilkinson and Margaret Taylor, and was baptized at Crossgate 19 April 1670. His father left him his lands at Seamer, co. York, and Stobilee and Eddercres, co. Pal., Durham, and £1750 ; admitted free of the Mercers' Company 10 Feb. 1690 ; died 22 and was buried at St. Oswald's 24 Nov. 1734, s.p. Will dated 25 Nov. 1725 ; proved at York 23 Dec. 1734. His wife was remarried 23 April 1735 at Chester-le-Street to Robert Hull. [MS. Ped. by E. A. W.]

REGISTER OF MARRIAGES IN THE

1719 Oct. 5 Humphr'y Arrowsmith, of ye Parish of Easington, & Eliz. Jurdison, of ye Parish of Pittington, Dioc. Dur.

Nov. 14 Will. Hallyman, of ye Parish of Easington, & Elisabeth Ord, of ye Parish of Middleham, Dioc. Dur.

Nov. 16 George Gibson, of St Nicholas in Newcastle, & Hannah Kelly, of Gateshead, Dioc. Dur.

Jo. Waring, Sacrist.

Nov. 20 Tho. Watson & Jane Wanless, both of ye Parish of Kelloe, Dioc. Durham.

Nov. 26 Jo. Corneforth, of ye Parish of Kelloe, and Mary Grainge, of ye Parish of Billingham, Dioc. Dur.

Dec. 3 Tho. Todd[1] & Ann Gregson, both of the Parish of Dalton, Dioc. Durham.

Dec. 3 Jo. Walton, of ye Parish of Gateshead, & Isabell Todd, of ye Parish of Washington, Dioc. Dur.

Dec. 12 Thomas Charleton, of ye Chappelrie of St Marg^{ts}, & Frances Ovington, of ye Parish of St Mary Lebow.

Jan. 25 John Allan & Marg^t Hood, both of All Saints in Newcastle, Dioc. Durh.

Jan. 30 Will. Gascoigne & Dorothy Bilton, both of ye Parish of Sunderland by ye Sea, Dioc. Dur.

Feb. 2 Mr. Tho. Bowlby, of ye Parish of St Mary Lebow, & Mrs Mary Burell, of ye Parish of little St Mary's.

Feb. 3 Jo. Toward[2] & Mary Burlison, both of the Parish of Wolshingham.

1720 April 4 Tho. Swainston & Alice Creyton, both of ye Parish of Gainford, Dioc. Dur.

April 23 Tho. Atkinson, of ye Parish of Brancepeth, & Jane Trotter, of ye Parish of Aukland St Andrew.

April 30 Will. Joplin & Isabell Busby, both of the Parish of Lanchester.

May 3 John Coultas & Sarah Abbs, both of ye Parish of Sunderland by ye Sea.

May 15 James Hutchinson, of St John's, and Frances Salkeld, of All Saints, both in Newcastle, Dioc. Dur.

May 26 Will. Gibson, of St Nicholas in Durham, & Thomasine Hutchinson, of St Marie's in ye South Bailey in Durham.

June 4 Robt Nicholson, of ye Parish of Staindrope, & Martha Wheatley, of ye Parish of Escomb.

June 7 Richd Thomlinson, of Bernardcastle, & Eliz. Hornsby, of ye Parish of Dalton.

June 7 Michael Dobbinson, of ye Parish of Seadgefield, & Mary Croft, of ye Parish of Witton on ye Wear.

June 14 Robt Smith & Mary Cooke, both of ye Parish of Hart, Dioc. Dur.

---

[1] She appears in a MS. pedigree of the family as dau. of Thomas Gregson, of Murton and Dalton, co. Pal., but as her parents were married 5 Feb. 1653-4, she is more probably granddau. of Thomas, and perhaps sister of William Gregson, whose marriage see 1 May 1714. [Ann, dau. of William Gregson, of Murton, baptized 23 April 1672, also occurs at Dalton-le-Dale.]

[2] Anne, their first child (others follow), baptized 18 June 1721 at Wolsingham.

1720 June 18 George Emerson & Elizabeth Burden, both of y^c Parish of Lanchester, Dioc. Dur.
June 21 John Cutter & Barbara Errington, both of Newcastle upon Tyne, Dioc. Dur.
July 18 Robt Southeron & Eliz. Cowle, both of the Parish of Greatham, Dioc. Dur.
Aug. 4 Philip Hall & Eliz. Milborne, both of the Parish of Monke Wearmouth, Dioc. Dur.
Aug. 11 John Hutchinson, of Bernardcastle, & Marg^t Armstron, of ye Parish of Gateshead, Dioc. Dur.
Aug. 11 Joseph Davison & Anne Craggs, both of y^c Parish of Sunderland by ye Sea, Dioc. Dur.
Aug. 13 Robt Whetherell, of St Nicholas in Durham, & Alice Wetherell, of Kirklevinton, Com. Ebor.
Sep. 8 Mr Will. Forster,[1] Minor Canon of y^c Cathedrall, & Mrs Joan Newby, of y^c Parish of Pittington.
Sep. 17 Will. Reed & Mary Ingo, both of ye Chappelric of Low Heweth, Dioc. Dur.
Sep. 22 Tho. Lynn & Jane Harrison, both of y^c Parish of Merrington, Dioc. Durh.
Sep. 25 Ju^o Dodds & Eliz. Chambers,[2] both of ye Parish of St Nicholas in Newcastle upon Tyne.
Sep. 27 Andrew Hutchinson, of All Saints in Newcastle upon Tine, & Cath. Milborn, of ye Par. of Gateshead.
Oct. 4 George Clapham, of ye Parish of Aukland St Andrew, & Cibelle Harper, of ye Parish of Sunderland by ye Sea, Dioc. Dur.
Oct. 6 Will. Scorer & Jane Allan, both of ye Parish of Pittington, Dioc. Dur.
Oct. 7 Ju^o Button, of y^c Parish of Branspeth, & Marg^t Lister, of ye College in Durham.
Oct. 8 George Lock, of ye Parish of Lesbury, & Marg^t Whithead, of ye Parish of Longhoughton, Com. Northumb., Dioc. Dur.
Oct. 15 Conon Stephenson & Anne Coatesworth, both of ye Parish of Middleton in Teasedale.
Oct. 20 Thomas Dobson & Mary Hillary, both of ye Parish of Stocton, Dioc. Dur.
Oct. 29 Ju^o Hutchinson, of ye Parish of Trimdon, & Mary Wilkinson, of ye Parish of St Nicolas in Durham, Dioc. Dur.

---

[1] He, then Vicar of Aycliffe, inducted into the Vicarage of St. Oswald's 24 Jan. 1725-6. Baptisms of his children occur there. [The Rev. Christopher Thompson, Vicar of Pittington, was married there 6 July 1691 to Ann Newby.]

[2] She dau. to Richard Chambers, of Newcastle, and, *jure uxoris*, of Warden Law, co. Pal., gent., by his wife Eleanor, youngest dau. and coheir of John Beckwith, of Newcastle, gent., and co. heiress to her cousin Judith Beckwith, an infant, of Warden Law. See Surtees, vol. i., and "Landed Gentry"—"Chambers of Clough House." No issue of this marriage is mentioned in wills of her relatives which have been examined. She was aunt of Sir Robert Chambers, Chief Justice of Bengal.

REGISTER OF MARRIAGES IN THE

1720 Nov. 21 Philip How, of ye Parish of Monk Wearmouth, & Isabel Pringor, of ye Parish of Sunderland by the Sea, Dioc. Dur.
Dec. 31 Jno Hazard & Rebec' Vipont, both of the Chapelrie of St Marg^ts in Durham.
Dec. 31 Julius Coniusby & Mary Welsford, both of ye Parish of Aukland St Andrew.
Jan. 9 Jno Humes & Eliz. Pate, both of All S^ts in Newcastle, Dioc. Dur.
Feb. 18 Will. Garth, of ye Parish of Witton on ye Wear, & Eliz. Cooling, of Witton Gilbert.
Feb. 19 Christopher Emmerson & Eliz. Walton, both of ye Parish of Hamsterly, Dioc. Dur.
Feb. 20 Jno Newton & Alice Downes, of ye Parish Tynemouth, Com. North., Dioc. Dur.
Feb. 25 Jno Redshaw & Jane Salkeild, both of ye Chapelrie of St Marger^ts in Durham.

1721 Mar. 26 Jno Mall, of ye Parish of Leuchester, & Dorothy Ogle,[1] of ye Parish of Woolsingham, Dioc. Dur.
April 11 Jno Blacklock, of ye Parish of Hexam, Dioc. Ebor, & Alice Shaw, of ye Parish of Ryton, Dioc. Dur.
April 11 Will. Potter, of ye Chapelrie of St Marg^ts, & Mary Raine, of ye Parish of St Mary Le bow, both in Durham.
April 15 Will. Baines & Eliz. Rooksby, both of ye Parish of Branspeth, Dioc. Dur.
April 20 George Middleton, of ye Parish of Darlington, & Marg^t Bishopbrig, of ye Parish of Haughton, Dioc. Dur.
May 20 Will. Carter, of ye Parish of Sunderland by ye Sea, & Mary Bilton, of ye Parish of Monk Wearmouth.
June 24 Jno Hutchinson, of ye Parish of Washington, & Mary Smith, of ye Parish of Lanchester.
July 11 John Webster & Jane Sum'erside, both of ye Parish of Aukland St Andrew.
July 15 John Borrow, of St John's in Newcastle, & Jane Proud, of ye Parish of Branspeth, Dioc. Dur.
Aug. 17 Will. Robson, of ye Parish of Chester in ye Street, & Elianor Watson, of ye Parish of Houghton in ye Spring.
Aug. 19 Bartholomew Andrew & Jane Henderson, both of ye Parish of Houghton Le Spring.
Sep. 4 John Goodchild, of ye Parish of Bp. Wearmouth, & Grace Nicholson, of ye Parish of Stainton.
Oct. 27 James Readshaw & Sarah Brown, both of All S^ts in Newcastle, Dioc. Dur.
Nov. 4 Robert Smith & Joan Whight, both of ye Parish of Sunderland by ye Sea, Dioc. Dur.
Nov. 9 Jno Brack, of ye Parish of Washington, & Marg^t Wheatly, of ye Parish of Houghton Le Spring.

---

[1] She dau. of George Ogle, gent., baptized 24 May 1698 at Wolsingham.

1721	Nov. 11	George Priestly & Eliz. Carter, both of Parish of Chester in yᵉ Street.
	Nov. 13	Jnᵒ Douthwait & Dorothy Dixon, both of yᵉ Chappelry of Bernardcastle.
	Nov. 17	Tho. Stothart, of yᵉ Parish of Haughton, & Anne Leivers, of yᵉ Parish of Houghton Le Spring.
		Wᵐ Parthericke Turner, Sacrist.
	Nov. 28	Robᵗ Snaith, of the Parish of Grundon, and Eliz. Robson, of yᵉ Parish of Sedgfield.
	Dec. 6	Jos. Sisson & Esther Sisson, of the Parish of All Saints in Newcastle-upon-Tyne, Dioc. Dun.
	Dec. 13	Henry Heaviside & Isabel Briggs, of yᵉ Parish of Hartinpoole, Dioc. Dunelm.
	Jan. 13	John Harrison & Eleanor Hobson, of the Parish of Chester in yᵉ Street, Dioc. Dunelm.
	Feb. 1	Humphrey Norton,[1] of yᵉ Colledge, & Ann Eyles, of the Parish of Sᵗ Oswald's.
1722	Mar. 27	Edward Ayre, of the chappelry of Sᵗ Helen's, & Mary Readhead, of yᵉ Parish of Whitworth.
	April 15	Wᵐ Milburne, of yᵉ Parish of Gateshead, & Margᵗ Newton, of yᵉ Parish of Sᵗ Nicholas in Newcastle upon Tyne, Dioc. Dunelm.
	May 29	Robᵗ Heath & Jane Graham, both of yᵉ Parish of Sᵗ Nicholas in Newcastle upon Tyne.
	May 31	Tho. Wilson, of yᵉ Parish of Fosset, Dioc. Ebor, & Eliz. Farrow, of yᵉ Parish of Brancepeth, Dioc. Dun.
	June 12	Dan. Albert, of yᵉ Parish of Gateshead, & Mary Procter, of yᵉ Chappelry of Benwell, Dioc. Dunelm.
	June 15	Robᵗ Wheat & Catherine Claxton, both of the Parish of Hartlepool, Dioc. Dun.
	June 19	Char. Nailor & Marg. Dawson, both of the Parish of Sᵗ Nicholas, Durham.
	June 30	Robᵗ Swalwell & Eliz. Smith, of the Parish of Easington, Dioc. Dun.
	July 5	Andrew Forsaith & Dorothy Prockter, of the Parish of Ryton, Dioc. Dun.
	July 9	Robᵗ Milbourn & Eliz. Browell, of the Parish of Sunderland by Sea, Dioc. Dun.
	July 14	Wᵐ Stell, of yᵉ Parish of Monk-Weremouth, & Eleanor Harrison, of yᵉ Parish of Houghton le Spring.
	July 21	Robᵗ Readhead, de Jarrow, & Is. Wilson, de Washington, Dio. Dun.
	Aug. 3	Edwᵈ Dickenson & Ann Ord, of the Parish of Sedgfield, Dioc. Dunelm.

---

[1] He, the son of Roger Norton by his first wife Catherine Hewitson, was baptized 1 Jan. 1692-3, was organist of Sedgefield; he was buried 9 May 1726 at St. Oswald's. His wife Ann was dau. of Thomas Eyles, of New Elvet, and was born on the 26 of March 1702. She re-married 22 June 1732, at St. Oswald's, "Mʳ" Robert Clifton. [MS. Ped. by E. A. W.]

1722 Aug. 19   Tho. Golbourn, of ye Parish of St Nicholas, Newcastle upon Tyne, & Ann Hall, of the Parish of Elsdon, Dioc. Dun.
Aug. 21   Thomas Elder & Jane Clark, of the Parish of Warkworth, Dioc. Dunelm.
Sep. 2   Joshua Colledge & Mary Martindale, both of ye Parish of St Nich., Durham.
Sep. 5   Cuthbert Forster & Mary Watson,[1] of the Parish of Wolsingham, Dioc. Dun.
Sep. 11   Geo. Hewison & Mary Henderson, both of the Chappelry of All Saints, Newcastle upon Tyne.
Sep. 20   John Hall, of St Andrew's Auckland, & Ann Nicholson, of ye Parish of Wolsingham.
Sep. 27   Geo. Vane,[2] Esq., of Long Newton, & Ann Machon, of ye Colledge, Durham.
Sep. 30   Cuthbert Davison & Johanna Stukeley, of ye Parish of Tyne-mouth, Dioc. Dunelm.
Oct. 8   Tho. Wake, of ye Parish of Sunderland by Sea, & Mary Shafto, of ye Parish of Gateshead, Dioc. Dunelm.
Oct. 26   Obadiah Emerson, of ye Parish of Stanhope, & Hanna Dickinson, of ye Parish of Alstone, Dioc. Dunelm.
Oct. 27   Wm Watson & Alice Dobinson, of ye Parish of Sunderland by Sea, Dioc. Dun.
Nov. 11   Robt Hawksworth & Marg^t Watson, both of ye Parish of Stranton, Dioc. Dun.
Nov. 16   Robt Makepeace, of ye Parish of St Nicholas, & Marg^t Wilkinson, of ye Chappelry of All Saints, widow, in Newcastle upon Tyne.
Nov. 23   Robt Mitchinson & Frances Atkinson, of ye Parish of Lanchester, Dioc. Dun.
Dec. 7   Wm Shaw & Muriel Green, both of ye Parish of Darlington, Dioc. Dunelm.
Dec. 10   Robt Ramsey & Cath. Morisby, of ye Parish of St Nicholas, Newcastle upon Tyne.
Dec. 11   John Errington, of ye Parish of Gosforth, and Ann Wright, of St Andrew's, Newcastle sup. Tyna'.
Dec. 26   John Webster, of ye Parish of St Nich., Newcastle upon Tyne, & Susanna Ayre, of ye Parish of Gateshead, Wid., Dioc. Dunelm.
Dec. 30   James Smith & Mary Barnes, of ye Chappelry of Lamesly, Dioc. Dunelm.

---

[1] She presumably a second wife, as "Abigail, wife of Cuthbert Forster," was buried 19 Jan. 1720-21 at Wolsingham.

[2] He eldest son of Lionel Vane, of Long Newton, co. Pal., Esq., and father, by this marriage, of the Rev. Henry Vane, of Long Newton, Prebendary of Durham (see the baptism of his dau. 12 May 1769), who was created a Baronet 1782. See Pedigree of VANE, of Long Newton, Surtees. She younger dau. and coheiress of Gilbert Machon, of Lichfield and Durham, Esq. (see the second marriage of her mother 30 Sep. 1706, and MACHON in Index). She was sole ex'or and residuary legatee of her father's cousin, the Rev. Gabriel Blakiston, Rector of Danby-upon-Wiske, Yorks, whose will was proved at York 21 Aug. 1721, and inherited his share of his "cole-mines" at Axwell and Swalwell.

1722	Jan. 21	John Carr & Mary Fowler, of ye Parish of Stockden, Dioc. Dunelm.
	Jan. 31	Rob. Thompson & Jane Lodge, of ye Parish of Darlington, Dioc. Dunelm.
	Feb. 21	John Benton, of ye Parish of Stockton, & Jane Stephenson, of ye Parish of Gateshead, Widow, Dioc. Dunelm.
	Mar. 6	David Kennebye, of ye Parish of Stanhop, & Eleanor Moor, of ye Chappelry of St Margarett's, Durham.
1723	April 1	Richard Warren & Isabel Brown, Widow, of ye Parish of Bishop-Middleham, Dio. Dun.
	April 7	Geo. Laws, of ye Parish of St Nicholas, and Ann Taylor, of the Chappelry of All Saints, Newcastle sup. Tinam, Dioc. Dunelm.
	April 23	John Dixon, of ye Parish of Haughton, and Mary Bell, of ye Parish of Staindrop, Dioc. Dun.
	May 6	Geo. Purvis & Marg^t Hall, of ye Chappelry of St Andrew, Newcastle upon Tine.
	May 7	John Thompson, of ye Parish of Chester in ye Street, and Grace Loftus, of ye Chappelry of St Margarett's, Durham, Dioc. Dunelm.
	May 11	Robert Mitchinson & Mary Thompson, of ye Chappelry of St Andrew's, Newcastle upon Tyne.
	May 15	Gerard Heckles & Isabel Pattinson, of the Parish of Gateshead, Dioc. Dunelm.
	May 23	John Wascoe & Eliz. Bradely, of the Chappelry of Witton upon Were. Dioc. Dunelm.
	May 30	Ralph Dunn & Eliz. Darnell, of the Parish of Lanchester, Dioc. Dunelm.
	June 3	Henry Stephenson and Eliz. Moffett, of the Chappelry of St Margarett's, Durham.
	June 4	John Willans, of Hamsterly, and Mary Bell, of ye Parish of St Andrew's Auckland, Dioc. Dun.
	June 8	Abraham Stout,[1] of ye Parish of St Nicholas, Durham, & Ann Brack, of ye Parish of Branspeth, Dioc. Dun.
	June 8	Ralph Hodgson, of ye Parish of Sedgfield, and Fortune Dixon, of ye Parish of Bishop-Weremouth, Dioc. Dunelm.
	June 11	John Harrison & Mary Taylor, Wid., both of ye Parish of Haughton, Dioc. Dunelm.
	July 8	Welbery Winshipp[2] & Eliz. Harrison, of ye Parish of Chester in ye Street, Dioc. Dun.
	July 9	William Morgan & Ann Grainger, of ye Chappelry of Bernard-Castle, Dioc. Dun.
	July 29	John Graham & Ann Coulson, widow, of the Parish of Wolsingham, Dioc. Dun.
	Aug. 2	Nicholas Jefferson, of ye Parish of Long-Newton, Dioc. Dunelm., and Ann Thompson, of the Parish of Crathorne, Dioc. Ebor.
	Aug. 31	Thomas Blenkinsopp & Susanna Rippon, Widow, of ye Parish of Lanchester, Dioc. Dun.

---

[1] The family of Stout, or Stott, has been long seated in Durham.
[2] He buried at Chester-le-Street 18 Aug. 1737. Of Whitehill, gent.

1723 Sep. 17 Christopher Kitchin & Marg^t Grosier, of the Chappelry of St Hilda (Shields), Dioc. Dun.

Sep. 18 Robert Major and Mercy Winshipp, of the Chappelry of St Hilda, Dioc. Dunelm.

Oct. 16 Joseph Stott & Mary Wilkinson, of the Parish of Darlington, Dioc. Dunelm.

Nov. 9 Andrew Wood, of ye Parish of Chester in ye Street, & Jane Selby, of ye Parish of Lanchester, Dioc. Dunelm.

Nov. 28 Thomas Taylor & Catherine Lewin, of ye Chappelry of All Saints, New-Castle upon Tyne.

Nov. 30 Thomas Parkin, of ye Parish of St Andrew Auckland, & Mary Browne, of ye Parish of Heighington, Dio. Dun.

Dec. 14 Joseph Turner & Mary Bell, widow, of ye Chappelry of All-Saints, Newcastle upon Tyne.

Jan. 10 Thomas Bailiffe & Esther Williamson, of ye Chappelry of All Saints, Newcastle upon Tyne.

Jan. 25 James Dobson & Marg^t Close, of the Parish of Kelloe, Dioc. Dunelm.

Jan. 27 Edward Milbourne & Ann Heads, Wid^w, of ye Parish of Gateshead, Dioc. Dun.

Feb. 2 John Wilkinson & Dorothy Simpson, of ye Parish of Darlington, Dioc. Dun.

Feb. 6 Mark Farrow[1] & Mary Beckfield, of ye Chappelry of St Helen's Auckland, Dioc. Dun.

Feb. 6 Robert Bamblett, of ye Parish of Ecclescliffe, Dioc. Dunelm., and Mary Harker, of ye Parish of Stoxley, Dioc. Eborac.

Feb. 15 George Craggs & Mary Layne, Wid^w, of ye Parish of Esh, Dioc. Dunelm.

1724 April 25 Thomas Marley, of ye Parish of Chester in ye Street, & Ann Corneforth, of the Parish of Branspeth, Dioc. Dunelm.

May 1 John Grainger, of the College, and Mary Errington,[2] of ye Parish of St Oswald, Dioc. Dunelm.

May 4 Richard Paul, of ye Parish of East Harlsley, Dioc. Ebor., and Jane Todd, of the Parish of Bolden, Dioc. Dunelm.

May 23 Thomas Wheatley, of the Chappelry of Kimblesworth, and Ann Appelby, of the Parish of Merrington, Dioc. Dunelm.

May 26 Wm Jackson, of ye Parish of Horton, and Dorothy Ingah, of ye Parish of Sedgfield, Dioc. Dunelm.

June 8 Samuel Ferguson & Jane Barrowman, of the Parish of St Nicholas, Newcastle upon Tyne, Dioc. Dunelm.

---

[1] He of Ramshaw in Evenwood, and the name is spelt variously in the Registers. This was probably his second marriage, as there are several children of his baptized before this date at St. Helen's. He appears to have been baptized 5 May 1678, the son of John Farrow by his marriage, 9 Sep. 1677, with Anne Bullock. William, oldest son of this Mark Farrah, Farrer, or Farrow, was baptized 30 Aug. 1724, and other children follow.

[2] She was probably Mary, dau. of William Errington, draper-taylor, of St. Oswald's (who has several other children baptized there), and was baptized 25 Jan. 1693-4.

CATHEDRAL CHURCH AT DURHAM. 69

1724	June 27	Thomas Ridley & Margaret Harker, of the Parish of Merrington, Dioc. Dun.
	July 25	George Edwards,[1] of the Chappelry of Barnard-Castle, and Anne Humble, of the Parish of Ryton, widow, Dioc. Dunelm.
	July 27	Tho. Craggs, of ye Parish of Bishop-Weremouth, and Hannah Allinson, of ye Parish of Houghton le Spring, Dioc. Dunelm.
	July 30	Jonathan Huck & Hannah Gamesby, of the Parish of Gateshead, Dioc. Dunelm.
	Aug. 21	John Newton & Eliz. Darnton, of the Parish of Staindropp, Dioc. Dun.
	Aug. 25	John Seddon, of Manchester in ye County of Lancaster, & Hannah Linskill, of the Parish of St Nicholas in ye City of Durham, widow.
	Aug. 27	John Robinson & Isabel Wilkinson, of ye Parish of Whickham, Dioc. Dunelm.
	Sep. 12	Wm Richardson & Jane Shipley, of the Parish of Morpeth, Dioc. Dunelm.
	Sep. 13	Geo. Shevill & Eliz. Turner, of the Parish of Boldon, Dioc. Dunelm.
	Oct. 9	Edward Brenkarn & Alice Metcalf, of ye Parish of Kirkby Stephen, Westmorland Dioc.
	Oct. 18	Anthony Taylor and Eliz. Langstaffe, of ye Chappelry of Witton Gilbert, Dioc. Dun.
	Oct. 20	Samuel Scroggs & Ann Smith, Widow, of the Parish of Houghton le Spring, Dioc. Dun.
	Oct. 22	Thomas Byers & Hannah Talentire, of ye Parish of Wolsingham, Dioc. Dunelm.
	Nov. 7	Cuthbert Rutter, of the Parish of Houghton le Spring, & Eliz. Averick, of ye Parish of Chester-le-Street, Dioc. Dun.
	Nov. 21	Wm Whitfield & Mary Reay, of the Parish of Houghton le Spring, Dioc. Dunelm.
	Nov. 24	Thomas Monkhouse, of ye Chappelry of All Saints, Newcastle upon Tine, and Ann Marley, of ye Parish of Chester le Street, Dioc. Dunelm.
	Nov. 26	Ric. Lawson & Is. Hearde, of the Chappelry of Auckland St Helen's, Dioc. Dun.
	Dec.	John Bainbridge & Dorothy Botcheby, of ye Parish of St Nicholas, Durham.

[1] He son of George Edwards, of Barnard Castle, tanner, who died intestate 1746, by his wife .... Garfoot. He married firstly Isabel Denison, and by her had several children, one of whom Isabella married General Hugonin, and was mother of General Hugonin, 4th Dragoons, and Charlotte, wife of Sir Roderick Impey Murchison, Bart., F.R.S. She was widow of .... Humble, of Ryton-on-Tyne (by whom she had a son Joseph Humble, whose dau. and heiress married Joseph Lamb, of Ryton, gent.), and dau. of .... Ornsby, of Lanchester, co. Pal., although she is not placed in that pedigree in Longstaffe's " History of Darlington." She had several children by her second marriage. Mr. Edwards's brother Ambrose died s.p. 1745, having married Anne, dau. of Thomas Norton, of Grantley, co. York, Esq., and aunt to the first Lord Grantley.

REGISTER OF MARRIAGES IN THE

1724 Dec. 22 Joshua Makepeace & Hannah Ranson, Widow, of ye Parish of Sunderland by Sea, Dioc. Dun.
Dec. 26 Ralph Lax & Eliz. Bonner, of ye Parish of Sunderland by Sea, Dioc. Dun.
Dec. 26 Charles Guy & Marg^t Atkinson, of ye Parish of Chester le Street, Dioc. Dunelm.
Jan. 26 Wm Curstt & Ann Waugh, of the Parish of Sunderland by Sea, Dioc. Dunelm.
Feb. 2 Richard Merrington & Eliz. Carter, of ye Parish of Long Newton, Dioc. Dun.
Feb. 6 John Harrison & Eliz. Adamson, of ye Parish of Easington, Dioc. Dun.
Feb. 6 Geo. Gibson, of the Parish of Whickham, and Ann Chapman, of the Parish of Houghton le Spring, Widow, Dioc. Dunelm.
Feb. 23 James Walker, of Gibside in the Parish of Whickham, & Eliz. Coates, of ye same Parish, Dioc. Dunelm.
Feb. 27 George Barker & Isabel Solley, of ye Parish of Jarrow, Dioc. Dun.
Mar. 2 Tho. Bowry & Barbara Thumble, of ye Parish of Long-Benton, Dioc. Dun.
1725 Mar. 31 John Todd, of the Parish of Aickliff, & Barbara Shipley, of ye Parish of Sunderland by Sea, Dioc. Dunelm.
April 27 Newark Hudson[1] & Eliz. Hobson, of the Parish of Chester in the Street, Dioc. Dun.
May 15 Edw. Rosby, of the Parish of Houghton le Spring, & Ann Mowbray, of the Parish of Chester le Street, Dioc. Dunelm.
May 20 John Collingwood & Sarah Harland, of ye Chappelry of Tanfield, Dioc. Dun.
June 3 John Barras & Jane Dunn, of the Parish of Greatham, Dioc. Dun.
June 29 Wm Taylor & Eliz. Baynes, Widow, both of the Parish of Sunderland, Dioc. Dun.
July 10 Richard Thompson & Sarah Dawson, of ye Parish of Gateside, Dioc. Dun.
July 19 Matthew Ingram & Rebecca Jurdison, of ye Parish of Pittington, Dioc. Dun.
July 27 Charles Hindmarsh & Sarah Cook, of the Parish of Sunderland, Dioc. Dun.
Aug. 3 Nicholas Straker, of the Chappelry of All Saints, Newcastle, & Frances Williamson, of the Chappelry of St Margaret's, Durham, Dioc. Dunelm.
Aug. 5 Mr Anthony Wilkinson,[2] of the Parish of St Margaret, and Mrs Deborah Machon, of the Colledge, Durham.

---

[1] [Matthew, son of Newark Hudson, buried 31 Dec. 1740; and Mr. Thomas Hudson, son of Mr. Newark Hudson, buried 11 Nov. 1770—Chester-le-Street.]

[2] He was the eighth son of William Wilkinson and Margaret Taylor, and was baptized at Crossgate 19 Sep. 1684. He was a Justice of the Peace for the County Palatine, and was a very

CATHEDRAL CHURCH AT DURHAM. 71

1725 Aug. 11 Michael Walton, of ye Parish of Kelloe, & Mary Usher, of ye Parish of Branspeth, Dioc. Dunelm.
Aug. 24 John Hixon, of ye Parish of Sedgfield, & Eliz. Johnson, of ye Parish of St Oswald, Dioc. Dunelm.
Aug. 26 Jo. Stout, Lay Clerk, and Ann Vasey, both of ye Parish of St Nicholas, Durham.
Aug. 30 Tho. Johnson & Ann Evening, of the Parish of Barnard Castle, Dioc. Dunelm.
Sep. 5 Tho. Cockaney & Jane Peers, of St Nicholas, Newcastle upon Tine.
Sep. 8 Wm Hinmers & Eleanor Horseley, Widow, of All Saints, Newcastle upon Tine.
Sep. 18 Israel Jeffryson & Grace Rutlis, of ye Parish of Sedgefield, Dioc. Dunelm.
Oct. 10 Robert Finch & Phyllis Forster, both of the Chappelry of Esh, Dioc. Dunelm.
Oct. 10 Andrew Turnbull & Ann Shute, Widow, both of the Chappelry of All Saints, Newcastle upon Tyne, Dioc. Dun.
Oct. 13 Edward Robson & Eliz. Ridley, of the Parish of Houghton le Spring, Dioc. Dunelm.
Oct. 28 Tho. Reed & Mary Cook, of the Parish of Seaham, Dioc. Dunelm.
Dec. 4 Rob. Gelson & Hannah Corneforth, of the Parish of Pittington, Dioc. Dun. Married by Bryan Turner.
Dec. 28 James Gregory & Eliz. Barker, Widow, of the Parish of All Saints, Newcastle upon Tine, Dioc. Dunelm. By Mr Waring.
Jan. 2 Mich. Taylor, of the Chappelry of All Saints, Newcastle, & Eliz. Baynes, of ye Parish of Tinemouth, Dioc. Dunelm. By Mr Waring.
Jan. 11 Wm Horseman[1] & Mary Smith, of ye Colledge. By Dr Mangey.
Jan. 13 Wm Maston, of the Parish of St Nicholas, & Jane Brack, of ye Parish of Brandspeth; by Mr Waring.
Jan. 15 Thomas Todd, of St Hellen's Auckland, and Christian Furbank, of All Saints, Newcastle, Wid.
Jan. 22 William Walton, of Kelloe Parish, & Elianor Whitfield, of ye Parish of Pittington, Dioc. Dunelm.
Jan. 23 Adam Reavely, of All Saints, New-Castle, & Dorothy Hanby, of St Nich., *ibidem*, Dioc. Dunelm.
Feb. 10 John Metcalfe, of Lauchester, & Ann Layburne, of Tanfield, Dioc. Dunelm.
Feb. 16 John Hodgson & Mary Gedlin, both of ye Parish of Bishop-Middleham, Dioc. Dun.

wealthy man. He died on the 26th and was buried with his father in the south aisle of Crossgates 28 March 1759. Will dated 3 April 1758 and proved at York. His wife the second dau. and coheiress of Gilbert Machon, of Lichfield and the City of Durham, Esq. She was buried 24 Sep. 1775. Her will, dated 1 April 1771, was proved at Durham 25 Sep. 1775. [MS. Ped. by E. A. W.]

[1] Also entered in Bow Register.

1725	Feb. 23	Geo. Peacock, of the Parish of Sunderland, & Mary Hutchinson, of ye Parish of Weremouth.
	Feb. 28	Anthony Hunter & Eliz. Clark, of the Parish of Pittington, Dioc. Dunelm.
	Mar. 12	Thomas Clarke & Abigail Wilkin, of the Parish of Chester le Street, Dioc. Dun.
1726	April 12	James Brankston & Jane Hall, of All Saints, Newcastle.
	April 16	John Ovington, of Brauspeth, & Marg^t Metcalf, of Lanchester, Dioc. Dunelm.
	April 28	Rowland Green, of Sunderland by Sea, & Barbara Robinson, of ye College.
	April 30	Wm Atkinson & Hilda Hodgson, of Brandspeth.
	May 3	Thomas Wren[1] & Ann Curry, of the Parish of Wolsingham, Dioc. Dunelm.
	May 5	John Richarby, of Croxdale, & Jane Brown, of Dalton, Dioc. Dunelm.
	May 21	Henry Thompson, of St Andrew's, New-Castle, & Marg^t Brittain, of Gateshead, widow.
	May 31	Robert Richmond, of Heighington, & Sarah Hutchinson, of St Helen's Auckland.
	June 11	Geo. Toward & Eliz. Willows, of Cockfield.
	June 12	Peter Pattison & Ann Earl, of Morpeth.
		(These two last married by Mr Waring.)
	June 16	Wm Morgan, of ye Parish of South Leath in Scotland, & Eliz. Green, of Houghton le Spring, Widow, Dioc. Dunelm.
	June 30	Samuel Watkin, of ye Parish of Bp. Wearmouth, & Mary Hogshon, of ye Parish of Sunderland by ye Sea.
	July 12	Robt Willson, of Whickham, Dioc. Dunelm., & Dorothy Charlton, of Hexham, Dioc. Ebor.
	Aug. 18	John Wilkinson, of Staindrop, Cl., & Eliz. Cole, of St Mary le Bow in Durham.
	Sep. 3	John Brown, of Escomb, & Eliz. Almond, of Aukland St Andrew.
	Sep. 7	Robt Skelton & Jane Maddison, both of ye Parish of Stanhope.
	Sep. 12	Tho. Davy & Ann Walton, both of ye Parish of Sunderland by ye Sea.
	Sep. 25	Tho. Sayer, of Yarum, Dioc. Ebor., & Ann Butterwick, of Eggs-cliff, Dioc. Dunelm.
	Nov. 3	Will. Wilkinson & Catherine Metcalf, both of ye Parish of Stockton.
	Nov. 5	Peter More, of ye Chappelry of St Margarett's, & Eliz. Dixon, of ye Parish of St Nicholas in Durham.
		(Robt Pigot, Sacrist, Nov. ye 20th, 1726.)
	Jan. 8	Henry Lyddel & Mary Carr, both of ye Parish of Whickham, Dioc. Dunelm.; by Mr Waring.

---

[1] Thomas Wren, of Wolsingham. He died (according to tombstone at Wolsingham) 20 Sep. 1771, æt. 74. She was the dau. of William Curry, of Scotch Eales, gent., by Barbara Walsh. She died (according to the tombstone) 28 Nov. 1770, æt. 70. [MS. Ped. by E. A. W.]

1726	Feb. 18	Lively Busby[1] & Elizabeth Wilkinson, of ye Parish of Pittington, were married by Mr Waring.
1727	May 23	John Dixon & Jane Sharp, both of ye Parish of St Nicholas, Durham.
	July 25	John Hutchinson, of ye Parish of St Nicholas, & Jane Weddell, of ye Parish of St Mary le Bow in ye City of Durham.
	Sep. 9	John Potts & Mary Hornsby, both of ye Parish of St Nicholas, Durham.
1728	April 21	Thomas Potter & Ann Brown, both of ye Parish of St Nicholas in Durham.
	May 14	Edward Charlton & Ann Kell, both of ye Parish of Brancepath in ye County of Durham, were married by Mr Newhouse.
	June 9	George Wheatley & Mary Askew, both of ye Parish of St Nicholas in Durham.
	June 11	John Spark & Ann Weams, both of ye Chappelry of Castle Eden, Dioc. Dunelm., were married by Mr Delaval.
	June 12	Thomas Clarke & Ruth Watson, both of ye Parish of Gainford, Dioc. Dunelm., were married by Mr Delaval.
	June 15	William Orfeur & Mary Glassington, Wid., both of ye Parish of St Nicholas, Durham, were married by Mr Delaval.
	Feb. 11	Thomas Hudson, of ye Parish of Hartlepool, & Margarett Hobson. of Lumley Park in ye Chappelry of Chester le Street, Dioc. Dunelm.
	Mar. 7	Robert Todd & Dorothy Ingoe, Wid., both of ye Parish of Jarrow, Dioc. Dunelm., were married by Mr Simon.
1729	April 19	William Wilson & Jane Dixon, both of ye Parish of Merrington, Dioc. Dunelm.
	Feb. 24	James Hesletine,[2] of ye Parish of St Mary le Bow, Durham, & Frances Wheler, of ye College, were married by Mr Waring.
1730	June 2	Robert Whitfeild,[3] of ye Parish of Wolsingham, & Osytha Wright, of ye Parish of Brancepath, were married by Dr Eden.

[1] "Lively, son of Mr. Henry Busbie," was baptized at St. Oswald's (born 20 Dec. 1707) 6 Jan. 1708-9. The father was probably a son or grandson of William Busby, of Cassop, gent., who married Mary, dau. of Rev. John Lively, B.D. (See note to baptism 12 Nov. 1625.)

[2] See his burial 23 June 1763.

[3] He the last heir male of his ancient family, seated at Whitfield in Northumberland from a very early time; he is said, by his extravagancies, to have caused the ruin of his house. He was eldest son of Matthew Whitfield, of Whitfield, Esq., by his wife Elizabeth, dau. of Sir Robert Eden, of West Auckland, first Baronet. She, dau. of .... Wright, was buried ("Osith Whitfield") 4 April 1752 at Wolsingham, where her husband lived in, and presumably built, a fine old mansion, "Whitfield House," still remaining. Elizabeth the dau. of this marriage, heiress of her line, married 29 Jan. 1750-51, at St. Andrew's Auckland (she then "of St. Oswald's par."), Hendry Hopper, of Wolsingham, gent., by whom she had twelve sons and seven daughters, and died at Sunderland 1807. This Mr. Hopper, elder brother of the ancestor of the Hopper-Williamsons (see "Landed Gentry"), appears to have been of quite a different family to the Hoppers seated at Todepotts in Wolsingham, temp. Henry VIII., represented by the late Rev. Edmund Hector Hopper, afterwards Shipperdson, J.P., D.L., of Hermitage, co. Pal., although the name of Hendry is common to both. The Hendry Hopper above (died 1796 at Wolsingham) descended from a John Hopper living at Shincliffe in 1574 as a tenant under the Dean and Chapter, and the Registers of St. Oswald's swarm with Hoppers from that date.

1731 Oct. 23 Robert Shadforth, of ye Parish of Sunderland by ye Sea, & Margarett Padman,[1] of ye Parish of St Nicholas, Durham.
Oct. 23 Robert Johnson & Dorothy Watson, of ye Parish of Stockton, Dioc. Dunelm.
1732 April 20 John Hutchinson[2] & Isabella Richmond, both of ye Chappelry of St Margarett's, Durham.
May 3 Robert Johnson, of ye Parish of Houghton le Spring, & Mary Bell, of ye Parish of St Mary le Bow in ye City of Durham, were married by Mr Waring.
May 16 James Watson & Winnifred Reddish, both of ye Chappelry of St Margarett's, Durham.
Nov. 4 Michael Robinson, of ye Parish of Brancepeth, & Elizabeth Trowlop, Wid., of ye Chappelry of St Marg^{tts} in ye City of Durham.
1733 May 17 Joseph Forster[3] & Elizabeth Yapp, both of ye Parish of St Mary in ye South Bailey in ye City of Durham.
Sep. 14 Robert Smith, of Whorlton in ye Parish of Gainford, & Margarett Harrison, of ye Parish of Staindrop, Dioc. Dunelm.
Sep. 24 John Wilkinson & Mary Gent, both of ye Parish of Sedgefield, Dioc. Dunelm.
Nov. 9 Thomas Nicholson, of ye Parish of Corbridge, & Susanna Willson, of ye Parish of Bywell St Andrew's, Dioc. Dunelm., were married by Mr Herne.
Dec. 8 Robert Hawksworth, of ye Parish of Strenton, & Margarett Noble, Wid., of ye Parish of Sunderland by ye Sea, Dioc. Dunelm., were married by Mr Bryan Turner.
Jan. 31 The Revd Mr John Branfoot,[4] Minor Canon of this Church, & Mrs Mary Hall.
1734 April 22 Peter Fea, of ye Parish of Jarrow, & Sarah Beals, of ye Parish of Monk Wearmouth, Dioc. Dunelm.
June 4 John Hodgson & Dorothy Bell, both of ye Chappelry of Witton le Wear in ye Diocese of Durham.

---

[1] She dau. of Mr. Richard Padman, barber.

[2] He son of John Hutchinson, Esq., of Framwellgate, Durham, who died 1715, being then Mayor, by Mary (marriage licence 6 Oct. 1706), dau. of Thomas Shadforth, of Durham, gent. He was buried at Crossgate 1 July 1749, and his will, dated 24 June 1749, was proved by his sister-in-law Elizabeth Richmond, as guardian to his younger son Christopher. See the marriage of his aunt Jane Hutchinson 2 Jan. 1704-5. She younger dau. and eventually sole heiress of Christopher Richmond, Esq., of High-head Castle in Dalston and of Catterlen in Newton, Cumberland, representative of the families of Vaux, of Catterlen and Tryermayne. She was buried in Crossgate Church with her husband and several of his ancestors and her mother 27 Nov. 1746. Her present representative is Rear-Admiral Thomas Hutchinson Martin, R.N. (Médjidie 5th Class), of Bittern, Hants, J.P.

[3] See his burial 15 May 1767.

[4] He Master of the Grammar School, Rector of St. Mary's, and afterwards Vicar of Bossall, co. York. He is called Jonathan by error in Surtees' Pedigree of HALL, vol. iv., part ii., p. 154. She (first wife) only dau. of John Hall of Hilton, co. Pal., gent., and sister of Anthony Hall, Esq., ancestor of the Standish family, late of Duxbury, co. Lancaster, and Cocken, co. Durham. See baptism 23 Oct. 1771.

1734	July 3	Ralph Emmerson & Dorothy Beach, both of the Parish of Gainforth in ye Diocese of Durham.
	Sep. 5	George Stott & Mary Sedgewick, both of ye Parish of Chester in ye Diocese of Durham.
	Sep. 28	Peter Watt & Jane Hudson, Widow, both of ye Chappelry of Hart le Pool in ye Diocese of Durham.
	Oct. 14	Thomas Grey & Margaret Blacket, both of ye Parish of Sedgefield & Diocese of Durham.
	Dec. 3	Ralph Bird, of ye Parish of Houghton le Spring, & Elizabeth Fewster, of ye College in Durham.
1735	Aug. 25	Richard Hayton, of ye Parish of Aisgarth in ye Arch-Deaconry of Richmond, & Eleanor Bowes.
1736	May 21	James Johnson & Ann Aisley, both of ye Parish of St Nicholas in Durham.
1738	Mar. 24	Thomas Hall, of Sunderland by Sea, Widower, & Mary Surat, of ye College in Durham, were married by Dr Sharp.
1741	Oct. 6	Henry Ibbotson,[1] of ye Parish of Leedes in ye Diocese of York, Esqr, & Mrs Isabella Carr, of ye Parish of St Mary le Bowe in Durham, were married by Mr Randolph.
	Nov. 12	John Ridley & Isabella Brown, Wid., both of ye Parish of St Mary le Bowe.
1742	Sep. 4	Joseph Smith[2] & Ann Horseman, both of ye Parish of St Nicholas in Durham.
	Sep. 25	Robert Hull & Jane Laxe, both of ye Parish of St Nicholas in Durham.
	Nov. 4	Braems Wheler, of ye Parish of Little St Mary, & Mary Smith, of ye Parish of St Mary le Bowe, were married by Dr Tho. Sharp.
1743	June 23	John Coulson, of ye Parish of Sunderland, Widower, & Catherine Finch, of ye Parish of St Nicholas in Durham.
	Feb. 2	John Barnes, of ye Parish of Middleton in Teasdale, & Margaret Musgrave, of ye College in Durham.
	Feb. 6	Tobit Finch & Mary Reah, both of ye Parish of St Nicholas in Durham.
1744	April 9	Robert White & Ann Reede.
	Aug. 26	Thomas White & Ann Hutchinson, Wid., both of ye Parish of St Nicholas in Durham, were married by Mr Huson.
1745	April 20	James Bullock & Elizabeth Davy, both of ye Parish of St Nicholas in Durham, were married by Mr Lamb.

---

[1] He created a Baronet in 1748. (See Burke's "Peerage and Baronetage.") She dau. of Ralph Carr, of Cocken, co. Pal., Esq. See that Pedigree in Surtees, vol. i. The second son of this marriage Henry Ibbetson married Miss Morton, who, as a widow, resided in the Bailey with her mother, her daughter, grand-daughter, and great-grandchildren, all occasionally being under the same roof at the same time. The Editor has considered this sufficiently curious and interesting to annex a tabular sketch of these five generations. Since he drew it up almost entirely from his mother's memory, the dates and circumstances have all been confirmed by Lady Northbourne, who writes that she herself visited her great-grandmother Mrs. Morton. (See page 81.)

[2] It will be noticed that from this date to Dec. 1748 nearly all the parties married are from St. Nicholas Parish.

1745	June 29	William Middleton & Sarah Atkinson, both of ye Parish of St Nicholas in Durham.
	July 27	Ralph Bates & Jane Stott, Wid., both of ye Parish of St Nicholas in Durham.
	Aug. 27	The Revd Mr William Williamson, Minor Canon of this Church, & Catherine Hornsby, of ye Parish of St Nicholas in Durham.
	Nov. 16	Richard Sommers & Mary Willson, Wid., both of ye Parish of St Nicholas in Durham.
1746	April 2	Robert Wilkinson[1] & Ann Willson, both of ye Parish of St Nicholas in Durham.
	April 4	Patrick Sanderson[2] & Mary Dowson, both of ye Parish of St Nicholas in Durham.
	May 8	John Huntley & Catherine Nicholson, both of ye Parish of St Nicholas in Durham.
	Nov. 13	William Brownbridge & Mary Pearce, both of ye Parish of St Nicholas in Durham.
	Dec. 2	Henry Wetherell,[3] of ye Parish of St Nicholas, & Mary Harle, of ye College in Durham.
	Jan. 6	William Watson & Hannah Wood, both of ye Parish of St Nicholas in Durham.
	Feb. 21	James Mewburn,[4] of ye Parish of Croft in ye Diocese of York, & Margaret Aisleby, of ye Parish of Darlington & Diocese of Durham, were married by Mr Lamb.
	Mar. 2	John Weybridge & Margaret Rashells, Wid., both of ye Parish of St Nicholas in Durham.
	Mar. 2	Joseph Simpson & Mary Wilkinson, both of ye Parish of Gateshead & Diocese of Durham, were married by Mr Williamson.
1747	May 16	Joseph Wallis, of ye Parish of Whickham, & Dorothy Marley, of ye College in Durham.
	June 4	George Bassnett & Margaret Ridley, both of ye Parish of St Nicholas in Durham.
	June 25	John Bewes & Mary Charlton, both of ye Parish of St Nicholas in Durham.

[1] Robert Wilkinson, of Claypath, Durham, innholder, sixth and youngest son of Martin Wilkinson, of Crossgate, by his wife Elizabeth Rennison; baptized at Crossgate 26 Jan. 1723-4; admitted free of Drapers' and Taylors' Companies 1745-6; buried at St. Nicholas, Durham, 17 July 1792. [Ann Wilkinson, widow, died 3 and buried 6 Aug. 1802, aged 83. St. Nicholas Register.] [MS. Ped. by E. A. W.]

[2] He was a well-known Durham bookseller, and published "Antiquities of Durham Abbey," 1767. He married secondly Sarah, dau. of Humphrey Norton, Organist of Sedgefield. See his marriage 1 Feb. 1721-2. [MS. Ped. by E. A. W.]

[3] He the son of Cornelius Wetherell, by Margaret his wife, was baptized 1 March 1714 at St. Nicholas Church; buried 23 July 1772. His wife was buried at St. Nicholas 8 Jan 1776. [MS. Ped. by E. A. W.]

[4] He a son of Thomas Mewburn, of Blackwell and Darlington, who died *ante* 1760. She one of the three daus. and coheirs of Michael Aislaby, of Monkend, Darlington, tanner and gentleman, who died 15 Jan. 1762, and was buried in the nave of Darlington Church. See a Pedigree of MEWBURN (incomplete) in Longstaffe's "Darlington." ["Francis Mewburn, of St. Nich. par., and Elizabeth Hornsby of this par." married 9 May 1773 at Crossgate.] There was issue of the above marriage.

CATHEDRAL CHURCH AT DURHAM. 77

1747 Feb. 13 George Langstaffe, of Bishop-Aukland, & Mary Shotton, of ye College in Durham ; by Dr Sharp.
1748 April 27 Ralph Taylor, of ye Parish of Monk-Wearmouth, & Alice Bainbridge, of ye Parish of St Nicholas in Durham.
 May 7 George Bone & Frances Aisley, both of ye Parish of St Nicholas in Durham.
 May 12 Thomas Johnson & Ann Reah, both of ye Parish of St Nicholas in Durham.
 Oct. 9 Thomas Chipchace & Elizabeth Willis, Wid., both of ye Parish of St Nicholas in Durham.
 Nov. 5 Thomas Thomson, of ye Parish of Grindon, & Ann Monkhouse, Wid., of ye Chappelry of St Margaret, Durham.
 Nov. 13 Thomas Bulman, of ye Parish of St Nicholas in Durham, & Ann Bird, of ye Parish of Houghton le Spring.
 Dec. 26 Robert Wolfe[1] & Margaret Emmerson, both of the Parish of St Nicholas in Durham.
1749 Oct. 26 Luke Athey, of Sunderland, & Jane Hardy, of ye College in Durham.
 Dec. 5 Francis Myddleton[2] & Grace Smith, both of ye College in Durham. By Dr Sharp.
1751 April 16 Thomas Attey & Hannah Dodds, both of ye Parish of Sedgefield in ye Diocese of Durham.
 Nov. 2 Michael Arrowsmith & Mary Emmerson, both of the chapelry of Barnard Castle.
 Sep. 17 Anthony Dobson, of ye Parish of St Giles, & Margaret Hunter. By Mr Davison.
1752 Jan. 15 Wm Boyes, of ye Parish of Gisborough in y^c County of York, & Ann Davison, of ye Parish of Redmarshall in ye Diocese of Durham ; by vertue of a Licence granted by Thos Gyll, esq^r, Surrogate.
 Feb. 4 George Emmerson, of ye Parish of Rombald-kirk in ye Archdeaconry of Richmond, & Alice Gascoigne, of the chapelry of All-Saints in Newcastle upon Tyne ; by vertue of a Licence.
 Feb. 27 Wm Topham, of ye Parish of Stranton in ye Diocese of Durham, & Dorothy Linn, of Trimden ; by vertue of a Licence.
 April 28 Geo. Pickering, of Stockton, & Jane Baker, of St Giles in Durham.
 May 16 Tho. Kilburn, of ye Parish of Witton le Wear, & Anne Buckton, of ye city of Durham. By Licence.
 May 18 Nicholas Bryan, of ye Parish of St Nicholas in Durham, & Hannah Chapman, of ye same Parish. By Licence.
 May 18 Peter Burrell, of ye Parish of St Helen Auckland, & Margery Allinson, of ye same Parish. By Licence.
 May 19 James Nicholson, of St Mary Le Bow in Durham, & Jane Smailes, of ye College in Durham. By License.

[1] A son of this marriage was Alderman John Wolfe, whose burial see 30 May 1832.
[2] See his burial 1 Aug. 1771.

1752 June 9 Edward Dagnia,[1] of y" Chapelry of S[t] Hild's in y[e] Diocese of Durham, & Hannah Johnson, of y[e] same. By Licence.

June 30 John Forster,[2] of Peter's cheap & city of London, & Marg[t] Wetherell, of S[t] Nicholas in Durham. By Nathan Wetherell.

June 22 W[m] Simpson, of Middleton Tyas in y[e] county of York, & Anne Peacock, of Dinsdale in y[e] Diocese of Durham. By Licence.

Oct. 24 John Dale,[3] of y[e] Parish of S[t] Oswald, & Lydia Maude, of y[e] college in Durham. By Licence.

1753 Jan. 29 Tho. Hunter, of y[e] chapelry of all-S[ts], & Jane Cowle, of y[e] chapelry of S[t] Andrew in Newcastle. By Licence.

Mar. 5 Benjamin Hunter, of S[t] Nicholas Parish in Newcastle, & Eliz. Rawlin, of S[t] Giles's Parish in Durham. By Licence.

May 14 Joseph Thomlinson & Jane Gibbon, both of y[e] Parish of Wolsingham in y[e] Diocese of Durham; by Licence.

July 8 Tho. Smith, of y[e] Parish of Seaham in y[e] Diocese of Durham, & Frances Hilton, of y[e] Parish & Diocese aforesaid; by Licence.

Dec. 6 W[m] Cummin & Ann Hills, both of y[e] Parish of Gainford in y[e] Diocese of Durham; by License.

Dec. 14 Geo. Morton, of y[e] Chapelry of S[t] John in Newcastle, & Frances Lowdon, of y[e] Parish of Stainton, both within y[e] Diocese of Durham; by License.

Dec. 22 Valentine Bowman & Mary Dent, both of y[e] Parish of Stockton and in y[e] Diocese of Durham; by Licence.

Dec. 31 John Smiles, of all S[ts], & Elionor Robson, of S[t] Nicholas in Newcastle upon Tyne; by Licence.

1754 Jan. 23 John Chrishop & Martha Rooksby, both of y[e] Parish of Stockton & Diocese of Durham; by Licence.

Feb. 9 R[d] Marshall & Jane Mofit, both of y[e] Parish of Brancepeth in y[e] county of D[m]. By Licence.

Feb. 16 John Atkinson, of Staindrop, & Mary Marshall, of Brancepeth in y[e] County of Durham; by Licence.

---

[1] He a younger son of John Dagnia, gent., of South Shields, who bought the Cleadon estate in 1738, and died 21 April 1743, aged 63, and was buried at South Shields. The above Edward died 24 Sep. 1799 according to his M.I. at South Shields. He had a son Benjamin Clayton Dagnia, baptized 2 Dec. 1756 at Sunderland; and "Jane, dau. of Edward Dagnia, gent.," was baptized 9 Oct. 1754 at St. Andrew's, Newcastle. Onesiphorus Dagnia (there were others of the name), of Newcastle gent., in his will dated 30 Sep. 1721, proved at Durham 24 March 1724-5, mentions his wife Margery; Christopher and John, sons of brother John, deceased; dear friend and relation John Dagnia; brother-in-law Edward Johnson, upholsterer, and Hannah his wife; nephew Edward Younghusband, and nieces Susanna and Hannah Younghusband; sister Hannah Johnson's children Edward, John, Elizabeth, and Rebecca; and niece Elizabeth Hilton.

[2] She was the dau. of Cornelius Wetherell by Margaret his wife. The clergyman performing was her brother and afterwards Dean of Hereford. [MS. Ped. by E. A. W.]

[3] John Dale, baker, and Mary Maud were married 8 June 1737 at St. Oswald's, where his previous wife Jane was buried 25 Dec. 1736, and her children baptized. This presumably was his third wife. He died 24 Dec. 1757, æt. 57, and was buried at St. Oswald's with a dau. Lydia. His M.I. affirms.

> This modest stone : What few vain marbles can :
> May truly say : Here lies an honest man.

CATHEDRAL CHURCH AT DURHAM. 79

1754 Mar. 21 Martin Dunn,[1] of Bp. Auckland & Diocese of D^m, & Jane Le:pla, of ye Chapelry of Croxdale in ye Diocese aforesaid. By Licence.[2]

1836 July 13 Henry Charles, Viscount Chelsea,[3] & Mary Sarah Wellesley, daughter of the Honble & Revd Dr Wellesley, were married in the Cathedral of Durham, by special licence, by me George Townsend, Preb^y of Durham. (This marriage is also register'd in the Church of St Mary le Bow in the City of Durham.)

1883 Aug. 2 Robert Thornewill, Widower, Esquire, of the Abbey, Burton-on-Trent, son of Robert Thornewill, Esquire, and Eliza Arabella Sarah Hamilton, Spinster, College, Durham, dau. of George Hans Hamilton, D.D., Archdeacon of Northumberland, Canon of Durham; by Licence.

1885 Oct. 1 Gerard Ford, Widower, Gentleman, Durham, son of John Ford (deceased), Solicitor, and Fanny Joan Atkinson, Spinster, Durham, dau. of Matthew Hall Atkinson (deceased), Shipowner; by Special Licence.

1888 April 12 Hugh Lupton, Bachelor, Engineer, Leeds, son of Francis Lupton, Merchant, and Isabella Simey, Spinster, Durham, dau. of Ralph Simey, Solicitor; by Licence.

1889 July 30 Henry William Michelmore, Bachelor, St. Leonard's Road, Exeter, son of Henry Michelmore, Clerk of the Peace, Devonshire, and Marian Simey, Spinster, The College, Durham, dau. of Ralph Simey, Clerk of the Peace, Durham; after banns.

1890 June 26 Percy John Heawood, Bachelor, Tutor of Durham University, Old Street, Durham, son of John Richard Heawood, Clerk in Holy Orders, and Christiana Tristram, Spinster, The College, Durham, dau. of Henry Baker Tristram, Canon of Durham; after banns.

1891 April 23 Henry Reginald Hutchings, Bachelor, Clerk in Holy Orders,

---

[1] [It is singular how the name of Martin runs through all the northern (and at least one completely southern) families of Dunn.]

[2] [After this time the Marriage Act of 1754, prohibiting marriages except in places licensed for the performance thereof, came into operation. The Cathedral being extra-parochial, the Chapter never applied for it to be licensed until quite a recent period after the date up to which these Registers have been brought. Since then there have been three marriages, all of residents in the College. The marriage of Lord Chelsea, immediately following, was by a special licence from the Archbishop of Canterbury, which enables the parties to be married anywhere and at any hour.]

[3] He eldest son of Admiral Henry Charles Cadogan, third Earl Cadogan, whom he succeeded, as fourth Earl, in 1864. He was born 15 Feb. 1812, and baptized by the Rev. Matthew Arnold, Chaplain to the English Forces, 8 Oct. 1813 at Palermo, and afterwards, 4 Feb. 1814 at St. Luke's, Chelsea. He was a Privy Councillor, and died 8 June 1873 and was buried at St. Luke's, Chelsea. She, cousin to her husband, was born 29 Nov. (Lodge's "Peerage" wrongly says 15th), and baptized at Hampton Court 1 Aug. 1809, and was the third dau. of Dr. Wellesley, whose burial see 27 Oct. 1848. Lady Cadogan died 11 Feb. 1873 and was buried at St. Luke's aforesaid. See the burial of their eldest dau. 9 Oct. 1843, and baptism of another 4 April 1844. Their eldest son George Henry, present and fifth Earl Cadogan, was also born in the College, but was baptized at St. James, Westminster, 25 July 1840.

		Warter, Yorkshire, son of William Henry Hutchings, Rector of Kirkby Misperton, and Dora Emily Body, Spinster, The College, Durham, dau. of George Body, Canon of Durham; after banns.
1894	Jan. 23	Charles Waring Darwin, Bachelor, Major in the Army, The College, Durham, son of Francis Darwin, Gentleman, D.L., Chairman of Quarter Sessions, West Riding Yorks, and Mary Dorothea Wharton, Spinster, Dryburn, Durham, dau. of John Lloyd Wharton, Gentleman, Chairman of Quarter Sessions, Durham, M.P., D.C.L.; after banns.
1894	Feb. 3	John Burnell, Bachelor, Gardener, The Bank's Mill, St. Margaret's Parish, son of John Burnell, Farmer, and Grace Greig Dall, Spinster, The College, dau. of Andrew Dall, Gardener; after banns.
1894	Aug. 13	Geoffrey Edward Hale, Bachelor, Physician, 26 High Street, Eton, son of Edward Hale, deceased, Clerk in Holy Orders, Assistant Master to Eton College, and Mary Kynaston, Spinster, The College, dau. of Herbert Kynaston, Canon of Durham; after banns.
1896	July 23	William Joseph Collings Merry, Bachelor, Doctor of Medicine, 1 Cleveland Square, Hyde Park, son of William Walter Merry, D.D., Rector of Lincoln College, Oxford, and Eleanor Charlotte Kynaston, Spinster, The College, Durham, dau. of Herbert Kynaston, D.D., Canon of Durham; after banns.

See Note (¹) page 75.

I. § SARAH BONNER, dau. of Joseph Bonner, of Howden=Andrew Morton. Buried 19 Aug. Panns, Wallsend, Northumberland, gent. Baptized 1798, aged 66.
27 Aug. 1732 at Wallsend; married 16 June 1755; buried ("Sarah Morton, widow, of Durham") 12 Aug. 1828, aged 96, at Wallsend.
Living, at the time of her death, with her daughter Mrs. Ibbetson, at 3 South Bailey, Durham.

§ Mrs. Morton used to recount to her descendants the passing through Newcastle of the Scotch troops in 1745. As she would then be thirteen years old she would well remember it.

II. GRACE ORD MORTON. Baptized 29 June=Henry Ibbetson, of St. Anthony's, Newcastle, 1756 at Wallsend; married 1784.
Living a widow in 1828 with her mother and daughter at 3 South Bailey.

Esq., second son of Sir Henry Ibbetson, first Bart., by his marriage with Isabella, dau. of Ralph Carr, of Cocken, Esq.

III. ISABELLA GRACE IBBETSON, elder dau. and coheiress.=Cuthbert Ellison, of Hebburn Hall, Married 21 July 1804.
Visiting with her mother in 1828 at South Bailey.

co. Durham, Esq., M.P. (See Landed Gentry—"Carr-Ellison.")

IV. 1. ISABELLA CAROLINE=(Hon.) ELLISON, eldest dau. and George coheir. Born 1805; John married 30 Oct. 1824. Vernon.
Used to visit with her mother, and accompanied by her child, at her grandmother Mrs. Ibbetson's house in the South Bailey 1828.

Succeeded as fifth Lord Vernon in 1835.

2. HENRIETTA=William ELLISON. Mar- Henry ried Jan. 1824. Lambton,
Used to visit her grandmother Mrs. Ibbetson at South Bailey, accompanied by her children, in 1828.

of Biddick Hall, co. Durham, Esq., brother of the first Lord Durham.

3. Louisa, Viscountess Stormont. ⊤ ⊥

4. Laura Jane, Lady Kensington. ⊤ ⊥

5. Sarah Caroline, Lady Northbourne.

V. CAROLINE MARIA VERNON, eldest child.=(Rev.) Frederick Born 2 Jan. 1826; married May 1845.
Used to accompany, as an infant, her mother when visiting her (C. M. Vernon's) great-grandmother Mrs. Ibbetson. Mrs. Anson herself is a grandmother now (1884).

Anson, Canon of Windsor. (See Burke's Peerage —" Lichfield, Earl of.")

HENRY RALPH LAMBTON, eldest child. Born Nov. 1824.
Used to accompany, as a child, his mother when visiting his great-grandmother Mrs. Ibbetson at South Bailey. ⊤

This is a remarkable instance of the number of generations of one family known to one person—the Editor's mother, whose father's town house in Durham was also in the South Bailey, Number 8. She has seen, and remembers distinctly, all the five generations set forth above; and what is more remarkable and perhaps uninstanced—at any rate in the higher classes—*all occasionally residing at the same time under one roof.* Mrs. Ibbetson lived in the South Bailey, and with her mother Mrs. Morton, then very old. Mrs. Ellison, her daughter, frequently visited her, and sometimes Mrs. Ellison's daughters and their children, there being thus at those times five generations under the same roof, and *three generations of grandmothers.* Mrs. Anson, who made the fifth generation, is now herself a grandmother, so that, should the Editor's mother meet Mrs. Anson's children and grandchildren, she would have known seven generations of the family, and could say to the last, "I remember your grandmother's grandmother's grandmother!" The period here referred to would be, say, 1824 to 1828, the date of Mrs. Morton's death. Mrs. Ibbetson's house, the only one in Durham which externally has any claim, architecturally speaking, to be termed a "mansion," was previously the town house of the Edens, in the days when the county gentry wintered in Durham for "the season," and it was afterwards the property successively of Mrs. Fawcett, Mr. Hopper (later by change of name Shipperdson), and Mr. William Henderson; and since (*quantum mutatus ab illo!*) it has been used by the University for lodging students, and again as a Girls' High School.

M

BURIALLS.

1611 Feb. 4 Edwarde Smythe,[1] Organiste of this Church, buryed the 4 daye of Februarie, Anno D'ni Jacobi Regis 9°, Annoque D'ni 1611.

1613 April 24 Anne Stobert,[2] dau. of M[r] Richard Stobert, was Buried the 24th of Aprell 1613.

July 19 John Barnes,[3] Esquier.

Nov. 27 Tymothy Colmer,[4] sonne of M[r] Docter Colmer, one of the prebends of this church.

1615 Mar. 8 Henrye Philpot,[5] sonn of M[r] John Philpot, peticannon in this Church.

Mar. 17 George Lightfoote,[6] Esquier, was Buried the 17th (19 *written above the* 17) of March Anno 1615.

---

[1] See the baptisms of his children, the first three entries in the Register. He is the third organist that occurs, counting John Brimley, whose quaint M.I. see in Carlton's "Inscriptions," etc.

[2] The marriage licence of her parents is dated 6 Dec. 1609. This was the father's only child. The mother Elizabeth, dau. of Stephen Hegg, Notary Public (see his burial 16 Feb. 1627-8), re-married 25 April 1611, at St. Mary's, Toby Ewbanke, Esq., of Staindrop, co. Pal. (see EWBANKE Pedigree, which this adds to, Surtees, vol. iv., part i., page 141), and made her will 1 Aug. following, and died same month, being buried 25 Aug. at the Cathedral, according to the missing Register.

[3] Also registered at St. Mary-le-Bow. He was son of Richard Barnes, Bishop of Durham 1577—1587 (who is buried in the Choir), by his first wife Fredismund, dau. of Ralph Gifford, of Claydon, Bucks, Esq. He was Clerk of the Peace of the Palatinate, and died numarried. His will, dated 18 July 1613, the day before his death, adds nothing to the Bishop's pedigree in Surtees. Mr. Edward Hutton and Mr. Barnaby Hutchinson were Ex'ors. One of the testator's brothers was named Barnaby, and it is possible that there was a relationship between the Barnes and Hutchinson families. The Bishop's second marriage is recorded at St. Oswald's thus: "Rychard Barnes, Bysshop of durham, & Jane dyllycote a french woman were maryed at his castle in durham vpon wednesday in the seconde weeke of lent, beinge the xxij of march a° 1582." This lady re-married Dr. Leonard Pilkington, brother of Bishop Pilkington, her husband's predecessor on the Palatinate throne.

[4] Tenth son of Rev. Clement Colmore, LL.D., Prebendary and Chancellor of the Diocese (see his burial 20 June 1619), by his second wife. He was born 18 Dec. 1591, and baptized at St. Mary-le-Bow. Sir Timothy Hutton, of Marske, Knt., Anne, Lady Calverley, of Littleburne (son and dau. of Dr. Hutton, then Bishop of Durham), and Thomas Chaytor, Esq., being sponsors.

[5] The parents ("S[r] John Philpott and Jane Wrangham") were married 13 July 1595 at St. Mary-le-Bow. The father was appointed Perpetual Curate of Whitworth 1599, and was buried 8 Jan. 1619-20 at St. Oswald's. [The marriage, 14 July 1592, of John Phylpott and Jane Forelesse occurs at St. Oswald's.]

[6] This burial, as "in the abbey," is also registered at St. Mary-le-Bow under 19 March. He was Counsellor-at-Law and son of Simon Lightfoote. In Jan. 1601-2 he acquired the manor of Greystones, co. Pal., from Francis Tunstall, of Scargill, Esq. His will, dated 1 July 1615, mentions his nephews William Smith, Counsellor (see his burial 17 Dec. 1631), James Smith,

1616	June	Mrs Margarett Walter,[1] widdow of Thomas Walter, of Whitwell, esquier.
	Mar. 19	James Philpot,[2] sonn of John Philpott, petycannon in this Church.
1617	May 12	William James,[3] Bushope of Durhame, Ætat. 75.
	Mar. 22	Mris Anne Huton,[4] wife of Mr Edwarde Huton, Balife of the broughe of Durham.
1618	Dec. 5	John Emmerson, gentelman, was buried in the cathedrall church of Durham.
1619	June 20	Clemens Colmore,[5] legu' doctor, prebendarius & cancellarius in sp'ualibus.

John, Simon, George, and James Lightfoote, sister Elizabeth, Anthony Dodsworth, brother James Lightfoote, deceased, and two daughters of his late sister Rydale. He left £20 to erect a school at Barnard Castle.

[1] She was previously widow of the Rev. Ralph Lever, Master of Sherburn Hospital 1577—1585. Her second husband was as above. [Surtees, vol. i., p. 82, has this wrong.] Her will is dated 18 May 1616. She desires "to be buryed in the cathedrall neere my late first husband," and mentions her son Ralph Lever; to Mr. Robert Lawrence "a silver cupp guilt," dau. Thomazine Lawrence, dau. Jane Follonsby "a silver tunn and £20," daus. Elizabeth Barton, Margarett Egglestone, and Jayne Watson; to Thomas, son of Robert Lawrence, her husband's signet ring; to Mr. Samson Lever 20 nobles; son William Dixon; to Anthony Maxton, of Sherburn-house, £10 for a token; sons Robert Lawrence, Henry Follonsby, Edward Barton, and Christopher Lever, Clerk, Ex'ors.

[2] See his brother's burial 8 March 1615-16.

[3] Said to have been born at Little Ore, Staffordshire. He was the son of John James, gent., of that place, by his wife Elenor, dau. of William Bolt, of Sandbach, Cheshire. Entered at Christ Church, Oxon, 1559; Master of University College 1572; Archdeacon of Coventry 1577; Dean of Christ Church 1584; Dean of Durham 1596; elected Bishop of Durham 5 Aug. and consecrated 2 Sep. 1606. His tenure of the See was uneventful, but we learn that in his "hospitallitie, which is a speciall grace in a Bishopp," he appears to have been very sparing; and he made enemies of both the county gentry and the citizens of Durham by his opposition to reform and his refusal to consider their petition to be represented in the Parliament of the country. He entertained King James I. in May 1617, and Surtees relates that His Majesty "scolded him [probably with reference to his difference from the Durham burgesses] so roundly and roughly on the 8th May, in his own castle at Durham, that he retired to Auckland and died of a violent fit of stone and strangury, brought on by perfect vexation three days afterwards [11th]." His will is dated 2 Oct. 1615. He was thrice married. By his first wife Catherine, dau. of William Risby, Mayor of Abingdon, Berkshire, he had an eldest son (who died vitâ patris), William James, M.A., of Christ Church, Oxon, Public Orator of that University. The Bishop was buried near the entrance to the Cathedral Choir. The brass is gone, but the epitaph may be read in Browne Willis's "Cathedrals." His arms remain on a mantelpiece in one of the state rooms of the Castle.

[4] She was dau. of Francis Lascelles, Esq., of Allerthorpe, co. York, and wife of Edward Hutton, Esq., B.C.L., Bailiff of the City of Durham 1615. Mr. Hutton was son of John Hutton, of Streatlam, co. Durham. His will bears date 7 Nov. 1629, and he was buried in Bishop Middleham Church 10th id. men., aged 72, his epitaph there recording: "Hæc juris præcepta, honeste vivere, alterum non lædere, jus suum cuique tribuere, hic juris peritus calluit." The baptisms of several children of Edward Huton (probably the same) appear in the Registers of St. Mary-the-Less. See the marriage of a great-granddau. 19 Feb. 1684-5.

[5] He, LL.D., was installed Prebendary of the eleventh stall 9 May 1590, and was Chancellor of the Diocese for thirty-seven years. He was second son of William Colmore, of Birmingham, co. Warwick (by Joan, dau. of Henry Hunt, of Tamworth), and grandson of another William, of

1619 Dec. 25 Anna Hegge,[1] uxor Stephani Hegge, sepulta est in ecclesia cathedrali Dunelm. vicesimo quinto die mensis Decembris (in die natalis D'ni) 1619.
1621 Mar. + Margaret, dau. of John Davies, Pettie-cannon of this Church.
1622 Jan. 8 Mr Jo. Rangall,[2] laye singingman of this cathedral church.
      Feb. 12 Mr Joseph Pilkinton,[3] of Middleston, was buried in this cathedral Church.
      Nov. 10 Nicholas Sheffeild.
1623 Aug. 28 Mr Thomas (John erased) Burdon, servant to ye right Reverend father in God Riched, Lo. Bushope of Durham.
      Aug. 10 Edward Bussye,[4] lay singingman of this cathedral Church.
      Nov. 10 Mr Robert Murrey,[5] Pettie can'on of this church.

Birmingham, by his wife A. Lane. The Colmore Pedigree, commencing with the Chancellor's father, appears in the "Visitation of Warwickshire, 1619" (Harleian Society's Publications, vol. xii., p. 335). Dr. Colmore was named by the Privy Council, Sep. 1596, to accompany Toby Mathew, Bishop of Durham, and meet Commissioners from the King of Scotland to settle disputes and disorders. In his will, proved at York, he desires to be buried in the Cathedral "betwixt my two wives." His second wife (to whom, according to a MS. note of Sir Cuthbert Sharp, he was married 8 Jan. 1579) was Mary, dau. of Thomas Barnard, of Purton, co. Oxford. She died in child-bed 1592, and Dean (afterwards Bishop) Mathew preached her funeral sermon from Gen. xxxv. 16-21. [The burial occurs at Richmond, Yorks, 25 Jan. 1587 of "Isabel, ux. Clem. Cowlemer."] Dr. Colmore had a very large family. See the burial of his tenth son 27 Nov. 1613.

[1] She was dau. of Robert Swyft, LL.D., Spiritual Chancellor of Durham, and wife of Stephen Hegg, Notary Public, of Durham, whose burial see 16 Feb. 1627-8. Her father and mother were both buried in the Cathedral. The latter Anne, dau. of the Rev. Thomas Lever, Master of St. John's College, Cambridge, and Master of Sherburn Hospital, near Durham, and sometime a sufferer by the Marian persecution, made her will 12 Nov. 1607, which was proved by the above Anne Hegge, sole Executrix, 6 May 1609.

[2] John Rangall was appointed, 22 Oct. 1582, Song Master "to exercyse and have ye said schole and the yearlye stipende thereunto belonginge so longe as he shall honestlye behave himself therein." He was Master, not of the Choir School, but of Bishop Langley's Song School, otherwise the "Petty School," the "Schola puerorum," the "Schola pro plano cantu et arte scribendi." (The Second Master of the present Grammar School is, as it were, the successor of John Rangall.) His burial is also registered at St. Mary-le-Bow, but there as on the 8th. See his son's burial 1 April 1635.

[3] Son of Leonard Pilkington, D.D., Master of St. John's College, Cambridge, Rector of Whitburn and Prebendary of the seventh stall, who was younger brother of James Pilkington, Bishop of Durham. He married Anne (baptized at St. Andrew's Auckland 30 April 1573; living 1628), dau. of William Trotter, of Helmedon, co. Pal., gent. (see "Visitation of Durham, 1615"), by his wife Catherine Saunders, and by her had several children whose baptisms are registered at St. Andrew's Auckland. In his will he desires burial in the Cathedral near his mother; his wife Anne sole Executrix. See his sister Mrs. Hutton's burial 23 Sep. 1632.

[4] ["Mrs Jayne Bussie, wedow, verie aiged," buried 6 Aug. 1624; and "Mr John Bussie, Esquire and Counsellor in law," buried 8 March 1607-8. St. Oswald's Register.]

[5] He was baptized 12 March 1594-5 at St. Giles, where his parents William Murrey and Elizabeth Ord were married 20 April 1591. The father was Curate of St. Giles 1584, and afterwards Vicar of Pittington, succeeding in 1594 his uncle Robert Murrey, a Minor Canon and Under Master of the School. The Robert here buried married 23 Jan. 1620-21, at St. Mary's, Barbara, dau. of Jarard Hopper. His tombstone, now gone, described him as dying aged 29, 10 Nov., and his merits in the hexameter—
    "Ingenium, pietas, candor, sapientia, virtus,
    Cuncta tibi, juveni, juncta fuere simul."

CATHEDRAL CHURCH AT DURHAM.   85

1623 Nov. 18   Robert Cowper,[1] lay singingman of this church.
       Nov. 25   Tho. Humble, lay singingman of this church, was buried in the church Novemb. 25, 1623.
       Jan. 12   M[r] Anthonie Cradock[2] was buried in the cathedral church.
       Sep. 15   Richerd,[3] sonne of M[r] James, Prebendarie.

[1] His burial is also recorded at St. Oswald's—"a verie honest, grave and wise nighbore, in the abbaie church yard." He married firstly 25 July 1591, at St. Mary's, Elizabeth, dau. of John Horne, who was buried 9 June 1592, the same day her infant twin sons Matthew and John were christened at St. Mary-le-Bow. He married secondly 19 Aug. following, at "Madlen chappell," but registered at St. Oswald's, Margaret (buried "wedowe, aged," 13 Aug. 1641 at St. Oswald's), dau. of Robert Brantingham (he was buried 18 March 1600-1 at St. Oswald's). His will is dated 11 Nov. 1623, and he desires burial at St. Mary's in the North Bailey (otherwise St. Mary-le-Bow, which at this time buried her dead in the Cathedral yard), "nigh the great north window of the cathedral church." He mentions his wife Margaret, son Matthew at the University of Oxford, Master of Arts, and son John. Matthew Cooper the elder son matriculated at Magdalen College (described as *fil. pleb.*), and graduated B.A. 3 July 1616. He appears to have been deprived of his commons for a day, 30 Aug. 1618, "quod campanas pulsaverit inter horas undecimam et duodecimam nocturnas." (Bloxam's "Register of Magdalen College," 1857.) He was Curate of St. Oswald's and Vicar of Dalton-le-Dale 1621—1662, when he resigned. He married 9 Oct. 1620, at St. Mary's, Alice Kyrby, and two of their children Francis and Matthew were christened at St. Oswald's 28 Aug. 1622 and 20 Feb. 1626-7 respectively. The Vicar had at least one dau. Katherine, buried 3 July 1645 at Esh, and another son Isaac Cooper, who married 4 May 1654, at Bishopwearmouth, Margaret, dau. of George Taylor, of Monk-Hesilden, and his will, as "of Elvet, surgeon" [buried 5 July 1697 at St. Oswald's], dated 4 March 1695-6, names his sons Francis, Robert, to whom his books, and Thomas, to whom a shilling, and dau. Catherine, Executrix. John Cooper, second son of Robert the singing-man, baptized 25 Dec. 1630 as "of Elvet, yeoman," and desires burial at St. Oswald's [buried 31 Dec. 1630, "a verie honest younge man"], near his grandfather John Horne ["John Horne buried 9 Dec. 1683"]; and he mentions his brother Matthew, "to whom my filial porc'on, which my mother-in-law hath yet unpaid," and his (Matthew's) wife Alice. There are many entries relating to these Coopers at St. Oswald's. There was another family of Cooper, very probably related, of whom Robert Cooper, Esq., Steward of the county Palatine, etc. ("vir pius, prudens, pacificus, variis officiis ac negotiis publicis decoratus"), entered his pedigree and had a confirmation of his arms by St. George in 1615. To him Surtees (vol. iv., part ii., p. 150) has wrongly affiliated the Matthew baptized as above 9 June 1592, but the Register of St. Oswald's clearly states that "Mathe Cooper and John Cooper, sons to Robin Cooper, were christened in Bow church, & there mother buried y[e] same day." *Fil. pleb.* decides to which Robert he was son.

[2] Of Woodhouses, Auckland, Esq., second son of John Cradock, of Newhouses, Baldersdale, co. York, and afterwards of Gainford, co. Pal. (by his wife, Anne, dau. of Anthony Latus, of Beck, Cumberland), and brother of Dr. John Cradock, Archdeacon of Northumberland, whose burial see 30 Dec. 1627. He married firstly .... dau. and sole heiress of .... Dickinson, of Salthouse, Cumberland, and had by her Joseph, of Bishop's Auckland (baptized 26 May 1594 at St. Andrew's Auckland, his father then "of the deanery"), who married at St. Andrew's, 10 June 1622, Margery Mawker, but died s.p., desiring burial near his mother at St. Helen's Auckland ; Cuthbert, baptized 1 Sep. 1598 at St. Andrew's ; and Mary, wife of Richard Curteis, of Durham, stationer, whose burial see 30 June 1670. Anthony Cradock married secondly Ann Williamson, of St. Helen's Auckland (where there was a respectable family of the name long settled), who administered to her husband Jan. 1629-30, and by whom he had William [buried 28 Feb. 1711-12?], and whose dau. Catherine was buried 12 Sep. 1716; Timothy, George, and John, all living 1633 ; Grace, buried 22 Jan. 1678-9 ; Rachel, buried 10 Feb. 1695-6 ; and (perhaps) Elizabeth, buried 5 April 1706, all at St. Andrew's. See Pedigree of CRADOCK in Surtees, to which all this adds, vol. iv., part i., p. 13.

[3] See his baptism 7 July 1622, and his father's burial 21 Jan. 1659-60.

REGISTER OF BURIALS IN THE

1624 Aug. 8 M⁺ Richard Cradocke.¹
     Nov. 27 M⁺ Doctor Birkett.²
1625 July 9 M⁺ Hurr. Neele.
1626 Aug. 9 Richerd,³ sonne of M⁺ Pleasance.
     Mar. 20 M⁺ⁱˢ Anne Richardson,⁴ the wife of M⁺ John Richardson.
1627 April 12 Thomas Tyler, Lay singing man of this church.
     April 12 Robert Grinwell,⁵ Lutenist.
     April 12 James,⁶ sonne of M⁺ Worlich (minister), was buried the said 12ᵗʰ day of Aprill (hi tres simul fuerunt sepulti die scilicet 12° Aprilis 1627).
     May 21 Jane,⁷ dau. of M⁺ Thomas Wrighte.
     Dec. 30 Johannes Cradocke,⁸ Sacræ Theologiæ p'fessor, Prebendarius, et dioces. Dunelm'ˢ Cancellarius in Spiritualib', morte' obiit 28° die Decembris, et sepultus fuit 30° die ejusdem mensis.

¹ Of Durham, Esq., Counsellor-at-Law, eldest son of Dr. Cradock, Prebendary, whose burial see 30 Dec. 1627; baptized 10 April 1592 at Gainford; married 3 June 1619, at Pittington, Dorothy, eldest dau. of Thomas Heath, of Kepyer, Esq., by whom he had 1, Margaret, baptized 21 March 1620-21 and buried 8 June 1630 at St. Giles; 2, Dorothy, baptized 2 Dec. 1621 at St. Mary-le-Bow and probably died young; 3, Anne, his heiress, christened 22 July 1623 at St. Oswald's (sponsors, "Mr. John Heethe the younger, mrs. . . . . Mydforth, and mrs. Francis Hilyard"), who married John Harrison, of Scarborough, Yorks, and had issue.

² He was D.D., and installed in the sixth prebend 14 July 1619, but removed (installed 5 Aug. 1620) to tenth prebend, in which at his death he was succeeded by Dr. Cosin, afterwards Bishop of Durham; Vicar of Egglescliffe 1610, and Vicar of Winston 1620. By his will, dated 24 Nov. 1624, he leaves to his dear wife Alice lands in Aislaby, co. Durham, for life, and makes her Executrix; mentions his dear mother Mary Birkhead, sister Mary Birkhead, brother Nathaniel Birkhead, to whom the Aislaby property was to go, sister Mary Bull and nephew Thomas Bull, sister Barber and her dau. Bridget Barber and her other five children, sister Thomson's children, sister Arrowsmith, sister Mrs. Place, Mr. Robert Place, and Mr. Lampton. Dr. Birkhead's wife was Alice (baptized at Dinsdale, co. Pal., 1561), dau. of Robert Place, of Dinsdale, Esq., and was living 1637. Her sister Mary is the "sister Arrowsmith" in the Doctor's will. "Mrs. Mary Birkhead, mother unto Mr. Doctor Birkhead, late Parson of Egslife," was buried at Egglescliffe about Feb. 1629. She presented a Bible to that church.

³ He was baptized at St. Mary's 22 May 1625, being the second son of Robert Pleasance, Esq., of the South Bailey, whose burial see 14 May 1635.

⁴ She was dau. of Richard Johnson of Durham. See her husband's burial 7 Feb. 1639-40.

⁵ Of the Cathedral Choir, no doubt. His burial is also registered at St. Mary-le-Bow, where occurs the baptism of his son John 10 Aug. 1623; the baptism 18 Jan. 1619-20, and the burial 26 April following, of his dau. Elizabeth; and the burial 21 Dec. same year of his dau. Margaret.

⁶ Baptized 31 Oct. 1626 at St. Mary-le-Bow, where the name is spelt Woldrige. There also is the burial. 17 March 1624-5, of George, son of John *Worliche*. Perhaps Timothy, son of John *Worley*, baptized at same church 23 Nov. 1621 is another child.

⁷ Baptized at St. Mary's 10 Oct. 1627. She was the eldest child of Thomas Wright, Esq., by his wife Jane Hutton, whose burial see 5 Oct. 1635.

⁸ Said to have been poisoned by his wife, for which she was tried but acquitted. He was third son of John Cradock, of Newhouses, Baldersdale, co. York (see his brother's burial 12 Jan. 1623-4); Vicar of Gainford 1594; Archdeacon of Northumberland 1619, but resigned it 6 Aug. same year, on being appointed Spiritual Chancellor to Bishop Noile, and was installed in the fifth prebend 18 Aug. (collated 7 Aug.) same year; and a Justice of the Peace. His wife was Margaret, dau. of William Bateman, of Wensleydale, and widow of . . . . Robinson. By her he had a large family, and was ancestor of a family of Cradock still existing. He died at Woodhorn Vicarage, which he held with Gainford, 28 Dec. See his eldest son's burial 8 Aug. 1624, and that of a grandson 8 Feb. 1689-90. See Ingledew's "Northallerton," of which Dr. Cradock was also Vicar.

CATHEDRAL CHURCH AT DURHAM.   87

1627 Feb. 16 Mʳ Steven Hegg¹ (Notarius Publicus).
      Mar. 24 George Summer (servant to Mʳ Deane).
1628 April 30 Richard,² sonne of Mʳ John Cosins, Prebendary.
      Oct. 12 Anne,³ the wife of George Barcroft.
      Nov. 21 Elizabeth,⁴ the daughter of Mʳ William James, Prebendary.
      Jan. 12 Mʳ John Lampton,⁵ Draper.

¹ Of Durham City and of Unthank. By his wife Anne (whose burial see 25 Dec. 1619) he had issue : 1, Robert (whose baptism the Editor has not found), who administered to his father, and is the author of the " Legend of St. Cuthbert." His grandmother Anne Swift, widow of the Chancellor, left to him by her will, dated 12 Nov. 1607, " the remainder of the lease of Sherborne tithes, so much as shall be unexpired at the hour of my death, for his better maintenance at school." We are told in Wood's " Athenæ " that this "prodigy of his time for forward and good natural parts was born within the City of Durham 1599." In 1614 he was admitted at Corpus Christi College, and became a Fellow in 1624. In 1626 he wrote the " Legend of St. Cuthbert," and his manuscript was, says Wood, " so exactly and neatly written, that many have taken it to be printed." He died of apoplexy, " to the great reluctancy of those who were acquainted with his admirable parts," 11 June 1629, and was buried in the chapel of his College. Stephen and Anne Hegg's other children were (the following dates are from St. Mary's) : 2, Frances, baptized 15 Oct. 1598 and buried Dec. 1599 ; 3, Stephen, baptized 30 Dec. 1599 ; 4, John, baptized 7 Dec. and buried 26 Dec. 1600 ; 5, Isabel, baptized 21 Feb. 1601-2, and married, 16 Feb. 1622-3, to John Calverley, gent. ; 6, Richard, baptized 3 July 1603 ; 7, Judith, baptized 18 Nov. 1604, married to Marmaduke Gibbons, Clerk, and administered to her father after her brother Robert's death ; 8, Elizabeth, wife of Richard Stobert (see the burial of their dau. 24 April 1613). Stephen Hegg, M.A., the second son, was presented to the Perpetual Curacy of Whitworth 1628, and married there, 19 Dec. 1641, Frances Wilkinson (buried at St. Andrew's Auckland 3 Feb. 1666-7), and by her had a son Robert, baptized at Whitworth 5 Aug. 1642. The Rev. Stephen was, presumably, also father of another Rev. Stephen Hegge, father of two children who occur at St. Andrew's Auckland, viz., Ralph, baptized 28 Nov. 1665, and buried (his father then dead) 4 Aug. 1688 ; and Stephen, baptized 26 Nov. 1667. The will of the second clerical Stephen is dated 21 July 1668, from his death-bed presumably ("these words spoken in the presence of Peregrina, wife of Charles Wren, Esq."), and was proved 5 Aug. following. He left his estate to his loving wife (Ann Coltpits—marriage licence 18 July 1663) and his son ; she Executrix. " Mr. Belt [the curate, died 1677] and my father to have a care of the education of my son ; Mr. Belt to choose out the best of my books to make him a schollar." The " loving wife " was married again, in the following November, to William Pratt, of Bishop's Auckland. [" John, son of Richard Hegge," buried 16 Oct. 1623 at St. Oswald's.]

² He was the second son of Dr. John Cosin, Prebendary of the tenth stall, Rector of Brancepeth, Archdeacon of Cleveland, and afterwards Bishop of Durham, whose burial see 29 May 1672.

³ George Barcroft and Ann Sheffield were married 10 Oct. 1626 at St. Mary-le-Bow. He married again. See his burial 10 Feb. 1638-9.

⁴ See her baptism 3 June 1627, and her father's burial 21 Jan. 1659-60. She was buried in the church.

⁵ Third son of Robert Lambton, of Lambton, co. Durham, Esq., by Frances, dau. of Sir Ralph Eure, who fell at Halydon Hill, v.p., only son of the first Lord Eure. He was a "draper and taylor " (of which Guild the present Earl of Durham is " free "), and Mayor of Durham in 1626. He was twice married. His first wife Alice .... was buried 18 Aug. 1620 at St. Oswald's, the Register of which records that she was " verie bountefull for house kepinge, both for riche and powre." He married secondly at St. Oswald's, 26 Aug. 1623, " Mrs. Kathrine Kirbie " (see her burial 1 Sep. 1641), who re-married Nicholas Briggs, of Broom Hall, gent. By his first wife Mr. Lambton had an only child Isabel, baptized 9 Sep. 1600 at St. Oswald's, and buried 7 Jan. 1600-1 ; by his second wife he had an only son John, for whom see Surtees' " Durham," vol. ii., p. 175. The gentle draper's burial is also recorded at St. Oswald's, as " draper, one tyme maiour of the Cittie of Durham, a verie honest and religious gen., good to the powre, of the aige of

1630 Jan.   3   Mʳ John Todd,¹ Minor Cannon of this Cathedrall Church.
1631 Mar. 25   Mʳⁱˢ Francis Walton,² the wife of Mʳ Nicholas Walton.
      Oct. 19   Margarett,³ the daughter of Mʳ Geers, was buried the 19ᵗʰ day of October 1631.
      Dec. 17   Gulielmus Smith,⁴ de Baliva Boreali, Armiger, Conciliarius, pius ac prudens, annum agens sexagesimum tertium naturæ concessit decimo sexto die Decembris, et sepultus est die sequente.
      Feb. 26   Richardus,⁵ filius Johannis Cosin, Doctoris & Sᵃᵉ Theologiæ professoris, diem extremum clausit vicessimo quinto die Februarii, et sepultus est die sequente anno domini 1631.
1632 Aug. 25   Robertˢ,⁶ filius Gulielmi Smith, Armigeri, egregiâ indole ac spe adolescens, annum agens 17, morte quievit placidâ vicessimo quarto die Augusti, et sepultus est die sequente.
      Oct. 13   Richardus,⁷ filius Thomæ Wright, generosi, bimulus, naturæ

---

lxxiiij yeares, was buryed in the abbaie Church." By his will he desires burial in the Abbey, nigh his brother James (whose will, dated 19 Jan. 1595-6, was proved 4 March following) ; and he mentions " my shop in the market-place," and his brother-in-law Mr. John Browne, Clerke [he was Vicar of St. Oswald's]. John Lambton, with some of the best blood of England in his veins, closely connected with the highest families in the county, and the great-great-great-grandson of King Edward IV., is certainly an interesting type of the merchant-shopkeeper of his day !

¹ He married, 12 Jan. 1607-8, at St. Mary's, Timosin Toft. [The burial of " Thomas Toft, gen.," occurs at St. Oswald's 1634.]

² Wife of Rev. Nicholas Walton, M.A. (his brother, Hugh Walton, several times Mayor of Durham, had a grant of arms from St. George in 1615), who was Master (" archididasculus ") of Bishop Langley's Grammar School, succeeding the Rev. John Inglethorpe (who, with the school, held the Rectory of Staintory), which post he resigned about 1628, retiring to his curacy at Croxdale, which he held with that of St. Nicholas in Durham. " Nicholas," relates Randall, " (puer ut videtur) orationem habuit coram Rege Jacobo, anno 1603, e Scotiâ in Angliam veniente." His will is dated 13 April 1639, and he was buried at St. Nicholas 17th id. men.

³ Dau. of John Geors, Bachelor of Music and Singing-man. See her baptism 14 Sep. 1631, and her father's burial 4 March 1641-2.

⁴ Of the North Bailey in the City of Durham, Counsellor-at-Law, Recorder of Berwick, and Attorney-General to Bishop Neile; son of Thomas Smith, of Barton, co. York, by his wife Margaret, dau. of Simon Lightfoote (see her brother's burial 17 March 1615-16). He was a man of substance, acquiring by purchase a considerable property in West Herrington, and receiving from St. George, at his Visitation in 1615, a grant of arms. His nephew James Smith, of Sneinton, co. York, entered his pedigree and shewed the same coat (differenced by a trefoil) at Dugdale's Visitation of Yorkshire 1665. Our Counsellor's will is dated 21 Feb. 1630-1, and he mentions a brother Francis Smith, then living, who is given neither in Surtees' nor Dugdale's pedigree. All the Counsellor's children, five, are baptized at St. Mary-le-Bow, and two of them are there buried. Margaret, his dau., married John Heath, of Kepyer, Esq., and her representative is the present Marquess of Londonderry, K.G. See his wife's burial 11 Dec. 1648 ; the marriage of his son Henry 10 June 1630 ; and the burial of his son Robert 25 Aug. 1632.

⁵ Born 6 and baptized 14 June 1629 at Brancepeth, Dr. Augustus Lindsell, Dean of Lichfield, being godfather. Third son of Dr. Cosin, afterwards Bishop of Durham.

⁶ Fourth son of his father, whose burial see 17 Dec. 1631. He was baptized 2 April 1616 at St. Mary-le-Bow ; that Register recording also that he was buried in the Cathedral. This burial is incorrectly given in Surtees.

⁷ Son of Thomas Wright, Esq., by his wife Jane Hutton, whose burial see 5 Oct. 1635. He

debitum soluit decimo tertio die Octobris, & sepultus est eodem die.

1632 Sep. 23 Gratia Hutton,[1] vidua, olim uxor Roberti Hutton, Sacræ theologiæ professoris, matrona religiosa ac pia, annos nata sexaginta tres, frigidâ paralyse in ecclesiâ inter precandum correpta, & non diu eâdem laborans, quietè naturæ concessit vicessimo secundo die Septembris, & sepulta erat die sequente 1632.

1633 Feb. 4 Gulielmus Lowthrop, generosus, mortem obiit tertio die mensis februarii, & sepultus fuit quarto 1633.

1634 April 3 Gulielmus,[2] filius Gulielmi James, Ecclesiæ cathedralis Dunelmensis prebendarii.

May 24 Elsabeth,[3] uxor Gulielmi James, Ecclesiæ cathedralis Dunelmensis præbendarii.

June 2 Johannis [sic], filius Thomæ Wright, generosi.

Aug. 15 Gulelmus Bridges,[5] filius Mris Badely.

was baptized at St. Mary's 28 Oct. 1630. His burial, as taking place at the Cathedral, is also recorded at St. Mary-le-Bow, but there the date is incorrectly given 27 Oct.

[1] Dau. of Dr. Leonard Pilkington, Master of St. John's College, Cambridge, and niece of James Pilkington, Bishop of Durham. She married Robert Hutton, D.D., Prebendary of the third stall (installed 13 Dec. 1589), and Rector of Houghton-le-Spring (4 Dec. 1589—1623), who was nephew of Matthew Hutton, Bishop of Durham, and afterwards Archbishop of York. See the burial of one of her daughters 5 Oct. 1635, and of her brother 12 Feb. 1622-3. Her husband was buried in the chancel of Houghton Church 19 May 1623.

[2] See his baptism 24 June 1632, and his father's burial 21 Jan. 1659-60.

[3] Second dau. of Henry Ewbanke, M.A., sometime Prebendary of the twelfth stall, Rector of Whickham, etc. (who died 1628 and was buried in the south aisle of the Cathedral, according to Brown Willis, though not here recorded), by his wife Anne, dau. of Dr. Thomas Sampson, Dean of Christ Church, Oxford. She was married at St. Mary's 3 Dec. 1620. See her husband's burial 21 Jan. 1659-60.

[4] Baptized 28 Jan. 1632-3 at St. Mary's. He was second son of his father and "Mistress Jane Hutton," whose burial see 5 Oct. 1635.

[5] Son of the first wife of Richard Baddeley, of the North Bailey, gent., by a previous husband named Bridges. See his brother's burial 6 Nov. 1636. Mr. Richard Baddeley published a reprint of Robert Hegg's "Legend of St. Cuthbert" (see Stephen Hegge's burial 16 Feb. 1627-8) "at London, 1663, in octavo, in a very bad letter, and worse paper, not without some derogation to the memory of the Author by concealing his name and putting the two first letters of his own, and with the writing a prologue to it."—Preface to reprint of the "Legend of St. Cuthbert," by Robert Henry Allan, Esq., F.S.A., 1824. The will of Richard Baddeley is dated the last of Sep. 1670. In it he desires burial in the Cathedral, near his former wife's children and niece. It is singular that there is no record of his burial, nor of his second wife Cassandra, who he states was "daughter to that blessed confessor of Christ Mr. John Mole, who after thirty-two years' imprisonment in the Inquisition, for the testimony of Christ's true religion, there died." He bequeaths money to the poor of Kirby Moorside and Keldholme "where I was borne." He accompanied Bishop Morton, whose life he wrote, from Lichfield to Durham as his Private Secretary and Amanuensis. The will of his second wife "Mrs. Cassandra Baddely, widow," is dated 12 April 1673. She likewise desires burial in the Cathedral. Besides her children, she mentions her niece Elizabeth, wife of Dr. Stanhope, "now at Waterford, in Ireland," and her two children; Mr. Thomas Stanhope and Mr. Anthony (or Arthur ?) Stanhope her kinsmen; her niece Annabella Hill, wife of Mr. John Hill, of Priston in Rutlandshire ; Mr. John Hill her kinsman, etc. In addition to the other children of Richard Baddeley, who will be found by consulting the Index, there was a dau. Mary, buried 5 Nov. 1634 at St. Andrew's Auckland, no doubt while the father was in attendance on the Bishop.

REGISTER OF BURIALS IN THE

1634 Sep. 7 Ricardus,[1] filius Eliæ Smith, minoris Canonici.
Sep. 11 Johanis[2] [sic], filius Henrici Palmar, lay singinma'.
Oct. 18 Elsabeth,[3] uxor Roberti Blakesto', Ecclesiæ cathedralis Dunelme'sis præbendarii.
Dec. 1 Jane Jackson,[4] widdow.
Jan. 19 Mr Robert Blakeston,[5] prebend of this Cathedral Church.
1635 April 1 George Ranghall,[6] beinge one of the lay singinge men of this Church.
May 14 Robertus Plesant,[7] senescallus hujus ecclesiæ.

[1] See his baptism 30 Oct. 1631, and his father's burial 9 Dec. 1676.
[2] See his baptism 27 March 1633, and his mother's burial 14 April 1638.
[3] Dau. and coheiress of John Howson, Bishop of Durham from 28 Sep. 1628 until his death, aged 75, 6 Feb. 1631-2. See the burial of her husband 19 Jan. 1634-5. Her father, the Bishop, who was Student and afterwards Canon of Christ Church, Oxon, Vicar of Brampton, Oxon, Rector of Brightwell, Berks, Canon of Hereford, and Bishop of Oxford before his translation to Durham, was a well-known writer in his day against Popery, and is recorded to have said that " he would loosen the Pope from his chair, though fastened thereto by a tenpenny nail." He died in London, and " over against the little North Door in the middle Ile, under a fair marble stone, without any inscription upon it, lieth buried " in St. Paul's Cathedral. Mr. John Caldcleugh, of Durham, has a good portrait of the Bishop, supposed to be by Cornelius Janssen.
[4] Her will, stating that she is the widow of Richard Jackson, Clerk, is dated 3 Sep. 1633. She desires burial in the Cathedral Yard in her mother's grave, and mentions Mr. William Smith; niece Elizabeth Jackson; James, Edward, Jane, and Sarah Moorecroft; and Mr. Ferdinand Moorecroft, Clerk, sole Ex'or. She was married, as Jane Tompson, 6 Jan. 1613-14, at St. Mary's, to Richard Jackson, clericus. [" Jane Tompson, widow," was buried 2 April 1605 at St. Mary's.]
[5] He was baptized at Sedgefield, co. Durham, 7 Jan. 1607-8, and was son of Marmaduke Blakiston (a descendant of one of the oldest territorial houses in the Bishopric—see his pedigree, Surtees, vol. iii., p. 163), Rector of Sedgefield, Prebendary of the seventh stall and Archdeacon of Cleveland, who resigned his Archdeaconry to his intended son-in-law John Cosin, afterwards Bishop of Durham, and his rectory and stall to this son, Robert, in 1631, so that he lost both son and preferment almost together. Robert Blakiston married Elizabeth (whose burial see 18 Oct. 1634), dau. and coheiress of Bishop Howson, but had no issue. He was one of the Prebendaries who held the canopy over King Charles I. when he visited Bishop Morton at Durham Castle 1 June 1633. His nuncupative will is dated 8 Jan. 1634-5. He was brother of John Blakiston, " the regicide," M.P. for Newcastle-on-Tyne.
[6] Son of John Rangall, whose burial see 6 Jan. 1622-3.
[7] Of the South Bailey, and a Barrister-at-Law of Gray's Inn. His will is dated 13 May and proved 21 July 1635. By his wife Jane (whose burial see 15 March 1676-7) he had issue seven children, all baptized at St. Mary's, viz., 1, Anne, 19 July 1618, living the widow of .... White in 1676, and sole Ex'or to her mother; 2, Grizell, 15 Aug. 1619, living 1676 ; 3, Mary, 18 Jan. 1620-21, living 1676, married to .... Morrice and having a son William; 4, Foster, 25 May 1623, living 1701 [buried 26 April 1704 at Northallerton], married [Grace, wife of Mr. Pleasance, buried 18 Aug. 1698 at Northallerton], and had a dau. Jane, living 1676 [Mr. Forster Pleasaunce and Mrs. Elizabeth Danby married 27 Nov. 1698 at Northallerton] ; 5, Richard, whose burial see 9 Aug. 1626 ; 6, Robert, 15 April 1627 ; 7, John, 17 May 1630, living 1644. Robert Pleasance, the sixth child, was of St. John's College, Cambridge, and afterwards of Bishop's Auckland, Clerk. He married, 4 Jan. 1655-6, at Boldon, " Mrs." Jane Wilkinson, who was buried at St. Andrew's Auckland Dec. 1687. His will, dated 21 April and proved by Robert Gowland 7 May 1701, states that he was born in the parish of Little St. Mary's, Durham, and mentions his nephew Mr. George Watson, his niece Elizabeth Hackworth, widow, and her children, and niece Mary White, spinster. He was buried with his wife 30 April 1701. The first-named Robert had a sister Mary Pleasance, living 1644.

CATHEDRAL CHURCH AT DURHAM. 91

1635 Oct. 5 M^ris Jane Hutton,[1] the wife of Mr Thomas Wright, gentleman.
1636 Nov. 6 Georgius Bridges[2] (Gulielmi Bridges, p'dicti frater).
1638 April 14 Katerne,[3] wife of Mr Henry Palmer, Lay singingman of this Church.
July 7 Richard,[4] sonn of Mr Henry Palmer, Lay singingeman of this Cathedrall Church.
July 6 [sic] Mr James Hilton,[5] gentleman.
Nov. 3 Richardus Hunt,[6] Sacræ Theologiæ professor, et Decanus hujus Ecclesiæ Dunelmensis.
Nov. 21 Mathew,[7] sonn of Mr John Geeres, laye singingeman of this church.
Feb. 10 George Barcroft,[8] lay singingeman of this church.
1639 Dec. 18 Dulcibella,[9] filia Eliæ Smith, hujus ecclesiæ, Minoris Canonici.
Feb. 7 Johannes Richardson,[10] Armiger.

[1] The importance of this lady's close relationship to the episcopal families of Hutton and Pilkington (see her mother's burial 23 Sep. 1633) perhaps accounts for the above rather unusual entry. She was married to Thomas Wright, Esq., at St. Mary's 21 Dec. 1624. See burials of her children in 1627, 1632, and 1634. She also had two daughters, Mary and Elizabeth, baptized at St. Mary's 5 Nov. 1627 and 4 Jan. 1628-9 respectively. Thomas Wright, of the North Bailey, was buried 4 Feb. 1640-41 at St. Oswald's, and Mary his dau. buried 12 Aug. 1638; also John, son of Thomas Wright, "laite deceased," 5 May 1642.
[2] See his brother's burial 15 Aug. 1634.
[3] See next entry, and that of 11 Sep. 1634.
[4] See preceding entry, and his baptism 16 July 1631.
[5] Second son of Lancelot Hilton, of Dyons, co. Durham, gent., by his wife Catherine, eldest dau. and coheiress of Ralph Alwent, of Dyons, Esq. He was baptized 28 April 1594 at Gainford. See further in the "History of Darlington," where the Hiltons have met with much careful attention from their descendant William Hylton Dyer Longstaffe, Esq., an exemplary and truthful genealogist and chronicler, and one of the most eminent and painstaking antiquaries the North has ever produced, and from whom the Editor has met with an ever hearty, ungrudging assistance in all matters genealogical.
[6] His monumental tablet of wood, with the inscription in gilt leters, having been taken down in the alterations of 1840, was, when the Editor copied it, lying a reproach to the authorities, neglected and dishonoured, in the south triforium of the choir. It seems incredible, but it is the fact, that the custodians of churches as a rule pay not the least respect to these memorials of the dead, their predecessors in office very often. Stoves are clamped down on beautifully carved marble slabs, or the inscriptions themselves ruthlessly and sacrilegiously cut away to make room for a pipe or a new stained "conventional" deal seat, itself perchance the successor of a fine old black oak but unconventional pew. A worse fate attends the Communion plate which the piety of our ancestors induced them to give to the church where they and their forbears had simply worshipped. The service is not of the orthodox shape, and charming seventeenth-century plate of pure, if plain, design is thrown into the melting-pot to reappear in the severest ecclesiastical form, covered with vulgar emblems and chasing of the most meretricious order, positively calculated to disgust the Communicant.
[7] See his baptism 4 March 1637-8, and his father's burial 4 March 1641-2.
[8] See his first wife's burial 12 Oct. 1628. He married secondly, at Houghton-le-Spring, 4 Aug. 1629, Elizabeth Ley, of Elvet in St. Oswald's parish [Elizabeth, dau. of William *Iley* was baptized there 17 Jan. 1601-2], by whom he had issue (all baptized at St. Mary-le-Bow) Jane, 6 May 1630; John, buried 25 May 1631; Thomas, 15 April 1632; Mary, 3 Dec. 1635; George, 19 Feb. 1636-7; and Elizabeth ("posthumous dau. of Eliz. Barcroft, widow"), 1 May 1639.
[9] See her baptism 15 March 1637-8, and her father's burial 9 Dec. 1676.
[10] Solicitor-General to Bishops Morton and James, and previously Deputy Solicitor-General

1639 Mar. 19 Georgius Cocknidge,[1] hâc in Ecclesiâ Lector Epistolæ, sepultus est (Ecclesiâ suâ p'ochiali).
Mar. 19 Tymotheo Commin,[2] paroch. prædict., Generoso, sepult. eodem die.
1640 Mar. 28 Anna,[3] uxor Venab[lis] Viri Thomæ Burwell, in spiritualib' Cancellarii.
1641 Sep. 1 Catherina,[4] uxor Nicholai Briggs, de Broomhall.
Mar. 4 Johannes Geers,[5] Musicæ Baccalaureus, et hâc in ecclesiâ psaltes.
1642 April 3 Cutb'us Marley, sacræ Theologiæ p'fessor.
June 28 Tobias Brooking,[6] hujus Ecclesiæ psaltes, qua eccedens, sepultus est [etc.].
June 28 Georgius,[7] filius Henrici Morecroft, Generosi.
Nov. 3 Francisca,[8] filia Pauli Neele, Militis.
Nov. 27 Elizabetha domina, uxor Alexandri Gordon, militis.
Jan. 12 Flora, uxor Eleaz. Duncon,[9] sacræ Theologiæ professor, et Prebend. hujus ecclesiæ.

to Bishop Hutton. His wife Anne, dau. of Richard Johnson, of Durham, was buried at St. Oswald's 16 Oct. 1615. By her he had 1, John, Counsellor and Escheator of the Bishopric [baptism not found, and, like many first children, was perhaps born at the mother's home] ; 2, Thomas, baptized 10 Oct. 1589 ; 3, Anne, baptized 6 Nov. 1590, married as second wife, 12 May 1607, Alderman George Walton, of Durham ; 4, William, baptized 22 March 1591-2 ; 5, Helme (or Helene), baptized 6 June 1594, and buried 28 Oct. 1696 ; 6, Elizabeth, baptized 11 Feb. 1601-2 —all registered at St. Mary-le-Bow. He had a confirmation of arms and a grant of a crest at St. George's Visitation 1615, when he entered his pedigree, commencing with himself. This appears in Surtees, vol. iv., part ii., p. 151, but is imperfect. He was the son of John Richardson, of Durham. He had a brother Bryan, baptized at St. Mary-le-Bow 10 Oct. 1572, who in his will, proved 14 April 1599, desires burial in the Cathedral, near his good friend Joseph Rudd. He mentions his sister Margaret Fairelas, Richard Fairelas, and his son Edward Fairelas ; sister Elizabeth Peart and her son George and three daughters ; brother-in-law James Eture and his wife Mary Eture (testator's sister) and Alice her dau. ; brother Michael Richardson ; sister Ann ; brother John Richardson (ex'or), his three sons and dau. Ann ; and mother Alice Watson. John Richardson's burial is also recorded at St. Mary-le-Bow.

[1] Clerk in Holy Orders. Occurs as Under Master (*hypodidascalus*) of the Grammar School 1604—1615 (perhaps longer), and as Rector, or, at any rate, Officiating Minister, of St. Mary in the South Bailey 1633. He first occurs as "lector epistolæ" at the Cathedral Sep. 1633.

[2] Receiver-General to Bishops Howson and Neile. He was oldest son of Simon Comyn, of Durham, Registrar to the Dean and Chapter, by his first wife Alice, dau. of John Robson, of West Morton, co. Durham (see pedigree in Surtees), and sister to Simon Robson, Dean of Bristol. Simon Comyn's second wife was Elizabeth, widow of Cuthbert Baynbrigg, of Middleton Teesdale, where he himself was buried, dying 13 April 1620. He had a grant of a crest from St. George in 1615. Francis Comyn, son of Timothy above, entered his pedigree at Dugdale's Visitation of Yorkshire 1665, but it is very scant, and his own father's death much antedated.

[3] See her marriage 19 Feb. 1632-3, and M.I. in Carlton ; also BURWELL Pedigree in Surtees, vol. iv., part ii.

[4] She was previously widow of Mr. John Lambton, whose burial see 12 Jan. 1628-9.

[5] He married at St. Mary's, 29 June 1630, Isabel Harrison. See his children's baptisms 14 Sep. 1631, 2 Oct. 1632, and 23 May 1635.

[6] See his wife's burial 22 Aug. 1645.

[7] An infant son of Henry Morecroft, of Durham, gent., by his wife Barbara, eldest dau. of James Hilton, of Dyons, gent., whose burial see 6 July 1638. See also the baptisms of other children 1641 and 1646, and the MORECROFT Pedigree in Surtees, vol. iii., p. 415.

[8] See her baptism on the previous day.

[9] Dr. Eleazer Duncan, a Scotchman, was installed in the fifth prebend 8 Jan. 1627-8. He

CATHEDRAL CHURCH AT DURHAM. 93

1642	Jan. 29	Elizabetha,[1] filia Pauli Neele, militis.
1643	May 19	Dina Bolt, vidua.
1644	Mar. 31	Captaine James Lindsey,[2] under Generall Kinge.
	Mar. 28	Richard,[3] sonn of Mr John Robson, prebend of this church.
	April 6	Thomas Malchin, servant to the Right Hon^{rble} the Lrd Mansfield.[4]
	June 20	Elizabeth Henekar, servant to the Lady Ham'on.[5]
1645	Aug. 14	Elizabeth,[6] dau. of Toby Brookin.
	Aug. 22	Magdalen,[7] wife of Toby Brookin.
	Aug. 29	Luke Huchinson,[8] lay singingman of this Church.
	April 12	Mr John Robson,[9] prebend of this Church.
	Sep. 9	Francis,[10] wife of Luke Huchinson.
1644	Dec. 22	Mr Francis Tempest,[11] brother to Sr Tho. Tempest.
1643	Feb. 8	Willia',[12] sonn of Mr Henrye Blakiston.
1647	Dec. 13	Deborah,[13] dau. of Mr Riched Badeley.
1648	Dec. 11	Marye Smith,[14] sometime wife to Mr William Smith, Councellor at lawe.

was Fellow of Pembroke Hall, Cambridge, and was preferred to a prebend at Winchester 1629, and York 1640. In 1633 he was collated to the rectory of Haughton-le-Skerne, co. Pal.; was Chaplain to King Charles I., and is said to have died in exile about 1650. There is a marriage licence at Durham, dated 6 Nov. 1680, for Eleazer Duncan, of Bear Park [Chapter land near Durham] and Phœbe Boyer. This Eleazar, who may have been a grandson of the Prebendary, has seven children baptized at St. Nicholas, Durham, between Jan. 1682-3 and July 1691.

[1] She was the dau. of Sir Paul Neile, Knt., by Elizabeth, dau. of the Rev. Gabriel Clarke, D.D., Archdeacon of Durham. [MS. Ped. by E. A. W.]

[2] Troops were constantly quartered in Durham at this time.

[3] He was admitted at St. Peter's College, Cambridge, 22 Oct. 1638. See his baptism 24 March 1621-2, and his father's burial 12 April 1645.

[4] Viscount Mansfield was the eldest son of Sir William Cavendish, Earl (afterwards Marquess and Duke) of Newcastle, the distinguished Royalist, who at this time was commanding the King's forces in the North.

[5] Regarding Lady Hammond see note to Stuarta Balcanquall's marriage 6 Sep. 1642.

[6] See her baptism 25 April 1631, and her mother's burial next entry.

[7] Tobias Brookin and Magdalen Dodsworth were married 11 July 1626 at St. Mary's. See her husband's burial 28 June 1642.

[8] See his wife's burial 9 Sep. 1645. ["Margaret, dau. of Luke Hutchinson," occurs as baptized at St. Nicholas 9 Aug. 1663.]

[9] He was installed in the sixth prebend 1 Aug. 1620, having previously been Rector of Morpeth 1611, and Rector of Whalton, Northumberland, 1615, and Chaplain to Charles I. He was returned as one of the Members of Parliament for Morpeth in the third Parliament of James I., but, as a clergyman, declared incapable of sitting. His will, dated 9 April 1645, names his wife Margaret Executrix; his only surviving son John (whose baptism see Feb. 1624-5); and his brother Joseph Robson. He bequeaths lands at "Quarie Hill," co. Durham. He married Margaret, dau. of Archdeacon John Cradock, whose burial see 30 Dec. 1627. See his son's burial 28 March 1644.

[10] See her husband's burial preceding entry but one.

[11] He was a Barrister-at-Law, of Gray's Inn, and appointed Recorder of Durham Nov. 1642, and was younger son of Rowland Tempest, Merchant, of Newcastle (third son of Thomas Tempest, Esq., of Stanley, co. Durham), and brother of Sir Nicholas Tempest, first Baronet, of Stella.

[12] Son of Henry Blakiston, gent., whose burial see 15 May 1683. He does not appear in Surtees' Pedigree of BLAKISTON, of Gibside, vol. ii., p. 255.

[13] See note to the burial of William Bridges 15 Aug. 1634.

[14] She was married as Mary Heron, at St. Mary-le-Bow, 28 Nov. 1592, to Oswald Baker, of

1648	Mar. 23	Margarett,[1] dau. to M[r] Henrye Blakistoun, gent.
1649	Oct. 25	Peregrina,[2] dau. to John Burrow.
1650	Nov. 8	Marye,[3] dau. of James Greene, minor Cannon of this Church.
1651	Jan. 20	Elizabeth,[4] dau. of M[r] Elias Smith, minor Cannon of this Church.
1652	Feb. 23	Thomas,[5] sonn of M[r] Richard Baddeley.
	Mar. 16	Patience Frickleton, M[r] Elias Smith's sister's daughter.
1653	Mar. 28	Joane Evans, servant to M[r] Devorax, minister.
	Nov. 21	John Hargrave, a minister.
	Jan. 25	Francis,[6] son of M[r] Francis Foster.
1658	April 29	John,[7] son of M[r] Francis Foster.
1659	Nov. 14	Mille,[8] wife of d[r] Clarke.
	Jan. 21	M[r] Willia' James,[9] prebend of this Church.
1660	June 27	Jane,[10] dau. of Ezechell Tonge, beinge the first that was buryed after the dissolution of y[e] Colledge.
	July 13	Elizabeth,[11] dau. of M[r] Robert Gray.
	Feb. 23	M[r] Robert Tempest.
1661	Mar. 31	Steven,[12] son of Ambrose Myars.
	June 2	Elizabeth, wife of Nicholaus Richardson.
	Nov. 29	George Blades, Steward to deane Balkanquall and to deane Barwicke.
	Oct. 30	Richard Wikelin,[13] a minor Cannon of this Church.
1662	April 9	Isabell,[14] dau. of John Drury.

Durham, and by him was mother of Sir George Baker, Knt., ancestor of the family of Baker, of Elemore, co. Pal. She married secondly, at the same church, 3 Oct. 1608, four months after Oswald Baker's death, William Smith, Esq. (whose burial see 17 Dec. 1631), Attorney-General to Bishop Neile.

[1] See her father's burial 15 May 1683.
[2] See her baptism 26 June 1648.
[3] See her baptism 1 March 1645-6, and her father's burial 14 May 1667.
[4] See her baptism 24 Feb. 1633-4, and her father's burial 9 Dec. 1676.
[5] See note to burial of William Bridges 15 Aug. 1634.
[6] See his baptism 5 Feb. 1652-3, and his eldest brother's 5 Feb. 1652-3.
[7] See his baptism 8 Dec. 1657.
[8] Mildred, wife of Dr. Gabriel Clarke, Prebendary (whose burial see 12 May 1662), and dau. of William Neile.
[9] Nephew of William James, Bishop of Durham, whose burial see 12 May 1617. Installed in the twelfth prebend 6 Oct. 1620, and made Vicar of Merrington 1629; was previously Public Orator at Oxford 1601; Rector of Crayke, Yorks, 1614; Rector of Washington 1616; Rector of Ryton 1617. He was one of the Prebendaries who held the canopy over King Charles I. on his visit to Durham. See his wife's burial 24 May 1634, and consult Index for the baptisms of his children.
[10] See her baptism 14 Dec. 1657.
[11] See baptism of another child 4 Oct. 1653.
[12] See the father's burial 18 March 1666-7.
[13] Married ("Richard Waiklinge, minister of Gods word") by licence, at St. Oswald's, 13 Feb. 1642-3 (where he was Curate in 1627), to Jane Sheffield. This marriage also entered at St. Mary-le-Bow (there "Wickelin"), of which he became Rector in 1645. See burial 21 Nov. 1668-9 of his son Richard, besides whom he had baptized at Bow James, born 28 Oct. 1659; Barbara, 24 Dec. 1651; Elizabeth, 15 Jan. 1648-9; Thomas, 23 Feb. 1645-6; and Ann, 18 Oct. 1643.
[14] See her baptism June 1655, and the marriage of her sister 29 Aug. 1682.

CATHEDRAL CHURCH AT DURHAM. 95

1662	May 12	Gabriell,[1] d{tr} Clarke, prebend of this Church.
	May 23	Doritye,[2] wife of Mr Henrye Graye.
	July 7	Henrye,[3] sonn of Mr Henrye Blakiston.
1663	June 2	Willia', son of Mr Robert Tempest.
	Nov. 8	An, wife of Robert Burrow.
	Mar. 14	Ralph Hedworth,[4] sometime of Pockerley.
1664	April 28	John, son of Mr Robert Tempest.
	May 15	Elizabeth, wife of Richard Blackett.
	Nov. 8	Anthony, son of Willia' West, or Mitford.
	Nov. 22	Elizabeth Thwing, wid.
	Feb. 4	George,[5] son of John Spearman.
	Feb. 10	An Bettles,[6] widow.
	Mar. 21	Thomas Savill, Beadsman of this Church.
1665	April 2	Willia' Robson, Cooke to our B{pp}.
	April 11	Margarett, wife to William Taler, joyner.
	Aug. 6	Sarah, wife of Anthony Glover, verger of this church.
	Nov. 17	Doritye Myers, widdow.
	Nov. 29	Matthew, son of Captain John Sissons.
	Dec. 11	Robert Dobson, translator.
	Dec. 30	Mary,[7] dau. of Thomas Massam.
	Jan. 8	Isabell, dau. of John Miller.
	Jan. 31	Willia' Lambe, glazier.
1666	July 26	Richard Huchinson.[8]
	Aug. 2	Kattern, dau. of Elizabeth Lambe, widdow.

[1] Son of John Clarke, of Clothall, Herts, yeoman, Chaplain to Bishop Neile. Installed in sixth prebend 1 Aug. 1623, and in first prebend 1 Aug. 1638; collated to Archdeaconry of Northumberland 7 Aug. 1619, and to that of Durham 11 Oct. 1620, and same year made Rector of Elwick; Master of Greatham Hospital 1624. He acted as proxy for Bishop Cosin at his enthronement, and he was one of the Prebendaries who supported the canopy of King Charles on his visit to Durham, going north, 1 June 1633. He married Mildred, dau. of William Neile, brother to the Archbishop; see her burial 14 Nov. 1659. Dr. Clarke died 10 May and was buried between the fourth and fifth pillars of the south aisle of the nave. His slab bears, On a bend between three roundlets as many swans; on a canton sinister a demi-ram salient between two fleurs-de-lys; over all a baton. Crest: A swan. Will dated 8 May and proved at York 9 July 1662.

[2] See her M.I. in Carlton. She was second sister of George Wytham of Cliffe, co. York, Esq., who was aged 36 in 1665. The monumental slab, of blue slate, in the centre aisle of the Galilee Chapel, bearing the arms of GREY impaling WITHAM, and inscription (where the name is Greye) is beautifully cut and as clear as new. The "Visitation of Yorkshire 1665" describes her husband erroneously as "*Hillary* Gray, of Bitchburne in co. Northumbr., son of Edward Gray, Esqr." He was buried at St. Oswald's 13 July 1710.

[3] See the father's burial 15 May 1683.

[4] Baptized at Chester-le-Street 2 April 1615, and son of Richard Hedworth, of Pokerley, co. Durham, gent. (who with his brother Christopher sold that estate to Sir William Blakiston *circa* 1638), by his first wife Alice Robinson.

[5] See his baptism 31 Jan. 1664-5, and his father's burial 22 Sep. 1703.

[6] This name, as Bettles, Bettels, Beckles, etc., often occurs at St. Oswald's. His son Robert Beckeles, "beare-bruer," was buried 1673. Mr. Richard Beckles, Attorney, was buried there 1702; and his son, again, Mr. Robert Beckles, innkeeper, 1730.

[7] See her father's burial 10 Sep. 1675.

[8] See baptism of James Huchinson 2 July 1615.

1666	Mar. 13	John Tinkler, beadsman of this Church.
	Mar. 18	Ambrose Myers,[1] plum'er of this Church.
1667	April 10	Samuell Rush,[2] son to the Right Reverend father in god John, Lrd B^{pp}'s sister was buryed in the Cathedrall Church.
	May 14	Mr James Greene,[3] one of the Minor Cannons and Sacrist of the Cathedrall, was buried on Tuesday.
	Aug. 2	Thomas Mudd, Ecclesiæ Cathedralis Eboracensis Organista.
1668	May 27	Mr Will. Tayler.
	May 31	Mrs Barbary Chapman.
	July 25	Mathew Tayler.
	Nov. 12	Margaret Stones,[4] dau. of Mr Christopher Stones.
1669	Aug. 29	Christopherus Mickleton,[5] Atturnatus et legum valde peritus, et in omnimodâ scientiâ eruditus.
	Nov. 21	Gulielmus,[6] Thomæ Massom filius; obiit vigesimo die novembris post vidie sepultus.
	Nov. 28	Timotheus Wilson, de baliva, hospes vicesimo octavo novembris sepultus fuit, pridie moriabatur.
	Jan. 1	Uxor[7] Davidis Ecyles.
1670	June 30	Richardus Curtise,[8] hujusce Cathdralis Dunel. vergifer obiit.
	July 26	Georgius Kipling,[9] Eclesiæ Cath. Duncl. vergifer obiit.
	Sep. 8	Katherina, Roberti Headley uxor.
	Sep. 17	Maria Robson, vidua, obiit.
1671	May 29	Joannes,[10] Dunel. Episcopus, mortuus fuit 15 Jan. & mense Maii proximo sequente sepultus fuit.

[1] Dr. Raine says that he gave, Jan. 1665, to the Chapter Library a copy of Walton's Polyglot, ed. 1657, in six folio vols. See his wife's burial 8 July 1687, and his dau. Mrs. Crosby's 19 Aug. 1696.

[2] He was son of Samuel Rush, of Norwich, by Mary (married 19 Nov. 1634 at St. Andrew's, Norwich), dau. of Giles Cosin or Cosyn, citizen of Norwich, and sister of Dr. John Cosin, Bishop of Durham, whose burial see 29 May [April] 1672. No will or adm'on can be found at Durham.

[3] See his widow's burial 19 Feb. 1691-2, and his children's baptisms 6 Jan. 1635-6 and 1 March 1645-6. Margaret Green occurs as a sponsor to Margaret Stones 28 Nov. 1665. Christopher Green occurs as hypodidascalus scholæ Dunelmensis 1577—1581.

[4] See her baptism 28 Nov. 1665.

[5] He purchased the Crookhall estate. His monumental inscription in the Cathedral no longer exists. See numerous other Mickletons in the Index, and MICKLETON Pedigree, Surtees, vol. iv., part ii., p. 140.

[6] See the father's burial 10 Sep. 1675.

[7] See her husband's burial 2 Oct. 1681.

[8] He was also a stationer and bookbinder, and was son-in-law to Anthony Cradock, Esq., whose burial see 12 Jan. 1623-4. See his son's baptism 9 Feb. 1625-6. The baptisms of Elizabeth, Margery, Anne, and Bridget, daughters of "Richard Courtiss, bookbynder," occur at St. Nicholas between 1627 and 1636. The office of verger appears to have been of some importance in the seventeenth century. Here we find the office filled by a well-to-do citizen, closely allied to one of the chief families in the county, and his wife being actually niece of one of the Archdeacons. Later we find a Mitford, son of an independent gentleman; and, again, early in last century, it was held by the father of the future Dean Wetherell, who was the son of a substantial yeoman ranking among the lesser gentry, and the nephew of the Rector of Dinsdale and Middleton-St. George.

[9] See his marriage 5 June 1667.

[10] Dr. John Cosin, Bishop of Durham Nov. 1660 to 15 Jan. 1671-2, when he died in London,

CATHEDRAL CHURCH AT DURHAM.

1673	May 15	Susanna,[1] Eli. Smith uxor; obiit decimo quinto die Maii.
	May 15	Thomas Cartheret,[2] filius Doc. Car.
	May 19	Sarah Robson, vidua, decessit decimo nono die Maii.
	June 1	Joyce Meggison, moriebatur primo die Junii.
1675	Dec. 24	Jana,[3] uxor Benjamini Borrow.
		filia W^{mi} Lorraine.
	April 14	Venerabilis & Egregius Vir Dr Joh'es Neile,[4] SS^æ Theologiæ Professor, et hujus Ecclesiæ Cathedralis Præbendarius Antiquus, naturæ concessit.
	April 18	Cuthbertus Sisson,[5] Gen^s, annos agens octoginta Septem. & Curiæ Consistorialis Dunelm. Procuratoru' unus, placidâ quievit Morte 17° die Aprilis, & die sequente sepultus est.
	July 4	Dorothea, uxor Lancæloti Hilton, Generosi.
	July 23	Margeria, filia W^{mi} Mathew, Gen^t.
	July 26	Joh'es, filius Joh'is Yapp.
	Aug. 11	Jana, filia Joh'is Yapp.
	Sep. 10	Thomas Massom,[6] hujus Ecclesiæ Cantor, obdormivit in Domino, nono die mensis Septembris, et die sequente sepultus est.
	Sep. 28	Richardus Wrench,[7] SS. Theologiæ Bacc'l'us et hujus Ecclesiæ Prebendarius; obiit 26° et 28° die mensis Octobris sep' fuit.
	Dec. 2	Mrs Maria Blakiston.[8]

where he was embalmed. The body was subsequently carried with great state to Durham, arriving 27th April. On the 29th it was taken to Bishop Auckland and buried in the chapel, which the Bishop had partly rebuilt. The date, May, given in the Register here is an error. The stall canopies in the Cathedral, the fine staircase and other carved wood-work in the Castle, are due to Cosin. See a brief but succinct memoir of him in Low's "Diocesan History of Durham" (S. P. C. K.); "The Correspondence of Bishop Cosin" (Surtees Society, where his will is printed, vol. lv.); and his pedigree (which is not quite correct) in Surtees' "History," vol. i., p. cxiv. See his dau. Mrs. Granville's burial 14 Oct. 1691.

[1] See her husband the Minor Canon's burial 9 Dec. 1676.

[2] *Recte* Cartwright. See his brother's baptism 7 June 1675, and his mother's burial 6 Jan. 1682-3.

[3] See her husband's burial 25 April 1676.

[4] Son of William Neile, Registrar to the Dean and Chapter of Westminster, by Catherine Stopes his wife. He was born 9 Dec. 1609; of Pembroke Hall, Cambridge, D.D. (Fellow 29 Oct. 1629); Prebendary of third stall in Durham Cathedral, collated 1 Aug. 1635; Archdeacon of Cleveland 1638; Prebendary of York 28 Jan. 1633-4; Vicar of Northallerton 1669; Dean of Ripon 25 May 1674; was also Prebendary of the Collegiate Church of Southwell 3 Aug. 1633, and Chaplain to Charles II. He was deprived during the Commonwealth of his preferments, but they were restored at the Restoration. Died 14 April 1675, and was buried in Ripon Cathedral. [MS. Ped. by E. A. W.]

[5] A proctor; died 17th, aged 87. See his widow's burial 4 April 1688, and his son's 19 Dec. 1680.

[6] See, probably, his widow's burial 20 March 1687-8, and his children's 1665, 1699, and 1700. [John Massam and Ellinor Thompson were married 13 Feb. 1609-10 at St. Oswald's.]

[7] See his marriage 16 Aug. 1664.

[8] She was fourth dau. and coheiress of William Blakiston, gent., and Attorney-at-Law, of York, who was buried 12 Nov. 1635 at St. Helen's, York, where she was baptized 18 Jan. 1617-18. This York Attorney is not in Surtees' Pedigree of BLAKISTON of Gibside, but he was probably of that family. See the burial, 15 May 1683, of his son-in-law Henry Blakiston.

o

98   REGISTER OF BURIALS IN THE

1675 Jan. 5 Will'us,[1] filius Thomæ Cartwright, S.T.P. et hujus Eccl'iæ Prebendarii.
     Mar. 23 Maria, filia Cuthberti Hilton, Gen^si.
1676 April 25 Thomas White.
     April 25 Benjaminus Borrow, annos agens octoginta novem., et hujus Collegii, Janitor senex & fidelis, naturæ concessit 24° die mensis Aprilis et die sequente sepultus est.
     June 29 Dorothea,[2] uxor Samuelis Martin, Clec'i & hujus Eccl'iæ Minoris Canonici, Naturæ concessit 28° die mensis Junii et die sequente sepulta est Anno D'ni (stylo Angliæ) 1676°.
     Aug. 14 Joh'es,[3] filius Thomæ Battersby, Gen^sl.
     July 27 Francisca, uxor Isaaci Basire, S.T.P., et hujus Eccl'iæ Prebendarii; naturæ concessit 26° die Julii et die sequente sepulta est.
     Oct. 8 Gracia Hutchinson, vidua.
     Oct. 14 Isaacus Basire, S.T.P., & hujus Eccl'æ Prebendarius Obdormivit in D'no 13° die Octobris, et die sequente sepultus est.
     Dec. 9 Elias Smith,[4] hujus Eccl'iæ Precentor.
     Feb. 20 Elizabetha,[5] filia Joh'is Foster, Organistæ.
     Mar. 15 Jana Plesence,[6] vidua, annos agens octoginta duos, vel eò circiter, fatis concessit 14° die Martii, et die sequente sepultus est.
1677 April 21 Joh'es Foster,[7] Organista, Naturæ concessit vicesimo die mensis Aprilis, et die sequente sep^ts est.
     May   1 Dorothea Barnes, Sp^r.
     May 18 Jana Smith, vidua.
     Aug. 17 Thomas Newton, Gen^s, Naturæ concessit 16° die Augusti, et die sequente sepultus est.

[1] See his brother's baptism 7 June 1675, and his mother's burial 6 Jan. 1682-3.
[2] She was baptized at St. Nicholas 12 March 1608-9, the dau. of Thomas Sonkey, gaoler, and Ann his wife, *gaolotrix*. Her children are all baptized at St. Mary-le-Bow. Samuel, the eldest son, was admitted at St. John's College, Cambridge, 21 Jan. 1661-2. See the husband's burial 20 April 1682.
[3] See his baptism 1675, and his father's burial 6 Nov. 1716.
[4] He was Master of the Grammar School 1640—1666, when he resigned; Librarian to the Dean and Chapter, Vicar of Bedlington, and Minor Canon (occurring as such in 1632, but was probably so earlier). The following curious record of the reverses of the School is extracted from the Mickleton MSS. in the Chapter Library: "Intravit Scholam circa Festum S^ti Petri ad Vincula A° 1640. Schola diruta, discipulos autèm docuit in Area Collegii, scilicet aliquandò in Domo pertinente ad tertium Præbe, juxta le Guest Hall ibid. aliquandò etiam in Domo pertinente ad primum præbend. Curam habuit dictus Elias, in nequissimis temporibus Librorum in Bibliothecâ Dec. & Cap. Dun. Etiamque Coparum & Vestimentorum & aliarum rerum ad Ecclesiam prædictam pertinentium, salvaque omnia in eisdem temporibus custodivit. Elias, variis negotiis distractus, substituit sibi Præceptores," etc. See his wife's burial 15 May 1673, and his children's baptisms and burials by consulting Index.
[5] See her father's burial 21 April 1677.
[6] Widow of the Seneschal, whose burial see 14 May 1635. She was dau. of Henry Ewbanke, Prebendary of the twelfth stall (see his burial 15 March 1676-7), and sister of the wife (see her burial 24 May 1634) of Prebendary James.
[7] He first occurs as Organist Feb. 1661. See his widow's re-marriage 29 Nov. 1677, and his son's baptism 25 Jan. 1664-5.

1677		Thomas Huchinson, sepult² est.
		.... Nelson, sepult² est.
	Jan. 26	Francisca,¹ uxor Cuth. Sisson, apothecarii, è vivis discessit 25° die Januarii, & die sequente sepultus est.
	Nov. 10	M' Johannes Brakenbury, Naturæ concessit nono die Novemb⁸, et die sequente sepult² est.
1678	May 2	Isaacus,² filius Isaaci Basire, Ar'.
	May 12	Anna,³ uxor Georgii Bullock.
	May 25	Isabella, filia Gulielmi Reed.
	June 22	Franciscus,⁴ filius Joh'is Spearman, Gen⁸.

¹ She was dau. of Henry Hutton, of Goldsborough, co. York, Esq., by his wife (see her burial 14 Jan. 1699-1700) Elizabeth (Lady Burton), dau. of Bishop Cosin. See her husband's burial 19 Dec. 1680.

² See his baptism 18 Feb. 1676-7.

³ She was married, as Ann Pattison, at St. Mary-le-Bow, "on St. Mark's day," 1665. See her sons' baptisms 25 Jan. 1665-6, 6 Jan. 1669-70, and 1 Nov. 1676; also the re-marriage, 22 Oct. 1679, of her husband (who appears to have been Churchwarden at Bow), by whom she had, also baptized at Bow, George, 29 May 1667, and Edward, *born* 1 June 1674.

⁴ See his baptism 26 Jan. 1668-9, and his father's burial 22 Sep. 1703.

A Register of all Buriallo

WITHIN THE CATHEDRALL CHURCH & CHURCHYARD OF DURHAM,

And of all Affidavits of the persons being buried in Woollen from the first Day of August Anno D'ni 1678, according to an Act of Parliament intituled an Act for Burying in Woollen, made Anno Tricesimo Caroli Secundi Regis Angliæ, etc., together with Memorialls entered against the Names of the Parties where noe such Affidavits were brought within the time limited in the said Act.

EDVARDUS KIRKBY, Sacrista.

1678 Aug. 26 Timothy Brigham.[1] (An Affidavit of his being buryed in Woollen, according to ye Act of Parliament, under ye hands & scales of two witnesses, & under ye hand of ye Magistrate before w^m ye same was sworne, was brought to me, September the 3^d —78º.)
Oct. 6 Robert Mitford,[2] sonn of John Mitford (Affidavit ut supra).
Dec. 5 Francis Wickliffe,[3] gentleman (Aff.).
Dec. 18 Richard Clerke,[4] sonn of Wilfrid Clerke (Aff.).
Jan. 9 Susanna Smith, dau. of Henry Smith, clerke (Aff.).
Jan. 6 Richard Rawe,[5] gent. Mem^{dum} y^t noe Affidavit of his being buried in Woollen was brought to me wthin eight days after his interment, and y^t I gave notice y^rof to George Bullock, Churchwarden, January ye 14th.
[*After this the Editor has omitted the words* " Aff." *or* " No aff."]
Mar. 4 Francis Frewin, gen.
Mar. 15 Dorothy Lowther,[6] widow.
Mar. 16 Georgius Lindsey.
Mar. 19 Mary, dau. of Cuthbert Bowes.
1679 April 3 Thomas Hull, gent.
April 4 Frances,[7] dau. of Mr Tho. Blakiston.
June 18 Elizabeth,[8] wife of Cuthbert Coulson.
June 21 ....[9] dau. of Cuthbert Bowes.

---

[1] He was baptized 14 Jan. 1609-10 at St. Nicholas, the son of Thomas Brigham, who has other children baptized there, and is elsewhere termed "Smith." See burial of his wife 4 May 1682, and of his dau. Horseman 7 Oct. 1698.
[2] Also registered at Bow. See his baptism 8 Feb. 1675-6, and his father's burial 4 Oct. 1704.
[3] Also in Bow Register, where the date is given as 1 Dec.
[4] See his baptism 8 Nov. 1675, and his father's burial 16 March 1679-80.
[5] He entered his pedigree (" No proofe of any armes ") at Dugdale's Visitation 1666, being then aged 46, and was described as of Plawsworth, co. Pal. See his widow's burial 24 Feb. 1697-8, and his son's 13 Feb. 1721-2. The name, originally Raw, appears to have become Rawe and finally Rowe.
[6] Also in Bow Register.
[7] Baptized at Darlington 19 Dec. 1669. See her father's burial 25 March 1711.
[8] Also in Bow Register.
[9] See her father's burial 22 Feb. 1714-15.

CATHEDRAL CHURCH AT DURHAM. 101

1679 Aug. 18 Dorothy, dau. of Mr John Cowle.
     Oct. 3 Christopher Bell, gent. (Mem^{dm} y^t noe Affidavit of his being buryed in Woollen was brought to me w^{t}hin 8 days after his interment; upon notice w^{r}of to ye Churchwardens I was certifyed by y^m of ye levying & receiving ye forfeiture in ye case made & provided, Octr 10th —79.)
     Dec. 3 Thomas Thompson, gent.
     Mar. 16 Wilfrid Clerk,[1] gent.
1680 April 5 Sarah Easter,[2] widow.
     April 13 Nicholas Fewster,[3] clerk, Minor Canon of y^s Church.
     July 3 Christopher Rashell.
     July 13 Rebecca Myres, sp^r.
     Aug. 9 Samuel Adamson.[4]
     Aug. 13 John Horsman.
     Aug. 25 Jane Weeres, wife of Tho. Weeres.
     Sep. 4 John, sonn of Ralph Midleton.
     Nov. 15 Mrs Cooper, widow.
     Dec. 4 Richard Lewen.
     Dec. 12 Thomas Bell,[5] prisoner.
     Dec. 19 Cuthbert Sisson,[6] gent.
     Mar. 13 John Hutchinson, prisoner.
1681 April 26 Jeronyma,[7] wife of Mr Thomas Battersby.
     May 30 Arthur Phillipps,[8] gent.
     June 6 John Nicholls,[9] gent.
     June 6 William,[10] sonn of Geo. Bullock.
     June 21 Barbara,[11] dau. of John Mitford.
                          (20th Julii 1681. Johannes Milner, Sacrista.)

[1] See his daughter's baptism 6 Feb. 1670-71. By his wife Mary he had, besides Maria, Ann and Richard, whose baptisms see 1670-71, 1673, and 1675; John, 10 March 1663-4; William, 16 July 1666; Dorothy, 11 May 1668; and Mary, 10 Feb. 1671-2, all baptized at Bow.

[2] Easter perhaps synonymous with Hester occurring before.

[3] Of Peterhouse, Cambridge, B.A. 1675; M.A. 1679. He was sometime Under Master of the Grammar School. See his son's burial 22 Aug. 1681. ["Nicholas Fewster and Margrett Wright" married 24 Nov. 1607 at St. Oswald's.]

[4] See note to burial of Samuel Adamson 24 July 1683.

[5] The gaol was then in the parish of St. Mary-le-Bow.

[6] See his wife's burial 26 Jan. 1677-8.

[7] See her husband's burial 6 Nov. 1716.

[8] See his widow's burial 17 March 1694-5. Arthur, son of Arthur Phillips, occurs in the Barber-Surgeons' books as bound apprentice 31 July 1665. See baptism (of his dau. ?) 6 Jan. 1666-7.

[9] Of Durham; not improbably a descendant of "my brother Nicholls" mentioned in the will, 12 Nov. 1607, of Anna, widow of Chancellor Swyft, and dau. of Thomas Lever, Master of Sherburn. His will is dated 5 March 1680-81, and was proved by the widow and sole ex'or Hester Nicholls, whose burial see 2 Oct. 1699. See his son's baptism 22 April 1662. [Cuthbert Nichols was, in 1576, a Minor Canon, and occurs as *hypodidascalus* in 1587—1589; and a John Nicholls was appointed *circa* 1666 Master of Bishop Langley's Song-School.]

[10] See his father's burial 2 Aug. 1699, and his mother's 12 May 1678.

[11] Born 6 and baptized 13 Oct. 1678 at St. Mary-le-Bow, where her burial also is entered. See her father's burial 4 Oct. 1704.

REGISTER OF BURIALS IN THE

1681
- Aug. 1   Anne, wife of Robert Smith, gent.
- Aug. 22 John,[1] son of Dorothy Fewster, widdow; on Monday.
- Sep. 15 Cuthbert,[2] son of Cuth. Bowes, Taylor.
- Oct. 2   David Eales.[3]
- Oct. 3   William, son of William Snawdon.
- Nov. 26 Martha,[4] dau. of Cuth. Hilton.
- Dec. 19 Jane Chipchase, of Norton, spinser.
- Jan. 7   Jane Hutchinson, widow.
- Jan. 7   Ralph,[5] the son of Dr Hen. Bagshaw, in ye 9 Altars.
- Feb. 27 Thomas,[6] son of Peter Nelson.
- Mar. 1   Henry Peirson.
- Mar. 3   Thomasin Horseman.
- Mar. 9   Mary Philips.

1682
- Mar. 31 Mary Mitchell, Spinst^r.
- April 13 John Jackson, Porter.
- April 20 Samuell Martin,[7] Minor Canon of this Church.
- May 4   Mary Brigham,[8] wid.
- June 10 Nicholas,[9] son of Mrs Dorothy Fewster, Wid.
- June 20 Isabell,[10] wife of Jo. Benson.
- July 7   Meriell,[11] wife of Mr Anthony Lodge.
- Aug. 9   Ra. Colepitt, gent., of Bishop Auckland.
- Aug. 18 William,[12] son of Jo. Bowman.
- Oct. 16 John,[13] son of Nicholas Barwick, Gent.
- Jan. 6   Sarah,[14] wife of Dr Tho. Cartwright, Deane of Rippon.
- Jan. 15 Priscilla,[15] dau. of Tho. Battersby, Clerke.

[1] See his baptism 5 Jan. 1678-9. The mother was dau. of John Martin, of Elvet, gent., and was baptized 13 April 1652 at St. Oswald's, where she married, 3 Feb. 1675-6, the Rev. Nicholas Fewster, whose burial see 13 April 1680. She was buried as "Mrs. Dorothy Feaster, widow," 22 June 1687 at St. Oswald's.

[2] See the father's burial 22 Feb. 1714-15.

[3] See his second marriage 20 June 1670, and his first wife's burial 1 Jan. 1669-70.

[4] See her baptism 23 July 1679, and her father's burial 28 April 1686.

[5] See baptism of his brother Henry 2 April 1684.

[6] See the father's burial 20 May 1703.

[7] He was Master of Bishop Langley's Petty-School (" pro plano cantu et arte scribendi "), in which he had officiated during the incarceration of the loyal Thomas Wandless, commonly called "cavalier," son of Alderman Edward Wandless. Martin himself, we learn, was nicknamed "Baggs" by his pupils. He occurs as Perpetual Curate of St. Nicholas 1663—1680. See his wife's burial 29 June 1676.

[8] "Tymothie Bridgham and Mary his wiff" married 14 July 1633 at St. Nicholas. See her husband's burial 26 Aug. 1678.

[9] See his brother's burial 22 Aug. 1681.

[10] See burial of her husband, to whom she appears to have been first wife, 19 Dec. 1696.

[11] See her husband's burial 21 July 1687.

[12] See his baptism 31 Dec. 1678, and his father's burial 27 Jan. 1695-6.

[13] See his baptism 31 Aug. 1682, and his father's burial 7 Dec. 1687.

[14] See her son's baptism 7 June 1675.

[15] See her baptism 17 July 1678, and her father's burial 6 Nov. 1716.

1682	Jan. 27	Richard Mathewes,[1] gent.
1683	April 4	Elizabeth Mitford,[2] widdow; Wednesday.
	April 23	John Archibald, gardiner.
	April 25	Anne Hunter, spinster.
	May 15	Henry Blakiston,[3] gent.
	June 29	Richard,[4] son of Jo. Raw, Esq.
	Nov. 26	Christian Foster;[5] on Monday.
	Dec. 29	Frances Gravelle, niece to Isa. Casaubon.[6]
	Jan. 9	Robert Hilton, Esq[r]; on Wednesday.
	Jan. 20	Katherine Hubbock; on Sunday.
	Mar. 18	Rebecca Mathewes; on Tuesday.
1684	May 15	Sarah, wife of Nicholas Hodgson; Thursday.
	June 20	John,[7] son of John Taylor.
	Aug. 10	Thomasin,[8] wife of Ro. Adamson, clerk; Sunday.
	Aug. 20	Robert,[9] son of John Mickleton, Esq[r]; Wednesday.

[1] See his widow's burial 21 Dec. 1687.

[2] She was married as Elizabeth Porter. 28 Oct. 1625, at St. Mary-le-Bow, to Robert Mitford, of the North Bailey, gent., to whose will, dated 24 Jan. 1666-7, she was Executrix, and who was buried 9 Feb. following at Bow. See the burial of their second son John Mitford 4 Oct. 1704. Their eldest son Christopher Mitford was baptized 9 Jan. 1627-8 at Bow, and died, *vitâ patris*, leaving two sons, Robert and William, the latter living with the grandfather in 1666-7, and both mentioned in his will. They also had Swinburne and Robert Mitford, baptized same place 1639 and Nov. 1646 respectively.

[3] Youngest son of Sir William Blakiston, of Gibside, co. Pal., Knt., by Jane, dau. of Robert Lambton, of Lambton, Esq., and brother of the first Baronet of Gibside (extinct). He married Elizabeth (her surname not given in Surtees), third dau. and coheir of William Blakiston, gent., Attorney-at-Law, of York, where she was baptized at St. Helen's 3 Oct. 1613. She was buried in the chancel of the church of Danby-upon-Wiske, co. York, of which her son Gabriel Blakiston was Rector. [See burials of her sister Mary 2 Dec. 1675, and her great-niece Mrs. Bowes 13 Nov. 1715.] See their children's burials 8 Feb. 1643-4, 23 March 1648-9, and that of their son Thomas Blakiston, Esq., 25 March 1711, and dau. Jane Blakiston 2 June 1714.

[4] Eldest child, apparently, of his father, whose burial see 13 Feb. 1721-2. His baptism is not at St. Oswald's, with those of all his brothers and sisters.

[5] See his baptism 29 Sep. 1667, and his father's burial 21 April 1677.

[6] Mons. J. de Gravelle du Pin was son-in-law of Isaac Casaubon, and signs the dedicatory epistle of Casaubon's "Commentary on Polybius," published in 1617, after the author's death, and the above Frances was, with scarcely any doubt, his dau., and granddau. of Isaac Casaubon— not niece, which is probably a slip of the transcriber, who would be accustomed to hear the names of Isaac and Casaubon in conjunction. "Niece" and "cousin" also, in those days, had a much wider signification than at present. She was actually niece, however, to Dr. Meric Casaubon, Prebendary of Canterbury. Isaac Casaubon died, aged 54, in 1614, so that he would hardly have a niece to represent him in 1683, but it may be fairly assumed that he was grandfather of Frances Gravelle. The territorial du Pin would naturally be relinquished in England. Isaac Casaubon married Florence, dau. of the most eminent of the great French printers who bore the name of Estienne, or Stephen, or Stephanus. See Michael Mattaire's "Stephanorum Historia," 1709.

[7] See his baptism 29 Jan. 1643-4, and his mother's burial 26 Jan. 1709-10.

[8] See baptism of her son 24 July 1683. The Rev. Robert Adamson was admitted 20 April 1672, then aged 18, at St. John's College, Cambridge. ["Mr. Robert Adamson, curate of Trimdon," buried 19 April 1709 at St. Oswald's.]

[9] He was baptized at Crossgate 14 June 1683. See his father's burial 16 Jan. 1708-9.

1684 Dec. 3 Jo. Sudbury,[1] Deane of Durham.
Dec. 7 Jo. Douthwaite, beadsman; Sunday.
Feb. 14 Henry,[2] son of Dr Henry Bagshaw.
Feb. 18 Dorothy,[3] wife of Jo. Mitford; Wednesday.
Feb. 28 Mary Hilton, widdow; Saturday.
1685 May 10 Miles Stapylton, Esqr; Sunday.
May 29 Lancelot Hilton, gent.
May 31 Dorothy Davison, wid.
Oct. 4 Elizabeth,[4] dau. of Jo. Simpson.
Dec. 12 Richard Jackson.
Dec. 28 Anne,[5] dau. of M^r Jo. Morton, Prebendary.
Jan. 9 Catherine,[6] dau. of Jo. Raw, Esqr.
Jan. 10 Elianor, dau. of Rob. Hilton.
Jan. 15 Jane, the dau. of Thomas Skepper.
1686 Mar. 30 Tho. Musgrave,[7] D.D.
April 28 Cuthbert Hilton, gent.
May 24 Richard,[8] son of Tho. Crosby, was borne & buryed.
Oct. 30 Jane Milner,[9] an infant.
Dec. 14 Michael Spearman,[10] gent.
Jan. 13 Ro. Adamson, prisoner.
Jan. 15 .... Bolton, prisoner.
Feb. 2 Joseph,[11] son of Henry Smith, Clerk.
Feb. 9 George Kirby,[12] gent.
1687 April 17 Thomas, son of Geo. Bullock.
July 8 Elizabeth Myres,[13] widow.

[1] He was made Dean 1661, succeeding Dr. Barwick, who had held the Deanery but a year. He turned the old refectory of the Monks into a library, and at the end of that chamber, over the door leading into the Deanery, his full-length portrait hangs. He was uncle of Sir John Sudbury, of Eldon, co. Pal., created a Baronet 1685, who died 1691 s.p. See note to baptism of John Wilson 17 Aug. 1684.

[2] See his baptism 2 April 1684.

[3] She died 17th, according to Bow Register. See her marriage 11 Nov. 1669, and her husband's burial 4 Oct. 1704.

[4] See her baptism 12 March 1682-3, and her father's burial 10 June 1688.

[5] See her baptism 19 Oct. 1684, and her sister Dulcibella's 22 Aug. 1682.

[6] Baptized at St. Oswald's 17 June 1684. Elder dau. by his first wife of John Raw, or Rowe, Esq., whose burial see 13 Feb. 1721-2.

[7] Of Queen's College, Oxford, matriculated 10 March 1656-7; B.A. 26 July 1659; M.A. 5 May 1662; B.D. and D.D. 10 Oct. 1685; Rector of Salkeld, Cumberland, 1669; of Whitburn, co. Pal., Durham, 1675; Canon and Archdeacon of Carlisle 1669; Canon of Durham 1675; of Chichester 1681; and Dean of Carlisle 1684 until his death 28 March 1686. He was sixth son of Sir Philip Musgrave, of Edenhall, second Bart., who was created Baron Musgrave after the Restoration, but the patent was never taken out. He married Mary, dau. of Sir Thomas Harrison of Copgrove, Knt., by Margaret, dau. of Conyers, Lord Darcy. See the baptism of a grandchild 20 June 1683, the son of one of Dean Musgrave's daughters and coheirs. Another dau., Margaret Musgrave, married Ralph Shipperdson, Esq., of Pittington Hallgarth, co. Pal., and her representative was the late Rev. Edmund Hector Shipperdson, formerly Hopper, D.L., J.P., of Pittington and Hermitage.

[8] See his father's burial 9 Nov. 1707.   [9] See her father's burial 5 June 1705.

[10] See his father's burial 22 Sep. 1703.   [11] See his father's burial 6 July 1696.

[12] See his widow's burial 11 March 1693-4.   [13] See her husband's burial 18 March 1666-7.

1687	July 21	Mr Antho. Lodge.¹
	Dec. 7	Nicholas Barwicke,² gent.
	Dec. 21	Isabell Matthews, widow.
	Dec. 23	Jo. Dun, porter.
	Jan. 5	Jane Hutchinson, widow.
	Jan. 11	George Campbell, gent.
	Mar. 20	Mary Massam, widow.
1688	April 4	Murial Sisson, widow.³
	May 30	Wm Skurfeild. (No affidavit brought to me, but as I suppose, to the Minister of Bow.)
	June 10	John Simpson.⁴ (The affidavit of his being buryed in Woollen delivered to Mr Kirton, Minister of Bow.)
	Sep. 22	Dulcibella Morton.⁵
	Oct. 17	Jane,⁶ wife of Wm Werdon, bookseller.
	Dec. 28	Mary,⁷ dau. of Wm Werdon.
	Jan. 1	Elizabeth Morley, spinster.
	Jan. 17	Anne,⁸ wife of John Darbyshire.
	Mar. 19	Mr Edward Kirkby,⁹ Præcentor of this Church.
1689	June 26	Mary Spooner, spinster.
		(Mr John Smith, Sacrista, Nov. 20, 1689.)
	Dec. 9	Margaret, wife of Mr Timothy Stott.
	Dec. 23	Richard,¹⁰ son of Dr Grayhm.

---

¹ He was son of Christopher Lodge, of Wolsingham, gent., who made his will 12 Nov. 1683. See his wife's burial 7 July 1682, and daughters' baptisms 15 May 1665 and 30 Nov. 1666.

² He was brother of Dr. Peter Barwick the Physician, and of Dr. John Burwick, first Dean of Durham after the Restoration 1660. In his will, dated 23 Nov. 1687, he is described as " of the college," and he mentions his brother Dr. Peter Barwick, son George, dau. Jane, and his brother-in-law Mr. John Milner, Mr. George Read, etc.

³ She was baptized 1597 at St. Mary-le-Bow, the eldest dau. of Robert Cooper, Esq., of Durham, Steward of the County Palatine, and a Master of the High Court of Chancery, who entered his pedigree and arms at Dugdale's Visitation 1615. See her husband's burial 18 April 1675.

⁴ He was a Notary Public. See his wife's burial 31 Oct. 1711, and his daughters' 4 Oct. 1685 and 15 July 1693. See also burial of Thomas Simpson 23 June 1710.

⁵ Wife of Dr. Thomas Morton, Prebendary, and Rector of Sedgefield, and previously wife of Rev. Thomas Dalton. She was baptized 21 Jan. 1643-4 at Sedgefield, and was, in the words of that Register, "filia venerabilis viri Josephi Naylor, sacræ theologiæ professoris, et ecclesiæ hujus rectoris vigilantissimi." Her mother was Dulcibella, dau. of Richard Baddeley, Esq. See note to burial of William Bridges 15 Aug. 1634. See her daughter's baptism 22 Aug. 1682 for an account of Dr. Morton; also her brother's baptism 18 Dec. 1637.

⁶ See her husband's burial 29 March 1703.

⁷ See preceding entry.

⁸ She was married, as Anne Borrow, 9 Jan. 1674-5 at St. Mary's, and was probably a grand-dau. of Benj. Borrow, buried 25 April 1676.

⁹ He was M.A., and admitted free of Mercers' Company, Durham, 15 Nov. 1681. See his widow's burial 16 July 1721.

¹⁰ See his baptism 17 Sep. 1689. The father William Graham, D.D., of Christ Church, Oxford, was brother of Richard, first Viscount Preston, and a younger son of Sir George Graham, second Bart., of Esk and Netherby, Cumberland, by his wife Lady Mary Johnstone, dau. of James, first Earl of Hartfell, and sister of the second Earl, created also Earl of Annandale. He succeeded Dr. Smith, on his promotion from the Deanery to the Bishopric of Carlisle in the

1689 Jan. 12 Barbara,[1] wife of William Snawdon.
     Feb. 28 Thomas Cradock,[2] Esq'.
     Mar. 19 Sarah Taylor, wid.
         [*Affidavits of being buried in woollen cease here.*]
1690 Mar. 25 Barbara,[3] wife of John Bowman.
     April 1 George Barkas,[4] Not. Pub.
     June 28 John,[5] son of John Lisle, Clerk.
     Dec. 7 William Wilson,[6] LL.B., Sp'ul Chancellor.
     Jan. 22 George,[7] son of John Morton, Preb^d.
     Feb. 18 Mary,[8] wife of Wm Wilson, ut sup.
     Feb. 19 Anne Green,[9] widow of Mr Green, M.C.
     Mar. 3 John Watson.
1691 Aug. 2 Margarett,[10] wife of John Eldridge.
     Oct. 14 Anne,[11] wife of Dr Granville, Dean of Durham.

first prebend, being installed 16 Aug. 1684, and succeeded Dr. Hartwell in the Rectory of Whickham 1685; made Dean of Carlisle 1686, and Dean of Wells 1704; Clerk of the Closet and Chaplain to Queen Anne. He died 5 Feb. 1711-12, and was buried at Kensington. From the Dean the present Baronets, both of Esk and Netherby, descend. See the marriage of his sister Lady Fenwick 18 May 1704.

[1] See her marriage 1 May 1678, and her husband's burial 15 Oct. 1692.

[2] Died 25th. Eldest and only surviving son of Sir Joseph Cradock, Knt., LL.D., Commissary of the Archdeaconry of Richmond, and grandson of Archdeacon Cradock, whose burial see 30 Dec. 1627. He was a Fellow of Trinity, Cambridge, and Barrister-at-Law of Gray's Inn, Attorney-General to Bishop Cosin, sometime M.P. for Richmond, Yorkshire. He married, firstly, Sibella, dau. of Archdeacon Gabriel Clarke (whose burial see 12 May 1662), who died 2 March 1669; and secondly, Dorothy (baptized 10 Sep. 1639 at Crossgate, and buried there 24 Feb. 1709-10), dau. of Nicholas Heath, of Little Eden, co. Pal., Esq., but had issue by neither. He is buried near his father-in-law, the Archdeacon, and his M.I. bears the arms: On a chevron three garbs. Crest: A bear's head couped and muzzled.

[3] See her husband's burial 27 Jan. 1695-6.

[4] See his widow's burial 10 Oct. 1693. [Richard Barkas occurs as Minor Canon in 1576.]

[5] See his baptism 1 Dec. 1689.

[6] He was a Notary Public and Registrar to the Chapter, LL.B. of Trinity Hall, Cambridge. He was accidentally drowned. See his wife's burial 18 Feb. 1690-91; son's baptism 17 Aug. 1684, and daughter's 15 Dec. 1685; and son's burial 6 Jan. 1700-1.

[7] See his baptism 30 Oct. 1683, and his mother's burial, if he was by the first wife, 22 Sep. 1688.

[8] See her marriage 18 Dec. 1677, and her husband's burial 7 Dec. 1690.

[9] See her husband's burial 14 May 1667.

[10] See her marriage 18 March 1688-9, and her husband's burial 24 Feb. 1697-8.

[11] She was fourth dau. of Dr. Cosin, Bishop of Durham (whose burial see 29 May, *valde* April, 1672), by his marriage (13 Aug. 1626 at Crossgate) with Frances, dau. of Marmaduke Blakiston, D.D., Prebendary of Durham, Rector of Sedgefield, and Archdeacon of Cleveland, which last preferment he resigned in favour of his son-in-law Cosin. There is a good memoir of Dr. Denys Granville in the "Diocesan History of Durham" (S.P.C.K.), p. 281, which gives a list of his preferments, etc., but where the editor, Canon Low, is a little wrong in his genealogy. Dr. Granville was born *circa* 1637, the youngest surviving son of the celebrated cavalier Sir Bevil Granville, of Stow, who has been termed " the Bayard of England," and brother of the first Earl of Bath, and uncle of the first Lords Lansdowne and Granville, all of which peerages are extinct. Notwithstanding his emoluments as a Prebendary, an Archdeacon, and the Rector of two good livings, all of which he afterwards held together with his Deanery, he became, from his extravagant way of life, much in debt, and was actually arrested in the cloisters as he was coming from service, in the presence,

1691	Dec. 2	John Yappe,[1] Bailiff to y[e] D. & C.
	Dec. 19	William Martiall, Clerk, M.A., Minor Can.
1692	June 6	Robert Thornton, Clerk, Rector of Bolden.
	Oct. 15	William Snawdon,[2] yeoman.
	Dec. 6	Anne Scourfield.
	Jan. 13	John Darby, yeom.
	Feb. 19	William Stagg,[3] Not. Pub.
1693	May 18	Elisabeth, dau. of Henry Smith.
	June 3	Golibright, dau. of Henry Smith.
	July 15	Mary,[4] dau. of Isabell Simpson.
	Aug. 4	James Mickleton, Esq[r].
	Aug. 7	Elisabeth Edmundson.[5]
	Oct. 10	Elisabeth Barkas,[6] wid.
	Nov. 27	Henry,[7] son of John Lisle, Clerk.
	Jan. 13	Catherine Foster, wid.
	Jan. 16	Thomas Were.
	Feb. 1	Anne,[8] wife of Arch-D. Booth.
	Feb. 26	Richard Mitchel, the Bishop's porter.
	Mar. 11	Mary Kirkby,[9] wid.
1694	April 12	Timothy Horseman.[10]
	Aug. 28	Edward, son of John Lisle, Clerk.
	Oct. 25	Samuel Eyre, D.D., Prebendary of y[e] 3[d] preb[d], & Rect[r] of Whitburn.
	Dec. 1	Elisabeth,[11] wife of Cuthbert Bowes.

we are told, of many of the chief gentry of the county. He was Dean from 1684 until the fall of James the Second, whom he followed to France (where he died), refusing to take the oaths to the new King. His preferments were not filled up until 1691.

[1] John Yapp graduated at Magdalen College, Oxon, B.A. 2 May 1662. See his wife's burial 4 Aug. 1718, and his son the Rev. Abraham Yapp's 23 Dec. 1728, and other children in Index.

[2] See his wife's burial 12 Jan. 1689-90, and baptisms of his children, — Jan. 1678-9 and 8 Jan. 1682-3.

[3] See his wife's burial 27 Feb. 1718-19, and the baptism of his son 2 May 1678.

[4] See her baptism — Nov. 1676, and her father's burial 10 June 1688.

[5] See note to burial of William Edmundson 8 Dec. 1704.

[6] See her husband's burial 1 April 1690.

[7] See his baptism 31 Aug. 1693.

[8] She was dau. of Sir Robert Booth, Chief Justice of the Court of Common Pleas in Ireland, and first wife of Robert Booth, Archdeacon of Durham, who was father, by his second wife, of the fourth and last Lord Delamere. Dr. Booth, who succeeded Dean and Archdeacon Granville in the lesser preferment in 1691, was a younger son of Sir George Booth, second Bart., of Dunham Massie, an eminent Royalist, who was created Baron Delamere 1661, by his second wife Lady Elizabeth Grey, dau. of the first Earl of Stamford. He was made Dean of Bristol 1708.

[9] She was dau. of .... Smith, Esq., of Burnhall (see Ped., Surtees, vol. iv., part ii., p. 187), and widow of George Kirkby, Esq., to whom she was married 14 April 1667 at St. Oswald's. See his burial 9 Feb. 1686-7.

[10] Son of William Horseman (whose burial see 17 Jan. 1723-4) by his wife Mary, dau. of Timothy Brigham.

[11] She was married, as Elizabeth Barcroft, 16 Nov. 1671 at St. Nicholas, and was probably dau. of George Barcroft (see his burial 10 Feb. 1638-9), and baptized 1 May 1639. See her husband's burial 22 Feb. 1714-15.

1694	Dec. 28	["M[rs] Elizabeth Shuttleworth[1] of this parish was buried in the Abbie Churchyard." St. Oswald's Register, 1694.]
	Mar. 17	Jane Philips,[2] widow.
1695	April 15	Richard, son of M[r] Mich. Mickleton.
	April 17	Elisabeth,[3] dau. of W[m] Horseman.
	June 25	Katherine Foster.
		(Franciscus Woodmas, Sacrista, Novemb. 20, 1695.)
	Oct. 12	Michaell, son of M[r] Mich. Mickleton.
	Jan. 27	John Bowman.[4]
	Feb. 22	Elizabeth,[5] dau. of M[r] John Spearman.
1696	June 19	Tamar,[6] wife of M[r] Henry Smith, Clerk.
	July 6	M[r] Henry Smith,[7] Clerk.
	Aug. 19	Elizabeth,[8] wife of M[r] Thomas Crosby.
	Oct. 20	Dorothy,[9] wife of John Clement, porter.
	Oct.	John,[10] son of John Clement, porter.
	Dec. 19	John Benson.[11]
	Jan. 16	Jane Yap.
	Jan. 23	Morton Blakeston; at Bow Church.
	Feb. 10	Abraham Yap, inf[t].
	Feb. 19	Elizabeth Martin.
		(Abra. Yap, sacrista, Feb. xi. succeeded M[r] Woodmas.)
1697	May 11	Ellenor Lewins; Tuesday.
	May 24	Elizabeth Morton,[12] dau. of D[r] Morton; Affidavit.
	Aug. 8	James Smart, sen., one of the lay-clerks of the Cathedr[l]; Sunday.
	Nov. 11	Jo. Martin, Minor Can'on of the Cath. Ch. of Durham.

---

[1] She was elder dau. and coheiress of Thomas Moore, gent., owner of large fisheries on the south side of the Tweed, and was widow of Nicholas Shuttleworth, of Forcet, co. York, and Durham, Esq.—the first of that family there settled—to whom she was married 28 Sep. 1671 at St. Oswald's. See the burials of her son 2 Oct. 1704, and her sister 22 March 1701-2.

[2] She was married, as Jane Hutchinson, at St. Oswald's, 12 Nov. 1643, to Arthur Phillipps, gent., whose burial see 30 May 1671.

[3] See her baptism 29 Sep. 1692, and her father's burial 17 Jan. 1723-4.

[4] See his wife's burial 25 March 1690, and baptisms of his children in Index.

[5] She was baptized 4 June 1695 at St. Mary-le-Bow. See her father's baptism 28 March 1672.

[6] See her husband's burial next entry.

[7] See his baptism 10 Feb. 1642-3. He was Rector of St. Mary's in the South Bailey. He appears to have been given to drink, and was often admonished by the Dean and Chapter on that head, and was perhaps suspended for some time. See preceding entry and his children's burials 9 Jan. 1678-9 and 2 Feb. 1687-8.

[8] See her marriage 9 Oct. 1681. She was a dau. of Ambrose Myers, whose burial see 18 March 1666-7. See her husband's burial 9 Nov. 1707.

[9] See her husband's burial 11 May 1710.

[10] See preceding entry.

[11] See his first wife's burial 30 June 1682, and his children's baptisms 21 July 1685 and 21 Sep. 1686.

[12] See her baptism 22 April 1688. She was youngest child of Dr. Morton by his first wife, whose burial see 22 Sep. 1688.

CATHEDRAL CHURCH AT DURHAM. 109

1697	Nov. 23	Will. Hawkins, one of the lay clerks of ye Cath. Ch. of Durh.
	Feb. 24	Mr John Eldridg.[1]
	Feb. 24	Mrs Jane Rowe,[2] widow of Rich. Rowe.
1698	Sep. 22	Eliz.,[3] dau. of Dr Dobson.
	Oct. 7	Mary,[4] wife of Will. Horsman.
	Nov. 21	Rich. Wakelin.[5]
	Dec. 5	Mary,[6] dau. of Dr Smith.
	Feb. 9	Mr Cuth. Hall.
	Feb.	A woman in ye jail.
1699	April 9	Mrs Longfield.
	April 13	Barbara,[7] wife of Abra. Yapp, Clerk.
	Aug. 2	George Bullock.[8]
	Aug. 9	....[9] son of Dr Smith.
	Sep. 27	John[10] (" Robert " *erased*), son of Gilbert Spearman.
	Oct. 2	Mrs Hester Nichols,[11] widow.
	Jan. 14	Dame Eliz. Burton.[12]

[1] See his wife's burial 2 Aug. 1691.

[2] She was the only dau. of Barnabas Hutchinson, Attorney and Proctor. Her M.I. says she died 14 Feb. 1700, which of course must be wrong, and was probably inscribed long after her death. The same altar-tomb, now almost illegible, described her father as dying 14 March 1633, and Jane his wife 28 Feb. 1699, æt. 102, but both were probably buried at St. Mary-le-Bow, to which Barnabas was a benefactor by will. See her husband's burial 6 Jan. 1678-9.

[3] See her baptism same day.

[4] She was dau. of Timothy Brigham, whose burial see 26 Aug. 1678, and was married at St. Oswald's 21 Sep. 1669. See her husband's burial 17 Jan. 1723-4. [Mary Horsman, widow, buried 26 Dec. 1684; and Mary Horsman, spinster, buried 9 Sep. 1684 at St. Oswald's.]

[5] He was baptized at St. Mary-le-Bow 29 March 1657, the son of the Rev. Richard Wikelin, or Waiklinge, Minor Canon, whose burial see 30 Oct. 1661.

[6] See her baptism 26 Jan. 1697-8.

[7] In her marriage licence, dated 24 Feb. 1693, she is termed Barbara Taylor, spinster. She is called sister, 1698, by John Taylor, a relation perhaps of Thomas Taylor, whose marriage with Mary Yapp see 13 Feb. 1699-1700. See burial of her husband, to whom she was first wife, 23 Dec. 1728.

[8] See burial of his first wife 12 May 1678, and his second marriage 22 Oct. 1679.

[9] See baptism same day.

[10] See his mother's burial 26 Jan. 1700-1.

[11] See her husband's burial 6 June 1681.

[12] She was the second dau. of Dr. Cosin, Bishop of Durham (whose burial see 29 May 1672), and was born 11 and baptized 17 June 1632 at Brancepeth. She married, firstly, Henry Hutton, of Goldsborough, co. York, Esq. (son of Sir Richard Hutton), by whom she had a dau. Frances, whose burial see 26 Jan. 1677-8; secondly, Sir Thomas Burton, Knt., of Brampton, Westmorland, by whom she had two sons, Richard Burton (of whom, for clearness sake, more below), and Henry Burton, who was buried 13 Jan. 1661-2 at St. Andrew's Auckland; thirdly, 23 Dec. 1662, at St. Andrew's Auckland, Samuel Davison, of Wingate, co. Pal., Esq., who was buried 15 April 1671 in the chapel at Auckland, much to the displeasure of the Bishop, his father-in-law, during his absence in London; fourthly she married Isaac Basire, Esq., the burial of whose son by her see 2 May 1678. The Rev. Richard Burton, mentioned above, left a widow, "Mrs. Mary Burton," buried at St. Oswald's 21 March 1720-21. Their son Richard Burton, Esq., lived, *jure uxoris*, at Elemore Hall, having married at Pittington, 21 April 1729, Frances, only dau. of Thomas Mitford, Esq. He died s.p. and was buried 24 Feb. 1740-41 at St. Oswald's, where his widow also was buried 6 Feb. 1758.

1700	Aug. 21	Jo., son of Henry Smith.
	Aug. 26	Tho. Crosby, son of Francis Crosby.
	Oct. 16	John,[1] son of M[r] Cuthbert's.
	Oct. 18	Charles,[2] son of M[r] Cuthbert's.
	Oct. 27	M[rs] Ann Guorden,[3] wife of M[r] Alderman Guorden's.
	Nov. 30	M[r] Tho. Sherman, Minor Canon; S[t] Andrew day.
	Dec. 16	John Fairlesse, Virger.
	Dec. 17	John Massam.[4]
	Dec. 18	Jane, y[e] wife of John Fairlesse.
	Jan. 6	Sudbury Wilson.[5]
	Jan. 26	Mary,[6] wife of M[r] Gilbert Spearman.
1701	April 16	Ellenor Shaw,[7] wife of Alexander Shaw.
	April 25	Gilbert,[8] son of M[r] Gilbert Spearman.
	Mar. 22	Marg. Huddleston,[9] widow, of Elvet Parish.
1702	May 6	Ann,[10] dau. of M[r] Geo. Dixon.

[1] Eldest son of John Cuthbert, Esq., by his wife Dorothy Spearman, whose baptism see 29 June 1670.

[2] Fifth son of John Cuthbert, Esq. See previous entry.

[3] Also entered in St. Nicholas Register—"in the Minster yard." She was second wife, and married as "Mrs. Anne Smith, sp[r]," to Mr. Gordon at St. Oswald's 29 July 1684. Alderman John Gordon, mercer, was son of James Gordon, gent., of Durham and Hurworth-on-Tees, was apprenticed 20 March 1663, and admitted free of the Mercers' Company 21 May 1672. He was made Alderman 24 May 1689, being then of Shacklock Hall (a house near "The Sands," Durham), and Mayor 1695. He married, firstly, Isabella, dau. and coheir of Robert Bromley, Esq., of Nesbett, co. Pal., at Hesilden 24 July 1677 (by whom he had two children), who was buried at St. Nicholas 1 Feb. 1679-80; secondly as above; and thirdly, "Mrs. Ann Tatam" [? widow of "Mr. Robert Tatam, of St. Nicholas, draper taylor," buried at St. Oswald's 17 Nov. 1699], at St. Nicholas 23 Nov. 1701, who was buried there 30 April 1706, dying 29th. The Alderman died 9 and was buried with his last wife 11 April 1713. See marriage also of Thomas Brumley and Anne Gordon 3 Feb. 1678-9.

[4] [Mary, dau. of Mr. John Massam, baptized 9 July 1693 at St. Nicholas.]

[5] Youngest son of William Wilson, Spiritual Chancellor of the Diocese (whose burial see 7 Dec. 1690), and was baptized at St. Mary-le-Bow 2 July 1688. See his brother's baptism 17 Aug. 1684.

[6] Died 23rd. She was dau. and coheiress of Robert Bromley, of Nesbett, co. Pal., Esq., and was married in 1697. Her descendants quarter, in right of her, Quarterly per fess indented gules and or. See her husband's second marriage 1 Sep. 1701, and her sister's burial 3 Feb. 1705-6, and note to Mrs. Gordon's burial 27 Oct. 1700.

[7] She died, according to Jacob Bee's Diary, 14th, and her burial is also registered, but as on 15th, at St. Oswald's, where also her husband "Mr. Alexander Shaw, musician," was buried 23 July 1706. See their marriage 29 Nov. 1677.

[8] See his mother's burial 26 Jan. 1700-1.

[9] Also registered at St. Oswald's. She was younger dau. and coheiress of Thomas Moore, gent., and widow of Ferdinando Huddleston, by whom she had a son Ferdinando, who married Sarah Watson (she re-married .... Christian) and died s.p., and a dau. Elizabeth, wife of Robert Bruce. See her sister Mrs. Shuttleworth's burial 28 Dec. 1694.

[10] Eldest dau. of George Dixon, of Durham, Attorney-at-Law, by his first wife, Elizabeth, dau. of Alderman Robert Grey, baptized at Bow 5 May 1696. See her mother's burial 6 June 1708, and her father's 3 June 1738. [MS. Ped. by E. A. W.]

CATHEDRAL CHURCH AT DURHAM. 111

1702	May 23	Ossytha,[1] or Psyche, dau. of ye Rev^d Jo. Morton, D.D.
	June 16	John Martin, of St Nicholas Parish.
	Aug. 11	William,[2] son of ye Rever^d Jno Smith, D.D., Prebendary of ye Cath. Church, Dunelm.
	Aug. 16	Mathew,[3] son of Mr Peter Nelson, writ. mast^r.
	Sep. 15	Thomas,[4] son of Abra. Yapp.
	Oct. 13	Jo.,[5] son of Mr Gilbert Spearman.
	Nov. 1	Ann, wife of Zadock Smith,[6] taylour.
	Mar. 16	John Yapp,[7] son of Ellenor Yapp, widow.
1703	Mar. 29	William Werdon,[8] bookseller.
	May 20	Mr Peter Nelson,[9] writing-master.
	Aug. 9	Theophilus,[10] son of Lawyer Cuthbert's.
	Aug. 26	Barbara Hall, a servant to Mrs Reed, wid., living in ye South Bailey.
	Sep. 22	Mr John Spearman,[11] Under-Sheriff.
	Jan. 21	Horatius,[12] son of Tho. Horsman.
	Feb. 23	Mr Robert Smith, widower.

[1] Dau. of Dr. Morton by his second wife, whose burial see 12 Feb. 1724-5. See her half-sister's baptism 22 Aug. 1682.

[2] Query by which wife. See his brother's baptism 25 Oct. 1696.

[3] He was baptized at Bow 30 Sep. 1688. See his father's burial 20 May.

[4] See his parents' marriage 28 Oct. 1700.

[5] Also entered in St. Nicholas Register as "in the Minster yard." See his parents' marriage 28 Oct. 1700.

[6] See baptisms St. Oswald's. She must have been his first wife, for he has children baptized and buried at St. Oswald's later.

[7] See the father's burial 2 Dec. 1691.

[8] See his wife's burial 17 Oct. 1688.

[9] He was Under or Writing Master at the Grammar School. Originally this school was two schools, under different masters who were not responsible to each other, but in time they became united, and the Master of the "petty school" (pro plano cantu et arte scribendi) was appointed and paid by the Master of the Higher School. To restore the schools to their former state was Nelson's great desire, and he was engaged in a long controversy with the Rev. Thomas Rudd, the Head Master, as to the stipend of the Writing or Under Master. Their letters display the rancour and personalities of any newspaper war of to-day. See some further remarks on the Schools in the Appendix. See the burial of Mr. Nelson's wife 28 Jan. 1721-2, and those of his sons' 21 Feb. 1681-2 and 16 Aug. 1702. He has three children baptized at St. Oswald's.

[10] Seventh son of John Cuthbert, Esq., by his wife Dorothy Spearman, whose baptism see 29 June 1670.

[11] Died 21st, aged 58. "A sound and judicious lawyer and antiquary"; he was for twenty-eight years Under Sheriff. He was baptized 16 Jan. 1645-6 at (Tynemouth?), the eldest son of Robert Spearman, gent., of Preston, near Tynemouth, Northumberland. He may be termed the *homo propositus* of his family, for he purchased in 1678 the manor of Thornley, co. Pal., which was for long the seat and is still the property of his descendants. He married 3 Nov. 1663. The births and baptisms of all his children except Michael (whose burial see 14 Dec. 1686) are entered at St. Mary-le-Bow, but consult also this Index. See Pedigree of SPEARMAN in Surtees, vol. i., p. 95, to which these Registers will be found to make some additions and corrections; also Burke's "Landed Gentry." Mr. Spearman's large collection of MSS. is in Bishop Cosin's library at Durham.

[12] The father afterwards Apparitor. See the burial of another child 31 Jan. 1710-11.

1704 April 25 Mrs Moor,[1] widow.
      Oct.   2 Richard Shuttleworth.[2]
      Oct.   4 John Midford,[3] apparitor.
      Nov. 14 Mrs Eliz. Mickleton,[4] wife of Mr Mich. Mickleton.
      Dec.   8 William,[5] son of John Edmundson.
      Jan. 16 Elizab.,[6] dau. of John Edmundson.
      Jan. 26 Mary,[7] dau. of Ellenor Yapp ; St. Paul.
1705 June   5 Mr John Milner,[8] Præcent^r.
      Sep. 15 Geo.,[9] son of Will. Graham, D.D.
      Oct. 14 Will.,[10] son of Mr George Dixon, attorney-at-law.
      Dec. 28 Robert,[11] son of Mr Michael Mickleton.
      Feb.   3 Phyllis,[12] dau. of Mr Brumly, of Nasebet.
      Feb.   5 Mrs Jane Compton, wid.
      Mar. 13 John Denton, barber.
1706 June   9 Higgons,[13] son of Sr Geo. Wheler.
      Dec. 13 Lancelot Lowther,[14] mercer.
1707 Sep.   2 Mrs Mary,[15] wife of Dr Finney.

[1] She was perhaps widow of Thomas Moore, Esq., and mother of Mrs. Shuttleworth and of Mrs. Huddleston, whose burials see 28 Dec. 1694 and 22 March 1701-2 respectively.

[2] He was baptized 17 Dec. 1672 at St. Oswald's, and was eldest son of Nicholas Shuttleworth, Esq. (younger brother of Sir Richard Shuttleworth, of Gawthorp, co. Lancaster), of Forcet, co. York, and Elvet, co. Pal., by his wife Elizabeth Moore, whose burial see 28 Dec. 1694. He died s.p., and his brother Nicholas Shuttleworth, Esq., of Durham, was his devisee.

[3] He was baptized 23 Oct. 1629 at St. Mary-le-Bow, the second son of Robert Mitford, of the North Bailey, gent., by his wife Elizabeth Porter, whose burial see 4 April 1683. He is named in his father's will of 24 Jan. 1666-7. See his wife's burial 18 Feb. 1684-5. He was perhaps married twice ; see burial of " Mrs. Jane Mitford, widow," 11 Feb. 1719-20. See also burials of his children 6 Oct. 1678, 21 June 1681, and 2 Jan. 1734-5. He had, besides, a dau. Dorothy, born 5 and baptized 10 March 1673-4 at Bow, and buried there 28 id. men.

[4] See her marriage 4 July 1687, and her husband's burial 19 Feb. 1710-11. She was dau. of John Spearman, the Under Sheriff, whose burial see 22 Sep. 1703.

[5] John Edmundson and Mary Lamb were married 6 May 1679 at Crossgate. The above child might have been either son or grandson of that marriage. See the burial of John Edmundson, *Senior*, 14 Sep. 1708.

[6] See preceding entry.

[7] See her mother's burial 4 Aug. 1718.

[8] He was perhaps a son of Thomas Milner, Master of the Grammar School, between Nicholas Walton, who resigned about 1628, and Richard Smelt, who occurs as Master in 1633. See his widow's burial 11 March 1730-31, his daughter's 30 Oct. 1686, and nephew's 3 Aug. 1708 ; also Nicholas Barwick's 7 Dec. 1687.

[9] See his brother Richard's baptism 17 Sep. 1689.

[10] Eldest son of George Dixon, Attorney-at-Law, by his first wife. See note to his sister's burial 6 May 1702. [MS. Ped. by E. A. W.]

[11] Baptized at St. Mary-le-Bow 7 March 1695-6. See the father's burial 19 Feb. 1710-11.

[12] Also outered at St. Oswald's, "at ye cathedral." She was dau. and coheiress of Robert Bromley, of Nesbitt, co. Pal., Esq. See her sister Mrs. Spearman's burial 26 Jan. 1700-1.

[13] See his father's burial 23 Jan. 1723-4.

[14] See his marriage 4 June 1698.

[15] She was dau. of .... Davison .... and was first wife to Dr. James Finney, Prebendary, whose burial see 13 March 1726-7.

CATHEDRAL CHURCH AT DURHAM. 113

1707	Oct. 22	Catherine,[1] wife of M[r] John Rawe.
	Nov. 9	Tho. Crosby.[2]
	Feb. 24	Joseph Dixon,[3] Verger.
	Mar. 10	One Mr Gravener, a Physician.
	Mar. 11	John, son of Abra. Yapp.
1708	May 31	John Saxton.[4]
	June 6	Eliz.,[5] wife of Mr Geo. Dixon; laid violent hands on herself, as was supposed.
	July 9	William Yapp.
	Aug. 3	Mr Tho. Milner,[6] nephew to M[r] Jo. Milner, olim Præc. Ecc. Dun[l].
	Sep. 14	John Edmundson,[7] sen[r].
	Oct. 10	Ann,[8] wife of Mr Rich. Baddely.
	Oct. 24	Mr Peter Burrell.
	Dec. 16	Dorothy,[9] wife of Ralph Wilkinson.
	Jan. 16	Mr John Mickleton.[10]
	Mar. 23	Theophilus,[11] son of Mr Gilbert Spearman.
1709	Jan. 26	Joyce Taylor.[12]
1710	May 11	John Clement,[13] College porter.
	June 23	Thomas Simpson,[14] son of John, and grandchild of old Tho. Simpson, then alive and above an 100 years old.

---

[1] She was married 21 Feb. 1688-9, at St. Oswald's, as "M[rs] Catherine Lisle, of Litle S[t] Maries," to Mr. Rawe, to whom she was second wife. Her M.I. states she died 21st, leaving her husband (whose burial see 13 Feb. 1721-2) "mœrens, deflens, dolens."

[2] He was baptized 1 June 1658 at St. Oswald's, the eldest son of Francis Crosby, Esq. (buried 23 Dec. 1700 at St. Oswald's), Clerk of the Peace, co. Pal., by Ann (buried 9 Oct. 1700 at St. Oswald's), dau. of John Richardson, Esq. (she was married 17 April 1655 at St. Oswald's). He was an Attorney-at-Law, and, according to Sir Cuthbert Sharp, succeeded his father 4 June 1679, when yet under age, as Clerk of the Peace. Ten children of "Mr. John Crosby," Attorney, evidently a brother of Francis above mentioned, occur at St. Oswald's. This Thomas Crosby had by his wife, whose burial see 19 Aug. 1696, three sons at least, Ambrose, Watson, and Thomas, who were baptized at St. Mary-le-Bow, besides Richard, whose burial see 24 May 1686.

[3] See his widow's burial 11 Nov. 1711.

[4] See a burial 5 Nov. 1758.

[5] She was the dau. of Alderman Robert Grey and Ann his wife, of Claypath, Durham. She was married 11 June 1695, and had three sons and four daughters. [MS. Ped. by E. A. W.] See also Pedigree of GREY, under "Scurfield of Hurworth," in Burke's "Landed Gentry."

[6] See his said uncle's burial 5 June 1705.

[7] See note to baptism of William Edmundson 8 Dec. 1704, and burial of "Widow Edmundson" 2 Feb. 1748-9.

[8] See her first marriage 8 Feb. 1678-9, and her second marriage 23 Dec. 1699 to Richard Baddely, whose burial see 16 Jan. 1713-14.

[9] See her marriage 2 Dec. 1697.

[10] He was baptized at Bow 5 March 1665-6, and was of Durham, gent. See his father's burial 29 Aug. 1669, and his two children's burials 20 Aug. 1684 and 16 July 1710.

[11] See his parents' marriage 1 Sep. 1701.

[12] See her marriage 29 Aug. 1682. She was dau. of the Rev. John Dury, or Drury, Epistoler. See the baptism of her sister June 1655, and that of a nephew 25 Sep. 1681.

[13] See his first wife's burial 20 Oct. 1696. He married secondly, 8 Sep. 1698, by licence, at St. Oswald's, Elizabeth Moss, "of Branspeth par." See his son's burial 4 March 1732-3.

[14] See note to burial of Jo. Simpson 10 June 1688.

Q

1710	July 16	Ann Mickleton,[1] dau. of M[r] John Mickleton, deceased.
	Sep. 21	Jane Langstaff, serv[t] to M[dm] Ann Bowes, in y[e] College.
	Jan. 31	Katherine,[2] dau. of Tho. Horsman, Appar[r].
	Feb. 19	Mr. Michael Mickleton,[3] of Crook Hall.
	Mar. 16	Sarah,[4] dau. of M[r] Geo. Dixon, attorney-at-law.
1711	Mar. 25	M[r] Thomas Blakiston.[5]
	June 13	Mary Bullock, wid.
	Aug. 19	Katherine Taylor, wid.
	Oct. 31	Isabel Simpson,[6] wid.
	Nov. 11	Joseph Dixon's[7] widow, late Virger.
		(Robert Lecke, Sacrist, Nov. 20, 1711.)
	Mar. 14	Tho. Smurfoot, a beadsman, aged 85.
1712	May 20	M[rs] Mary Hilton.
	Aug. 1	Francis,[8] son of M[r] Geo. Dixon, attourney.
	Dec. 2	M[r] Ralph Clark.
	Dec. 9	Horace Alston,[9] Esq[r], nephew to the L[d] Crew.
1713	June 6	Margaret,[10] wife of W[m] Turner, Clerk.
	Aug. 20	William,[11] son of W[m] Turner, Clerk.

[1] See her baptism 9 Aug. 1681, and her father's burial 16 Jan. 1708-9.

[2] The father (probably a son of William Horseman, buried 17 Jan. 1723-4), apparently succeeded John Baty as Apparitor 1710. See the burial of another child 21 Jan. 1703-4.

[3] See his wife's burial 14 Nov. 1704.

[4] Baptized at Bow 26 Dec. 1710. She was the eldest dau. of Mr. George Dixon by his second wife Sarah, dau. of Francis Johnson, of Newcastle, to whom he was married 2 Feb. 1709. See the mother's burial 6 March 1765. [MS. Ped. by E. A. W.]

[5] Son of Henry Blakiston, whose burial see 15 May 1683, by his wife Elizabeth, second dau. and coheiress of William Blakiston, of York, gent. He was Bailiff of Darlington in 1699. He married Frances, dau. and coheiress of Bishop Cosin, and widow of Charles Gerard, Esq. (buried at Darlington 15 April 1665), by whom he had an only child Frances, whose burial see 4 April 1679. The place of their marriage is not known, and it has truly been said that the Bishop "was not altogether happy in his family" (Low's "Diocesan History," p. 281), for, in a letter to Miles Stapylton, Esq. (see his burial 10 May 1685), 19 March 1667-8, he says, "I rec[d] the draught of the lease for Bedbourne parke, etc. You have mentioned my daughter, not as the relict of Charles Gerrard, but as the wife of T. B., which I have not yet acknowledged, nor was it ever made knowne to mee that they were legally married, and whensoever it shall be so made knowne I professe beforehand that I am extreamly displeased with it, for I was most treacherously used, and for my part shall never owne it." "T. B." died 22 March, æt. 73, and his will is dated 2 Aug. 1706. His wife Frances was buried at Darlington 10 March 1668-9.

[6] See her husband's burial 15 May 1683.

[7] See her marriage 19 July 1699, and her husband's burial 24 Feb. 1707-8.

[8] Baptized at Bow 22 May 1712. He was the eldest son of Mr. George Dixon by his second wife. See note to his sister's burial 16 March 1710. [MS. Ped. by E. A. W.]

[9] He was *great*-nephew to Lord Crew, Bishop of Durham, being the son of Sir Rowland Alston, second Bart., of Odell, Beds, by his wife Temperance, dau. of Thomas, second Lord Crew, older brother of the Prelate and his immediate predecessor in the title. He was appointed Under Sheriff on the death of Spearman 1703, "during the Bishop's pleasure." See the Bishop's marriage 23 July 1700.

[10] First wife of the Rev. William Parthericke Turner, Minor Canon. See her marriage 1 Nov. 1708.

[11] See preceding entry.

1713	Jan.	16	Mr Richard Baddelye.[1]
			Elizabeth Lamb, widow.
1714	June	2	Mrs Jane Blakiston.[2]
	Nov.	1	George, son of John Bullock.
	Dec.	18	Dorothy,[3] dau. of Mr Robt Spearman.
	Feb.	22	Cuthbert Bowes,[4] taylor.
	Mar.	13	Mr Phinehas Baddeley.
	Mar.	15	Mr Geo. Mitford,[5] a Clergyman.
	Mar.	18	Mr Thomas Skepper.[6]
1715	Sep.	8	Mary,[7] dau. of Mr Geo. Dixon.
	Nov.	7	Mr Benjamin Jackson, singing-man.
	Nov.	13	Madam Anne Bowes.[8]
1716	April	27	Mary,[9] daughter of Mr Gilbert Spearman.
	Nov.	6	Mr Tho. Battersbye.[10]
			(John Powell, Sacrist, 9^{ber} ye 20th, 1716.)
	Feb.	21	John Bell, Virger, & Steward to Dean Mountagu.
1717	May	17	Jane,[11] dau. of Sr George Wheler.
	Sep.	28	Susanna Smith.[12]
1718	April	15	Mr Christopher Mickleton,[13] on ye Palace Green.

[1] Son of Mr. Richard Baddeley, of whom see note to burial of William Bridges 15 Aug. 1634. See his wife's burial 10 Oct. 1708.

[2] She was dau. of Henry Blakiston, Esq. (whose burial see 15 May 1683), by his wife Elizabeth Blakiston. Her brother Gabriel Blakiston, Rector of Danby-upon-Wiske, co. York, in his will, dated 17 Sep. 1719, and proved at York 21 Aug. 1721, leaves to "my friend Mrs. Rowell, widow of Mr. John Rowell, late of Durham, for and in respect of her care of my dear sister Mrs. Jane Blakiston in her last sickness," 10 guineas.

[3] See her father's burial 20 Oct. 1728.

[4] Cuthbert Bowes, son of Edward Bowes, of Darlington, admitted free of Draper and Taylors' Company, Durham, 15 June 1666. See his wife's burial 1 Dec. 1694; see also burials of his children 21 July 1679 and 15 Sep. 1681. Edward, son of Cuthbert Bowes, was admitted Draper and Taylor 1699.

[5] A George Mitford graduated at Christ College, Cambridge, B.A. 1688.

[6] He was baptized 12 Feb. 1634-5 at St. Mary-le-Bow, the fourth son of Moses Skepper, Clerk of the Halmote Court, and grandson of Christopher Skepper, who entered his pedigree and arms at St. George's Visitation 1615. See his daughters' burials 15 Jan. 1685-6 and 15 Jan. 1733-4.

[7] Baptized at Bow 27 Dec. 1713. See note to her sister's burial 16 March 1710. [MS. Ped. by E. A. W.]

[8] See her second marriage 30 Sep. 1706.

[9] Dau. of Mr. Spearman by his second marriage, which see 1 Sep. 1701.

[10] He was appointed Master of the Grammar School, about 16 July 1666, in succession to the Rev. Elias Smith, and resigned about 1690. He is buried in the Cathedral Yard near the north porch. His grave-cover has clearly never had an inscription, but bears the arms, a saltire paly, and a ram passant for crest. See his wife's burial 26 April 1690, and consult Index. [Richard Battersby was an "intruder" to the Rectory of Haughton. Surtees, vol. iii., p. 342.]

[11] See her father's burial 23 Jan. 1723-4.

[12] Perhaps a dau. of the Rev. Elias Smith (see his burial 9 Dec. 1676) and his wife Susanna, but her baptism is not here.

[13] See his baptism 19 June 1664, and his father's burial 29 Aug. 1669. The name of his father, who had been dead nearly fifty years, being given is unusual, but it was doubtless to distinguish him from his great-nephew, whose burial see 1720.

1718	Aug. 4	Ellenor Yapp,[1] widow.
	Feb. 27	Alice Stagge,[2] widow.
1719	April 19	M[r] John Powell,[3] Minor Canon of the Cathedral & Sacrist thereof.
	April 19	.... Massam.

(Jo. Waring, Sacrist, Nov. 20, 1719.)

	Dec. 15	Anne Rydley, serv[t] to M[rs] Eliz. Burrell, widow.
	Feb. 11	M[rs] Jane Midford,[4] widow.
1720	April 2	Anne Denton,[5] widow, a beadswoman, aged 106.
	April 7	Marg[t], daughter of M[r] Christopher Mickleton.
	April 30	M[r] Christopher Mickleton.
	June 15	M[r] Peter Burrell,[6] of South Bailey.
	July 10	Thamar, wife of Will. Laye, singing-man.
	Aug. 25	Christopher, son of M[r] Christopher Mickleton.
	Oct. 12	M[rs] Smith, wife of M[r] Posthumus Smith.
	Jan. 28	Thomas,[7] son of D[r] Morton, Prebendary of Durham.
	Mar. 23	M[r] Ralph Hutton.
1721	May 8	John,[8] son of John Waring.
	July 16	M[rs] Kirkby,[9] widow.
	Nov. 17	Cath. Wilson.

(W[m] Parthericke Turner, Sacrist, Nov. 20, 1721.)

	Dec. 19	M[rs] Robinson, a midwife.
	Jan. 16	D[r] John Bowes, Prebendary.
	Jan. 28	M[rs] Nelson,[10] a widow.
	Feb. 7	M[r] John Mickleton,[11] of Crookhall.
	Feb. 13	John Rowe,[12] Esq.
1722	July 4	John,[13] son of M[r] Peter Burrell.

---

[1] See her marriage 3 Feb. 1667-8, and her husband's burial 2 Dec. 1691.
[2] See her marriage 29 Aug. 1677. See Surtees, vol. iv., part ii., p. 160.
[3] See his daughter's burial 8 July 1784.
[4] Perhaps second wife of John Mitford, buried 4 Oct. 1704.
[5] See note to burial of John Denton 13 March 1705-6.
[6] See his father's burial 24 Oct. 1708. He married, firstly, 12 Oct. 1686, at St. Giles, Elizabeth, dau. of Lancelot Hilton, Esq., of Durham. See his second marriage 16 Feb. 1709-10. See the burial of his son-in-law John Garth 27 Jan. 1723-4, and the marriage of his dau. 2 Feb. 1719-20.
[7] See his baptism 26 June 1694.
[8] See his baptism 13 March 1720-21.
[9] See her marriage 27 May 1674, and her husband's burial 19 March 1668-9.
[10] Her burial is also entered at St. Oswald's (" widow of M[r] Peter Nelson, schole-master, dy'd here, & was bury'd in y[e] Cathedr[l] "). She was married at Long Newton, co. Pal., 1 June 1669— " Peter Nelson, of Durham, scrivener, and Ann Thorp, of Yarm."
[11] See his father's burial 19 Feb. 1710-11. He was born at Crookhall 1689, and died unmarried.
[12] Died 11th. He was aged 18 at Dugdale's Visitation Aug. 1666. His first wife, Annabella, was buried 16 Oct. 1688 at St. Oswald's, where he has four children by her baptized, and eight by his second wife (whose burial see 22 Oct. 1707), and he is there invariably called " John Raw, Esq." See burials of his father 6 Jan. 1677-8, a son 29 June 1683, a dau. 9 Jan. 1685-6, and another son 29 Oct. 1769.
[13] See his father's burial 15 June 1720.

CATHEDRAL CHURCH AT DURHAM. 117

1722	Sep. 13	Wm Smith, son of Mr Posthumus Smith, Register to the Dean & Chapt.
	Dec. 2	Mrs Jane Hilton, wife of Mr Cuth. Hilton.
	Feb. 18	Eliz.,[1] wife of Geo. Garry, bellringer.
	Feb. 23	Abigail,[2] Relict of Mr John Mickleton.
	Mar. 2	Geo,[3] son of Geo. Garry, bellringer.
1723	Jan. 17	Wm Horseman,[4] a beadsman.
	Jan. 23	Sr Geo. Wheler,[5] Prebendary, Rector of Houghton-le-Spring.
	Jan. 27	Mr John Garth,[6] of Headlam.
	Mar. 2	Mary Bullock,[7] wife of Jo. Bullock, taylor.
1724	Sep. 8	Mr Cuthbert Hilton, son of Mr Robt Hilton, Register.
	Nov. 22	Tho. Stonehewer, son of Mr Rich. Stonehewer.
	Dec. 25	Ann, daughter of ye Revd Mr Ab^m Yapp.
	Feb. 2	George Garry,[8] bellringer.
	Feb. 12	Ositha,[9] 2^d wife of Jo. Morton, D.D., Preb.
1725	June 4	Dr William Hartwell,[10] Prebendary.
		Mr Posthumus Smith, Register to ye Dean & Chapter.
	Dec. 25	Isabel Featherstone.
1726	April 5	Eleanor Barwicke,[11] widow.
	April 22	Sam. Clarke, writing-master.
	May 1	Margarett Scruton.[12]
	June 30	Mrs Read, wid.
	July 31	Mr Brabant.
	Sep. 25	James Garth.[13]

(Robt Pigot, Sacrist, Novr ye 20th, 1726.)

[1] See the husband's burial 2 Feb. 1724-5.
[2] See her husband's burial 16 Jan. 1708-9.
[3] See the father's burial 2 Feb. 1724-5.
[4] See his wife's burial 7 Oct. 1698, and other baptisms and burials of his family in Index.
[5] He was born at Breda 1650, where his Royalist parents were in exile. He was the son of Colonel Charles Wheler of the King's Guards, and of Charing, Kent, by Anne, dau. of John Hutchin, Esq., of Egerton. He was knighted at Winchester 11 Sep. 1682. He married Grace (she died 20 April 1703), dau. of Sir Thomas Higgons, Knt., by Bridget, dau. of Sir Bevil Granville and sister to Dean Granville, the burial of whose wife see 14 Oct. 1691. See burial of a son 9 June 1706. M.I. (See also Le Neve's "Knights," Harleian Society's Publications, Vol. VIII., p. 366.)
[6] He married at St. Mary-le-Bow (also entered at St. Oswald's), 2 Feb. 1713-14, Margaret, dau. of Peter Burrell, Esq., whose burial see 24 Oct. 1708. She re-married, as fourth wife, James, first Lord D'Arcy, of Navan, Ireland, but died s.p. 1758. See burial of her sister Mrs. Bowlby 15 Aug. 1783.
[7] The husband perhaps a son of George Bullock, whose burial see 2 Aug. 1699.
[8] See his wife's burial 18 Feb. and his son's 2 March 1722-3.
[9] Her maiden name was Robinson. See note to Dulcibella Morton's baptism 22 Aug. 1682, and her children's burials 23 May 1702 and 28 Jan. 1720-21.
[10] He married, 18 Aug. 1702, at St. Nicholas, Newcastle, "Mrs Frances Marley," sole Ex'or and legatee of Henry Marley, of Newcastle, merchant, who died 1700.
[11] See her marriage 21 Sep. 1667, and her husband's burial 7 Dec. 1687.
[12] A fragment of her headstone still remains, recording that she died May 1, aged 67.
[13] A son of John Garth, Esq., whose burial see 27 Jan. 1723-4.

1726	Dec. 17	Margarett,[1] dau. of y⁰ Rev⁴ M⁰ John Waring, Præcentor.
	Mar. 13	D⁰ James Finney,[2] Prebendary.
1727	Mar. 28	Elizabeth Waugh.
	April 2	M⁰⁰ Ann Barkhurst.
	May 9	Mary,[3] dau. of M⁰ Tho. Bowlby.
	June 27	Isabel,[4] dau. of Jacob Readshaw.
	Mar. 22	Mary, wife of M⁰ Tho. Hopper.
1728	Mar. 27	Jane Bell.
	Oct. 7	Elizabeth, dau. of y⁰ Rev⁴ M⁰ John Rymer.[5]
	Oct. 20	M⁰ Robert Spearman.[6]
	Dec. 23	M⁰ Abraham Yapp,[7] formerly Minor Canon of this Church.
1729	May 11	M⁰⁰ Mary Smith, wid. of y⁰ late D⁰ Smith, Prebend. of this Church.
	Aug. 4	John, son of John Bullock.
	Aug. 21	Thomas, son of Francis Walker.
	Sep. 21	Margarett,[8] dau. of Hammond Clement.
1730	Aug. 24	Ann Clarke, wid.
	Oct. 26	M⁰ Thomas Bowlby.[9]
	Nov. 4	George Snowden.
	Nov. 24	M⁰ William Smith.
	Mar. 8	George Readshaw.
	Mar. 11	M⁰⁰ Joanna Milner,[10] wid.
1731	April 27	Isabel Wood,[11] wid.

[1] See her brother's baptism 13 March 1720-21.

[2] He was third son of William Fynney, or Finney, Esq., of Cheddleton, Staffs., by his wife Mary, dau. of Richard Bateman, Esq., of Hartington Hall, Derbyshire. See his first wife's burial 2 Sep. 1707, and his second marriage 6 Oct. 1709. He died s.p., and by his will, dated 20 Feb. 1726-7, left £2500 for two £40 Fellowships and two £10 Scholarships at Worcester College, Oxon, for natives of Staffordshire, and, in default, natives of co. Durham, but the Court of Chancery decided, 25 Jan. 1738, that only the former are eligible. ("Liber Scholasticus.")

[3] Born 22nd and baptized 26 July 1725 at St. Mary-le-Bow, eldest dau. of Mr. Thomas Bowlby, of the City of Durham, Attorney-at-Law (see his burial 26 Oct. 1730), by Mary his wife, dau. and coheiress of Peter Burrell, Esq., of Durham. [MS. Ped. by E. A. W.]

[4] See (presumably) the father's burial 25 July 1744.

[5] See her baptism 15 Nov. 1715, and her father's burial 15 Feb. 1732-3.

[6] He was younger brother of John Spearman the Under Sheriff, whose burial see 22 Sep. 1703. See his marriage 11 Dec. 1701; his widow's burial 14 March 1737-8; that of a dau. 18 Dec. 1714; and that of his granddau. Mrs. Fenwick 19 June 1838.

[7] Probably born at his mother's home, Hilton in Staindropshire, co. Pal. He entered at Trinity College, Cambridge, 8 Feb. 1686-7, aged 18, and graduated B.A. 1690; M.A. 1695; Minor Canon and, Feb. 1697, Sacrist. See his father's burial 2 Dec. 1691, his first wife's 13 April 1699, and his widow's 17 Oct. 1732.

[8] See her baptism 14 July 1729, and father's burial 4 March 1732-3.

[9] Son of Richard Bowlby, merchant, of Stockton, and Mayor thereof in 1707, by Frances, dau. of Nicholas Swainston (marriage licence 18 Oct. 1697). Mr. Thomas Bowlby married Mary, youngest dau. and coheiress of Peter Burrell, Esq., of Durham (by his wife Elizabeth, dau. of Lancelot Hilton, of Durham), whom he married at St. Giles 23 May 1688. [MS. Ped. by E. A. W.]

[10] See her marriage 4 Nov. 1675, and husband's burial 5 June 1705.

[11] Widow (presumably) of John Wood, College gardener. See baptism of their children 12 June 1684 aud 20 Jan. 1686-7.

CATHEDRAL CHURCH AT DURHAM. 119

1731	June 9	Frances,[1] wife of M[r] James Hesletine.
	Aug. 20	Robert Denton.[2]
	Sep. 26	Exton Sayer,[3] LL.D., & Spiritual Chancellour.
	Oct. 8	James Hayes.
	Nov. 24	M[r] John Smith.
	Jan. 19	John Forster.
1732	Oct. 17	M[rs] Ann Yapp,[4] wid. of y[e] Rev[d] M[r] Abr. Yapp.
	Dec. 7	M[rs] Jane Hilton, wid.
	Jan. 11	Mary, wife of y[e] Rev[d] M[r] Edward Gregory.
	Feb. 15	Y[e] Rev[d] M[r] John Rymer.[5]
	Mar. 4	Hammond Clement.[6]
1733	April 2	Alice Massam,[7] wid.
	Nov. 27	Grace, wife of M[r] William Lofthouse.
	Jan. 8	Robert,[8] son of M[r] Robert Dixon.
	Jan. 15	Frances Schepper.[9]
	Mar. 18	Robert Johnson.
1734	Nov. 30	Dorothy,[10] wife of y[e] Rev[d] D[r] Tho. Eden, Prebend. of this Church.
	Jan. 2	Mary Mitford.[11]
1735	April 25	John,[12] son of John Denton.
	Jan. 6	Elizabeth Stagg.[13]
1736	Feb. 7	D[r] William Watts,[14] Prebendary.

[1] See her marriage 24 Feb. 1729-30, and her husband's burial 23 June 1763.
[2] See other Dentons in Index.
[3] See EXTON Pedigree in Le Neve's "Knights" (Harleian Society, Vol. VIII., p. 303). He married Catherine, younger dau. of William Talbot, Bishop of Durham 1722—1730 (grandfather of the first Earl Talbot, and ancestor of the present Earl of Shrewsbury and Talbot).
[4] See her marriage, 20 April 1700, to Mr. Yapp, and his burial 23 Dec. 1788; and consult Index for her children and other numerous Yapps.
[5] Died 13th, aged 49. M.A., "Scholarcha Sedgefeldensis"; Master of the Grammar School 1711, on resignation of Rev. Thomas Rud; Lecturer at St. Nicholas 29 Feb. 1719. See baptism of his dau. 15 Nov. 1715, and his widow's burial 2 Jan. 1747-8.
[6] See his baptism 4 Sep. 1692, and his daughter's 14 July 1729; his wife's burial 28 March 1739, and his father's 11 May 1710.
[7] Widow, perhaps, of John Massam, buried 17 Dec. 1700.
[8] The father was, perhaps, an apothecary, and identical with Robert, baptized at Bow 17 Sep. 1700, son of Mr. Robert Dixon (baptized at Crossgate 14 March 1670-71), fourth son of Robert Dixon, gent., of Ramshaw.
[9] Born 23 June 1667 and registered at St. Mary-le-Bow. See her father's burial 18 March 1714-15.
[10] She was previously widow of Robert Shafto, of Whitworth, co. Pal., Esq., M.P., who died s.p., and was dau. of Henry (Dawnay), second Viscount Downe. See her second husband's burial 6 March 1754.
[11] Eldest dau. of John Mitford, whose burial see 4 Oct. 1704. She was born 15 and baptized 19 Aug. 1670 at St. Mary-le-Bow.
[12] See, perhaps, the father's burial 13 March 1705-6.
[13] See other Staggs in Index.
[14] His name is spelt Wats on his monument, which states that he was born "in villâ de Barns-Hall, in agro Eboracensi." He was a Fellow of Lincoln College, Oxford, and Rector of Wolsingham, which he held with his stall. His arms, Or, three bucks passant azure; impaling Gules, a plain cross or, are on his monument. He was aged 50. See his widow's burial 3 Aug. 1748.

REGISTER OF BURIALS IN THE

1737	May 1	Mr Richard Stonehewer, Alderman.
	Nov. 24	Eleanor Horseman.
	Dec. 6	Ann Bell,[1] wid.
	Mar. 14	Mrs Hannah Spearman,[2] wid.
1738	April 22	Ann,[3] dau. of ye Revd Dr Thomas Sharp, Prebendary of this Church.
	May 29	Wadham Chandler, M.A., Spiritual Chancellour & Prebendary of this Church.
	June 3	George Dixon,[4] attorn.
	Oct. 14	The Revd Mr Bryan Turner,[5] Præcentor.
	Dec. 10	Mrs Ann Hunter.
	Feb. 20	Mary, wife of Mr James Hallyburton.
1739	Mar. 28	Priscilla Clement,[6] widow.
	May 30	Catherine,[7] wife of ye Revd Mr Richard Dongworth.
	Jan. 27	Mr Jonathan Storey.
1741	July 21	Mary Atkinson, wid.
	July 26	Mrs Elizabeth Burwell, wid.
	Aug. 30	Elizabeth,[8] dau. of ye late Revd Mr Bryan Turner.
	Dec. 29	Esther Hawkins,[9] wid.
1742	April 13	Richard, son of Mrs Frances Middleton, wid.
	April 25	Mr Thomas Faucet.
	May 7	Mrs Margaret Hilton.
	Nov. 28	Robert Renison.
	Dec. 21	Elizabeth Snowden.
1743	April 28	Walter Pearson.
	April 28	Mrs Mary Stonehewer, wid.
	June 15	Jonathan Hall, S.T.P., Prebendary of this Church.
	June 18	Elizabeth, wife of Joseph Chesterman.
	Oct. 21	Mr Charles Whitaker.
	Dec. 9	Mrs Elizabeth Whitaker, wid., moth. of Char.
1744	July 25	Jacob Readshaw.[10]

[1] See her marriage 23 May 1670.
[2] See her marriage 18 July 1701, and her husband's burial 20 Oct. 1728.
[3] See her baptism 19 April 1737.
[4] Baptized at Crossgate 7 April 1663, was of Durham and of Aykleyheads, Attorney-at-Law, and sometime Town Clerk of Durham. He married, 11 June 1695, Elizabeth, dau. of Alderman Robert Grey, by whom he had three sons and four daughters. See her burial 6 June 1708. He married secondly, 2 Feb. 1709, Sarah, dau. of Francis Johnson, of Newcastle. She died 3 and was buried at the Cathedral 6 March 1765, aged 89. By his second wife he had two sons and three daughters. By his will, dated 2 March 2 George II., his children by his first wife are ignored. [MS. Ped. by E. A. W.]
[5] See also burials of his married daughters 1 Feb. 1791 and 18 Aug. 1808. See the burials of his widow 27 Feb. 1771, and daughters 30 Aug. 1741, 1 Feb. 1791, and 18 Aug. 1808.
[6] See her husband's burial 4 March 1732-3.
[7] She died 27th, aged 29, and was the only dau. of John Cosens, of Waltham Cross, Herts, by his wife Sarah, whose burial see 31 Dec. 1747. See her husband's burial 26 Feb. 1761.
[8] She was baptized at St. Oswald's 17 March 1730-31. See her father's burial 14 Oct. 1738.
[9] See, perhaps, her husband's burial 23 Nov. 1697.
[10] See burial of his dau. (?) 27 June 1727, and of his widow (?) 6 March 1744-5.

1744	Aug. 24	Eleanor Richardson, wid.
	Oct. 23	Margaret Simpson.
	Dec. 17	Mr John Smith.
	Feb. 22	Elizabeth,[1] wife of Arthur Baty.
	Mar. 6	Mary Readshaw,[2] wid.
1745	May 29	Alice Denton,[3] wid.
	Aug. 9	Thomas Baty.[4]
	Dec. 15	Mrs Jane Smart.
	Jan. 2	John Schneeberger, a Swiss Captain of Hirzel's Regiment, & of ye Canton and City of Zurich.
	Feb. 11	Sam. Dav. Joseph de Monceaux d'Autin, a Captain in ye Dutch service, of Hirzel's Regiment.
1746	April 14	Mrs Jane Bowes.[5]
	Sep. 26	Francis Walker.
	Dec. 12	Mr Hilton Shaw,[6] Alderman of Durham.
1747	Aug. 1	Arthur Baty.[7]
	Sep. 2	Mrs Ann Forster, wid.
	Dec. 31	Mrs Sarah Cosins,[8] wid.
	Jan. 2	Mrs Michal Rymer,[9] wid. of ye late Revd Mr John Rymer.
1748	Mar. 28	Thomas Baty.[10]
	May 11	Mrs Elizabeth Hunter.
	Aug. 3	Mrs Mary Watts, wid. of ye late Revd Dr Watts, Prebend. of this Church.
	Sep. 19	Mr John Pye.[11]
		(Samuel Dennis, Sacrist, Nov. 20, 1748.)
	Nov. 28	Martha Turvey.
	Feb. 2	The Widow Edmundson.[12]
1749	June 21	Mary Bell.[13]

[1] See burial of her husband 1 Aug. 1747.
[2] Widow (perhaps) of Jacob, buried 25 July 1744.
[3] Perhaps widow of John Denton, buried 13 March 1705-6.
[4] A Thomas Baty was appointed Master of the Song School 14 Oct. 1720. The marriage, 23 Sep. 1701, of "John Baty and Thomasine Croft, both serv^{ts} to ye Bishop, at ye Castle," and the burial, 28 June 1707, of "John Baty, apparitor;" of "Mrs Thomasine Baty, widow," occur at St. Oswald's.
[5] Also entered at St. Oswald's.
[6] Son of Geoffrey Shaw, of Barnard Castle, by his wife Barbara (whose baptism see 27 Oct. 1670), dau. of Cuthbert Hilton, of Durham, gent. He married, at Stanhope, co. Pal., 3 April 1739, "Mrs. Catherine Rickaby, of Durham," who re-married, at St. Giles, 15 April 1751, "Mr. Richard Lowdon, wid^r."
[7] See burial of his wife (?) 22 Feb. 1744-5, and burial of Thomas Baty 9 Aug. 1745.
[8] Widow of John Cosens, of Waltham Cross, Herts, and mother of Mrs. Dongworth, whose burial see 30 May 1739.
[9] See her husband's burial 15 Feb. 1732-3.
[10] See note to burial of Thomas Baty 9 Aug. 1745.
[11] He married, by licence, at St. Mary's, 6 June 1723, "Mrs. Margaret Burton," who was buried at St. Oswald's 7 Nov. 1727. [A burial of "Mrs. Pye, of Durham, widow," occurs 30 Aug. 1711 at Northallerton.]
[12] See note to burial of William Edmundson 8 Dec. 1704.
[13] Perhaps a dau. of Ann Bell, buried 6 Dec. 1737.

R

REGISTER OF BURIALS IN THE

1750	June 18	Elizabeth Bullock.
	Jan. 27	Geo.,[1] son of M[r] Christ. Johnson.
1751	April 19	Eliz. Rainsford, granddaughter of S[r] Jno. Dolben,[2] Baron[t], Prebendary of this Church.
	Dec. 13	Eliz. Rawlin.
1753	Jan. 4	M[r] W[m] Pye.[3]
	Aug. 18	Elizab[th] Robinson.
1754	Feb. 28	Christopher Readshaw.
	Mar. 6	Rev[nd] D[r] Tho[s] Eden,[4] Prebendary of this Church.
	April 5	M[rs] Jane Mowbray.
	July 20	Walter Pearson.
	Aug. 3	Dorothy Paxton.
1755	Mar. 10	Rev[nd] D[r] Tho. Mangey,[5] Prebendary of this Church.
1756	Jan. 18	Margaret Thompson, widow.
	Jan. 24	Michael Conduit (drown'd).
1757	April 9	Grace Whitaker.
	May 7	John Poole.
	July 2	M[rs] Judith Sharp.[6]
1758	Feb. 2	Thomas Foster, attorney-at-law.
	Mar. 23	Rev[nd] D[r] Thomas Sharp,[7] Prebendary of this Church.
	Nov. 1	M[rs] Jane Rowe.
	Nov. 5	Elioner Sexton, widow.
1760	July 13	Miss Mary Barker.
	Aug. 4	George Elleray.

[1] Born 19 July and baptized 11 Aug. 1749 at St. Mary-le-Bow, eldest son of Christopher Johnson, of Durham, Attorney-at-Law, by Tabitha his wife, youngest dau. of George Dixon, of Aykleyheads, who were married at St. Mary-le-Bow 27 Aug. 1747. [MS. Ped. by E. A. W.]

[2] Sir John Dolben, second Bart., married Elizabeth, dau. of William, fifth Lord Digby, and aunt of William Digby, LL.D., Dean of Durham 1777—1788 (grandfather of the present Peer), and his dau. by her, Elizabeth, married John Nicholls Raynsforth, Esq., of Brixworth, Northants, and was mother of the child above. Sir John Dolben died at Fineden 20 Nov. 1756. ["Dictionary of National Biography," vol. xv., p. 193.]

[3] He was Registrar to the Chapter. His wife Mary was buried at St. Oswald's 15 April 1728.

[4] He was baptized at St. Helen's Auckland, 27 Sep. 1682, the fourth son of Sir Robert Eden, first Bart., of West Auckland, by his wife, Margaret, dau. and heir of John Lambton, of Durham, Esq. He was LL.D., Prebendary of the seventh stall and Official (Feb. 1723-4) to the Dean and Chapter. He died s.p. See his wife's burial 30 Nov. 1734.

[5] Died 6th March 1755-6. D.D., LL.D., and Rector of St. Mildred's, Bread Street, London. He married, in 1728, Dorothy, dau. of John Sharp, Archbishop of York. She died at Dunmow, Essex, 6 March 1755.

[6] Dau. of the Rev. Sir George Wheler, Prebendary of Durham and Rector of Houghton-le-Spring (whose burial see 23 Jan. 1723-4), wife of Archdeacon Sharp, who she married on the 19th of June 1722, and mother of the celebrated philanthropist, Granville Sharp. Born 1700; buried in Galilee Chapel next her father.

[7] Born 12 Dec. 1693 and baptized 1 Jan. 1693-4 at St. Martin's in the Fields; of Trinity College, Cambridge, B.A. 1712; M.A. 1716; D.D. 1729; Rector of Rothbury, Northumberland, 1720; one of Lord Crewe's trustees; Archdeacon of Northumberland (collated 27 Feb. 1722-3); Prebendary of the tenth stall in Durham Cathedral (installed 1 Dec. 1732), and Prebendary of York and Southwell; Official to the Dean and Chapter of Durham 1755. Died 16 March 1758, buried in the Galilee Chapel.

1760	Dec. 31	R^d Dr Wadham Knatchbull.[1]
1761	Feb. 26	The Revnd Mr Richd Dongworth.[2]
1762	Jan. 14	Mrs Margaret Moubray.
	April 15	Mrs Elizabeth Davison.[3]
1763	May 31	Mrs Martha Fielding.[4]
	June 1	Mrs Frances Middleton, widow.
	June 11	Elizabeth Pearson.
	June 23	Mr James Hesletine,[5] Organist.
1764	April 11	Mr John Dixon,[6] attorney-at-law.
	Sep. 26	Mr Robert Doddesly,[7] stationer in London.
1765	Mar. 6	Mrs Sarah Dixon,[8] widow.
	Oct. 7	Mrs Dorothy Mickleton, widow.
1766	Nov. 24	Mrs Sarah Dennis,[9] wife of the Revnd Mr Dennis, Sacrist of this Church.
1767	May 15	Mr Joseph Foster.[10]
	June 26	Mrs Cuthbert,[11] widow.
	Sep. 2	W^m,[12] the son of Thomas Hogg.
	Dec. 20	Thomas Paxton.
1768	April 21	Elizabeth Wardle.[13]

[1] He was a younger son of Sir Edward Knatchbull, M.P., fourth Bart. (ancestor of the present Baronet and of Lord Brabourne), by his wife Alice, dau. of John Wyndham, Esq., and granddau. of Sir Wadham Wyndham, a Judge of the Common Pleas Court. He (then "of Chilham, Kent"), married, 8 July 1743, at the private chapel of Somerset House, London, Harriett, dau. of Charles Parry, Esq. ("of Oakfield, Berks," she is described). He was LL.D. and Spiritual Chancellor of the diocese.

[2] M.A. and Master of Grammar School Dec. 1732, and Vicar of Billingham; he died 23rd, aged 58. His altar-tomb exists, but the inscription is nearly illegible. See his wife's burial 30 May 1739, and sister's 17 June 1779.

[3] Died 10th. She was dau. of William Davison, of Beamish, co. Pal., Esq., by his first wife Elizabeth, sister of Sir Benjamin Rawling. Her father re-married Dulcibella Morton, whose baptism see 22 Aug. 1682. Her will is dated 1 March 1762. M.I. at St. Oswald.

[4] Of the North Bailey; dau. of Israel Feilding, of Startforth, Esq., who was buried at St. Martin's in the Fields, London, 5 June 1723. [MS. Ped. by E. A. W.]

[5] See his marriage 24 Feb. 1729-30, and his wife's burial 9 June 1731.

[6] Born and baptized 11 March 1714-15 at Bow, second son of George Dixon, of Durham, by his second wife Sarah Johnson. See their burials 3 June 1738 and 6 March 1765.

[7] *Recte* Dodsley, the publisher and poet, born in 1703. [See "Dictionary of National Biography," vol. xv., p. 170.]

[8] Second wife of George Dixon, Esq., of Durham and Aykleyheads, whose burial see 3 June 1738. She was the dau. of Francis Johnson, of Newcastle, Esq., by his wife Eleanor, dau. of Richard Bowser, of Auckland. [MS. Ped. by E. A. W.]

[9] See her husband's burial 14 Nov. 1775.   [10] See his marriage 17 May 1733.

[11] Dorothy, widow of the Rev. Richard Cuthbert, Vicar of Kendal (to whom she married 16 June 1735 at Houghton-le-Spring), and dau. of Christopher Mickleton, of Durham, gent. She was baptized 21 March 1715-16; see also the baptism of her husband's mother, Dorothy Spearman, 29 June 1670. Mrs. Cuthbert had a son George, who died about 1733, and a dau., whose burial see 6 Sep. 1796. Her husband died 7 Nov. 1744, æt. 48, at Kendal.

[12] See his baptism 13 March 1767.

[13] She was the dau. of Christopher Mickleton, of Durham, gent., and married first (articles before marriage dated 11 Sep. 1735) Richard Wilkinson, of New Elvet, who died in 1737. She married secondly, 5 June 1759, at St. Mary-le-Bow, Christopher Wardell, gent. [MS. Ped. by E. A. W.]

REGISTER OF BURIALS IN THE

1768 May 12   The Revnd Dr Bland,[1] Prebendary of this Church.
      June 29   Ch^{l},[2] the infant dau. of ye Revnd Mr Weston, Prebendary of this Church.
      July 25   Dr Thos. Bradford, Physician.
1769 Oct. 29   The Revnd Mr Richard Rowe.[3]
1771 Feb. 8   Anne Cordery.
      Feb. 27   Mrs Elizabeth Turner.[4]
      June 15   Mr William Dennis.
      July 7   Mr Thos. Hornsby,[5] Alderman & apothecary.
      Aug. 1   Francis Middleton,[6] Esq.
1772 Mar. 22   Mrs Grace Middleton, widow.
      April 7   Mrs Catherine Russel, widow.
      June 14   Thomas,[7] son of Mr Thomas Hogg.
                 (James Deason, Sacrist, Nov. 1772.)
1774 April 2   The Honourable & Revd Dr Spencer Cowper,[8] Dean of Durham.
      Aug. 20   Christopher Walker.
1775 Mar. 8   Thomasin,[9] widow of Mr Hornsby, apothecary.
      Nov. 14   Samuel Dennis,[10] Minor Canon of this Church, Curate of S. Shields, & Rector of Beford in Yorkshire.
      Dec. 5   George Bullock,[11] batchelor.

---

[1] Born 1703. Henry, elder son of Dr. Henry Bland, Dean of Durham 1728—1746, Canon of Windsor and Provost of Eton College, by his wife Anne, dau. of Peter Hudson, Alderman and J.P. for Doncaster, by his wife Ursula, dau. of Robert Wildbore, of Arksey, near Doncaster. He was educated at Eton ; B.A. Christ Church, Oxford 1726 ; Prebendary of Lincoln and Rector of Gadway 1731 ; Rector of Washington and Bishopwearmouth 1735 ; installed in sixth prebend of Durham 2 Aug. 1737 ; D.D. 1747. Died 6 May, worth £80,000, which all went to his sisters. His epitaph was written by Dr. Louth, Bishop of Oxford. He is stated to have been buried " in the transept," but his M.I. is in the Nine Altars.

[2] Charlotte, dau. of Mr. Charles Weston, who was no relation to Dr. Phipps Weston, another Prebendary, whose burial see 24 April 1794.

[3] Baptized at St. Oswald's 14 Jan. 1689-90, the eldest son by his second wife of John Raw, or Rowe, Esq., whose burial see 13 Feb. 1721-2.

[4] Widow of the Rev. Bryan Turner (whose burial see 14 Oct. 1738), to whom she was married as " Mrs. Elizabeth Forster " 21 June 1722 at Crossgate.

[5] See his widow's burial 8 March 1775.

[6] See his marriage 5 Dec. 1749.

[7] See his baptism 17 Nov. 1763.

[8] Died 25 March. He was younger son of Sir William Cowper, third Bart., who was afterwards Lord Keeper of the Great Seal and Baron Cowper, and Lord High Chancellor of Great Britain, and created, 1718, Earl Cowper (and is ancestor of the present Peer), by his second wife Mary, dau. and heiress of John Clavering, Esq., of Chopwell, co. Pal. He graduated B.A. 14 March 1731-2 ; M.A. 1734 ; B. and D.D. by diploma 25 June 1746. He married, May 1743, Dorothy, elder dau. (by his second wife, sister of the Minister, Sir Robert Walpole) of Charles, second Viscount Townshend. He was made Dean of Durham 1746. His portrait hangs in the Chapter Library.

[9] She was married as " Mrs. Thomasine Foster " 31 Aug. 1732 at St. Oswald's.

[10] Poulson says, in his " History of Holderness," that he obtained the Rectory of Beeford through the interest of his sister, who was housekeeper to Archbishop Blackburn. He appears to have resigned it before his death, as Poulson states that the Rev. Robert Evans was instituted 24 Nov. 1766, but query if correct. He graduated at New College, Oxford, B.A. 1723 ; M.A. 1726.

[11] Perhaps a son of George Bullock, buried 2 Aug. 1699.

1776	Jan. 25		Margaret Wright, virgin, Claypath.
	June 23		Elizabeth Allan, widow, of Elvet.
1777	Jan. 8		Elizabeth Elleray, widow, housekeeper to the Bishop.
	June 3		Sarah Dennis,[1] virgin, daughter of Mr S. Dennis, late M. Canon.
1778	Feb. 27		Mrs S. Wright, widow, of Claypath.
	Mar. 5		Adam Scott, butler to Dr Sharp, Prebendary.
	June 7		Abraham Foster, batchelor.
1779	May 7		Isabella Wright, virgin, of Claypath.
	June 3		Mrs Ann Fielding,[2] virgin ; Bailey.
	June 17		Mrs Dongwith,[3] old virgin ; Elvet.
1780	Mar. 3		John King,[4] a trumpeter in the Huntington Militia.
	Aug. 2		The Revd James Douglass,[5] D.D., Prebendary of Durham.
1782	April 14		John,[6] son of John Pearson.
	May 2		The Revd Dr Fawcett,[7] Prebendary here.
	June 27		Tabitha,[8] daughter of Christopher Johnson, Esqr, of Akleyheads; virgin.
	Sep. 4		Jane,[9] widow of Dr Douglass, late Prebendary of this Church.
1783	July 7		Donald MacPen, an old Scotchman ; pauper.
	Aug. 15		Mary Bowlby,[10] widow, mother of Dr P. Bowlby.
	Dec. 26		Widow Inmman (Mary),[11] sister to Dr Bowlby.
1784	July 8		Sarah Powel.[12] Her father died M. Canon in 1719.

Stamp Duty paid.

[1] See her father's burial 14 Nov. 1775.

[2] Dau. of Israel Fielding by Margery his wife. Will dated 20 July 1772, wherein she says, "I desier to be kept four nights after I am dead. I would be buryed in woolling & a plain weinscot coffin, neather lined or covered." Proved at Durham in 1779. [MS. Ped. by E. A. W.]

[3] Sister of the Rev. Richard Dongwith, buried 26 Feb. 1761.

[4] The Huntingdon Militia were quartered in Durham at this period, and there were barracks on the Palace Green. Several of the soldiers took wives from Durham, and their weddings occur at St. Nicholas.

[5] *Recté* Douglas. Vicar of Kelloe ; Rector of Long Newton 1742 ; Rector of Stainton 1760 ; Prebendary of the fifth and fourth stalls successively. He became, by the death of his elder brother in 1774, head of the Cavers family of Douglas (see " Landed Gentry "), but died issueless. See his widow's burial 4 Sep. 1782.

[6] According to the tombstone, which is much the more likely to be correct, *John* is in error for *James* in both instances. See the father James Pearson's burial 7 Sep. 1801. The date of the son's death on the tombstone is given as 18th.

[7] Baptized 8 Oct. 1714, he was second son of John Fawcett, Esq., Recorder of Durham (whose portrait is in the Town Hall), by his wife Elizabeth, dau. of Richard Stonehewer, Esq., of Durham. He was Rector of Gateshead and Vicar of Newcastle. He married Miss Elizabeth Brown, his elder son by whom assumed the name of Pulteney. See Burke's " Landed Gentry."

[8] Born 20 Jan. 1752, second dau. of Christopher Johnson, of Durham, Attorney-at-Law, whose burial see 13 Dec. 1787, by his wife Tabitha, dau. of George Dixon, of Aykleyheads, co. Durham (see her burial 18 March 1798). [MS. Ped. by E. A. W.]

[9] The " Landed Gentry " states that she was Jean, dau. of Halyburton, of Pitcur, co. Forfar. See her husband's burial 2 Aug. 1780.

[10] Baptized at St. Mary-le-Bow 2 Feb. 1697-8, youngest dau. and coheiress of Peter Burrell, Esq., of Durham, and widow of Thomas Bowlby, gent., and Attorney-at-Law. See their marriage 2 Feb. 1719-20. [MS. Ped. by E. A. W.]

[11] Baptized at St. Mary-le-Bow 29 June 1727 ; married there (as second wife), 23 Oct. 1755, Charles Inmman. [MS. Ped. by E. A. W.]

[12] See her father's burial 19 April 1719.

1784	Nov. 19	Ann Loadman, widow.
1786	May 22	Elizabeth, daughter of the late Revd Mr Hopper.
	Aug. 15	Margaret Foster, widow.
1787	Dec. 13	Christopher Johnson,[1] attorney-at-law, of Akleheads.
		Stamp Duty paid to Oct. 1, 1788, viz. 3^d *a head for baptisms & funerals.*
		(James Deason, Sacrist.)
1788	Nov. 6	Elizabeth Marsden,[2] widow.
1789	Sep. 1	Anthony Pearson,[3] batch^r.
1790	April 16	Mrs Ann Davison[4] (sister to Lady Eden), of the Bailey.
1791	Feb. 1	Ann,[5] wife of Mr Willm Walker, of Gilligate.
1792	Mar. 21	William Ambler,[6] Counsellor-at-Law, South Bailey, Recorder of Durham.
	May 3	The Revd John Sharp,[7] D.D., Archdeacon of Northumberland & Prebendary (the 11th stall) here.
1793	April 25	Eliza, dau. of the Revd Dickens Haslewood, Minor Canon.
	Oct. 20	Henry, son of the Revd D. Haslewood, M. Canon & Rector of Little St Mary's (an infant).
	Dec. 13	Margaret, wife of James Bullock, taylor.
	Dec. 20	Ann,[8] widow of the late Willm Ambler, Counsellor.
1794	Jan. 9	Agnas, wife of Thomas Curry.
	April 24	The Revd Phipps Weston,[9] Prebendary here & Rector of Witney, Oxfordshire.

[1] Born 7 April 1718; of Durham, Attorney-at-Law, and afterwards (*jure uxoris*) of Aykleyheads. He married, at St. Mary-le-Bow, 27 Aug. 1747, Tabitha, youngest dau. of George Dixon, of Aykleyheads, Esq., and sister and heiress of John Dixon, of Aykleyheads. See her burial 18 March 1798. [MS. Ped. by E. A. W.]

[2] Baptized at St. Mary-le-Bow 31 Jan. 1730-31; married there, 1 July 1754, to Thomas Marsden, of Barnsley, co. York. [MS. Ped. by E. A. W.]

[3] A hairdresser, and died 30 Aug.; baptized at Crossgate 16 Jan. 1748-9. See his father's burial 21 Sep. 1806.

[4] Dau. of William Davison, Esq., of Beamish, co. Pal. See Pedigree of DAVISON of Beamish in Surtees, vol. ii.

[5] She died on Sunday, 30 Jan., and was a dau. of the Rev. Bryan Turner, M.A., whose burial see 14 Oct. 1738.

[6] He died 15 March and is buried in the Nine Altars. He was son of William Ambler, a London conveyancer. See his widow's burial 20 Dec. 1793, and daughter's 4 March 1829. He was appointed Recorder of Durham.

[7] Born 21 March 1722-3; Vicar of Hexham Jan. 1759-60; Archdeacon of Northumberland (collated 21 April) 1762; Prebendary of the ninth stall (installed 11 Aug.) 1768; P.C. of Barmbrough 1773; of Trinity College, Cambridge (B.A. 1743; M.A. 1747; D.D. 1759); was also Vicar of Hartburn, and Lord Crewe's senior Trustee. Buried in the Galilee. [MS. Ped. by E. A. W.]

[8] She died 14 Dec., and was dau. of William Steele, gent., of Newcastle. Her sister Elizabeth, marrying Hauxley Surtees, of Newcastle, was grandmother of Surtees the historian of Durham.

[9] He died 20 April, in his 56th year. He matriculated at Magdalen College, Oxford, 28 July 1753, then aged 15. His father, the Rev. Phipps Weston, matriculated (son of John Weston, of Oxford, "pleb.") at Brasenose 17 March 1730-31, then aged 17; B.A. Christ Church 1734; M.A. 1737; B.D. and D.D. New Inn Hall 1772. The Prebendary married, *circa* June 1790, the dau. and sole heiress of Thomas Clarke, of Hammersmith, deceased. He was installed in the third prebend 17 July 1789; was also Rector of Witney, Oxon.

1794	June 19	Jane,[1] wife of John Pearson, bellringer.
	Sep. 17	Boulby, son of D. Haslewood, Minor Canon.
	Sep. 25	Thomas, son of Dick. Haslewood, Minor Canon.
	Oct. 9	Martha,[2] wife of the Rev[d] Joseph Watkin, Vicar of Merrington & Minor Canon.
	Oct. 26	Henry Howard,[3] batchelor.
1795	Jan. 20	John Pearson,[4] a bellringer & shoemaker.
1796	Mar. 15	Mary Cook, a servant in the College.
	Sep. 6	Miss Cuthbert. Her father was Vicar of Kendal in Westmoreland in 1745, & left the town as the Rebels came in.
1798	Jan. 31	Mary Sharp,[5] of the South Bailey in Durham, widow of the late Rev[d] John Sharp, D.D., Prebendary of 9th and afterwards of the 11th stall in this Cathedral, and daughter of the Rev[d] Heneage Deering, formerly Dean of Ripon. Died, in the 77th year of her age, on 26th & was buried on 31st day of January 1798 in the Galiley.
	Mar. 18	Tabitha,[6] widow of the late Christopher Johnson, Esq[r], attorney-at-law, of Aklcheads; died at her house in Queen Street March 15th.
	Sep. 23	Ann,[7] wife of William Brecknell, Virger to the Dean of Durham.
	Dec. 14	Ann Pearson, spinster, aged 92.
1799	June 9	Elizabeth,[8] widow of Captain Bright, & daughter of the late D[r] Stonehewer, Rector of Houghton-le-Spring, aged 72.
1800	April 22	Charlotte Fielding,[9] spinster, aged 96.
1801	May 26	James Bullock, bellows-blower to the Organist.
	Aug. 8	Uvedale Robert,[10] infant son of the Rev[d] Robert Price, LL.D., Prebendary of Durham, & Mary Ann his wife.

[1] See her husband's burial 20 Jan. 1795.

[2] Died 8th. She was married 9 June 1773. He married secondly Anna Maria, dau. of —— Owen, who died his widow, aged 80, and was buried at St. Mary-the-Less 20 Jan. 1838. He was afterwards Vicar of Norham, where he was buried.

[3] "In his 64th year." ("Newcastle Advertiser.")

[4] See his wife's burial 19 June 1794.

[5] Born 7 March 1720-21; married, 4 Dec. 1752, to the Rev. John Sharp, D.D. See his burial 3 May 1792.

[6] Youngest dau. of George Dixon, of Aykleyheads, co. Durham; married at St. Mary-le-Bow, 27 Aug. 1747, Christopher Johnson, Attorney-at-Law. See his burial 13 Dec. 1787. [MS. Ped. by E. A. W.]

[7] She died 20th. The Verger [a freeman of Durham] died 11 Jan. 1806, aged 76, and was buried at Wolsingham 13th. His son William Brecknell was a surgeon there, and had, by Jane Hall his wife, a dau. Jane, who married, 25 Jan. 1837, Joseph Snaith Wooler, gent., of Wolsingham.

[8] In Surtees' pedigree she is wrongly called Margery. Her sister was Margery, and the second wife of Nicholas Halhead, Esq.

[9] Of the North Bailey, third dau. of Israel Feilding by Margery his wife. See her sisters' burials 3 June 1779 and 31 May 1763. Their tomb in the Cathedral Yard has a fine carving of the Feilding arms, in a maiden lozenge borne on the breast of the double-headed eagle of the House of Hapsburg. [MS. Ped. by E. A. W.]

[10] Also Canon Residentiary of Salisbury. This child, according to a newspaper, was born 21 July 1801.

1801 Sep. 7   James Pearson,[1] shoemaker ; Sadler Street.
1803 Mar. 25   Mary,[2] dau. of John Smith, Virger.
1804 Jan. 12   The Rev[d] Newton Ogle,[3] D.D., Dean of Winchester & Prebendary of Durham.
      April 18 Philip Vavasor,[4] infant son of the Reverend David Durell & Anne his wife. M[r] Durell is Prebendary of Durham.
      Dec. 5   John,[5] 4th son of the Reverend George Barrington, Prebendary of Durham and Rector of Sedgefield, & Elizabeth his wife.
1805 Mar. 30   Ann,[6] wife of Ambrose Wallice, Porter at the Castle.
      Oct. 28   Christopher Johnson,[7] attorney-at-law ; Queen Street.
1806 April 24 Elizabeth Hutchinson, housekeeper to D[r] Zouch.[8]

[1] Perhaps a brother of William Pearson the Verger, buried 21 Sep. 1806. See his widow's burial 20 Oct. 1829.

[2] See her father's burial 19 Dec. 1813.

[3] "Father of the College." He was installed Prebendary 27 Oct. 1768, and made Dean of Winchester 21 Oct. 1769. He died 6 Jan., aged 78. See his daughter's burial 26 Feb. 1825, and Burke's "Landed Gentry"—"Ogle of Kirkley."

[4] Baptized 25 Jan. 1804 at Mongewell, Oxfordshire, of which the father was about sixty years Rector, and fifty years Prebendary of Durham, where he was appointed to the ninth stall in 1801, and removed to the eighth in 1809. A native of Jersey, he was born 18 June 1762, a younger son of Thomas Le Vavasseur-dit-Durell (the representative of one of the oldest families in Jersey, and the direct descendant of John Le Vavasseur-dit-Durell, born *circa* 1497, and his wife Anne Messervy) by his first wife Mary, dau. of John Aubin, Denunciator of the Royal Court of Jersey, and niece of the Rev. Philip Falle, Prebendary of Durham, Rector of Shenley, Herts, and Chaplain to the King. He married Anne, dau. of Philip Robin, of another old Jersey stock, and by her, who died at Mongewell, Sunday, 16 Oct. 1836, had with other issue a son Thomas Vavasour Durell, who succeeded him in the Rectory of Mongewell. Dr. Durell's family present a curious instance of the ancient nomenclature of the Channel Islands. He used the ordinary arms of Vavasour, "Or, a fess dancetté sable," but some of the family now use "Azure, a lion rampant erminois ducally crowned," which bearing differs but slightly from that of the English Darells. He graduated at Christ Church, Oxon, B.A. 1785 ; M.A. 1789 ; D.D. of Durham University. He died 15 Jan. 1852 and was buried at Mongewell. [David Durell, who graduated M.A. at Pembroke College, Oxon, and afterwards B.D. and D.D. at Hertford College, and Prebendary of Canterbury, was uncle of Dr. David Durell, and son of another Thomas Le Vavasseur-dit-Durell. John Durell, likewise a native of Jersey, of Merton College, Oxon, received a prebend from Bishop Cosin.]

[5] The father (see the "Peerages") succeeded in 1815 as fifth Viscount Barrington, and was nephew of the Hon. Shute Barrington, Bishop of Durham. He married, 1788, Elizabeth, dau. of Robert Adair, Esq., by Caroline, dau. of the second Earl of Albemarle. He died 5 March 1829, and his wife 2 March 1841. All their numerous children were born at Sedgefield Rectory, it is believed.

[6] She was married, as Ann Scott, 4 April 1775 at St. Mary's. See her daughter-in-law's burial 24 March 1837.

[7] Second son of Christopher Johnson, Attorney-at-Law, who was buried at the Cathedral 13 Dec. 1787, by his wife Tabitha, dau. of George Dixon, of Aykleyheads, co. Durham, whose burial see 18 March 1798. He was born 10 Sep. and baptized at St. Mary-le-Bow 9 Oct. 1750, and died s.p. 25 Oct. 1805. He married Mary, dau. of Thomas Carr, 17 July 1800. See her burial 16 March 1837. [MS. Ped. by E. A. W.]

[8] Dr. Zouch was one of the Prebendaries and Rector of Wycliffe-on-Tees. He married firstly Isabella, dau. and coheir of the Rev. John Emerson, Rector of Winston, whose other dau. and coheir Frances Emerson married Thomas Emerson Headlam, Esq., father of the late Archdeacon Headlam. He married secondly, Aug. 1808, at Sandall, near Wakefield, Miss Brooke, sister of William Brooke, Esq., of Wakefield, the Doctor being then about 73. He died, aged 80, at Sandal, 17 Dec. 1815.

CATHEDRAL CHURCH AT DURHAM. 129

1806	July 20	Betty Smith, servant to D[r] Price.
	July 26	Margaret,[1] wife of Rev[d] John Pitchford, A.M.
	Sep. 21	William Pearson,[2] late Virger; born in 1722.
	Oct. 12	Margaret Cummins, servant to M[r] Woodifield.
	Oct. 27	Gibson Yarrow, spirit-merchant.
1808	Jan. 14	Elizabeth, wife of Hendry Hopper, Esquire.
	Feb. 12	Ann,[3] wife (widow) of the late Virger, Will[m] Pearson.
	Feb. 29	Francis Danes, infant son of the Rev[d] M[r] Barrington,[4] Prebendary of Durham & Rector of Sedgfield, & Elizabeth his wife.
	Aug. 18	Jane,[5] wife of John Roddam, of Gateshead.
1809	Jan. 21	Mary Hunter, housekeeper to the Bishop of S[t] David's.[6]
	Mar. 25	Judith Sharp,[7] virgin, sister to D[r] Sharp, late Prebendary of the eleventh Stall.
	Sep. 22	Richard Samuel,[8] son of D[r] & M[rs] Prosser. D[r] Prosser was [sic] Prebendary & Archdeacon of Durham.
1812	Feb. 21	Harriet Sibylla,[9] fourth dau. of Rev[d] Henry Phillpotts, Prebendary of the ninth stall, & of Deborah Maria his wife. Aged twenty weeks.
	April —	Edmond,[10] son of Rev[d] Rob[t] Gray, Prebendary of the .... stall, & of Elizabeth his wife. Aged 4 days. Born April 2nd; died April 6th.
	June 25	Hendry Hopper, Esq., of Hendon in the parish of Bishop-Wearmouth; died June 21st.

[1] The "Newcastle Advertiser" states that she "died at Durham, in child-bed, in the very bloom of life." Although not in the Register, was buried in the Nine Altars, where her M.I. states she was aged 26 years and her infant two days.

[2] Died 20th. The "Newcastle Advertiser" stated that he "had held different situations about the Cathedral for upwards of 60 years." See burials of his wife 12 Feb. 1808, his dau. 28 April 1825, and his son Anthony 1 Sep. 1789, and other Pearsons in Index. [Possibly Mr. Anthony Pearson, who was appointed Under Sheriff of the county 1663, and was buried 24 Jan. 1665-6 at St. Mary's, was his ancestor.]

[3] See her husband's burial 21 Sep. 1806.

[4] See burial of a son, John, 5 Dec. 1804.

[5] Aged 80, according to "Newcastle Advertiser," and died 15th. She was dau. of Rev. Bryan Turner (see his burial 14 Oct. 1738).

[6] The Bishop of St. David's, John Bankes Jenkinson (a name so familiar as coming in the "bidding" prayer at the Cathedral), was also Dean of Durham 1827—1840.

[7] See her baptism 25 Nov. 1733.

[8] Only son of his parents; died at Bamborough 15 Sep., aged 13 ("Newcastle Advertiser"). The father (Balliol College, Oxford) was Archdeacon of Durham 1808—1831, when he resigned, and Prebendary for thirty-five years. He died at Belmont, Herefordshire, æt. 91, 8 Oct. 1839, bequeathing his estates to his sister's grandson, the present Francis Richard Wegg-Prosser, of Belmont, Esq. See the mother's burial 11 March 1824.

[9] See her baptism 6 Oct. 1811.

[10] Dr. Gray was Rector of Bishopwearmouth and Prebendary of the seventh stall, and afterwards Bishop of Bristol; graduated B.A. 1784; M.A. 1787; B.D. 1799 and D.D. 1802. He married Elizabeth, sister of Alderman Camplin, of Bristol. He died at Rodney House, Clifton, 28 Sep. 1834. See his dau. Mrs. Mowbray's burial 18 Feb. 1823.

1812 Sep. 21 Jane,[1] dau. of John Hall, Silver Street, parish of S[t] Nicholas, currier, & Elizabeth his wife. Aged 5 years.
1813 Feb. 9 Faith,[2] dau. of John Smith, Virger, and of his wife; Queen Street, in the parish of North Bailey; 2 years & 4 months; D. Haslewood, Sacrist.
       Mar. 28 Sarah, second dau. of Dickens Haslewood, Sacrist, and of Elizabeth his wife; South Bailey; 20 years 11 months and 19 days; Jn[o] Clarke, Minor Canon.
       April 2 Elizabeth,[3] third dau. and fourth child of James Wallace, flax-dresser, and of Ann Wallace his wife; Claypath, in the Parish of S[t] Nicholas, Durham; 5 years; Jno. Clarke, Minor Canon.
       May 3 Elizabeth,[4] dau. of John Hall, Currier, and of Elizabeth his wife; Silver Street, parish of S[t] Nicholas, Durham; one year; D. Haslewood, Sacrist.
       Nov. 16 Jane,[5] dau. of Robert and Ann Hall (their second child and first dau.); Chapelry of S[t] Margaret, Durham; eleven weeks; D. Haslewood, Sacrist.
       Dec. 19 John Smith,[6] Virger; Queen Street, in the parish of North Bailey; 35 years; D. Haslewood, Sacrist.
1814 April 27 John Handy, footman to the Hon[ble] and Rev[d] A. Grey, Prebendary; College; 37 years; D. Haslewood, Sacrist.
       Dec. 15 Mary Atkinson;[7] Dun Cow Lane, parish of S[t] Mary le Bow, Durham; 70 years; D. Haslewood, Sacrist.
1815 April 14 Christopher Sanders (servant with M[r] Woodifield, Sub-Treasurer); College; 22 years; D. Haslewood, Sacrist.
       May 31 Edward Griffith,[8] son of John and Mary Griffith; S[t] Mary le Bow, Durham; one year and twelve weeks; D. Haslewood, Sacrist.
1816 Jan. 25 Mary Walker, widow (servant as housekeeper in) the prebendal house of D[r] Price; 64 years; D. Haslewood, Sacrist.
       Jan. 26 Ann Jemima Sharp,[9] spinster; South Bailey; 53 years; D. Haslewood, Sacrist.

[1] Died 19 Sep. Second dau. and third child of her parents, whose burials see 13 May 1841 and 23 Feb. 1851. She was born 2 Dec. 1806.
[2] See her father's burial 19 Dec. 1813.
[3] See her mother's burial 24 March 1837. Her father, James, was son of Ambrose and Ann Wallace; see the latter's burial 30 March 1805.
[4] Born 30 March 1812. Third dau. and fifth child o[f] John Hall, whose burial see 13 May 1841.
[5] Died 14th. See her father's burial 2 Oct. 1816.
[6] See his daughters' burials 25 March 1803, 9 Feb. 1813, and 3 March 1831, and his wife's 2 Feb. 1840.
[7] She died 12 Dec. She was housekeeper to the Dean, Bishop of St. David's.
[8] Born 6 March and baptized 22 May 1814. Son of John Griffith, of Durham, Under Sheriff of the Palatinate, by Mary, dau. of John Hays, Esq. See their burials 19 May 1845 and 21 Oct. 1850. [MS. Ped. by E. A. W.]
[9] Born 15 Nov. 1762. Only child of her parents, whose burials see 3 May 1792 and 31 Jan. 1798. She was buried near them in the Galilee Chapel. [MS. Ped. by E. A. W.]

CATHEDRAL CHURCH AT DURHAM. 131

1816	June 4	John Hall,[1] son of John and Elizabeth Hall; Silver Street, parish of S[t] Nicholas; 6 years; D. Haslewood, Sacrist.
	Oct. 2	Robert Hall;[2] chapelry of S[t] Margaret, Durham; 29 years; D. Haslewood, Sacrist.
1817	Feb. 22	Henry Evans Holder,[3] M.D.; North Bailey; 35 years; Dickens Haslewood, Sacrist.
	Mar. 22	Ann Hall,[4] dau. of John & Elizabeth Hall; Silver Street, parish of S[t] Nicholas; 12 years; D. Haslewood, Sacrist.
	Nov. 23	Thomas Acton;[5] Queen Street, S[t] Mary-le-Bow; 62 years; P. Penson, off. Min.
1818	Oct. 25	Mary, wife of William Evance; Bow Lane, North Bailey; 67 years; Dickens Haslewood, Sacrist.
1819	Oct. 6	Arthur Johnston; Palace Green; twelve years; Dickens Haslewood, Sacrist.
1820	April 6	Richard Buttler;[6] parish of S[t] Nicholas; forty years; Dickens Haslewood, Sacrist.
1821	Oct. 7	Dickens Haslewood, Sacrist and Librarian; South Bailey; 61; John Clarke, offic[g] Min[r].
	Dec. 30	Robert Hall;[7] Framwellgate; 70; Tho[s] Ebdon, Sacrist.
1822	April 20	Anne Bennett;[8] Gilesgate; 6 months; Tho[s] Ebdon, Sacrist.
	June 11	Stephen George Kemble;[9] Grove, South Street; 64; W. N. Darnell, offic[g] Min[r].

[1] Second son and fourth child. See the father's burial 13 May 1841. Tombstone says *buried* 2nd, but that is the date of his death, also the sixth anniversary of his birth.

[2] A tanner; died 29 Sep. Son of Robert Hall, whose burial see 30 Dec. 1821. He married Ann (born 15 April 1792), dau. of Ralph and Sarah Jackson (see burial of Mary Dickens 6 April 1857).

[3] Physician to the Durham Infirmary; died 18th. His eldest dau. Ashley married, 5 Nov. 1831, at Clifton, Gloucester, R. W. Elton, Esq., 16th N.I., nephew of Admiral Sir William Young.

[4] Eldest dau. and second child, born 8 Dec. 1804; died 20th, which tombstone wrongly gives as burial date. See her father's burial 13 May 1841.

[5] The "Durham Advertiser" says he died 21st, aged 60, and was a "gentleman" chorister. He married, 3 July 1796 ("Newcastle Advertiser"), at Chester-le-Street, Eliza Marshall, of Durham.

[6] Described as of Sunderland on his tombstone. He married Margaret-Pearson (whose burial see 19 Feb. 1861), dau. of Alderman John Wolfe, of Durham, by his wife Elizabeth Pearson. His widow re-married the Rev. Edward Davison at St. Oswald's 11 May 1824.

[7] Died 28th; of Framwellgate, tanner and shoemaker. See his wife's burial 23 Feb. 1827, and those of his sons, Robert and John, and dau. Mrs. Wallace. Mr. Ebdon, the Sacrist, was Vicar of Billingham, and died in Claypath 18 Nov. 1852, aged 65, and buried at St. Oswald's.

[8] Dau. of George Bennett, a singing-man, afterwards a painter, who died, aged 71, 7 Oct. 1864 in Gilesgate. See burial of another infant 6 Feb. 1824.

[9] The least good actor of the Kemble family, and chiefly celebrated for being able to play Falstaff without padding. He was born 3 May 1758 at Kingstown, Herefordshire, the second son of Roger Kemble (a Roman Catholic), by his wife Sarah, dau. of Mr. Ward, also an actor and a contemporary of Quin. Roger Kemble, who died about 6 Dec. 1802, very early in life appeared on the stage, but only once acted in London, and then for his son Stephen's benefit, but he was long a Manager of strolling companies. Mrs. Kemble played, the very night Stephen was born, the part of Anne Boleyn, which was just at the time when the Queen is supposed to give birth to the Princess Elizabeth. Stephen Kemble, who was brother to John and Charles Kemble and Mrs.

REGISTER OF BURIALS IN THE

1822 Dec. 10 Hannah Spoor (housekeeper in the) prebendal house of Dr Gray; 66; Thos Ebdon, Sacrist.
1823 Feb. 18 Elizabeth Mowbray,[1] wife of George Isaac Mowbray, Esq., of Yapton House, Sussex, and eldest daughter of the Revd Dr Gray; Rectory, Bishop-Wearmouth; 24; F. Haggitt, offic^g Min^r.
Mar. 11 Anthony Hopper,[2] Esquire; Silksworth; 85; W. N. Darnell, offic^g Min^r.
April 15 Francis Baker,[3] Captn in the Royal Navy; prebendal house of Dr Price (College) his father-in-law; 37; Thos Ebdon, Sacrist.
July 2 George Isaac Mowbray,[4] Esq., of Yapton House, Sussex (and son-in-law of the Rev. Dr Gray); prebendal house of Dr Gray; 31; Rev. W. N. Darnell, offic^g Min^r.
Dec. 5 Elizabeth Russell; prebendal house of Dr Gray (College) in whose service she had lived; 65; Thos Ebdon, Sacrist.
1824 Feb. 6 Ann Bennett; Gilesgate; 5 months and 10 days; Thos Ebdon, Sacrist.
Feb. 28 John Wilton,[5] College Cook; North Bailey; 54; Thos Ebdon, Sacrist.
Mar. 11 Sarah Prosser,[6] wife of the Revd R. Prosser, D.D., Archdeacon and Prebendary of Durham; Dr Prosser's house, College; 70; R. G. Bouyer, offic^g Min^r.
June 22 Jonathan Linslay; Mr Woodifield's house, College (with whom he lived as servant); 29; T. Ebdon, Sacrist.
July 22 Ann Phillips;[7] Sunderland; 7 weeks; T. Ebdon, Sacrist.

Siddons, was firstly apprenticed to a surgeon at Coventry, and was afterwards Manager of the Edinburgh, Glasgow, Liverpool, Newcastle, and other theatres. When he settled in Durham he lived at "The Grove," near the present Grammar School. In Feb. 1820 he advertised as "Shortly to be published, 'Durham College; or, Portraits of the Living: a Poem. By S. G. Kemble. Dedicated to Viscount Barrington.'" He died 5 June and is buried in the Nine Altars. See his wife's burial 28 Jan. 1841.

[1] She was married, in Nov. 1821, to George Isaac Mowbray, Esq., whose burial see 2 July 1823. She died at the birth of her only child, Elizabeth-Gray, now the wife of the Right Hon, Sir John Robert Mowbray (formerly Cornish), Bart., M.P. for Oxford, who sat for Durham City 1853—1868. She is buried in the Nine Altars (M.I.).

[2] Buried in the Nine Altars.

[3] Died 11th. He was buried in the outer south aisle of the Galilee. See his son's baptism 10 Jan. 1817 and his daughter's 9 Feb. 1821.

[4] He was elder son of George Mowbray, Esq., of Ford, co. Durham, and Mortimer, Berks, by Jane, dau. and heiress of Oliver Coghill, of Coghill, co. York, Esq., and grandson of George Mowbray, Esq., of Ford, whose wife was Elizabeth, dau. of Anthony Wilkinson, Esq., of Crossgate. See the burial, 18 Feb. 1823, of Mrs. Mowbray, with whom he lies in the Nine Altars.

[5] Died 24th.

[6] Died 4th. She was the youngest dau. of Samuel Wegg, Esq., of Bloomsbury Square, London, and Acton, Middlesex, and was her brother's sole heiress. She was married 20 June 1796, by the Rev. Dr. Parker, Rector of St. James, Westminster, to Dr. Richard Prosser, then Rector of Gateshead. See her son's burial 22 Sep. 1809.

[7] The mother was Mary Ann, dau. of James Wallace, of Claypath, grocer, by his wife Ann Hall, whose burial see 24 March 1837. She married, at St. Nicholas, 15 July 1823, Alexander Phillips, of the Sunderland Pottery.

CATHEDRAL CHURCH AT DURHAM. 133

1824	July 28	Mary Jane Phillips;[1] Sunderland; 8 weeks; T. Ebdon, Sacrist.
	Dec. 6	Mary Cowens; Visc[t] Barrington's prebendal house, College (with whom she lived as servant); 20; W. S. Temple, offic[g] Min[r].
	Dec. 20	Jane Logan,[2] wife of Alex[r] Logan, Esq.; Old Elvet; 79; W. N. Darnell, offic[g] Min[r].
1825	Feb. 26	Susannah Ogle,[3] sister of the Rev[d] J. S. Ogle, Prebendary of Durham; College; 66; W. N. Darnell, offic[g] Min[r].
	April 28	Ann Pearson;[4] Gilesgate; 80; T. Ebdon, Sacrist.
	July 5	Elizabeth Haslewood, relict of the late Rev[d] Dickens Haslewood, Sacrist of this Cathedral; Bishop-Wearmouth; 65; T. Ebdon, Sacrist.
	Sep. 6	William Tyler;[5] College; 10; T. Ebdon, Sacrist.
	Dec. 6	Anne Matilda Feilding,[6] eldest daughter of the late George Feilding, Esq., of Startforth Hall, in the County of York; North Bailey, Durham; 77; T. Ebdon, Sacrist.
1826	Jan. 21	Andrew Philip Skene,[7] Esq., of Hallyards, in Fife, and of Kilmacoe, in the County of Wicklow, Ireland, Officer in His Majesty's Army; Church Street, Durham; 73; T. Ebdon, Sacrist.
	Feb. 4	The Rev[d] Reynold Gideon Bouyer,[8] LL.B., Prebendary of this

[1] See last entry.

[2] Buried in the Galilee. She was first wife to Alexander Logan, who married secondly, at St. Oswald's, 15 April 1827, Jane, dau. of Matthew Davison, of East Burdon. ("Durham Advertiser.")

[3] She was dau. of the Very Rev. Newton Ogle, D.D., of Kirkley Hall, Northumberland, Dean of Winchester and Prebendary of Durham (whose burial see 12 Jan. 1804) and sister of the Rev. John Savile Ogle, D.D., of Kirkley. Dr. J. S. Ogle died at Kirkley, 1 April 1853, aged 86, and his wife Catherine-Hannah, dau. of Edward Sneyd, Esq., of Dublin (and aunt of the Rev. Edward Sneyd, Minor Canon, of whom hereafter, under 11 Sep. 1837), died 18 March same year, aged 83.

[4] Dau. probably of William Pearson, the Verger, whose burial see 21 Sep. 1806.

[5] See his baptism 16 Dec. 1814, and his father's burial 14 July 1849.

[6] Baptized at Startforth, co. York, 15 May 1748. Her father was buried there 13 June 1783; her mother, Ann, buried there 18 Nov. 1782.

[7] Died 18th. Formerly Captain 9th Light Dragoons and Major of Brigade in Canada. He was the only son of Captain Philip [Wharton] Skene, Lieutenant-Governor of Crown Point and Ticonderoga, Colonel of a regiment of Militia in America (Commission as Ensign 1st Royals 11 Sep. 1741 or 1742; Second Lieut. 26 Sep. 1745), and sometime Captain 27th Foot, by Katharine, only child of Samuel Heyden, of Arklow, co. Wicklow, by his wife Katherine Byrne, of Ballymanus. He was born 25 March 1753 in Dublin Barracks, and baptized by the Chaplain of the Royals and afterwards at Maynooth. Commission as Ensign 27th Regiment 1762, and 30 Oct. same year, Lieut. 72nd Regiment (being then nine years of age!), and Lieut. 43rd Regiment 1774. He married, at St. Dunstan's, Fleet Street, Henrietta, only child of David James, Solicitor, of Serjeants' Inn (where she was born), and of Golygoed, Carmarthenshire, and by her had, with other issue, a dau. Henrietta, married to William Trotter, Esq., of Bishop's Auckland. Captain Andrew Philip Skene, who was the twenty-ninth head in male succession of the ancient Scotch house of Skene, of Skene and Hallyards, is buried in the outer south aisle of the Galilee (M.I.).

[8] Died 30th Jan. Vicar of Northallerton, LL.B. Buried in the Nine Altars, where his M.I. displays the arms: "Azure, a lion rampant or; impaling Azure, a bull passant argent." See his widow's burial 15 Aug. 1831.

Cathedral, Archdeacon of Northumberland, etc.; Prebendal House, College; 84; The Very Revᵈ Charles Henry Hall, Dean of Durham.

1826 Mar. 8 William Browning, coachman to the late Archdeacon Bouyer; the Archdeacon's prebendal house, College; 55; T. Ebdon, Sacrist.

Mar. 30 Hannah Reed,[1] widow; Old Elvet, Durham; 90; T. Ebdon, Sacrist.

April 11 Ellen Elizabeth Carr,[2] dau. of John and Rosetta Anne Carr; Palace-Green, Durham; 4 months; James Raine, Rector of Meldon.

Nov. 3 Robert Wallace;[3] Providence Row, Durham; 14 months; T. Ebdon, Sacrist.

1827 Jan. 24 John Pearson;[4] Durham; 53 yʳˢ; T. Ebdon, Sacrist.

Feb. 22 Elizabeth Bowlby,[5] wife of Captⁿ P. Bowlby, and dau. of the late Revᵈ D. Haslewood; North Bailey, Durham; 29; T. Ebdon, Sacrist.

Feb. 23 Ann Hall;[6] Durham; 75. T. Ebdon, Sacrist.

Mar. 22 The Very Revᵈ Charles Henry Hall,[7] D.D., Dean of Durham; Deanery, College; 63; W. N. Darnell, Prebendary of Durham.

1828 Jan. 11 Elizabeth Gargrave; Dʳ Fenwick's, North Bailey; 65; T. Ebdon, Sacrist.

July 9 William Pearson;[8] Gilesgate, Durham; 69; T. Ebdon, Sacrist.

---

[1] She was dau. of Utrick Reay, Esq., of Newcastle. "March 14, 1757. William Reed, of Durham, Esq., was married at All Saints' in this town to Miss Reay in Pilgrim Street, a young lady celebrated for beauty, and distinguished for many valuable accomplishments, with £10,000 fortune." ("Newcastle General Magazine.") Her husband William Reed, Esq., was buried 22 April 1763 at Crossgate, where are the baptisms of their children Hannah-Jane 3 April 1759 and Margaret 21 Jan. 1762. Mrs. Reed is buried in the inner south aisle of the Galilee.

[2] Born 19 Nov. 1825. See the father's burial 6 Nov. 1833.

[3] Youngest son of James Wallace, junior (by his wife Lucy Sanderson), son of James Wallace, by his wife Ann (Hall), whose burial see 24 March 1837. See his brother's burial 30 July 1818 and sister's 4 Nov. 1849.

[4] A maltster, and died 21st, according to newspaper, and "formerly a shoemaker in Pullin Corner." "At St. Nicholas, 17 Sep. [1803], Mr. John Pearson, an eminent ladies' shoemaker, to Miss Thwaites, milliner, both of Durham." ("Newcastle Advertiser.") See his widow's burial 14 June 1839. He was probably a son of John Pearson, buried 20 Jan. 1795.

[5] Dau. of the Rev. Dickens Hazlewood, M.A., of Christ Church, Oxon, Minor Canon of Durham Cathedral; born 22 Oct. 1798. Married, 24 March 1819, at St. Mary the Less, to Captain Peter Bowlby of the 4th Regiment, with which he was present at Waterloo. He died 8 Nov. 1877 at Cheltenham. [MS. Ped. by E. A. W.]

[6] Died 18 Feb. See her husband's burial 30 Dec. 1821.

[7] He died suddenly, 16th March, in Edinburgh. He was son of Charles Hall, Dean of Bocking, and was educated at Westminster School; Vicar of Broughton, Yorks, 1794; Canon of Christ Church, Oxford, 1799 (D.D. 1800); Vicar of Luton, Beds, 1804; Regius Professor of Divinity, Oxford, 1807; Dean of Christ Church 1809; and Dean of Durham 26 Feb. 1824, succeeding Earl Cornwallis, who held the Deanery with the Bishopric of Lichfield and Coventry. He married, 29 Aug. 1794, the Hon. Anna-Maria-Bridget Byng (who died 30 Oct. 1852), dau. of the fifth Viscount Torrington.

[8] Son of James Pearson, whose burial see 7 Sep. 1801. He was brother to Mrs. Wolfe, whose burial see 4 Feb. 1847.

CATHEDRAL CHURCH AT DURHAM. 135

1828	Dec. 21	Isabella Hall;[1] Silver Street; 10; T. Ebdon, Sacrist.
	Dec. 27	James Miller,[2] son of the Rev[d] J. Miller, Minor-Canon of this Cathedral; Queen Street; 6 years; T. Ebdon, Sacrist.
1829	Mar. 4	Elizabeth Ambler,[3] dau. of the late Will[m] Ambler, Esq , Recorder of this City; Old Elvet; 61; W. S. Gilly, Prebendary of Durham.
	Oct. 4	Ann Esther Forster;[4] Market Place; 91; T. Ebdon, Sacrist.
	Oct. 20	Elizabeth Pearson;[5] Church Street; 84; T. Ebdon.
	Dec. 13	Jane Lambert;[6] Queen Street; 42; T. Ebdon.
1830	Jan. 6	Henrietta Skene,[7] relict of A. P. Skene, Esq[r]; Church Street; 65; T. Ebdon.
	April 8	Ann Chaytor,[8] dau. of the late Rev[d] Henry Chaytor, Prebendary of this Cathedral; South Bailey; 61; W. N. Darnell, Prebendary of this Cathedral.
	Dec. 29	Mary Chaytor,[9] sister of the above; Palace Green; 60; W. N. Darnell.
1831	Feb. 2	Elizabeth Woodifield,[10] wife of Matthew Woodifield, Esq.; South Bailey; 25; T. Ebdon, Sacrist.

[1] Died 19th. She was born 5 Aug. 1818, eighth and youngest child of John Hall, whose burial see 13 May 1841.

[2] Died 25th; born 5 Oct. 1822. The father was born at Cruff, Scotland, about 1782; was a Licentiate of the Scotch Church, but ordained by Bishop Barrington at Auckland 22 Sep. 1811, and became Minor Canon of Durham, and Vicar of Pittington, where he died 15 Jan. 1854 and is buried. He was D.D. of St. Andrew's University. He married at St. Andrew's, 23 Oct. 1821, Burnett, dau. of John Hunter, LL.D., Professor of Humanity of St. Andrew's (his portrait hangs in the Library there), and afterwards Principal of the United Colleges of St. Salvadore and St. Leonard. Mrs. Miller, who was born 11 Nov. 1789, died 24 Feb. 1873 at North Street, St. Andrew's, where she was buried. Besides the children buried here (they were all baptized at St. Mary-le-Bow, probably), there were Elizabeth Miller, born 18 May 1824, died 25 July 1850 and buried at Pittington; John Burnett Miller, born 3 Nov. 1828, died 12 Oct. 1845 and buried at St. Andrew's; and Henrietta B., living unmarried at North Street, St. Andrew's, in 1877.

[3] Died 26th Feb. She was the only dau. of the Recorder (whose burial see 21 March 1792), and is buried in the Nine Altars.

[4] Died 30 Sep. Called "Mrs." in newspaper.

[5] Died 18th. She was widow of James Pearson (whose burial see 7 Sep. 1801), and mother of Mrs. Wolfe, whose burial see 4 Feb. 1847.

[6] Died 10th. Was formerly housekeeper to Archdeacon Prosser.

[7] Died 30 Dec. See her husband's burial 21 Jan. 1826. She is buried in the same vault in the Galilee.

[8] Died 30 March. The second dau. of the Rev. Henry Chaytor, LL.D., Prebendary, by his second wife Ann, dau. of Charles Robinson, Esq., of Appleby, Westmorland. She was born 13 April and baptized 5 May 1768 at Kirkby Stephen, of which her father was then Vicar. Buried in inner north aisle of the Galilee (M.I.) with her sisters, whose burials see next entry, 20 Oct. 1843, and 8 Nov. 1849. See Pedigree of CHAYTOR, Longstaff's "History of Darlington," and Surtees, vol. iv., part ii.

[9] Buried with her sister; see last entry. Born 20 Sep. and baptized 27 Oct. 1769 at Kirkby Stephen.

[10] Born 14 Sep. 1805 and baptized 18 Aug. 1806 at Houghton-le-Spring. She was second of the three daughters and coheiresses of Anthony Tilly, of Pittington and Durham (where he died, aged 70, 28 June 1826), by Sarah Haswell, of Cornforth (married 17 Sep. 1802—"Newcastle Advertiser"—and died in Church Street, Durham, 26 May 1839, aged 71). She was first wife of

1831	Mar.	3	Mary Ann Smith,[1] dau. of the late John Smith, Virger; Queen Street; 25; T. Ebdon.
	Mar.	8	Rosetta Anne Carr,[2] dau. of the Rev[d] John Carr and Rosetta Anne his wife; Palace Green; 12; T. Ebdon.
	June	2	George Cayley,[3] M.D.; Old Elvet; 68; Thomas Ebdon.
	Aug.	15	Elizabeth Bouyer,[4] widow of the late Rev[d] R. G. Bouyer, Prebendary of this Cathedral; North Bailey; 80; Charles Thorp, Prebendary of this Cathedral.
1832	May	30	John Wolfe,[5] Alderman of this City; Framwellgate; 74; T. Ebdon, Sacrist.
	Oct.	31	Anne Elizabeth Colberg;[6] prebendal house of the Rev. W. S. Gilly, College; 57; Thomas Ebdon, Sacrist.
	Dec.	5	George James Miller,[7] son of the Rev. J. Miller; Queen Street; 7 months; Thomas Ebdon.
1833	Mar.	19	Margaret Charlton,[8] widow of W. Charlton, Esq., Hesleyside; Old Elvet; 75; T. Ebdon, Sacrist.
	Mar.	27	Grace Hunter Miller,[9] dau. of the Rev. J. Miller; Queen Street; 7; T. Ebdon.

Mr. Woodifield (whose burial see 6 April 1857), and died 28 Jan., having given birth to a dau. (baptized at St. Mary's) on the 19th. She is buried in the outer north aisle of the Galilee. Her older sister, Ann Tilly (born 23 July 1803 and baptized at Houghton 26 June 1804), was wife of John Burrell, Esq., of Durham, and is buried at Crossgate with her husband. Her younger sister, Sarah Tilly (born 17 March 1806 and baptized at Houghton 25 Sep. 1809), became the wife successively of George Appleby, Esq., of Durham, and of Robert Ingram Shafto, Esq., of Durham, head of the Shaftos of Bavington, and is, with both her husbands, buried at Crossgate.

[1] See her father's burial 19 Dec. 1813.

[2] Born 1 Feb. 1819; died 5 March and buried in the aisle of the north transept, next her father, whose burial see 6 Nov. 1833.

[3] Died 27 May (M.I.) and buried at the end of the nave, close to the great doors leading to the Galilee Chapel. He was born in 1763, the third son of John Cayley, Esq., Consul-General at St. Petersburg, and was great-grandson of Sir William Cayley, of Brompton, first Bart. He was Physician to the Russian Army, and elected Physician to the Durham Infirmary 13 Dec. 1798; Cornet Yorkshire Hussars 6 June 1803, resigning 6 Dec. following. Burke's "Peerage" says he died s.p.

[4] Her husband's monument (see his burial 4 Feb. 1826) in the Nine Altars records: " uxorem duxit Elizabetham Ponton, de Ponton Parvâ, in agro Lincolniensi, A.D. MDCCLXXI." Her own name does not appear thereon.

[5] The son of Robert Wolfe, of Durham (whose marriage see 26 Dec. 1748), he was baptized at St. Nicholas 12 Dec. 1758; was Governor of the Gaol, and commonly therefore known as "Jailer Jack;" was an Alderman, and served as Mayor. He married firstly, 7 May 1786, at Crossgate (where she was buried 6 Dec. 1789), Caroline Wilson. See burial of his second wife 4 Feb. 1847, and of his dau., Mrs. Davison, 19 Feb. 1861. Died 15th and buried in centre of nave (M.I.).

[6] She was oldest dau. of Captain Samuel Colberg (by his wife Mary Relph), Barrack-Master at Liverpool, and was born in London. She was aunt to the second wife of Dr. Gilly the Prebendary, and was a considerable legatee in Bishop Barrington's will.

[7] Born 16 May 1832. See his brother's burial 27 Dec. 1828.

[8] Died 12th and is buried in the centre of the nave (M.I.). She was dau. of John Fenwick, Esq., M.D., of Morpeth (see "Fenwick of Long Framlington," Burke's "Landed Gentry"), and sister of John-Ralph Fenwick, Esq., M.D., whose burial see 17 Jan. 1855. She married, 1778, William Charlton, Esq., of Hesleyside, Northumberland, who died 1797. See "Landed Gentry."

[9] Died 23rd; born 6 Feb. 1826. See her brother's burial 27 Dec. 1828.

1833 May 9 Emily Charlotte Henshaw,[1] dau. of M[r] W. Henshaw, Organist of this Cathedral; Bow Lane; infant; T. Ebdon.
Nov. 6 The Rev[d] John Carr,[2] Master of the Grammar School, and Professor of Mathematics in the University of Durham; Master's House; 47; G. Townsend, Prebendary of Durham.
Nov. 6 Charles Carr,[3] son of the above; Master's House; infant; G. Townsend.
Nov. 22 William Harland,[4] Esq., Recorder of the Corporation of Durham; North Bailey; 83; T. Ebdon.
1834 Mar. 8 Mary Salt,[5] wife of George Salt, Virger of this Cathedral; Bishop's Palace, Durham; 60; T. Ebdon, Sacrist.
Aug. 19 Mary Chaytor;[6] South Bailey; 30; S. Gamlen, offic[g] Min[r].
1835 Feb. 2 The Rev[d] Thomas Bowlby,[7] late Curate of Painshaw; North Bailey; 74; T. Ebdon, Sacrist.

[1] Born 3rd of same month. The father, William Henshaw, Mus. Doc., Organist of the Cathedral, son of Joseph Henshaw, of Marylebone, London, by his wife Anne, dau. of Thomas Tomlins, of Marylebone, was born 1792. He married, 6 July 1825, at St. Clement Danes, London, his cousin Emily, dau. of James Tomlins, of Lambeth, who died 1 July 1877, at North Road, Clapham, aged 79. Dr. Henshaw was appointed Organist 1 Jan. 1814 and resigned 1 Jan. 1863, when he was succeeded by Dr. Philip Armes, the present Organist (ex inform. Dr. Henshaw).
[2] Died 30 Oct. A native of Stackhouse, in Giggleswick, co. York; formerly Fellow of Trinity College, Cambridge (M.A. 1810); Vicar of Hatfield Broad Oak, Essex; Vicar of Brantingham, Yorks, 1818, on presentation of Dean and Chapter of Durham. He married at Scarborough, 8 Jan. 1817, Rosetta-Anne (baptized 12 March 1795 at Witton-le-Wear), eldest dau. of John-Thomas-Hendry Hopper, of Witton Castle, co. Pal., Esq. [The newspapers announced her death, 12 Aug. 1876, aged 81, at Harley Rectory, Salop, as *Anne* only.] See the baptism of Dorothy Spearman, her great-great-grandmother, 29 June 1670. He is interred under a Gothic monument in the aisle of the north transept, with a coat of arms: On a chevron three mullets, a martlet for difference. M.I. on brass plate near. See burials of his children, 11 April 1826, 8 March 1831, and next entry.
[3] Buried in the same coffin with his father. See preceding entry.
[4] Died 16th. He was the eldest son of George Hoar, gent., of Middleton St. George, co. Pal., and Deputy-Keeper of the Jewels in the Tower, by his first wife Frances (married at Redmarshal 1 Jan. 1749-50), dau. of William Sleigh, Esq., of Stockton-on-Tees, and he assumed the name of Harland, and had a grant of arms 25 Aug. 1802. Was gazetted Captain in the Durham Volunteers 18 Oct. 1803, and was a Bencher of Lincoln's Inn. His younger brother Charles also assumed the name of Harland, and received in 1808 a Baronetcy, which died with him 1810. The late William Charles Harland, of Sutton Hall, co. York, M.P. for Durham City, was son of the above Mr. William Harland by his wife Anne, whose burial see 21 Jan. 1842. See also baptism of his sister Mrs. Dickens' child 27 March 1787.
[5] Formerly Mary Bee, upper-nurse and afterwards housekeeper to Lord Barrington, the Prebendary.
[6] Died 13th. Born 10 July 1804; she was younger dau. of Lieut.-Colonel Henry Chaytor, Grenadier Guards, by his wife Jane, dau. of William Marriott, Esq. She is buried in the inner north aisle of the Galilee Chapel with her brother, sister, and aunts. (M.I.) The Rev. Samuel Gamlen, Vicar of Heighington, Perpetual Curate of Croxdale, a Minor Canon, and afterwards Rector of Kirkley Mall, Leicestershire, died 2 June 1855.
[7] Born 27 Sep. 1762 and baptized at St. Mary the Less the same day. Of Trinity College, Cambridge, B.A. 1784, M.A. 1787. Perpetual Curate of Painshaw, co. Pal., for many years. Died, aged 73, 28 Jan. 1835. He married 3 March 1786, at Croxdale Chapel, co. Durham, Eleanora-Elizabeth, dau. of Anthony Salvin, of Sunderland Bridge, co. Pal., Esq. See her burial at the Cathedral 20 Aug. 1842, aged 82. They had seven sons and six daughters. [MS. Ped. by E. A. W.]

1835	Mar. 12	Charles Surtees Marsden,[1] infant son of T. Marsden, Esq., Proctor, & Dorothy his wife; Elvet Cottage; 8 months; T. Ebdon.
	April 28	Robert Hall;[2] Silver Street; 32; J. Cartwright, offic^g Min^r.
	Dec. 10	Elizabeth Townsend,[3] wife of the Revd G. Townsend, Prebendary of this Cathedral; College; 48; The Right Revd J. B. Jenkinson, Dean of Durham.
1836	Feb. 27	Caroline Henshaw;[4] Bow Lane; infant; T. Ebdon, Sacrist.
	Mar. 1	The Right Revd William Van Mildert,[5] D.D., Bishop of Durham; Episcopal Palace, Bishop Auckland; 70; The Right Revd J. B. Jenkinson, Dean of Durham.

[1] Born at Elvet Cottage 16 July 1834, son of Thomas Marsden, of Durham, Proctor, and his wife Dorothy, elder dau. of John Thomas Christopher, of Norton. See his burial 3 July 1857.

[2] A currier; died 23rd; tombstone incorrectly says buried 23rd. He was born 11 May 1803, eldest child of John Hall, whose burial see 13 May 1841. By his wife (whose burial see 21 June 1875) he had an only son Ovington Hall, who died 10 March 1869, aged 37, and was buried at Chester-le-Street, leaving issue.

[3] Died 3 Dec. She was the only surviving dau. of Samuel Fyler, Esq., Barrister-at-Law, of Twickenham, Middlesex, by his wife (and cousin) Mary, only child of John l'Anson, Esq., and niece of Sir Thomas Bankes l'Anson, Bart., of Corfe Castle, Dorset. She was married 8 July 1813, at the Parish Church, Brighton, to Dr. Townsend (see his burial 28 Nov. 1857), to whom she was first wife. She is buried in the Nine Altars. (M.I.)

[4] Died 24th. Born 14 Jan. 1836 and baptized at St. Mary-le-Bow. See her sister's burial 9 May 1833.

[5] Baptized 8 Dec. 1765 at St. Mary, Newington. Educated at Merchant Taylors; of Queen's College, Oxford, where he matriculated, then aged 18, 21 Feb. 1784 (B.A. 23 Nov. 1787; M.A. 17 July 1790; B. and D.D. 13 Oct. 1813). His first Curacies were at Sherborne, Hants, and Lewknor, Oxon, and afterwards at Witham, Essex, where he married. Rector of Braddon, Northampton, April 1795; Rector of St. Mary-le-Bow, London, 1796—1819; Vicar of Farningham, Kent, 1807; Precentor of Lincoln's Inn April 1812; Regius Professor of Divinity at Oxford and Canon of Christ Church Sep. 1813—20; consecrated Bishop of Llandaff 31 May 1819; Dean and Canon Residentiary of St. Paul's 1820; Bishop of Durham 3 April 1826, confirmed at St. James's Church, Piccadilly, 17 April, and installed in Durham Cathedral 30 May. He made his formal entry into the county on the 14th of July, and was attended by much pageantry, the falchion of the Lord of Sockburn being presented to the Bishop on Croft Bridge, and another falchion of the owners of Pollard's Lands at Auckland Castle, the Bishop wearing a coat and waistcoat of the Palatinate purple. His public entry into the City of Durham and enthronement in his Cathedral took place 21 July. He died at Auckland Castle 21 Feb. and was buried 1 March 1836 in his Cathedral in a vault within the altar rails. The styles and titles of the deceased Prelate were proclaimed over the tomb by the Principal Surrogate.

"The Herald breaks the Wand, while he proclaims
The sainted Palatine's puissant names;
Yon Kingless throne is now for ever bare."—(Faber.)

He was the second and only surviving son of Mr. Cornelius Van Mildert, of Newington, co. Surrey, who died there, aged 76, 29 April 1799, by his wife Martha (who died at Newington, aged 86, 21 Sep. 1818), dau. of Mr. William Hill, of Vauxhall. The Bishop had married, 22 Dec. 1797, Jane, youngest dau. of Lieut.-General Archibald Douglas, Colonel 13th Dragoons, and M.P. for the Dumfries Burghs in 1771. See her burial 28 Dec. 1837. [MS. Ped. by E. A. W.]

The Bishop, in conjunction with the Dean and Chapter, founded in 1834 the University of Durham. See a brief account of the changes the Ecclesiastical Commission made during this episcopacy in the constitution of the Bishopric and Chapter in Low's "Diocesan History of

CATHEDRAL CHURCH AT DURHAM. 139

1837	Mar. 16	Mary Johnson;[1] South Street; 76; T. Ebdon, Sacrist.
	Mar. 24	Ann Wallace;[2] Claypath; 62; T. Ebdon.
	April 10	John Leybourne,[3] deputy-Treasurer and Receiver of the Dean and Chapter; College; 63; J. S. Ogle, Prebendary of Durham.
	Sep 11	Joseph Boruwlaski,[4] the celebrated little Polish Count; Banks' Cottage, Durham; 98; Edward Sneyd, offic^g Min^r.
	Dec. 28	Jane Van Mildert,[5] widow of William, late Bishop of Durham; Harrogate; 77; G. Townsend, Prebendary of Durham.
1838	April 2	William Henshaw;[6] Bow Lane; infant; T. Ebdon, Sacrist.
	April 26	Phillis Georgiana Marsden;[7] Shincliffe; infant; T. Ebdon.
	April 28	Francis Johnson,[8] Esq^e; Aykley Heads; 80; W. S. Gilly, Prebendary of Durham.

Durham" (S.P.C.K.).* In Canon Low's account of Dr. Van Mildert it is well to correct an error. He says, "the last Palatine was carried to his tomb in the Chapel of the Nine Altars." There indeed is erected the public monument, a sitting effigy of the Bishop, but he was buried in a vault within the altar rails, the covering slab bearing his initials and those of his wife.

[1] Widow of Christopher Johnson, who died 1805.

[2] Died 17th. She was wife of James Wallace, of Claypath, grocer (whose burial see 9 April 1843), and dau. of Robert Hall, whose burial see 30 Dec. 1821; and the burials of her dau. Elizabeth 2 April 1813; her grandchildren (Phillips) July 1824; and a grandson 3 Nov. 1826.

[3] He came from about Cotherstone, Yorkshire. He married at Crossgate (described as " junior " in the register), 15 Feb. 1810, Ann Mowbray, of Witton Gilbert. Ann. his only child, married 1 Dec. 1835, at St. Mary-the-Less, John Grace, third son of John Grace, Esq., of Felling Hall, co. Pal. See also next entry.

[4] Died 5th. He was a native of Pokucia, in Poland. Refer to the Count's Memoirs of himself, which, however, must be taken in parts *cum grano*. He was a polished gentleman, but vain and bombastic. He was only three feet three inches in height, and an exact life-size statue of him (some of his clothes are there also) is in the Museum on the Palace Green, and there is an oil portrait extant, now the property of Mr. Alan Greenwill. The "Count's Corner" on the banks is so called from the cottage, now demolished, where he lived with the Miss Ebdons—sisters of the Rev. Thomas Ebdon, Minor Canon—and which was situated in the lower garden (not then enclosed) of the last house (the Chaytors') in the South Bailey. The Count is buried in the north aisle of the nave, under the north-western tower, the slab marked J. B. Curiously enough his last earthly neighbour is Mr. Leybourne (see last entry), who was an unusually tall man.

[5] See the Bishop's burial 1 March 1836.

[6] Died 29 March; born 2 July 1837 and baptized at St. Mary-le-Bow. See his sister's burial 9 May 1833.

[7] Dau. of Thomas Marsden, of Durham, Proctor, by his wife Dorothy, dau. of John Thomas Christopher, of Norton. See her brother's burial 12 March 1835.

[8] Born 23 July and baptized at St. Mary-le-Bow 16 Aug. 1757; entered at Lincoln's Inn 1779; a Justice of the Peace and Deputy-Lieutenant, co. Durham, and Major (commission dated 16 July 1804) of the Durham Volunteers; died 23 April 1838. Will dated 9 Dec. 1835, and proved at Durham 1 Oct. 1838. He married at St. Nicholas, Durham, 29 Dec. 1801, Mary, second dau. of the Hon. Richard Hetherington, President of the Virgin Island, West Indies, and of the Hill at Burton in Lonsdale, co. York. She was born 10 Oct. 1777; died 5 and was buried at the Cathedral 11 April 1851. [MS. Ped. by E. A. W.]

---

* This very readable little work contains a good account of the great temporal powers exercised by the Bishops of Durham down to as late a time as that of Bishop Barrington, powers which will be hardly credited by readers distant from "the bishoprick," as that part of the diocese bounded by the Tyne and Tees was generally termed.

1838	June 19	Dorothy Fenwick,[1] wife of J. R. Fenwick, Esq., M.D.; North Bailey; 85; C. Thorp, Prebendary of Durham.
1839	June 14	Mary Pearson;[2] Crossgate; 67; T. Ebdon, Sacrist.
	Sep. 22	Ann Wallace;[3] Claypath, Durham; 14 months; T. Ebdon, Sacrist.
1840	Feb. 2	Elizabeth Smith;[4] Market-place, Durham; 60; T. Ebdon, Sacrist.
	Nov. 26	William Hughes,[5] student of the University of Durham; University House, Palace Green; 20; The Very Rev[d] George Waddington, Dean of Durham.
1841	Jan. 23	Harriet Chaytor,[6] youngest dau. of the Rev[d] Henry Chaytor, Prebendary of Durham; North Bailey; 62; The Very Rev[d] George Waddington, Dean of Durham.
	Jan. 28	Elizabeth Kemble,[7] relict of Stephen George Kemble, Esq[e]; Grove, near Durham; 78; The Rev[d] G. Townsend, Prebendary of Durham.
	May 13	John Hall,[8] tanner; Framwellgate, Durham; 62; T. Ebdon, Sacrist.
	July 11	Sarah Moor;[9] University House, Palace Green; 3; T. Ebdon.
	Sep. 27	Jane Serpell, servant to the Bishop of Chester;[10] College, Durham; 24; T. Ebdon.
	Nov. 1	Henry Griffith,[11] youngest surviving son of John Griffith, Esq[e], North Bailey, Durham; No. 1 Little Argyll Street, Hanover Square, London; 31; T. Ebdon, Sacrist.

[1] Died 11th. Born 19 Jan. 1753. She was eldest dau. and coheiress of Robert Spearman, Esq., of Old Acres, co. Pal. (see Pedigree in Surtees), and was married 3 Aug. 1788 at St. Mary-le-Bow. See her husband's burial 17 Jan. 1855, and her grandfather Spearman's 20 Oct. 1728.

[2] Died 11th. See her husband's burial 7 Sep. 1801. Her mother kept a school in Framwellgate.

[3] See her brother's burial 3 Nov. 1826.

[4] Died 29 Jan. See her husband's burial 19 Dec. 1813.

[5] Died 22nd. Born 23 Oct. and baptized 3 Dec. 1820 at St. Chad's, Shrewsbury. He was the fourth son of Mr. Philip Hughes, of that town, wine merchant, by his wife Anne Palmer (married at Stockland, Dorset, 27 Oct. 1806), of Devonshire. (M.I.)

[6] Died 16th. Born 5 Dec. 1778; probably baptized at Croft, Yorkshire. See her sister's burial 8 April 1830.

[7] Died 20th. Formerly Miss Satchell, of the Covent Garden Theatre. She was married about Nov. 1783 to Mr. Stephen Kemble, whose burial see 11 June 1822. She lies with her husband in the Nine Altars on the north of St. Cuthbert's Shrine.

[8] Died 9th. Was an Alderman of Durham. See his father's burial 30 Dec. 1821, and his wife's 23 Feb. 1851. His tombstone says erroneously buried 9th. See also the burial of his son-in-law John Robson 23 Dec. 1866. Besides the children already occurring as buried here (consult Index), John Robson had another child Mary, born 2 June 1814, who married Thomas White.

[9] Died 8th. Elder child of John Moor, Verger, whose burial see 12 Jan. 1875. She was born 2 and baptized 11 Oct. 1837, and christened 15 March 1838.

[10] The Bishop of Chester, Dr. John Bird Sumner, held a stall at Durham until his preferment to the Archbishopric of Canterbury.

[11] Born 4 March and baptized 1 April 1810 at St. Mary-le-Bow. See his brother's burial 31 May 1815, and his parents' burials 19 May 1845 and 21 Oct. 1850. [MS. Ped. by E. A. W.]

CATHEDRAL CHURCH AT DURHAM.   141

1841 Dec. 16 Thomas Heming;[1] prebendal house of the Rev[d] G. Townsend, College, Durham; 63; T. Ebdon.
1842 Jan. 21 Anne Harland,[2] relict of the late William Harland, Esq[e]; North Bailey, Durham; 81; T. Ebdon, Sacrist.
     Feb. 5 Margery Burgess,[3] relict of the late D[r] T. Burgess, Bishop of Salisbury; North Bailey, Durham; 77; The Vener[e] Archdeacon Thorp.
     Mar. 11 Elizabeth Eleanor Feilding;[4] North Bailey, Durham; 84; T. Ebdon, Sacrist.
     July 24 Jane Jackson;[5] Dun Cow Lane, Durham; 3; T. Ebdon, Sacrist.
     Aug. 20 Eleanora Elizabeth Bowlby,[6] relict of the late Rev[d] Thomas Bowlby; North Bailey, Durham; 82; T. Ebdon, Sacrist.
     Aug. 30 George Jackson,[7] Clerk of the Works to the Dean and Chapter; Dun Cow Lane, Durham; 37; John Cartwright, offic[g] Min[r].

[1] Died 13th. He was an artist, and, according to the "Durham Chronicle," of Magdalen College, Oxford; was Author of "Scripture Geography" and other works. He was on a visit to Dr. Townsend when he died.
[2] Died 16th. Younger dau. of John Wilkinson, merchant, of Stockton-on-Tees and of Worcester. See "Landed Gentry"—"Wilkinson, of Harperley." She was baptized at Stockton 18 April 1758, and married there, 30 Nov. 1780, to William Hoar, afterwards Harland, Esq. (whose burial see 22 Nov. 1833), with whom she rests in the same vault in the north transept. (M.I.)
[3] Died 27 Jan. The only dau. of John Bright, Esq. She was baptized at St. Oswald's 5 April 1764; is buried in the Nine Altars near her mother, whose burial see 9 June 1799 (M.I.). Her husband (married 1796), the Bishop, Thomas Burgess, D.D., F.R.S., F.S.A., was born at Odiham, Hants, where his father William Burgess was a grocer; was M.A. and Fellow (1787) of Christ Church College, Oxford; Rector of Winston, co. Pal.; Prebendary of Salisbury 1787; Prebendary of Durham (second stall) 1791; Bishop of St. David's 1803, and of Salisbury 1825, succeeding Dr. Fisher. He owed his advancement in life and preferments to his ever staunch friend and supporter Bishop Barrington, to whom he was Chaplain. He died 19 Feb. 1837, aged 80, at Southampton, and is buried in his Cathedral. Mrs. Burgess used to drive out in a coach and four, and so narrow are the streets of Durham that for safety, when she went into Elvet, her equipage was driven into the market-place, and the horses turned there.
[4] Baptized at Startforth 13 Dec. 1757. Fourth dau. of George Feilding, of Durham and Startforth, Esq. Her aunt Anne Feilding left her her "common Prayer book with cuts in it, hair buttons set in gold, ring with the Duchess of Marlborough's hair, & silver shoe bukills." Died unmarried 11 March 1842, æt. 81 (of the North Bailey). [MS. Ped. by E. A. W.]
[5] Died 20th. See her father's burial 30 Aug. 1842.
[6] She was the dau. of Anthony Salvin, of Sunderland Bridge, co. Pal., Esq.; baptized 1 March 1761, and married 3 March 1786 at Croxdale Chapel, co. Durham; died 15 Aug. 1842. This lady, through the families of Belasyse, Fairfax, Gascoyne, Percy, and Mortimer, was fifteenth in direct descent from King Edward the Third. [MS. Ped. by E. A. W.] See her husband's burial 2 Feb. 1835.
[7] Died 26th. A natural son of Mary Jackson, afterwards Dickons (whose burial see 6 April 1857), and was born 24 July 1805. He married Ann Robson, of Durham, who died, aged 65, 23 Jan. 1873, at Holloway, London, and is buried at Highgate Cemetery. Their son Thomas George, born *post pat. mort.*, whose death is also recorded on the tombstone (died 28 Aug. 1872, aged 29), is buried at Edinburgh. They had three other daughters and a son. See a daughter's burial 24 July 1842.

1842	Oct. 28	Sarah Flintoff;[1] North Bailey, Durham; 12; T. Ebdon, Sacrist.
	Nov. 26	Francis Augustus Liddell,[2] 3rd son of the Hon^e and Revd Robt Liddell; prebendal house of Dr Wellesley, College, Durham; infant; The Very Revd George Waddington, Dean of Durham.
1843	Jan. 26	John Wright, footman to the Hon^e and Revd Dr Wellesley; College, Durham; 28; T. Ebdon, Sacrist.
	Feb. 19	Catherine Phillips;[3] Sunderland; 6 months; T. Ebdon.
	Mar. 27	Bridget Beckett,[4] relict of Thos Beckett, Esq^e, of Thornton-le-Moor, in the County of York; North Bailey; 77; G. Townsend, Prebendary of Durham.
	April 9	James Wallace;[5] Gilesgate, Durham; 66; T. Ebdon.
	Oct. 9	The Hon^e Emily Frances Geraldine Matilda Cadogan,[6] eldest dau. of Viscount Chelsea; prebendal house of the Hon^e and Revd Dr Wellesley, College, Durham; 5; The Right Revd Bishop of Chester.
	Oct. 20	Isabella Chaytor,[7] fourth dau. of the late Revd Henry Chaytor, Prebendary of Durham; Old Elvet, Durham; 72; T. Ebdon, Sacrist.
1844	June 7	Gustavus Adolphus Chaytor,[8] M.D.; South Bailey; 38; Thomas Ebdon, Sacrist.
	Nov. 19	The Revd James Frederick Townsend,[9] son of the Revd G. Townsend, Canon of Durham; Twickenham, Middlesex; 29; The Very Revd George Waddington, Dean of Durham.

[1] Died 24th. Born 16 Aug. 1829 at Osmotherley, co. York. See her father's burial 19 May 1864.

[2] Died 22nd. Third son and fourth child; born 11 May and baptized 25 July 1842 at Barking, Essex. The father, fifth son of Thomas Henry, first Lord Ravensworth, was born at Farnacres 24 Sep. 1808, and baptized at Lamesley, co. Pal.; of Christ Church, Oxon (B.A. 1829), and of All Souls (M.A. and Fellow 1834); Vicar of Barking, Essex, 1836—51, when he went to St. Paul's, Knightsbridge. He died 29 June 1888. The mother, Emily Ann Charlotte, eldest dau. of Dr. Wellesley (whose burial see 27 Oct. 1848), was born at Hampton Court 23 Oct. and baptized there 22 Nov. 1803. She was married at St. Mary-le-Bow, Durham, 26 Jan. 1836, and died in Wilton Place, London, 22 Oct. 1876, being buried 26 id. men. at Woking Cemetery. This child is buried in the Nine Altars.

[3] See burials 22 and 28 July 1824.

[4] Died 21st. Formerly Bridget Peacock. She married at Northallerton, 6 Jan. 1784, Thomas Beckett, Esq. (then described as "of Westminster, bach^r"), of Thornton-le-Moor, whom she survived.

[5] A grocer. See his mother's burial 30 March 1805, his wife's 24 March 1837, a daughter's 2 April 1813, and that of a grandchild 3 Nov. 1826.

[6] Died 5th. She was the first child of her parents (whose marriage see 12 July 1836); was born at Naples 23 Feb. 1838 and baptized there. She is buried in the Nine Altars. (M.I.)

[7] Died 12th. Born 1 Aug. 1771 and probably baptized at Croft. See her sister's burial 8 April 1830.

[8] Died 1st. Nephew of preceding; born 1 June 1844; the fourth son of Lieut.-Colonel Henry Chaytor, Grenadier Guards, by his wife Jane, dau. of William Marriott, Esq. He was unmarried.

[9] Died 14th. He was second child (by his first wife) of Dr. Townsend (whose burial see 28 Nov. 1857); was born 26 July and baptized 15 Sep. 1815 at Hackney Church, Middlesex. Of University College, Oxon, B.A. 1837; unmarried. Buried in Nine Altars. (M.I.)

CATHEDRAL CHURCH AT DURHAM.   143

1845 April 2   Frances Amelia Bowlby,[1] youngest dau. of the late Rev[d] Thomas
                  Bowlby; North Bailey; 44; Thomas Ebdon, Sacrist.
       April 11 Joseph Buchan;[2] Framwellgate, Durham; 45; Thomas Ebdon.
       April 12 Michael Pearson;[3] The Castle, Durham; 35; Thomas Ebdon.
       May 15   James Moor;[4] Coldwell, Northumberland; 36; Thomas Ebdon.
       May 19   Charles Rowlandson;[5] College, Durham; infant; Thomas Ebdon.
       May 19   John Griffith,[6] Esq[e], solicitor; North Bailey, Durham; 81;
                  Thomas Ebdon, Sacrist.
1846 June 6   Jane Moor,[7] wife of M[r] John Moor, Virger; University House,
                  Durham; 43; Bolton Simpson, Minor Canon of Durham.
1847 Feb. 1   Elizabeth Inman,[8] niece of the late Rev[d] Doctor Bowlby; Old
                  Elvet, Durham; 82; Thomas Ebdon, Sacrist.
       Feb. 4   Elizabeth Wolfe,[9] widow of John Wolfe, Esq[e]; Hartlepool, in
                  the County of Durham; 80; Thomas Ebdon, Sacrist.
       Mar. 4   Elizabeth Davison,[10] son of Joseph Davison, Esq[e]; South Bailey,
                  Durham; Infant; Bolton Simpson, Minor Canon of Durham.
                  (By a slip, Son is written instead of Daughter. Thomas
                  Ebdon, Sacrist.)

[1] Born 27 Nov. 1800 and baptized 20 May 1801 at Houghton; died 28 March 1845. See her father's burial 2 Feb. 1835.

[2] Died 8th; a mason at the Cathedral. He was perhaps a son by his first wife of one John Buchan, who married secondly Ellen Banks, widow of William Rigby, of Framwellgate. John Buchan returned to his native place, Flodden Field, and died there. William and Ellen Rigby had a son, also a mason, who fell from the scaffolding of the Cathedral and was killed.

[3] Probably son of Michael Pearson (see his burial 18 Aug. 1851), who was butler at the Castle.

[4] Died 12th; a farmer. Third son of Thomas Moor, of Kirkharle, Northumberland, and was born at Bavington in that parish. His tombstone records his age as 39. See his brother's burial 12 Jan. 1875.

[5] Died 17th. The father Samuel Rowlandson, gent., was appointed Deputy-Treasurer to the Dean and Chapter April 1837, at the death of Mr. John Leybourne. The son (by Sarah his wife, whose burial see 17 Dec. 1864) of Christopher Rowlandson, of West Shaws, near Barnard Castle, he was born 27 Nov. 1805. He died in the College 22 Feb. 1883 and was buried in the Cathedral Yard. His wife (formerly Miss Hannah Kipling) died 21 Sep. 1884, and was buried with her husband and children.

[6] Born 30 Dec. 1763 and baptized 14 Feb. 1764. Attorney-at-Law; Under Sheriff of the Palatinate; Deputy Prothonotary of the Palatinate Court of Common Pleas; gazetted Captain in Durham Volunteers 18 Oct. 1803. Married, 3 March 1795, at St. Mary-le-Bow, Durham, Mary, eldest dau. of John Hays, Esq., Senior Proctor of the Palatinate Consistory Court, by his wife Eleanor, dau. and coheir of Richard Wetherell, Dean of Hereford, and Master of University College, Oxford. See her burial 21 Oct. 1850. [MS. Ped. by E. A. W.]

[7] Died 2nd. Youngest dau. of Robert Morrell, of Heighington, co. Pal. (who died there, aged 79, 14 July 1839). She was born 6 June 1803, and was married to John Moor (whose burial see 17 Jan. 1875) at St. Mary's, Durham, 15 March 1836.

[8] See her mother's burial 26 Dec. 1783.

[9] Died 29 Jan. Dau. of James Pearson, cordwainer and shoemaker, whose burial see 7 Sep. 1801. [Elizabeth, dau. of James and Elizabeth Pearson, baptized at Crossgate 29 April 1770.] She was second wife to Mr. Wolfe (whose burial see 30 May 1832), to whom she was married at St. Nicholas 11 July 1790.

[10] Baptized 10 Dec. 1846 at St. Mary's. See the father's burial 17 Dec. 1868.

1847 Mar. 10 Elizabeth Marsden,[1] second dau. of Thomas Marsden, Esq[e]; Old Elvet, Durham; 18; Bolton Simpson.
Mar. 16 Catherine Thompson,[2] youngest dau. of the late Rev[d] John Thompson, Vicar of Thornton-Steward, Yorkshire; College, Durham; 23; Bolton Simpson, Minor Canon of Durham.
Mar. 27 Francis Morris, butler of the Rev[d] Canon Douglas; College, Durham; 19; Bolton Simpson.
May 8 Catherine Bowlby,[3] third dau. of the late Rev[d] Thomas Bowlby; North Bailey; 49; Thomas Ebdon, Sacrist.
Sep. 19 Robert Hall;[4] Gilesgate, Durham; 35; Thomas Ebdon, Sacrist.
Oct. 21 George Henry Bowlby,[5] Esq., Lieutenant in the Royal Navy, 3rd son of the late Rev. Thomas Bowlby, of Durham; Edinburgh; 54; Thomas Ebdon, Sacrist.
Dec. 11 John Mingay,[6] head-butler at Bishop Hatfield's Hall, University of Durham; North Bailey, Durham; 31; Thomas Ebdon, Sacrist.
1848 Feb. 7 John Humble Waite,[7] Esq[e], a Member of the University of Durham; Framwellgate, Durham; 21; Thomas Ebdon, Sacrist.
Mar. 8 Edith Elder,[8] infant dau. of the Rev. Edward Elder, Head Master of the Durham Grammar School; New Grammar School, Durham; 10 months; Thomas Ebdon.
May 13 George Salt,[9] late Verger of this Cathedral; Old Elvet, Durham; 74; The Venerable Charles Thorp, Archdeacon of Durham.
June 2 Mary Dickons,[10] second dau. of M[r] Thomas Dickons, builder; Claypath, Durham; 23; Thomas Ebdon, Sacrist.
July 30 Jabez Wallace,[11] second son of M[r] James Wallace; Claypath, Durham; 17; Thomas Ebdon.

[1] Born 5 May, baptized 2 June 1828 at St. Mary-le-Bow. See her brother's burial 12 Oct. 1835.
[2] Died 13th, aet. suae xxii, and youngest dau. (M.I.)
[3] Born 11 Nov. 1798, baptized 10 June 1799 at Houghton. See her father's burial 2 Feb. 1835 and her mother's 20 Aug. 1842. [MS. Ped. by E. A. W.]
[4] Died 16th. See his father's burial 30 Dec. 1821.
[5] Born and baptized 17 Jan. 1793, according to the Houghton Register. Lieut. Royal Navy; Commander 21 May 1814; half-pay 28 Feb. 1817; served in the Expedition to Copenhagen in H.M.S. "Ganges" in 1807, and at the Siege of Sebastian in H.M.S. "Andromac" in Sep. 1813. Died 15 Oct. 1847, s.p. See his father's burial 2 Feb. 1835 and his mother's 20 Aug. 1842. [MS. Ped. by E. A. W.]
[6] Died 8th. (M.I.)
[7] Died 7 Feb. He was son of the Rev. Joseph Waite, M.A., sometime Curate of St. John's, Weardale. His elder brother is the Rev. Joseph Waite, D.D., Vicar of Norham (1873), Canon of Newcastle-on-Tyne, formerly Fellow and Tutor of University College, Durham, and afterwards the popular Master thereof.
[8] Died 4th. See her father's burial 14 April 1858.
[9] Died 8th. He was twenty-two years Verger of the Cathedral, and was previously butler to Bishop Barrington. He had a sister housekeeper to Archbishop Whately, and she was living, old and infirm, at the Palace, Dublin, some years since. See his wife's burial 8 March 1834.
[10] Died 30 May. Born 2 Oct. 1824 (twin with Miss Sarah Dickons, now living, 1880), and probably baptized at St. Nicholas. See her brother's burial 6 April 1857.
[11] Son of the younger James Wallace. See his brother's burial 3 Nov. 1816.

1848 Oct. 27   The Hon^r and Revd Gerald Valerian Wellesley,[1] D.D., Canon of Durham, and Rector of Bishop-Wearmouth; College, Durham; 77; The Very Revd George Waddington, D.D., Dean of Durham.
1849 Mar. 9   Samuel Rowlandson,[2] second son of Samuel Rowlandson, Esq^e; College, Durham; 2; Thomas Ebdon, Sacrist.
      July 14   Anthony Tyler,[3] late Verger at this Cathedral, & Porter at the College gates; College gates, Durham; 80; Thomas Ebdon, Sacrist.
      Nov. 4   Jane Wallace;[4] Saint Nicholas; 20 years; Bolton Simpson, off^g Sacrist.
      Nov. 8   Juliana Chaytor;[5] North Bailey; 76 years; Bolton Simpson, off^{ng} Sacrist.
1850 Feb. 20   Henry Rennet Relton,[6] student of the University; University College, Durham; 19; Edwd Greatorex, Sacrist.
      Oct. 21   Mary Griffith,[7] widow of the late John Griffith, Esq.; North Bailey; 78; Edwd Greatorex, Sacrist.

[1] Died 21st. He was born (probably at Dangan Castle) 7 Dec. 1770, the fourth son of Garret, first Earl of Mornington, by his marriage, 6 Feb. 1759, at St. Mary's, Dublin (in the Register of which his name is spelt Garrett), with Anne, eldest dau. of Arthur (Hill) first Viscount Dungannon; M.A. of St. John's College, Cambridge, 1792; Chaplain at Hampton Court 1793; Rector of Chelsea 1805; Rector of Therfield, Hants, 1822; Rector of Bishopwearmouth and Prebendary of Durham (in which he held the stall at his death) 1827. He married, 2 June 1802, at St. George, Hanover Square, Lady Emily Mary Cadogan, eldest dau. (by his second wife) of Charles, first Earl Cadogan. Lady Emily Wellesley, who died at Boulogne 22 Dec. 1839, is buried at St. Luke's, Chelsea. Dr. Wellesley (he was D.D. Lambeth) was next younger brother to the first Duke of Wellington, to whom he bore an extraordinary likeness. His portrait hangs in the Castle Hall. He was buried in the Nine Altars. See his daughter's marriage 12 July 1836.
[2] Died 6th. Born 26 June and baptized 7 Aug. 1846. See his brother's burial 19 May 1845.
[3] Died 10th. A native of Essex (probably Dunmow or Heybridge); he was born *circa* Feb. 1769. He was "of St. Mary-le-Bow, Durham, bachelor," at his marriage 1804. His portrait appears in Mr. Edmund Hastings' picture, hanging in the Chapter Library, of the Judges at the Cathedral service. See his wife's burial 20 Aug. 1861, and that of his son 27 Jan. 1871, and others in Index. His eldest child Elizabeth, the only one not baptized at the Cathedral, was born 15 Dec. 1804, baptized at St. Mary-le-Bow, and was living at Durham, unmarried, 1886.
[4] See her brother's burial 3 Nov. 1826.
[5] Fifth dau. of the Rev. Henry Chaytor, LL.D., Vicar of Kirkby Stephen, Rector of Croft, and Prebendary of Durham. She was born 6 Aug. and baptized 29 Sep. 1773 at Kirkby Stephen. See her sister's burial 8 April 1830.
[6] Died 18th. His second name should be Rennett. He was born 12 Feb and baptized 15 March 1831 at Down-Ampney, Gloucestershire, where his father the Rev. John Rudge Relton, M.A. (Queen's College, Oxon), was Curate. His mother was Sophia, dau. of the Rev. James Boyer, Rector of Colne Engain, Essex, and was married *circa* 1814. This youth, previously a chorister, Magdalen College, Oxford (admitted 10 Nov. 1842); matriculated at Durham University Oct. 1847. He was first class in classics in his first and second years' exams.; Foundation Scholar Oct. 1848; and classical prizeman Oct. 1849.
[7] Eldest dau. of John Hays, Esq., Senior Proctor of the Palatinate Consistory Court, by his wife Eleanor, elder dau. and coheir of Richard Wetherell, Esq., of Durham; married 3 March 1795 at St. Mary-le-Bow, Durham. See her husband's burial 19th May 1845. [MS. Ped. by E. A. W.]

1850 Oct. 23 Sarah Woodifield,[1] wife of Matthew Woodifield, Esq.; South Bailey, Durham; 50; Edw[d] Greatorex, Sacrist.
1851 Feb. 23 Elizabeth Hall;[2] North Road, Durham; 71; Edw[d] Greatorex, Sacrist.
  April 11 Mary Ann Johnson;[3] Aykleyheads; 73; J. Cartwright, Minor Canon.
  June 28 Caroline Bowlby;[4] Bailey, Durham; 56; Edw[d] Greatorex, Sacrist.
  June 28 Augusta Elder,[5] infant dau. of the Rev[d] Edward Elder; Bellasis, Durham; infant; Edw[d] Greatorex, Sacrist.
  Aug. 18 Michael Pearson;[6] Hallgarth St., parish of S[t] Oswald, Durham; 74; Edward Sneyd, Vicar of S[t] Oswald.
  July 6 Charlotte Davison;[7] South Bailey; infant; Edw[d] Greatorex, Sacrist.
  Aug. 29 Alice Maude Robson;[8] North Road; 1¾; Edw[d] Greatorex, Sacrist.

[1] Married at the British Legation, Naples, as Miss Sarah Fitch, 8 Oct. 1835 (Durham Newspapers). See the burial of her husband, to whom she was second wife, 6 April 1857.

[2] Formerly Elizabeth Wood, of Kimblesworth, co. Pal. Married at Chester-le-Street, 22 Aug. 1802, to John Hall, whose burial see 13 May 1844.

[3] Widow of Francis Johnson, Esq., of Aykleyheads. Her name was not Ann, and she was married as Mary only.

[4] *Recte* Caroline-Sophia. Widow of George Henry Bowlby, Esq., and dau. and coheiress of Henry Salvin, of Castle Eden, co. Pal., Esq. (see Surtees, vol. iv., p. 2). Married at Alston, Cumberland, 29 June 1844. Died 24 June 1851 and was buried by her husband (see his burial 21 Oct. 1847). [MS. Ped. by E. A. W.]

[5] Died 26th. See her father's burial 14 April 1858. Bellasis is the name of the fields on which the new grammar school was built. The present Head Master's house, though now enlarged by a wing and second storey, was already there. The situation of Durham School is perfect; it is beautifully placed in a bracing part, conveniently near and yet at a discreet distance from the City, close to the river, and but a few minutes' walk from the Cathedral, its *Alma Mater*, for the Dean and Chapter are Governors.

[6] Died 14th. Formerly butler at the Castle (University College), and previously butler to Dr. Burgess the Prebendary, Bishop of Salisbury. He was perhaps unconnected with the other numerous Pearsons buried here. See, however, his son's burial 12 April 1845. The officiating Minister, the Rev. Edward Sneyd, M.A.—who it may be presumed owed his appointment partly to his being nephew by marriage to Dr. J. S. Ogle (see Miss Ogle's burial 26 Feb. 1825)—was son of Rev. William Sneyd (nephew of Nathaniel Sneyd, Esq., M.P., Lord-Lieutenant of co. Cavan, who was assassinated in 1833, and son of Edward Sneyd, Esq., of Dublin, who was son of Archdeacon Wettenhall Sneyd, of Kilmore and Ardagh, by his wife Barbara, dau. of Dr. Marsh, Bishop of Limerick and Kilmore, by his wife Mary, dau. and coheir of the eminent Bishop Jeremy Taylor), a descendant of the Sneyds of Keele, co. Stafford, and his wife Maria (died 5 Nov. 1863, æt. 90), dau. of Sir Ralph Fetherston, of Ardagh, first Bart. Mr. Sneyd was presented to the Vicarage of St. Oswald's 20 July 1848, resigning it in 1862. He was previously Perpetual Curate of Wokey, Somersetshire, and of Cowes, I.W.; Chaplain to Lord Radnor; and Rector of Witton Gilbert. He died 3 Aug. 1866, æt. 71, and was buried at Elvet Hill Cemetery (registered at St. Mary-the-Less) with his mother. Mr. Sneyd will be long remembered in Durham for his moderate but Low-Church views, and his dignified person and manners.

[7] Charlotte is an error for Caroline. She was baptized 2 Feb. 1851 at St. Mary's. See her father's burial 17 Dec. 1868.

[8] Died 26th. Born 26 Oct. 1849 and baptized 11 March 1850 at Crossgate, but entered in Register (the baptism being private, doubtless) 3 April. See her father's burial 23 Dec. 1865.

1851 Sep. 24 William Jones;[1] Divinity House, Palace Green, Durham; 63; Edwd Greatorex, Sacrist.
Oct. 24 Annie Sarah Rowlandson;[2] College; 10; Bolton Simpson, off^{ng} Min^r.
Nov. 11 Kate Marion Rowlandson;[3] College; 7; Edwd Greatorex, Sacrist.
Dec. 30 Edward Farley Elder;[4] Bellasis, Durham; 2¾; Edwd Greatorex, Sacrist.
1852 May 18 George Griffith;[5] North Bailey; 47; Edwd Greatorex, Sacrist.
Dec. 20 Frances Harriett Robinson;[6] Sniperley, Durham; Geo. Townsend.
1853 May 25 Anne Jane Chaytor;[7] South Bailey; 55; Edwd Greatorex, Sacrist.
July 26 Elizabeth Bowlby;[8] Bailey, Durham; 66; Edwd Greatorex, Sacrist.
Dec. 2 Sophia Elizabeth Feilding;[9] North Bailey, Durham; 65; Edwd Greatorex, Sacrist.
Dec. 31 Elizabeth Margaret Anne Holden,[10] wife of the Revd Henry Holden, Head Master of the Durham Grammar School; Bellasis, Durham; 27; Edwd Greatorex, Sacrist.
1854 May 15 George Murray,[11] student of the University of Durham; Bishop Cosin's Hall, Durham; 20; Edwd Greatorex, Sacrist.

[1] Died 20th. Was formerly butler to Dr. Gray, Bishop of Bristol, and during the Reform Bill riots there was of much service to his Master. His son is Mr. Thomas Jones, of Queen Street, Official to the Archdeacons of Durham, etc., and a Proctor.

[2] Died 21st. Born 27 Sep. and baptized 1 Dec. 1842 at St. Mary's. See her brother's burial 19 May 1845.

[3] Died 14th. Born 4 Jan. and baptized 1 Feb. 1844 at St. Mary's. See her brother's burial 19 May 1845.

[4] Died 20th. See the father's burial 14 April 1858.

[5] Born 17 Jan. and baptized 13 Feb. 1805. Son of John Griffith by his wife Mary Hays. See their burials 19 May 1845 and 21 Oct. 1850. He was an Attorney of Durham, and died unmarried 18 May 1852. [MS. Ped. by E. A. W.]

[6] Died 7th. She was last surviving of ten children and youngest dau. of Sir William Pennyman, of Ormesby, in Cleveland, Yorkshire, sixth Bart., M.P., by Elizabeth, dau. of Sir Henry Grey, of Howick, Northumberland, first Bart. The Pennyman Baronetcy is now extinct. She married firstly, at Walton Abbey, 29 Nov. 1808, Charles-John Berkeley, Esq., M.D., of Beverley, Yorks; and secondly, 26 Aug. 1820, at Bishopwearmouth, John-Christopher-Wall Robinson (who died by a fall from his horse 6 April 1823), of Sniperley, near Durham, Esq. See burial of her adopted daughter's husband (through whom she acquired burial in the Cathedral yard) 17 Dec. 1868. She died issueless, aged 76.

[7] Died 18th. Born 4 Dec. 1797. She was the eldest dau. of Lieut.-Colonel Henry Chaytor, Grenadier Guards. See other burials of her family in Index. She was perhaps the last lady in Durham of her class who assumed "brevet-rank," desiring to be addressed as "Mrs."

[8] Dau. of the Rev. Thomas Bowlby by his wife Eleanora-Elizabeth, dau. of Anthony Salvin, Esq. Born 22 Sep. 1787; baptized 25 Jan. 1788 at Houghton; died unmarried 23 July 1853. See her parents' burials 2 Feb. 1835 and 20 Aug. 1842. [MS. Ped. by E. A. W.]

[9] Dau. of Charles Israel Feilding, of High Holborn, silk mercer, in 1778. She lived at Durham with her sister Charlotte-Anne, who kept a ladies' school in New Elvet. [MS. Ped. by E. A. W.]

[10] She was born 5 Jan. and baptized 10 Aug. 1826 at Woodleigh, co. Devon, and was eldest dau. of the Rev. Richard Edmonds, of Magdalen College, Oxford, B.A., Rector of Woodleigh, by his wife Elizabeth Nicholls, dau. of Robert Pell, Esq., of Tiverton, Devon, to whom she was married at Tormohun, same co., 27 Aug. 1824.

[11] Drowned 11 May, while boating. He was second son of John Dalrymple Murray, Esq., of

1854 Nov. 23 Mary Bowlby;[1] North Bailey, Durham; 57; Edwd Greatorex, Sacrist.
1855 Jan. 17 John Ralph Fenwick,[2] Esq., M.D.; North Bailey, Durham; 94; Edwd Greatorex, Sacrist.
1856 Mar. 16 Editha Maude Greatorex,[3] third dau. of the Revd Edward Greatorex, Sacrist of Durham; The Grove, Durham; infant; John B. Dykes, officiating Minister.
    Dec. 9 Thomas Dickons;[4] Claypath, Durham; 34; Edwd Greatorex, Sacrist.
1857 Mar. 4 Elizabeth Procter;[5] Gilesgate, Durham; 54; Edwd Greatorex, Sacrist.
    April 6 Mary Dickons;[6] Claypath, Durham; 72; Edwd Greatorex, Sacrist.
    April 6 Matthew Woodifield,[7] Esquire; South Bailey, Durham; 54; Edwd Greatorex, Sacrist.
    July 3 Thomas Marsden,[8] Esquire; South Bailey, Durham; 66; Edwd Greatorex, Sacrist.
    July 15 Granville Baker;[9] College; 19; The Reverend Edward Sneyd, officiating Minister.

Murraythwaite, Ecclefechan, Dumfries-shire, by his second wife Anne Elizabeth, eldest dau. of the Rev. Henry Askew, of Redheugh, co. Pal., Rector of Greystock, Cumberland. He was born 15 Oct. 1833, according to the "Landed Gentry."

[1] Dau. of the Rev. Thomas Bowlby by his wife Eleanora Elizabeth, dau. of Anthony Salvin, Esq. Born 1 Dec. 1796 and baptized 21 Jan. 1797 at Houghton; died unmarried 20 Nov. 1854. See her parents' burials 2 Feb. 1835 and 20 Aug. 1842. [MS. Ped. by E. A. W.]

[2] Died 11th, s.p. He was born 14 Nov. 1761, and was second son of John Fenwick, Esq., M.D., of Morpeth, by Mary, youngest dau. of John Thornton, Esq., of Netherwitton, Northumberland. He was D.L. and J.P., co. Durham, and was gazetted Lieut.-Colonel of the Durham Volunteers 18 Oct. 1803. He lived in the house, North Bailey, now the residence of the Misses Fawcett. See his wife's burial 19 June 1838 and the "Landed Gentry"—"Fenwick of Longframlington."

[3] Died 14th, aged one day, "a chrisom child." Her baptism, 14th, is entered in Crossgate Register. See her sister's baptism 6 Jan. 1853.

[4] Died 5th. Born 17 Nov. 1822 and probably baptized at St. Nicholas; the eldest child of his parents. See his father's burial 26 Dec. 1862.

[5] Died 28 Feb. Dau. of Alderman John Wolfe (whose burial see 30 May 1832) by his second wife. She married at St. Oswald's, 26 Feb. 1825, Robert Procter, of Newcastle, general merchant.

[6] Died 3rd. Born 21 Sep. 1784 (probably at Brandon, co. Pal.); third dau. of Ralph Jackson and Sarah Robson, who were married 19 May 1777. She married 20 Sep. 1821, at Crossgate, Thomas Dickons, builder. The newspaper describes her as "of Framwellgate." See burial of her husband 26 Dec. 1862 and of George Jackson 30 Aug. 1842.

[7] Died 29 March. See his baptism 1 July 1802 and the burials of his wives 2 Feb. 1831 and 23 Oct. 1850.

[8] Of Durham, Proctor; born 5 Feb. and baptized 21 March 1791. He married 29 Aug. 1825 Dorothy, elder dau. of John Thomas Christopher, gent., of Norton. See their son's burial 12 March 1835 and a dau. 26 April 1838.

[9] Died 12th. Born 17 May 1838 and baptized at Nuneham Courtenay, Oxon. He was the third surviving son of the Rev. James Baker, M.A., of New College, Oxford, Chancellor of the Diocese of Durham, Rector of St. Mary-the-Less, and afterwards Rector of Nuneham Courtenay, by his second wife Sarah Janetta, youngest dau. of the Rev. Frederick Ekins, Rector of Morpeth and J.P. Northumberland (son of Dr. Jeffery Ekins, Dean of Carlisle), by Anne, eldest dau. of Philip Baker, Esq., Deputy-Secretary of War, and Anne his wife, dau. of Dr. Dawson, Canon of

1857 Nov. 28 The Revd George Townsend,[1] D.D., Canon of Durham; College; 69; The Very Revd George Waddington, D.D., Dean of Durham.
1858 Jan. 28 George Lionel Andrew Dykes;[2] South Bailey; 3 months; Edwd Greatorex, Sacrist.
      April 14 The Revd Edward Elder,[3] D.D., Head Master of Charterhouse School, London, and formerly Head Master of the Durham Grammar School; Charterhouse, London; 45; Edwd Greatorex, Sacrist.
      April 15 Martha Bell;[4] College, Durham; 67; The Reverend John B. Dykes, officiating Minister.

Windsor. Chancellor Baker died 6 Sep. 1854 and was buried at Nuneham Courtenay. His arms, Argent, a tower between three keys erect sable, are in the Town Hall, Durham.

[1] Died 23rd. Born at Ramsgate 12 Sep. 1788. He was the eldest son of the Rev. George Townsend (his portrait *penes* his grandson Rev. George Fyler Townsend), a well-known Independent Minister at Ramsgate, who was brother to John Townsend, founder of the Deaf and Dumb Asylum, Old Kent Road, London, by his wife Susannah Morris (portrait *penes* G. F. T.). He graduated at Trinity College, Cambridge (B.A. 1812, M.A. 1816); ordained Deacon and Priest by Bishop of Ely 1812; Curate of Littleport, Isle of Ely, 1813-14, and of Hackney, Middlesex, 1814-15; Professor at the Royal Military Academy, Sandhurst, with the Curacy of Farnborough, 1817; Domestic Chaplain to Bishop Barrington 1822; installed in the tenth Prebend of Durham 1825; Vicar of Northallerton 1826, resigning 1839, when he took the Perpetual Curacy of Crossgate, Durham. He preached Bishop Van Mildert's funeral sermon. See his first wife's burial 10 Dec. 1835. He married secondly, 19 Dec. 1839, at St. George, Hanover Square, Charlotte Charlton, eldest dau. of J. Hollingbery, Esq., of Lamberhurst, Sussex, and grand-dau. of Thomas Hollingbery, D.D., Prebendary of St. Paul's, who was living s.p. 1877. By his first wife Dr. Townsend (he was D.D. of Durham University) had issue: 1, (Rev.) George Fyler Townsend (see the baptism of his son 1 Jan. 1849): 2, (Rev.) James Frederick Townsend (whose burial see 19 Nov. 1844); 3, Mary Susan, born 25 Sep. 1816, and married 12 Feb. 1840, at St. Mary's, Durham, George Albemarle Cator, Esq., and was living with issue 1877. A portrait of the Doctor hangs in the Chapter Library and another in the Castle hall. His arms, Argent, fretty sable, on a cross gules five estoiles or, are in the Town Hall, Durham. Perhaps no Prebendary of Durham was ever better known than Dr. Townsend, and his memory is yet green in the Palatinate City. His principal works were: "Armageddon," a poem, 8vo; "Edipus Romanus;" "The Old and New Testaments," historically and chronologically arranged, 4 vols. 8vo; "Accusations of History against the Church of Rome," 8vo—a work written under the supervision of Bishop Barrington, and which gained him his stall; "Life and Defence of Bishop Bonner," 8vo (anonymously); Pamphlets on Church Reform and Abolition of Pluralities; two vols. of Sermons; "Ecclesiastical and Civil History, philosophically considered," 2 vols. 8vo, 1847; "Communion with God" (an enlarged edition of his previous arrangement of the Bible); "Letter to Samuel Butler, Esq., on the Roman Catholic Relief Bill." He printed also "Journal of a Tour in Italy," in which is contained an account of his visit to Pius the Ninth.

[2] Born 2 and baptized 30 Nov. 1857 at St. Mary's, Durham. His father was John Bacchus Dykes, of St. Catherine's College, Cambridge, B.A. 1847, M.A. 1850. Minor Canon of Durham and Precentor until 1862, when he was appointed to the Vicarage of St. Oswald's, Elvet. Composer of several Anthems and of many of the Hymns "Ancient and Modern;" Mus. Doc. He died at St. Leonard's 22 Jan. 1876 and was buried at St. Oswald's 28 Jan. 1876. [MS. Ped. by E. A. W.] See also "Dictionary of National Biography," xvi., 292.

[3] Died 1st. Born 1 Oct. 1812.

[4] Died 12th. She was "empty-housekeeper" to Dr. Phillpotts, Bishop of Exeter and Prebendary of Durham.

1858	July 8	William Charles Chaytor,[1] Esquire, Registrar to the Dean and Chapter of Durham; South Bailey; 57; The Reverend H. Jenkyns, D.D., Canon of Durham.
	Dec. 9	The Rev. James Raine,[2] D.C.L., Librarian to the Dean and Chapter of Durham, Rector of Meldon and S. Mary in the South Bailey; Crook Hall; 67; The Reverend J. B. Dykes, officiating Minister.
1859	Mar. 15	Ann Evett;[3] Palace Green, Durham; 57; Edwd Greatorex, Sacrist.
	May 24	Anna Elizabeth Johnson;[4] Aykley Heads; 57; The Reverend J. Cartwright, officiating Minister.
	June 23	Alice Jane King;[5] Grove House, Gilesgate; infant; Edwd Greatorex, Sacrist.
	July 20	The Revd Henry Douglas,[6] M.A., Canon of Durham; College,

[1] Died 1st. He was born 23 Oct. 1800. The second son of Lieut.-Colonel Henry Chaytor, Grenadier Guards, by his wife Jane, dau. of William Marriott, Esq. See the burials of his brothers, sisters, and aunts in Index.

[2] Died 6th; the eminent antiquary and historian of North Durham. He was born 25 and baptized 30 Jan. 1791 at Forcett, North Riding of Yorks, and was second son of James Raine, of Ovington, same shire, by his wife Anne, dau. of William Moore. He was Second Master of Durham School 1812—27; Rector of Meldon, Northumberland, 1822; Rector of St. Mary's (in the South Bailey) 1828; he was also Librarian to the Dean and Chapter for thirty-seven years, and Principal Surrogate of the Consistory Court of the Diœcese; M.A. (Lambeth Degree) and D.C.L. of Durham University. He married 28 Jan. 1828, at Denton, co. Durham, Margaret, eldest dau. of the Rev. Thomas Peacock, Perpetual Curate of that place, and sister of the Very Rev. George Peacock, Dean of Ely, by whom he had a son and three daughters. His widow died 4 Nov. 1874 and is buried at Elswick Cemetery, Newcastle-on-Tyne. Dr. Raine, says the "Gentleman's Magazine" (vol. li., p. 156), was "one of the last survivors of the old race of County Historians, whose works were produced in stately folios, and the founder of one of the most successful and useful of our printing clubs, the Surtees Society." Besides his "History of North Durham," he was Author of "St. Cuthbert, with an Account of the state in which his remains were found upon the opening of his Tomb in Durham Cathedral," Durham, 1828, and was the Editor for the Surtees Society of fourteen of its volumes. The antiquarian mantle of the historian fitly fell on the shoulders of his son the late Rev. Canon James Raine, D.C.L., of York, the indefatigable Secretary to and Editor of many volumes of the Surtees Society. Dr. Raine's second dau. Margaret, wife of the late Alfred William Hunt, Esq., A.R.A., the distinguished artist, is the Author of several novels. [See also "Dictionary of National Biography," vol. xlvii., p. 175.]

[3] Died 11th. Wife of William Evett, butler at the Castle (University College), whose burial see 18 Jan. 1864.

[4] Born 26 Nov. 1802 and baptized at Crossgate 22 Jan. 1803. Dau. of Francis Johnson, of Aykleyheads, Esq. (by his wife Mary, dau. of the Hon. Richard Hetherington). See the parents' burials 28 April 1838 and 11 April 1851. [MS. Ped. by E. A. W.]

[5] Died 21st. The father the Rev. Charles William King, M.A., was son of the Rev. William Clark King, Hon. Canon of Durham and Vicar of Norham, by his wife Sarah, eldest dau. of John Hodgson, Esq., of Elswick House, Northumberland (see "Landed Gentry"—"Hodgson-Hinde," and in later editions "Archer-Hinde"). He was Rector of St. Mary-le-Bow; Principal of the Durham Training College for Schoolmistresses, and afterwards one of Her Majesty's Inspectors of Schools; he died 1872. The mother (living 1890) was Mary Anne, third dau. of Canon Douglas, whose burial see next entry.

[6] Died 15th. He was born 17 April 1793, and was eldest son of the Rev. Robert Douglas (previously an officer in the Army), Rector and Patron of Salwarpe, Worcestershire, and was

			Durham; 66; The Very Rev[d] George Waddington, D.D., Dean of Durham.
1860	May	7	Elizabeth Cartwright;[1] Old Elvet, Durham; 86; The Reverend Edward Sneyd, officiating Minister.
	May	26	Ann Clues;[2] College, Durham; 50; Edw[d] Greatorex, Sacrist.
	Dec.	25	Elizabeth Ann Robson;[3] North Road; 22; Edw[d] Greatorex, Sacrist.
1861	Feb.	19	Margaret Pearson Davison;[4] Church Street, Durham; 66; The Reverend Edward Sneyd, Vicar of S. Oswald's.
	Mar.	2	Henry Bradley,[5] student at the University; Bishop Cosin's Hall; 20; Edw[d] Greatorex, Sacrist.
	June	1	Frances Bell, cook and housekeeper; University College; 67; Edw[d] Greatorex, Sacrist.
	July	25	Annie Martha Chaytor;[6] South Bailey, Durham; 51; The Reverend J. B. Dykes, Precentor of Durham.
	Aug.	20	Elizabeth Tyler;[7] Old Elvet, Durham; 86; Edw[d] Greatorex, Sacrist.

brother of the late Robert Archibald Douglas-Gresley, Esq., of Salwarpe and High Park, same co. (see " Landed Gentry "—" Douglas-Gresley "), and grandson of Lieut.-General Archibald Douglas, Colonel of the 13th Dragoons, and M P. for the Dumfries Burghs 1771, who was father of Mrs. Van Mildert (see her burial 28 Dec. 1837). Mr. Douglas was sometime Rector of Salwarpe and Prebendary of Durham. He married in 1823 Eleanor, who died 24 April 1879, dau. of the Rev. Thomas Birt, Vicar of Newland, Gloucestershire, and had issue seventeen children, of whom the eldest dau., who died 1887, was wife of Dr. William Walsham-How, first Bishop of Wakefield. See the burial of a grandchild, preceding entry.

[1] Died 2nd. She was the only child of James Tinkler, merchant of London, by his wife Mary Atkinson (died, aged 97, and buried at Norton, co. Pal.), sister of Thomas Atkinson, of Mold Green and Bradley Mills, Huddersfield, and was granddau. of John Tinkler, of Kirk-Oswald, Cumberland, gent., and his wife Barbara, third dau. of the Rev. George Lowthian, of Staffold, Cumberland, and sister and coheiress in her descendants of Richard Lowthian, of Staffold, Esq., who died, aged 90, 1 May 1784, s.p., at Dumfries. She married, about 1801, John Cartwright, of Norton, Esq., D.L. and J.P. co. Durham, who was a native of Halifax, and died at Bath 5 March 1854 and was buried 10th in the Abbey Cemetery there. The issue and only surviving child of this marriage was the late Rev. John Cartwright. He was born at Halifax 20 June 1804; of Christ's College, Cambridge (B.A. 1827 ; M.A. 1830) ; Precentor and Minor Canon of Durham 1834; Perpetual Curate of Ferryhill 1843-4; Rector of Witton-Gilbert 1849—1851. He was the author of several translations from Greek and German authors. He died unmarried, having given up his Minor Canonry some years before, 15 Dec. 1879, and was buried 19th at Elvet Hill Cemetery, being registered at St. Mary-the-Less.

[2] Died 24th. " Empty-housekeeper " to the Bishop of Exeter, Dr. Philipotts.

[3] Died 18th. She was born 30 April 1838. See her father's burial 23 Dec. 1865.

[4] Wife of the Rev. Edward Davison, Vicar of St. Nicholas and Rector of Harlington, Middlesex (who died 22 May 1863); lived in Church Street, Durham. She was the dau. of Alderman John Wolfe, of Durham, by his wife Elizabeth, who was the widow of Richard Buttler, of Sunderland. Mrs. Davison was married at St. Oswald's 11 May 1824. She died 14 Feb. 1861 and was buried next her father and grandfather Pearson and Mr. Buttler. [MS. Ped. by E. A. W.]

[5] Died 27 Feb. Only son of Henry Bradley, of Blackheath, Kent.

[6] Died 20th. She was the only dau. of Thomas Greatorex, Esq., F.R.S., Organist of Westminster Abbey (the burial of whose widow see 30 July 1868). She married, 8 Sep. 1836, Colonel John Chaytor, R.E., whose burial see 12 Feb. 1862.

[7] Died 16th. Born 14 Nov. 1774, being the dau. of William Bates, of that parish, by his wife Elizabeth Bullock, whom he married at Marylebone 23 April 1767. See her husband's burial 14 July 1849 and her son's 27 Jan. 1871.

1862	Feb. 12	John Chaytor,[1] Colonel Royal Engineers; South Bailey, Durham; 60; The Reverend J. B. Dykes, Precentor of Durham.
	April 8	The Revd John Edwards,[2] M.A., Canon of Durham, & Professor of Greek in the University of Durham; College, Durham; 73; The Very Revd George Waddington, D.D., Dean of Durham.
	Dec. 26	Thomas Dickons;[3] Claypath; 70 y^{rs}; J. C. Lowe, Sacrist.
1863	Nov. 24	Rosamond Evans; The College; 35 y^{rs}; George Bland, Archdeacon of Northumberland.
	Nov. 28	The Revd Henry Joseph Maltby,[4] Canon of Durham; The College; 51 y^{rs}; George Waddington, Dean of Durham.
1864	Jan. 18	William Evett;[5] The Old Gram. School; 54 y^{rs}; J. Conran Lowe, Sacrist.
	April 7	Elizabeth Darnell;[6] The Rectory, Stanhope; 76 y^{rs}; The Ven. Archdeacon Bland.
	May 19	David Flintoff;[7] Banks Cottage; 71 y^{rs}; The Ven. Archdeacon Coxe.

[1] Died 8th. He was born 28 Jan. 1802, the third son of Lieut.-Colonel Henry Chaytor, 1st Foot Guards, by his wife Jane, dau. of William Marriott, Esq. His sons are the representatives of the Chaytors "of Butterby." He died very suddenly of heart disease. See his wife's burial 25 July 1861.

[2] Died 1st. He was born 14 Nov. 1789 and baptized at Huntingdon, being the son of the Rev. Edward Edwards, of that place, by his wife Sarah, dau. of Colonel Freeman, of Apsley, Bedfordshire. He graduated, B.A. 1812, M.A. 1815, at St. John's College, Cambridge, moving to Jesus College, and was for sometime Head Master of Bury St. Edmunds Grammar School; Canon of Durham, and Professor of Greek in that University 1841. He married at Huntingdon Church, 9 July 1816, Louisa (who died 13 April 1831 and is buried at Bury St. Edmunds), dau. of Robert Cooch, Esq., of Huntingdon, by his wife Ann, dau. of Samuel Wells, of Biggleswade, Beds. See his granddaughter's baptism 20 Oct. 1856.

[3] Died 23rd. Native of Sedgefield. He signed the Marriage Register at Crossgate "Dickins," and was described "of Brancepeth." See his wife's burial 6 April 1857; his daughter's 2 June 1848; and his sons' 9 Dec. 1856 and 21 May 1875.

[4] Died 24th. He was born at Buckden (of which his father was then Vicar), Hunts, 2 July 1814, and was the fifth and youngest son of Dr. Edward Maltby, Bishop of Durham 1836–1856, by his first wife Mary, dau. of —— Hervey, Esq., of Norwich (who died at Buckden 2 May 1825); of Caius College, Cambridge (B.A. 1835; M.A. 1838); Vicar of Eglingham, Northumberland, Rector of Egglescliffe, co. Pal., and Canon of Durham. He married first, 13 Feb. 1840, at Long Horsley, Northumberland, Julia Katherina (she died 27 April 1843 and is buried at Long Horsley), third dau. of Charles-William Bigge, of Linden, Northumberland, Esq., D.L., J.P., by whom he had issue; and secondly, 13 June 1847, at St. Paul's, Knightsbridge, Elizabeth Mary, eldest dau. of Lieut.-General Sir Thomas Bradford, G.C.B., G.C.H., by his first wife Mary Anne, only dau. of James Atkinson, Esq., of Newcastle, and widow of Lieut.-Colonel Philip Ainslie, 4th Dragoons. See his sons' burials 20 June 1864 and 24 Aug. 1866. His father, who was the first Bishop after the Palatinate powers were transferred to the Crown, resigned the Bishopric in 1856; died in London 3 July 1859, and was buried at Kensal Green. He was previously Bishop of Chichester. He had a grant of arms, viz.: Argent, on a bend gules, between a lion rampant in chief azure and a Maltese cross in base of the second, three garbs or. Crest: A garb, charged with a Maltese cross between two laurel branches.

[5] Died 14th; butler at the Castle. See his wife's burial 15 March 1859.

[6] Wife of the Rev. William Nicholas Darnell, whose burial see 24 June following—dau. of the Rev. William Bowe, M.A., of Scorton, co. York—married 15 June 1815. [MS. Ped. by E. A. W.]

[7] Died 16th; woodman and choir porter for forty-five years to the Dean and Chapter, and formerly steward to Dr. Townsend at Northallerton, where he was probably baptized. He was

1864	June 20	Ralph Howard Maltby;[1] The College; 9 y^{rs}; Julius Conran Lowe, Sacrist.
	Dec. 17	Sarah Rowlandson;[2] Gilesgate; 86 y^{rs}; Julius Conran Lowe, Sacrist.
1865	June 24	Rev. William Nicholas Darnell;[3] Stanhope; 89 y^{rs}; The Venerable Archdeacon Bland.
	Aug. 23	Vere Holden; Bellasis; infant; Edward Greatorex, off. Min^r. [Cemetery.]
	Dec. 3	Charles Thorp Greatorex;[4] The Grove; infant; J. C. Lowe, Sacrist.
	Dec. 18	Christopher Hardinge Fenwick;[5] South St., Durham; 12 y^{rs}; Edward Greatorex, off. Min^r. [Cemetery.]
1866	Mar. 20	William Nixon;[6] The Grammar School (a native of Windsor); 17 y^{rs}; J. C. Lowe, Sacrist; Died March 18. [Cemetery.]
	Aug. 24	Henry Charles Bradford Maltby;[7] The College; 17 y^{rs}; J. C. Lowe, Sacrist.
	Dec. 23	John Robson;[8] Neville House; 52 years; J. C. Lowe, Sacrist.

third son of Thomas Flintoff, of Romanby, near Northallerton, and grandson of David Flintoff, of Holdstead Hall, near Northallerton, gent. He had by his wife Beatrice (whose burial see 30 Jan. 1871), besides the daughters buried 28 Oct. 1842 and 19 Oct. 1867, Jane, born 21 March 1816, married, living with issue 1877; Thomas, born 28 Aug. 1817, ob. infant; Marianne (from whom this information), born 14 Jan. 1821 (whose burial see 2 Dec. 1878); James, born 22 July 1824, ob. infant—all probably baptized at Northallerton. Little did the Editor think, as a boy at Durham School, when he and his fellow scholars were teasing "old Davy," that it would be his lot one day to write this!

[1] Died 16th. Third and youngest son, by his second wife, of Canon Maltby, whose burial see 28 Nov. 1863.

[2] Died 14th. Mother of Mr. Samuel Rowlandson, agent to the Dean and Chapter. See her grandson's burial 19 May 1845.

[3] Baptized 16 April 1776 at All Saints, Newcastle; of Christ Church, Oxon (B.A. 1796, M.A. 1800); Rector of St. Mary-le-Bow, Durham (June 1809); Vicar of Stockton-on-Tees; Prebendary of Durham Jan. 1816; Rector of Stanhope, succeeding Bishop Phillpotts. When Dr. Phillpotts, then Rector of Stanhope (the richest living the Bishop of Durham possessed, which is now vested in the Bishop of Ripon), was offered the Bishopric of Exeter, of so much smaller value than his own preferment, he exchanged his Rectory with Mr. Darnell for that gentleman's Prebend. [MS. Ped. by E. A. W.]

[4] See his baptism 15 May 1864 and his sister's 6 Jan. 1853.

[5] His headstone records that he died same day. He was a pupil of the Rev. Julius Conran Lowe, M.A., Minor Canon and Sacrist, in whose house he died. He was eldest child of Thomas Fenwick, Esq. (now Fenwick-Cleunell, of Harbottle Castle, Northumberland), by his wife Frances, eldest dau. of Frederick Hardinge, Esq., of Coatham Mundeville, co. Pal., younger brother of the first Viscount Hardinge.

[6] *Recté* William Yates Nixon; died 13th. He was born 17 March and baptized 2 May 1849 at St. John's, New Windsor, Berkshire, and was seventh son of Thomas Nixon, of that place, by his marriage at St. John's aforesaid, 2 May 1829, with Mary Ann, dau. of William Collison, of Leicester. He was a King's Scholar of Durham School.

[7] Died 19th. The eldest son, by his second wife, of Canon Maltby (whose burial see 28 Nov. 1863). He was born 9 April 1849 and baptized at St. Paul's, Knightsbridge.

[8] Died 19th. He was the eldest son and second child of Thomas Robson by his wife Ann Stokeld (married 1812), and was baptized privately 16 Sep. 1814, and afterwards at St. Nicholas 9 July 1815. He married at Witton Gilbert, 20 June 1837, Frances (living 1877), fifth dau. and

REGISTER OF BURIALS IN THE

1866 Dec. 25 Jane Bond;[1] The Deanery; 32 y^{rs}; J. C. Lowe, Sacrist. [*Cemetery.*]
1867 Jan. 27 Thomas Kaye,[2] lay clerk; Sadler St.; 52 years; J. C. Lowe, Sacrist. [*Cemetery.*]
       Oct. 19 Elizabeth Flintoff;[3] Halgarth St.; 34 years; J. C. Lowe, Sacrist.
       Dec. 27 Agnes Harrison Johnson;[4] Aykleyheads; 56 y^{rs}; Rev. Canon Evans.
1868 Feb. 14 Alice Pedder;[5] The College; 7 m^{ths}; J. C. Lowe, Sacrist.
       July 30 Elizabeth Greatorex;[6] The Grove; 87 y^{rs}; J. C. Lowe, Sacrist.
       Dec. 17 Joseph Davison;[7] Greencroft, Lanchester; 60 y^{rs}; The Bishop, assisted by Archdeacon Bland.
1869 June 4 Phillis Hartley;[8] College Gates; 54 y^{rs}; Canon Chevallier.

seventh child of John Hall, currier, whose burial see 13 May 1841. He was proprietor of the Durham flour mills, and elder brother of the late Robert Naisbitt Robson, Esq., M.R.C.S. and J.P. for the City, who died 1888. See his daughters' burials 29 Aug. 1851 and 25 Dec. 1860.

[1] Died 21st. She was cook and housekeeper to Dean Waddington.

[2] Died 23rd. He was nineteen years a Lay Clerk of the Cathedral.

[3] Died 15th. Born (according to family information supplied) 12 July 1825 at Northallerton, and her age, therefore, must be wrongly stated here. See her father's burial 19 May 1864.

[4] Wife of Francis-Dixon Johnson, of Aykleyheads, Esq., whose burial see 22 Nov. 1893. She was the dau. of John Greenwood, of Polefield, co. Lancaster, Esq., by his wife Agnes Harrison, of Poulton on the Fylde; born 30 Aug. 1811; married at Prestwich 18 Jan. 1838; died 22 Dec. 1867. Arms: Sable, a chevron between three saltires argent. There is an oil portrait of her with her younger dau. at Aykleyheads. [MS. Ped. by E. A. W.]

[5] Died 11 Feb. Dau. of Rev. John Pedder by his wife Harriet, eldest dau. of the Rev. Henry Jenkyns, D.D., Canon of Durham and Professor of Divinity in the University, and of Botley Hill, Southants. She was born 23 June 1867.

[6] Died 26th at the residence of her son the Rev. Edward Greatorex, Minor Canon. She was married to Thomas Greatorex, Esq., F.R.S. This gentleman, the only son of Anthony Greatorex, of Derbyshire, by his wife Miss Bingley, and grandson of Daniel Greatorex, was born at Wingfield, near Chesterfield, 5 Oct. 1758; he was Organist of Westminster Abbey from 1819, and Conductor of the King's Concerts for Ancient Music for thirty-nine years. Not more distinguished for his great musical talents than for his refined manners and knowledge of mathematics, astronomy, and even military science. As an archer, almost the first bowsman in England; as an artist, chemist, and botanist, equally distinguished. In short, "he was one of those gifted beings who appear to have the power of excelling in whatever they undertake." As such he was acceptable to the highest society, and received in the warmest friendship, not only by the Earl of Sandwich, the celebrated Lord Chesterfield, the "old" Pretender, and a host of other well-known men of genius, but by George the Third and his Queen, as also George the Fourth. He died at Hampton, Middlesex, 18 July 1831 and was buried 25 July in the west cloister of Westminster Abbey. See his grand-daughter's baptism 6 Jan. 1853 and others in Index. [See "Dictionary of National Biography," xviii., p. 33, and "Westminster Abbey Registers," Harleian Society's Publications, vol. x., p. 504.]

[7] Died 13th. He was son of Thomas Davison, agent to Bishop Barrington (who left him £100), of Sedgefield, Croft, and Durham City (he died 1862), by his wife (died 1862) Miss Barker, of Sedgefield, who brought her husband the Diamond Hall property at that place. He was Registrar to the Bishop of Durham and Registrar of the Probate Court, Durham, and latterly was resident at Greencroft Park, Lanchester. He married at Witton Gilbert, 1 June 1842, Anne-Caroline Robinson, natural and adopted dau. of J. C. W. Robinson, Esq., of Sniperley, and heiress of his wife, whose burial see 20 Dec. 1852. Mrs. Davison died at Brighton 13 and was buried at Durham Cathedral 18 Sep. 1879, aged 70.

[8] Died 1st. She was born 10 May 1815 at Breadsall, Derbyshire, and was dau. of John

CATHEDRAL CHURCH AT DURHAM. 155

1869 July 24 The Very Revd George Waddington,[1] D.D., Dean of Durham; The Deanery; 75 y^{rs}; The Bishop, assisted by Canon Chevallier, Sub-Dean.
1870 Jan. 18 Thomas Griffith;[2] The Bailey, Durham; 74 y^{rs}; J. C. Lowe, Sacrist.
May 16 Arthur Thomas Fabian Evans;[3] College; 8 y^{rs}; The Very Revd W. C. Lake, Dean of Durham.
1871 Jan. 27 Edwin Tyler;[4] Old Elvet; 62 y^{rs}; J. C. Lowe, Sacrist.
Jan. 30 Beatrice Flintoff;[5] North Road; 82 y^{rs}; J. C. Lowe, Sacrist.
1872 Jan. 10 Elleanor Griffith;[6] North Bailey; 65 y^{rs}; J. C. Lowe, Sacrist.
Jan. 16 Elizabeth Bowlby;[7] Old Elvet; 78 y^{rs}; J. C. Lowe, Sacrist.
1873 May 14 Frances Griffith;[8] North Bailey; 72 y^{rs}; W. H. Robertson, Sacrist.

Rowland, of that place, where she was married 22 Sep. 1840. See her husband's burial 25 April 1876.
[1] Died 20th. He was born 7 Sep. 1793 at Tuxford, Notts, the elder son of the Rev. George Waddington, M.A. (died 1824), Vicar of that place, by his wife Anne, youngest dau. of Peter Dollond, the well-known optician, of St. Paul's Churchyard (married 13 May 1790), and grandson of the Rev. Joshua Waddington, Vicar of Harworth, and of Walkeringham, Notts, and his wife Ann, dau. (but not heiress, although the Dean quartered her arms) of the Rev. Thomas Ferrand, of Bingley, Yorks. He graduated (B.A. 1815; M.A. 1818) at Trinity College, Cambridge, of which he was Fellow; Vicar of Masham, co. York, and, 1840, Dean of Durham. Notwithstanding the changes made by the Ecclesiastical Commission, the Deanery during Dr. Waddington's tenure was of much greater value than at present. The Dean, who refused the Bishopric of Manchester, was brother of the Right Hon. Horatio Waddington, for long Permanent Under-Secretary of State, Home Department, and M. Waddington, the late French Ambassador, is of the same family. The arms his family used (Argent, on a fess sable between three fleurs-de-lys azure, a lion passant of the field), and which are in the Durham Town Hall, are wrong. This is the coat of Thwaites (whose heiress married into the Waddington family) differenced by the lion, though it was "confirmed" to William Waddington, Esq., uncle of the Dean, in 1769. The mistake first arose in 1665 through an error of the Herald Warburton. The right arms of Waddington are: Argent, a chevron between three martlets gules (sometimes sable).
[2] Of North Bailey, Durham, and Morden, Esq., sometime an Attorney and Under Sheriff, eldest son of John Griffith, of Durham, by Mary, dau. of John Hays (see their burials 19 May 1845 and 21 Oct. 1850). Born 8 and baptized 23 Dec. 1795. Will dated 22 Dec. 1869, proved in London 10 Feb. 1870. [MS. Ped. by E. A. W.]
[3] Died 12th. Youngest son of the Rev. Thomas Saunders Evans, Canon of Durham, and Professor of Greek in the University.
[4] Died 22nd. See his baptism 24 Oct. 1808. He was a Surgeon, and Surgeon to the North Durham Militia. He married at St. James's, Paddington, Maria (his cousin), third dau. of John-William Burt, of Westbourne Terrace, London (by his wife Phyllis, dau. of William Burt, of Marylebone). See his father's burial 14 July 1849, and his mother's 20 Aug. 1861.
[5] Died 26th. She was the third dau. of James Sharpe, of Aycliffe, co. Pal., farmer. See her husband's burial 19 May 1864.
[6] Born 10 Nov. and baptized 5 Dec. 1806; died unmarried at North Bailey 6 Jan. 1872. Third dau. of John Griffith, of Durham, by his wife Mary, dau. of John Hays, Esq. (see their burials 19 May 1845 and 21 Oct. 1850). [MS. Ped. by E. A. W.]
[7] Born 10th, baptized privately 20 July 1793 and publicly 26 Sep. 1793 at St. Mary-the-Less. Eldest dau. of John Bowlby, Registrar to the Dean and Chapter of Durham, by Sarah, dau. of John and Dorothy Elliot. She died unmarried at Old Elvet 13 Feb. 1872. [MS. Ped. by E. A. W.]
[8] Born 18 March, baptized 14 April 1801. Third son of John Griffith, of Durham, Esq., by his wife Mary, dau. of John Hays, Esq. (see their burials 19 May 1845 and 21 Oct. 1850). Died

1873	Nov. 4	David Lambert;[1] Saddler St.; 40 y^{rs}; J. C. Lowe, Minor Canon. [Cemetery.]
1874	Feb. 4	Wm James Martin;[2] North R^d; 55 y^{rs}; W. H. Robertson, Sacrist. [Cemetery.]
1875	Jan. 12	John Moor[3] (for upwards of 37 years Verger of this Cath^l Church); The Palace Green; 78; John B. Dykes, off^g Min^r.
	May 21	John Ralph Dickons;[4] Claypath; 48; Th. Rogers, offic. Min^r.
	June 21	Mary Hall;[5] Old Elvet; 67; W. H. Robertson, Sacrist.
1876	April 25	William Hartley,[6] Dean's Verger for 37 years; College Gates; 70 y^{rs}; Edward Prest, The Archdeacon of Durham.
1878	July 16	Willoughby Waite;[7] College; 15 weeks; H. B. Tristram, Canon.
	Nov. 4	James Lambert;[8] Old Elvet; 68 years; The Ven. the Archdeacon of Northumberland.
	Dec. 2	Marianne Flintoff;[9] North Road; 57 years; W. H. Robertson, Sacrist.
1879	July 28	Mary White; North Road; 65 years; W. H. Robertson, Sacrist.
	Sep. 18	Anne Caroline Davison;[10] Brighton; 70 years; H. B. Tristram, Canon.
1880	Feb. 20	The Ven^{ble} George Bland,[11] Archdeacon of Northumberland and Canon of Durham; The College; 75 years; The Bishop, assisted by the Dean.

unmarried at the North Bailey 10 May 1873. Will dated 12 March 1868, proved 7 Aug. 1873 under £20,000 personalty. [MS. Ped. by E. A. W.] The Griffiths occupy a long row of nine nameless graves, extending from the Abbey towards the railings arranged in the order they died. [A small headstone has lately, 1885, been placed at the father's grave.]

[1] Died 30 Oct. in the Cathedral, during evening service. He was a son of James Lambert, also a Lay Clerk, the possessor of a magnificent bass voice, whose burial see 4 Nov. 1878. He was formerly in the choir of the Chapel Royal, Windsor. He is buried at Elvet Hill Cemetery.

[2] Died 30 Jan.; was for thirty-five years a Lay Clerk. He is buried at Elvet Hill Cemetery. His children are baptized at Crossgate.

[3] Died 8th. He was born at Kirkharle, Northumberland, 26 June 1796, the eldest of nine children of Thomas Moore (who died at Coldwell, aged 81, 23 May 1841), farmer, and many years land agent to Sir William Loraine, of Kirkharle, Bart., by his wife Sarah Hedley, who died at Coldwell, same co., aged 73, 3 July 1841. By his wife (whose burial see 6 June 1846) he had an only dau. Jane Catherine, born 7 Feb. 1841 and baptized at St. Mary's 2 Jan. 1842.

[4] Died 17th. Born 19 Feb. 1827; he was younger son of Thomas Dickons, whose burial see 26 Dec. 1862. He was a retired stationer and bookseller.

[5] See her husband's burial 28 April 1835.

[6] Died 22nd. He was born at Knightsbridge, Middlesex, 31 March 1806.

[7] Son of the Rev. Joseph Waite, D.D., Vicar of Norham, Hon. Canon of Newcastle, and his wife Rosamond, dau. of Rev. T. S. Evans, Canon of Durham, and Professor of Greek in the University of Durham.

[8] See his son's burial 4 Nov. 1873, and his daughter's 12 Sep. 1888.

[9] Dau. of David Flintoff, woodman and choir porter to the Dean and Chapter. See her parents' burials 19 May 1864 and 30 Jan. 1871.

[10] She was a dau. of Mr. Robinson, whose widow's burial is recorded 20 Dec. 1852. She was the widow of Joseph Davison, who was buried 17 Dec. 1868.

[11] Son of Michael Bland, Esq., F.R.S., by his wife Sophia, youngest dau. of George Maltby, Esq., of Norwich, and sister of the late Bishop Maltby. He was educated at the Grammar School of Bury St. Edmunds under Dr. Benjamin Heath Malkin; graduated at Caius College, Cam-

CATHEDRAL CHURCH AT DURHAM. 157

1880 June 5 Frederick John Copeman;[1] University College, Durham; 40 years; The Very Rev. W. C. Lake, Dean of Durham, assisted by Canon Evans. Cath. Yard.
   Oct. 21 Rosamond Waite;[2] Norham Vicarage, Northumberland; 10 years; H. B. Tristram, Canon. Cath. Yard.
1881 Feb. 19 Dorothy Marsden;[3] Altrincham, Cheshire; 83 years; W. H. Robertson, Sacrist. Cath. Yard.
   Sep. 7 Thomas White; North Road; 78 years; W. H. Robertson, Sacrist. Cath. Yard.
1883 Feb. 27 Samuel Rowlandson;[4] The College; 77 years; W. H. Robertson, Sacrist; Lesson read by Rev. Canon Evans. Cath. Yard.
   Aug. 29 Mary Griffith;[5] North Bailey; 84 years; H. B. Tristram, Canon. Cath. Yard.
1884 Sep. 25 Hannah Rowlandson;[6] The College; 74 years; Rev. D[r] Tristram, Canon of Durham, & Rev. W. H. Robertson, Sacrist. Cath. Yard.
1885 Mar. 14 William Darnell;[7] S. Leonards on Sea; 68 years; Rev. E. Greatorex, Precentor, & Rev. W. H. Robertson, Sacrist. Cath. Yard.

bridge, B.A. 1828; M.A. 1831; ordained in 1829; appointed in 1836 by Bishop Maltby, then Bishop of Chichester, to the Rectory of Slinfold in Sussex. When Bishop Maltby was translated to Durham in 1844 Mr. Bland was appointed to the newly created Archdeaconry of Lindisfarne, and held the living of Eglingham. In 1853 Bishop Maltby transferred him to the Archdeaconry of Northumberland, and he was at the same time presented to a Canonry of Durham Cathedral. In 1856 he became Incumbent of St. Mary-le-Bow in Durham, which was then in the gift of the Archdeacon of Northumberland. In Dec. 1862, on the death of Archdeacon Thorpe, he was appointed Official of the Officialty of the Dean and Chapter of Durham. He married at Boldon, in 1846, Frances Sybel, eldest dau. of the Rev. John Collinson, Rector of that place, and sister to Admiral Collinson. He died at his residence in the College on the 17th Feb. 1880.

[1] Second son of James Robert Copeman, of Worcester, Esq.; matriculated at Christ Church, Oxford, 19 Oct. 1859; Servitor 1859; Student 1860—1865; B.A. 1864; M.A. 1865; Classical Tutor in the University of Durham 1865; Proctor 1873—1875. Died 31 May 1880.

[2] See her baptism 13 July 1870.

[3] Widow of Thomas Marsden, of Durham, Proctor, whose burial see 3 July 1857. She was the elder dau. of John Thomas Christopher, of Norton, co. Pal., by his wife Dorothy, second dau. of Crosier Surtees, of Redworth and Merry Shields, Esq. Married at Gainford 29 Aug. 1825; died at Newcastle. Arms: Per chevron wavy azure and erminois, a chart of Chesterfield's Inlet between two estoiles in chief argent, and on a mount in base vert a beaver passant proper. Mrs. Marsden was granddau. of the Navigator, William Christopher. [MS. Ped. by E. A. W.]

[4] Appointed Deputy-Treasurer to the Dean and Chapter April 1837 at the death of Mr. John Leybourne. The son (by Sarah his wife, whose burial see 17 Dec. 1864) of Christopher Rowlandson, of West Shows, near Barnard Castle. He was born 27 Nov. 1805; died 22 Feb. 1883. See his wife's burial 25 Sep. 1884.

[5] Dau. of John Griffith, of Durham, Esq., by Mary, eldest dau. of John Hays, Esq.; born 17 Sep., baptized 12 Oct. 1798 at St. Mary-le-Bow; died 25 Aug. 1883, unmarried, in the house she was born in. [MS. Ped. by E. A. W.]

[6] Widow of Samuel Rowlandson, whose burial see 27 Feb. 1883 (formerly Miss Hannah Kipling).

[7] The Rev. William Darnell, son of the Rev. William Nicholas Darnell, B.D., by his wife Elizabeth, eldest dau. of Rev. William Bowe, M.A. (see their burials 24 June 1865 and 7 April 1864). He was born 19 Nov. 1816 at Stockton Vicarage; of Christ Church College, Oxford, B.A. 1838; M.A. 1843; Vicar of Bamborough, Northumberland; J.P. [MS. Ped. by E. A. W.]

1885 Aug. 6 William Henry Robertson;[1] South Street; 45 years; Ven. G. H. Hamilton, Archdeacon of Northumberland, & Rev. V. K. Cooper & Rev. J. C. Lowe, Minor Canons, & Rev. H. B. Tristram, Canon of Durham. Elvet Cemetery.

1887 Aug. 8 Julius Conran Lowe;[2] South Bailey; 65 years; Very Rev. The Dean of Durham, Rev. G. Body, Canon of Durham, Rev. W. M. Smith-Dorrien, Precentor of Durham. Elvet Cemetery.

1888 April 3 Elizabeth Greatorex;[3] Croxdale Rectory; 60 years; The Ven[ble] The Archdeacon of Durham, The Ven[ble] Archdeacon of Northumberland, The Rev. W. M. Smith-Dorrien, Minor Canon of Durham. Cath. Yard.

Sep. 4 John Alder Bedser; Prebend's Cottage; 72 years; George William Anson Firth, Sacrist. Elvet Cemetery.

Sep. 12 Ann Beckwith;[4] Walker on Tyne; 45 years; The Ven[ble] The Archdeacon of Northumberland & V. K. Cooper. Elvet Cemetery.

Oct. 25 Mary Jones;[5] Queen Street, Durham; 96 years; V. K. Cooper, Precentor, G. W. A. Firth, Sacrist. Cath. Yard.

1889 Jan. 3 Maria Cooch;[6] North Bailey; 87 years; Rev. Canon Farrar, D.D., Rev. Canon Evans, Rev. Archdeacon Hamilton, Canon of Durham, Rev. G. W. Anson Firth, Sacrist. Cath. Yard.

May 21 Thomas Saunders Evans,[7] D.D., Senior Canon; The College; 73 years; H. B. Tristram, Canon. Cath. Yard.

1890 May 26, died May 24. Kate Tuke; Crossgate, Durham; 38 years; V. K. Cooper, Precentor. Buried in Cemetery, Elvet Hill.

June 16, died June 14. Edith Mary Tuke; Crossgate, Durham; 20 years; V. K. Cooper, Precentor. Buried in Cemetery.

Sep. 26 Robert Kirkup Liddle; 14 years' Dean's Verger; Palace Green, Durham; 60 years; W. C. Lake, Dean. Bow Cemetery.

1893 Mar. 7 Francis Allan Ker;[8] South Street, Durham; 34 years; Rev. H. B.

---

[1] Born at Buxton, Derbyshire, 14 Feb. 1840, son of William Henry Robertson, Esq., M.D., F.R.C.P., J.P., of Buxton, by his wife Eliza, dau. of John Slater Gill, of Chesterfield; of Christ Church, Oxon (B.A. 1863; M.A. 1866); successively Curate of Thorpe Mandeville and Houghton-le-Spring; Minor Canon of Durham Sep. 1866 and Sacrist 20 Nov. 1872, and also Sub-Librarian. He married Frances Henrietta, second dau. of the late Francis Jones, M.A., Vicar of Morton Pinkney, Northamptonshire. He died at Buxton 2 Aug. 1885.

[2] Son of the Rev. Richard Lowe, of Marylebone, Middlesex; of Queen's College, Oxford, matriculated 28 May 1841, B.A. 1845; M.A. 1854; Sacristan 1854—1872; Minor Canon 1854; Chaplain of the Durham County Prison from 1873 until his death 4 Aug. 1887.

[3] Wife of the Rev. Edward Greatorex, Minor Canon and Precentor of the Cathedral, Rector of Croxdale, co. Durham. She was the dau. of Charles Thorp, D.D., Archdeacon and Canon of Durham.

[4] Dau. of James Lambert, Lay Clerk, who was buried 4 Nov. 1878, and wife of James Sadler Beckwith, Vicar of Walker-on-Tyne, whose burial see 23 Jan. 1895.

[5] Widow of William Jones, buried 24 Sep. 1851.

[6] Sister of Rosamond Evans, buried 24 Nov. 1863.

[7] Professor of Greek in the University of Durham.

[8] Second son of Claud Buchanan Ker, M.D., of Cheltenham; of New College, Oxford, matriculated 26 Jan. 1878, B.A. 1882; M.A. 1886.

CATHEDRAL CHURCH AT DURHAM. 159

		Tristram, Canon of Durham, Rev. V. K. Cooper, Precentor, Rev. J. M. Marshall, Head Master. Elvet Hill Cemetery.
1893	Nov. 22	Francis Dixon Johnson;[1] Aykley Heads; 89 years; Rev. H. B. Tristram, D.D., Canon of Durham, & Rev. G. W. Anson Firth, Sacrist. Cath. Yard.
1894	Aug. 30	Henry Bond Bowlby,[2] Bishop of Coventry; S[t] Philip's Rectory, Birmingham; 71 years; J. J. S. Worcester. Cath. Yard.
1895	Jan. 23	James Sadler Beckwith;[3] Walker Vicarage, Walker on Tyne; 51 years; G. W. Anson Firth, Sacrist. Elvet Hill Cemetery.
1896	April 29	William Henry Grice, Layclerk; John Street, Durham; 61 years; H. B. Tristram, D.D., Canon of Durham Cathedral, & V. K. Cooper, M.A., Precentor of Durham Cath. Elvet Hill.
	Dec. 11	Arthur Ernest Harcourt Armes;[4] 17 North Bailey; 24 years; Geo. Body, D.D., Canon of Durham, J. T. Fowler, D.C.L., Lecturer in Hebrew. Elvet Hill.

[1] Born 25 Dec. 1803 and baptized at Crossgate 24 July 1806; of St. John's College, Cambridge, B.A. 1827; Barrister-at-Law, of Gray's Inn and afterwards of Lincoln's Inn (called to the Bar 1833); was a Justice of the Peace and Deputy-Lieutenant for the County of Durham. Died 19 Nov. 1893, having married, 18 Jan. 1838, Agnes Harrison, third dau. of John Greenwood, of Polefield, co. Lancaster, Esq. See her burial 27 Dec. 1867. [MS. Ped. by E. A. W.]

[2] Son of Major Peter Bowlby by his wife Elizabeth, dau. of Rev. Dickens Hazlewood, M.A. (see her burial 22 Feb. 1827). Born 23 Aug. 1823, baptized 18 Sep. following at Bishopwearmouth; late Fellow of Wadham College, Oxford; B.A. 1844; M.A. 1849; Vicar of Oldbury, co. Worcester, 1850; Vicar of Dartford 1868; Rector of St. Philip's, Birmingham, 1875; Hon. Canon of Worcester Cathedral; consecrated Bishop Suffragan of Coventry 1891. He married first, at St. Hilda's, South Shields, Catherine, eldest dau. of Thomas Salmon, of South Shields; she died 22 Jan. 1875 and was buried at the cemetery, Dartford, co. Kent. He married secondly, at St. Oswald's, Chester, 21 Sep. 1886, Sarah, third dau. of Harry King, Esq., of Windsor, Nova Scotia, and widow of Frederic Allison, Esq. He died at Edinburgh 27 Aug. 1894. [MS. Ped. by E. A. W.]

[3] Late Scholar of University of Durham; ordained Deacon 1876; Priest 1877; Curate of Ryhope, co. Durham, 1876—1878; of St. Matthew, Newcastle, 1878—1880; of Benfieldside, co. Durham, 1880-81; B.A. 1880; M.A. 1883; Vicar of Walker 1881; married Ann, dau. of James Lambert. See her burial 12 Sep. 1888.

[4] Son of Philip Armes, Mus. Doc., Organist of the Cathedral.

INDEX.

The names in the Text are in SMALL CAPITALS, those in the Notes in ordinary type, and the italic letter *n* indicates that the references are in the Notes.

ABBS, SARAH	62	AISLEY, ROBERT	36
Aboyne, Charles, Earl of..	20	AISLEY, ROBERTI	5
Acton, Eliza	131	Albemarle, Earl of	26, 128
ACTON, THOMAS	131	ALBERT, DAN.	65
Adair, Caroline	128	ALBERT, MARY	65
Adair, Lady Caroline	26	ALDERSON, ELIZABETH	57
Adair, Elizabeth	26, 128	ALDERSON, JANE	48
Adair, Robert	26, 128	ALDERSON, JOSEPH	48
Adams, Dr. Fitz-Adams, Prebendary of Durham	18	Aldham, Georgiana Bailey	31
ADAMSON, ANNA'	43	ALLAN, ELIZABETH	125
Adamson, Blythman	53	ALLAN, JANE	63
Adamson, Cuthbert	53	ALLAN, JOHN	62
ADAMSON, DOROTHEAM	44	ALLAN, MARGT.	62
ADAMSON, DOROTHY	53	ALLAN, MARY	61
Adamson, Rev. Edward Hussey	53	Allan, Robert Henry	89
ADAMSON, ELIZ.	53, 70	ALLEN, FRANCES	53
Adamson, Elizabeth	53	Allenson, Alice	15
Adamson, Isabel	60	ALLENSON, ANNAM	45
ADAMSON, ISABELLAM	40	Allenson, Anthony	15
Adamson, Jane	53	ALLENSON, GULIELMUS	40
ADAMSON, JOHAN'ES	44	ALLENSON, JANNAM	40
ADAMSON, MARIAM	40	ALLENSON, MARIA'	42
Adamson, Ralph	53	ALLENSON, MARMADUCO	15
ADAMSON, RANDULPHUS	40	Allenson, Marmaduke	15
ADAMSON, RO.	104	Allenson, Mary	15
ADAMSON, REV. RO.	103	Allenson, Ralph	15
ADAMSON, ROBERT	53	ALLENSON, ROBERTUS	45
ADAMSON, REV. ROBERTI	14	ALLINSON, ANNAM	39
ADAMSON, SAMUEL	101 : *n*. 14	ALLINSON, HANNAH	69
ADAMSON, SAMUELL	14	ALLINSON, MARGERY	77
ADAMSON, THOMASIN	103	ALLISON, ELIZABETH	53
Adamson, William	60	Allison, Frederic	159
Adamson, Lieut.-Col. William	53	Allison, Sarah	159
Adamson, William Blythman	53	ALLISON, VALENTINE	53
AGAR, AN	38	ALMOND, ELIZ.	72
AGAR, GULIELMS	41	ALSTON, HENRY	114
AGAR, JANAM	41	Alston, Sir Rowland	114
Agar, Mary Elizabeth	27	Alston, Temperance	114
AGAR, WILLIA'	38	Alwent, Catherine	91
AINSLEY, MARGARETAM	38	Alwent, Ralph	91
Ainslie, Mary Anne	152	AMBLER, ANN	126
Ainslie, Lieut.-Col. Philip	152	AMBLER, ELIZABETH	135
AIRE, ALICIAM	41	AMBLER, WILLIAM	126
AIRE, GULIELMS	41	AMBLER, WILLM.	126, 135
AIRE, JANE	57	ANDERSON, ANNAM	39
AIRE, WM.	57	ANDERSON, ELIZABETH	57
AIRSON, FRANCISCAM	39	ANDERSON, GULIELMUS	39
Airson, John	39	ANDERSON, MARY	61
Aislaby, Michael	76	ANDREW, BARTHOLOMEW	64
AISLEBY, MARGARET	76	ANDREW, ELIZABETH	54
AISLEY, ANN	75	ANDREW, JANE	64
AISLEY, FRANCES	77	ANDREW, MARY	48
AISLEY, JOANNA'	36	Annandale, Earl of	105
AISLEY, MARGARETA	5	Annandale, Marquess of	49

Y

REGISTERS OF DURHAM CATHEDRAL.

Anne, Queen of England 106
Anson, Caroline Maria 81
Anson, Rev. Frederick, Canon of Windsor 81
Antrim, Anne Katherine, Countess of 22
APEDAIL, ANN 47
APEDAIL, WILLIAM 47
APLEBY, REBECCAM 42
APLEBY, RICH'US 42
APPELBY, ANN 68
Appleby, George 136
Appleby, Sarah 136
APPLEGARTH, ANNA' 45
APPLEGARTH, GULIELMUS 45
ARCHER, ANNE 56
Archer-Hinde, — 150
ARCHIBALD, JOHN 103
Arcy, see D'Arcy.
ARMES, ARTHUR ERNEST HARCOURT 159
Armes, Philip 159
Armes, Dr. Philip 137
ARMSTRON, MARGT 63
ARMSTRONG, ELIZABETH 60
ARMSTRONG, ROB 50
ARMSTRONG, SARAH 50
ARMSTRONG, THOMAS 60
Arnold, Rev. Matthew 79
ARROWSMITH, ANN 50, 59
ARROWSMITH, ELIZ. 49, 62
ARROWSMITH, ELIZABETHAM 39
ARROWSMITH, HENRICUS 39
ARROWSMITH, HUMPHR'Y 62
ARROWSMITH, MARIAM 39
ARROWSMITH, MARY ...... 54, 77; n. 86
ARROWSMITH, MICHAEL 77
ARRUNDELL, MARGERIAM 40
ARRUNDELL, RICHARDUS 40
ARTUS, MARY 55
Arundell, Alice 40
Arundell, Christopher 40
ASKEW, ANNAM 44
Askew, Anne Elizabeth 148
Askew, Rev. Henry 148
ASKEW, MARY 73
ATHEY, JANE 77
ATHEY, LUKE 77
Atkin, Elizabeth 55
Atkin, Mariam 40
Atkin, Wm. 55
ATKINSON, ANNAM 41
ATKINSON, BRYAN 47
ATKINSON, FANNY JOAN 79
ATKINSON, FRANCES 66
ATKINSON, GULIELMUS 41
ATKINSON, HILDA 72
Atkinson, James 152
ATKINSON, JANE 62
ATKINSON, JOHN 78
ATKINSON, MARG'TAM 41
ATKINSON, MARGT. 70
ATKINSON, MARY ...... 78, 120, 130: n. 151
Atkinson, Mary Anne 152
ATKINSON, MATTHEW HALL 79
ATKINSON, RACHEL 44
ATKINSON, SARAH 76
ATKINSON, SARAM 41
ATKINSON, SUSAN 47
ATKINSON, THO. 62
Atkinson, Thomas 151
ATKINSON, WM. 72
ATTEY, HANNAH 77
ATTEY, THOMAS 77

Aubin, John 128
Aubin, Mary 128
Aubone, Elizabeth 58
Aubone, William 58
Aubrey, Alice 2
Aubrey, John 2
Aucher, Anthony 37
Aucher, Margaret 37
Aucher, — 37
Auckland, Lord 13, 22
Audley, George, Lord 37
Austen, Edward 20
Austen, Jane 20
Anstin, see D'Austin.
AVERICK, ELIZ. 69
AWBREE, JO. 2
AWBREE, MARIAN 2
AWBREY, ELIZABETH 2
AWBREY, JO. 2
AYRE, ANTHONIUS 39
AYRE, EDWARD 65
AYRE, JANAM 38
AYRE, KATHERINAM 39
AYRE, MARY 65
AYRE, SUSANNA 66
AYTUS, MARY 55

B., J. 139
BADDELEY, AN 37
BADDELAY, RICHARD 6, 94
BADDELAY, THOMAS 94
BADDELEY, ANN ...... 47; n. 113
BADDELEY, CASSANDRA ...... 5; n. 89
Baddeley, Dulcibella 5, 105
Baddeley, Mary 89
BADDELEY, PHINEHAS 115
BADDELEY, RICHARD 47; n. 5, 89, 105, 113, 115
Baddeley, — 89
BADDFLEYE, RICHARD 115
BADDELY, ANN 113
Baddely, Cassaudra 89
BADDELY, RICH. 113
BADELEY, DEBORAH 93
BADELEY, RICHED 93
BADELY, — 89
BADYLEY, RICHARD 5
Bagshaw, Anne 15
BAGSHAW, EDWARD ...... 16; n. 14, 15
BAGSHAW, ELISABETHA 16
Bagshaw, Elizabeth 15
BAGSHAW, DR. HEN. 102
BAGSHAW, HENR., PREBENDARY OF DURHAM 16
BAGSHAW, DR. HENRICI, PREBENDARY OF DURHAM 14
BAGSHAW, HENRICUS 14
BAGSHAW, HENRY ...... 104: n. 15, 16, 102
BAGSHAW, DR. HENRY 104
Bagshaw, Mary 15
Bagshaw, Prudence 15
BAGSHAW, RALPH ...... 102; n. 15
BAGSHAW, SARAH ...... 17: n. 15
BAGSHAW, DR. — 16, 17
Bagshawe, Dr. — 15
BAILES, DINAH 54
BAILES, JOHN 57
BAILES, MARGARET 57
BAILES, THOMAS 54
BAILIFFE, ESTHER 68
BAILIFFE, THOMAS 68
BAINBRIDGE, ALICE 77

BAINBRIDGE, DOROTHY	69	BARKER, JOH'ES	41
BAINBRIDGE, JANAM	41	BARKER, MARG.	49
BAINBRIDGE, JOHN	69	BARKER, MARY	122
BAINBRIDGE, MARGARETAM	40	Barker, —	154
BAINBRIDGE, SUSANNAM	39	BARKHURST, ANN	118
BAINES, ELIZ.	64	Barnard, Mary	84
BAINES, WILL.	64	Barnard, Thomas	84
Baiter, Eleanora	33	Barnes, Barnaby	82
Baiter, Dr. J. G.	33	BARNES, DOROTHEA	98
Baiter, Susanna	33	Barnes, Fredismund	82
BAKER, AMELIA CATHERINE	28	Barnes, Jane	82
Baker, Anne	148	BARNES, JOHN	1, 75, 82
BAKER, CAROLINE	28	BARNES, MARGARET	75
BAKER, CAROLINE MARY ANNE	28	BARNES, MARY	66
Baker, Catherine	25	Barnes, Richard, Bishop of Durham	82
BAKER, CAPT. FRANCIS	28, 132	Barnes, Rychard, Bishop of Durham	82
Baker, Sir George	94	Barnes, —	1
BAKER, GRANVILLE	148	BARRAS, ELIZ.	51
BAKER, JAMES	28	BARRAS, JAMES	51
Baker, Rev. James	25, 148	BARRAS, JANE	70
BAKER, JANE	77	BARRAS, JOHN	70
Baker, Mary	93	BARRINGTON, CHARLOTTE BELASYSE	26
Baker, Oswald	93	BARRINGTON, ELIZABETH	27, 128, 129 : n. 26
Baker, Philip	148	BARRINGTON, FRANCES DANES	129
BAKER, ROBERT	28	BARRINGTON, FRANCIS DAINES	27
Baker, Sarah Janetta	148	BARRINGTON, REV. GEORGE, PREBEND-	
Baker, Sybella	28	ARY OF DURHAM	27
BAKER, THOS.	28	BARRINGTON, REV. GEORGE, VISCOUNT,	
Bakiston, Elizabeth	3	PREBENDARY OF DURHAM	26, 128
Bakiston, Dr. Robert	3	BARRINGTON, JOHN	128
Balcanquall, Dame Elizabeth	37	Barrington, Maj.-Gen. Hon. John	26
Balcanquall, Stuarta	37, 93	Barrington, Hon. Sarah	24
Balcanquall, Dr. Walter, Dean of Durham	37	Barrington, Shute, Bishop of Durham	24, 26
Balcanquall, —.	6	Barrington, Hon. Shute, Bishop of Dur-	
Balcanquall, Dean of Durham	6	ham	128
BALES, JANE	76	Barrington, Bishop of Durham	135, 136, 139,
BALES, RALPH	76		141, 144, 149, 154
Balkanquall, Dean of Durham	94	Barrington, Lord, Prebendary of Durham	137
BALLCANQUALL, GUALTERI, DEAN OF		BARRINGTON, REV. —, PREBENDARY OF	
DURHAM	37	DURHAM	129
BALLCANQUALL, STEWARTAM	37	Barrington, Viscount	26, 132
BALQUANCALLO, GUALTERO, DEAN OF		Barrington, Viscount, Prebendary of Dur-	
DURHAM	6	ham	133
BAMBLETT, MARY	68	BARROWMAN, JANE	68
BAMBLETT, ROBERT	68	Barton, Edward	83
BAMBROUGH, ISABEL	52	Barton, Elizabeth	83
Barber, Bridget	86	BARTRAM, EMMETTAM	42
Barber, —	86	Barwick, Elizabeth	10
BARCHAS, GEORGE	7, 8	Barwick, George	105
BARCHAS, —	9	BARWICK, GEORGIUS	10
BARCROFT, ANNE	87	BARWICK, HELLENEN	38
Barcroft, Eliz.	91	BARWICK, JANA	10
Barcroft, Elizabeth	91, 107	Barwick, Jane	105
BARCROFT, GEORGE	87, 91 : n. 91, 107	BARWICK, JOHAN'ES	13
Barcroft, Jane	91	BARWICK, JOHN	102
Barcroft, John	91	Barwick, Dr. John, Dean of Durham	105
Barcroft, Mary	91	BARWICK, NICHOLAI	10, 13
Barcroft, Thomas	91	BARWICK, NICHOLAS	102 : n. 112
Barecroft, Ann	87	BARWICK, NICHOLAUS	38
Barecroft, George	87	Barwick, Dr. Peter	105
BARKAS, ANNE	53	Barwick, Dean of Durham	104
BARKAS, ELISABETH	107	BARWICKE, ELEANOR	117
BARKAS, ELIZABETHÂ	9	BARWICKE, NICHOLAS	105
BARKAS, GEORGE	106 : n. 9	BARWICKE, DEAN OF DURHAM	94
Barkas, Richard, Minor Canon of Durham	106	BASIERE, FRANCES	9
BARKAS, WM.	53	BASIERE, ISAAC, D.D., PREBENDARY OF	
Barkas, —	8, 9	DURHAM	9
BARKER, ELIZ.	54, 71	BASIERE, DR. —	38
BARKER, FRANCISCAM	41	Basire, Lady Elizabeth	12
BARKER, GEORGE	70	BASIRE, FRANCISCA	98
BARKER, ISABEL	70	BASIRE, ISAACI	12, 99

BASIRE, ISAACI, PREBENDARY OF DUR-
  HAM.. 98
BASIRE, ISAACO, PREBENDARY OF DUR-
  HAM.. 11
BASIRE, ISAACUS 12, 99
BASIRE, ISAACUS, PREBENDARY OF DUR-
  HAM.. 98
Basire, — 9
Basire, Dr. —, Prebendary of Durham...... 12
BASSNETT, GEORGE 76
BASSNETT, MARGARET 76
BATEMAN, HANNAM 40
Bateman, Margaret 86
BATEMAN, MARY.................... 47 : n. 118
Bateman, Richard 118
BATEMAN, THOMAS 47
Bateman, William 86
BATERSBY, JOH'ES 12
BATERSBY, THOMÆ 12
BATES, ELIZABETH .... 27 : n. 151
BATES, WILLIAM................... 27 : n. 151
Bath, Earl of.. 106
Bath, Marquess of 37
Bathurst, Allen, Earl 25
Bathurst, Benjamin, M.P. 25
BATHURST, CAROLINE 25
Bathurst, Catherine................................. 25
Bathurst, Charles Henry 25
Bathurst, Charles William........................ 25
BATHURST, COOTE 26
Bathurst, Frances 25
Bathurst, Grace 25
BATHURST, DR. HENRY, PREBENDARY OF
  DURHAM, BISHOP OF NORWICH 25
Bathurst, Hester 25
Bathurst, Jane 25
Bathurst, Katherine............................... 25
Bathurst, Mary 25
Bathurst, Robert 25
BATHURST, REV. ROBERT 25
Bathurst, Selina 25
Bathurst, Susannah............................... 25
Bathurst, Tryphena............................... 25
BATHURST, REV. DR. —, PREBENDARY OF
  DURHAM 26
BATTERSBIE, ELIZABETHA..................... 11
BATTERSBIE, PRYSCILLA 12
BATTERSRIE, THO. 11, 12
BATTERSBY, ANN 47
BATTERSBY, JERONYMA 101
BATTERSBY, JOH'ES 98
BATTERSBY, PRISCILLA 102
Battersby, Richard 115
BATTERSBY, REV. THO. 102
BATTERSBY, THOMÆ 98
BATTERSBY, THOMAS .... 101 : n. 13
BATTERSBYE, THO. 115
BATY, ARTHUR.................................... 121
BATY, ELIZABETH 121
Baty, John........................... 114, 121
BATY, THOMAS 121
Baty, Thomasine 121
Bax-Ironside, Henry George Outram 43
Baynbrigg, Cuthbert 92
Baynbrigg, Elizabeth 92
Baynes, Eliz................................ 70, 71
BEACH, DOROTHY 75
BEACHMAN, ELIZABETH......................... 61
BEADNELL, MARY................................. 58
BEALS, SARAH 74
Beaufort, Henry, Duke of 30

BEAUMONT, DELAVAL............................ 55
BEAUMONT. ELIZ.................................. 55
Beaumont, Hammond 55
Beckeles, Robert 95
BECKETT, BRIDGET 142
BECKETT, ELIZ. 142
BECKFIELD, MARY 68
Beckles, Richard 95
Beckles, Robert 95
BECKWITH, ANN .... 158 : n. 159
Beckwith, Eleanor 63
BECKWITH, JAMES SADLER ...... 159 : n. 158
Beckwith, John.................................... 63
Beckwith, Judith 63
Bede, — 46
BEDSER, JOHN ALDER 158
BEE, FRANCISCAM 43
Bee, Jacob 6, 110
Bee, Mary 137
Bee, — 10, 14, 137
Belasyse, — 141
BELL, ANN .... 120 : n. 13, 121
BELL, ANNA 13
BELL, ANNAM 39
BELL, CHRISTOPHER 101
BELL, CHRISTOPHERUS 39
BELL, DOROTHY 74
BELL, FRANCES................................. 151
BELL, GEORGE 61
BELL, ISABEL 52
BELL, JAMES 52
BELL, JANE 55, 118
BELL, JOHN.............................. 51, 115
BELL, MARIAM 39
BELL, MARTHA 149
BELL, MARY 51, 55, 61, 67, 68, 74, 121
BELL, THOMAS 101
BELLAMYE, CUTHB................................ 6
BELLAY, JANE 37
BELLAY, THOMAS 37
Belli, Caroline Howley Turner 32
Belli, William Hallows 32
Belt, Rev. — 87
BELWOOD, CATHERINE 57
BENNETT, ANNE 131, 132
Bennett, George 131
BENSON, ELISABETHA........................... 16
BENSON, ISABELL................... 102 : n. 15
BENSON, JACOBUS................................ 15
BENSON, JO. 15
BENSON, JOH'IS. 15, 16
BENSON, JOHN 108
BENTON, JANE 67
BENTON, JOHN 67
Berkeley, Charles John, M.D. 147
Berkeley, Frances Harriott..................... 147
Besant, Walter 48
Best, Dorothy 24
Best, James 24
Best, Jane 24, 45
Best, Richard 45
BETTLES, AN 95
Bettles, — 95
BEWES, JOHN 76
BEWES, MARY 76
Bigge, Charles William 152
Bigge, Julia Katherina 152
BILTON, DOROTHY 62
BILTON, MARY 64
Bingley, —..................................... 154
BIRD, ANN 77

BIRD, ELIZABETH	75
BIRD, RALPH	75
BIRKET, —	1
Birkett, Alice	86
Birkett, —	1
BIRKETT, DR., PREBENDARY OF DURHAM	86
Birkhead, Alice	86
Birkhead, Mary	86
Birkhead, Nathaniel	86
Birkhead, Dr. —	1. 86
Birt, Eleanor	151
Birt, Rev. Thomas	151
BISHOPBRIG, MARGT.	64
BISHOPRICK, ELIZ.	41
BITLESTON, JOSEPHUS	41
BITLESTON, MARG'TAM	41
Blackburn, Archbishop	124
BLACKET, MARGARET	75
BLACKETT, ELIZABETH	95
BLACKETT, RICHARD	95
BLACKLOCK, ALICE	64
BLACKLOCK, JNO.	64
BLADES, GEORGE	5, 94
BLAIKESTON, ELIZABETHÂ	3
BLAIKSTON, ELIZABETHÂ	4
BLAIKSTON, ROBERTI, PREBENDARY OF DURHAM	4
Blakesley, Alice Anne	29
Blakesley, George Holmes	29
Blakesley, Rev. Joseph Williams, Dean of Lincoln	29
BLAKESTO', ELSABETH	90
BLAKESTO', ROBERTI, PREBENDARY OF DURHAM	90
Blakeston, Rev. Francis	52
BLAKESTON, MORTON	108
BLAKESTON, ROBERT, PREBENDARY OF DURHAM	90
BLAKISTON, ANN	52
BLAKISTON, ELIZ.	13
Blakiston, Elizabeth	13, 90, 103, 114, 115
BLAKISTON, FRANCES	100 : n. 106, 114
Blakiston, Rev. Gabriel	66, 103, 115
BLAKISTON, HENRY	103 : n. 13, 93, 97, 114, 115
BLAKISTON, HENRYE	93, 95
BLAKISTON, JANE	61, 115 : n. 103
Blakiston, John, M.P.	90
BLAKISTON, MARIA	97
BLAKISTON, MARMADUKE, PREBENDARY OF DURHAM	3
Blakiston, Marmaduke, D.D., Prebendary of Durham, Archdeacon of Cleveland	90, 106
Blakiston, Mary	15, 103
Blakiston, Ralph	61
Blakiston, Robert	90
BLAKISTON, THO	100 : n. 14
BLAKISTON, THOMAS	114 : n. 103
BLAKISTON, WILLIA'	93
Blakiston, William	97, 103, 114
Blakiston, Sir William	61, 95, 103
Blakiston, —, Prebendary of Durham, Archdeacon of Cleveland	15
BLAKISTONN, HENRYE	94
BLAKISTONN, MARGARETT	94
BLAKLOCK, BENJAMIN	57
BLAKLOCK, MARY	57
Bland, Anne	124
BLAND, GEORGE, ARCHDEACON OF NORTHUMBERLAND	33, 152, 156
Bland, Henry	124
Bland, Dr. Henry, Dean of Durham, Canon of Windsor	124
Bland, Michael	156
Bland. Sophia	156
BLAND, ARCHDEACON —	153, 154
BLAND, REV. DR., PREBENDARY OF DURHAM	124
BLARTON, ELLENORA'	41
BLENKINSOPP, SUSANNA	67
BLENKINSOPP, THOMAS	67
Bliss, —	11
BLITHMAN, ANNAM	40
Bloxam, —	85
BLUNT, ALICE	36
BLUNT, MATTHEW	36
Blythman, Elizabeth	53
Blythman, Mary	53
Blythman, William	53
BOASMAN, ANNAM	41
BODY, DORA EMILY	80
BODY, REV. G., CANON OF DURHAM	158
BODY, GEO., D.D., CANON OF DURHAM	159
BODY, GEORGE, CANON OF DURHAM	80
Bolt, Dina	93
Bolt, Elenor	83
Bolt, William	83
BOLTON, JOHN	8
Bolton, Robert	37
BOLTON, SAMUELL, MINOR CANON OF DURHAM	7, 8, 37
BOLTON, SARAH	37
BOLTON. SUSANNA	7
BOLTON, —	104
BOND, JANE	154
BONE, FRANCES	77
BONE, GEORGE	77
Bonham, Francis Warren	19
Bonham, Joyce	19
Bonham, Mary Ann	19
BONNER, ELIZ.	70
Bonner, Joseph	81
Bonner, Sarah	81
Bonner, Bishop	149
BOOTH, ANNE	107
Booth, Lady Elizabeth, Baroness Delamere	107
Booth, Sir George, Baron Delamere	107
Booth, Robert, Archdeacon of Durham, Dean of Bristol	107
Booth, Sir Robert	107
Booth, —, Lord Delamere	107
Borrow, Anne	105
Borrow, Benj.	105
BORROW, BENJAMINI	97
BORROW, BENJAMINUS	98
BORROW, JANA	97
BORROW, JANE	64
BORROW, JOHN	64 : n. 6
BORUWLASKI, COUNT JOSEPH	139
BOTCHEDY, DOROTHY	69
BOUCKE, CHRISTOPHER	2
Boulay, see Du Boulay.	
Boutflower, Elisabetham	44
Boutflower, Gulielmus	44
Boutflower, Ven. Samuel Peach, Archdeacon of Carlisle	44
Boutflower, Thomas	44
BOUYER, ELIZABETH	136
BOUYER, REV. R. G.	132
BOUYER, REV. R. G., PREBENDARY OF DURHAM	136

BOUYER, REV. REYNOLD GIDEON, PREBENDARY OF DURHAM, ARCHDEACON OF NORTHUMBERLAND 133, 134
BOUYER, — 24
Bowe, Elizabeth 29, 152, 157
Bowe, Rev. William 29, 152, 157
Bowes, Andrew Robinson 24
BOWES, ANN 50, 114
Bowes, Anne 50
BOWES, MADAM ANNE 115
BOWES, CUTH. 102
BOWES, CUTHBERT 100, 102, 107, 115
Bowes, Edward 115
BOWES, ELEANOR 75
BOWES, ELISABETH 107
BOWES, GEORGE 50
BOWES, JANE.. 121
BOWES, DR. JOHN, PREBENDARY OF DURHAM .... 116 : n. 50
Bowes, Lady Maria 24
BOWES, MARY 100
Bowes, Lady Mary 24
Bowes, Thomas 50
BOWES, — .... 100 : n. 103
BOWLBY, CAROLINE.................................. 146
Bowlby, Caroline Sophia........................... 146
BOWLBY, CATHERINE .... 144 : n. 159
BOWLBY, ELEANORA ELIZABETH 141 : n. 137, 147, 148
BOWLBY, ELIZABETH 134, 147, 155 : n. 23, 159
Bowlby, Frances 118
BOWLBY, FRANCES AMELIA 143
Bowlby, Frances Eliza................................. 34
BOWLBY, GEORGE HENRY .... 144 : n. 146
BOWLBY, HENRY BOND, BISHOP OF COVENTRY 159
Bowlby, John 155
BOWLBY, MARY 62, 118, 125, 148
BOWLBY, CAPT. P. 134
BOWLBY, DR. P. 125
Bowlby, Capt. Peter 134
Bowlby, Maj. Peter 159
Bowlby, Richard 118
Bowlby, Russell 23
Bowlby, Sarah 155, 159
BOWLBY, THO. 62, 118
BOWLBY, THOMAS .... 118 : n. 125
BOWLBY, REV. THOMAS ... 137, 141, 143, 144 : n. 147, 148
Bowlby, — 117
BOWLBY, DR. — 125
Bowlt, Rev. Andrew 19
BOWMAN, BARBARA 106
BOWMAN, CUTHBERTUS 15
BOWMAN, JANA 14
BOWMAN, JO. 102
BOWMAN, JOD'ES 12
BOWMAN, JOH'IS 12, 14, 15
BOWMAN, JOHN 106, 108
BOWMAN, MARY 78
BOWMAN, VALENTINE................................. 78
BOWMAN, WILLIAM 102
BOWNAS, ISABELLA 42
BOWNAS, JOH'ES 42
BOWNAS, LUCYE 55
BOWNAS, MARY... 50
BOWNAS, THOM. 50
BOWRY, BARBARA 70
BOWRY, THO.. 70
Bowser, Eleanor 123
Bowser, Jana' 43

BOWSER, MARIAM 41
Bowser, Richard 123
BOWSER, THOMAS....................................... 41
Bowser, William 43
Boyce, Ann... 38
Boycke, Anne 2
Boycke, Rev. —.. 2
Boyer, Rev. James 145
Boyer, Phœbe 93
Boyer, Sophia 145
BOYES, ANN 77
BOYES, WM. 77
BRABANT, JANE .... 50 ; n. 45
Brabant, John 45
Brabant, Margareta' 45
BRABANT, MICHAEL 50
BRADANT, — 117
Brabin, Jane 50
Brabin, Michael 50
Brabourne, Lord 123
BRACK, ANN 47, 67
BRACK, ANNAM... 41
BRACK, DOROTHY 60
BRACK, JANE... 71
BRACK, JNO. 64
BRACK, MARGT. 64
BRACKE, ISABELL.. 38
BRACKENBURY, JANA' 43
BRADELY, ELIZ. 67
BRADFORD, DOROTHEAM 39
Bradford, Elizabeth Mary 152
Bradford, Mary Anne 152
BRADFORD, DR. THOS............................... 124
Bradford, Lieut.-Gen. Sir Thomas 152
BRADLEY, HENRY 151
BRAKENBURY, JOHANNES 99
BRANFOOT, ELIZABETH 22
BRANFOOT, REV. JOHN, MINOR CANON OF DURHAM .... 74 : n. 22
Branfoot, Jonathan 74
BRANFOOT, REV. JONATHAN 22
BRANFOOT, MARY 74
BRANFOOT, THOMAS JOHN 22
BRANKSTON, JAMES................................... 72
BRANKSTON, JANE 72
Brantingham, Margaret 85
Brantingham, Robert 85
BRASS, ANN .... 60 ; n. 11
Brass, Cuthbert... 11
BRASS, JOHN 8
BRASS, KATTERN 8
BRASS, THOMAS 60
BRASSE, CUTHBERT 11
BRASSE, JOHANNIS 11
Bray, Reginald 47
Bray, Temperance....................................... 47
BRECKNELL, ANN 127
Brecknell, Jane 127
BRECKNELL, WILLIAM 127
BRENKARN, ALICE 69
BRENKARN, EDWARD 69
BREVENT, DANIELL, D.D., PREBENDARY OF DURHAM 9
Brevint, Ann 11
BREVINT, D'NA ANNA 11
Brevint, Dr. Daniell, Prebendary of Durham, Dean of Lincoln 9
BREWER, ANNAM 39
BREWER, MATTHÆUS 39
Bridges, Sir Brook 22
BRIDGES, ELIZAB. 6

BRIDGES, GEORGIUS	91	Brown, Johannes	10
BRIDGES, GULELMUS	89	Brown, Johannis	10
BRIDGES, GULIELMI	91	BROWN, JOH'E	9
Bridges, Harriet Mary	22	BROWN, JOHN	72 : n. 10, 44
Bridges, William	5, 93, 94, 105, 115	BROWN, SARAH	64
Bridgewater, Francis, Earl of	24	BROWNBRIDGE, JOSEPH	58
Bridgewater, John, Earl of	24	BROWNBRIDGE, MARY	58, 76
Bridgham, Mary	102	BROWNBRIDGE, WILLIAM	76
Bridgham, Tymothie	102	BROWNE, ANNE	54
Brien, see O'Brien.		BROWNE, ELIZ.	51
BRIGGS, CATHERINA	92	BROWNE, ELLINOR	49
BRIGGS, ISABEL	65	BROWNE, GERRARDS	12
Briggs, Kathrine	87	BROWNE, JANAM	44
BRIGGS, NICHOLAI	92	BROWNE, JOH'ES	12
Briggs, Nicholas	87	BROWNE, JOH'IS	12
BRIGHAM, MARY	102 : n. 107, 109	Browne, Rev. John	88
Brigham, Thomas	100	BROWNE, MARY	68
BRIGHAM, TIMOTHY	100 : n. 107, 109	BROWNE, THO.	49, 54
BRIGHT, ELIZABETH	127	BROWNE, WILL.	51
Bright, Frances	12	Browning, William	134
Bright, John	141	Bruce, Elizabeth	110
Bright, Col. Sir John	12	Bruce, Robert	110
Bright, Margery	127, 141	BRUMLEY, ANNA'	42
BRIGHT, CAPT. —	127	Brumley, Anne	110
Brimley, John	82	BRUMLEY, THOMAS	42, 110
BRITTAIN, MARGT.	72	BRUMLY, PHYLLIS	112
BRITTON, ELIZA	24	BRUMLY, —	112
BRITTON, HARRIOT JANE	26	BRYAN, HANNAH	77
BRITTON, ISABELLA	23, 24, 26	BRYAN, NICHOLAS	77
BRITTON, JAMES	23	Buchan, Ellen	143
BRITTON, REV. JAMES	24, 26	Buchan, John	143
BRITTON, REV. JAMES, D.D.	23	BUCHAN. JOSEPH	143
BRITTON, MARY ANN	26	BUCKTON, ANNE	77
Brocket, Elizabeth	42	Bull, Mary	86
BROCKETT, ELIZ.	42	Bull, Thomas	86
BROCKETT, GULIELMS.	42	Bullmer, Alice	40
Brockett, Isabella	13	BULLOCK, ANNA	99
Brockett, William	13, 42	Bullock, Anne	68
Brodrick, Katherine	25	Bullock, Edward	99
Brodrick, Dr. Laurence, Prebendary of Westminster	25	BULLOCK, ELIZABETH	75, 122 : n. 151
		BULLOCK, GEO.	101, 104
BROMELY, ANN	61	BULLOCK, GEORGE	100, 109, 115, 124 : n. 99, 117
Bromley, Anne	11	BULLOCK, GEORGII	10, 12, 99
Bromley, Isabella	110	BULLOCK, GEORGIUS	43
Bromley, Mary	110	BULLOCK, GULIELMUS.	12
Bromley, Phyllis	112	BULLOCK, JAMES	75, 126, 127
Bromley, Robert	11, 110, 112	BULLOCK, JO.	117
BROMWELL, MARGARETAM	40	BULLOCK, JOHN	115, 118
Brooke, William	128	BULLOCK, MARG'TAM	43
Brooke, —	128	BULLOCK, MARGARET	126
BROOKIN, ELIZABETH	93	BULLOCK, MARY	114, 117
BROOKIN, MAGDALEN	93	BULLOCK, NICHOLAUS	10
Brookin, Tobias	93	BULLOCK, THOMAS	104
BROOKIN, TOBY	93	BULLOCK, WILLIAM	101
BROOKING, ELIZABETH	3	BULLOCKE, GEORGE	8
BROOKING, TOBIAS	92	BULLOCKE, JOHN	8
BROOKING, TOBY	3	BULMAN, ANN	77
BROUGH, ANNAM	44	BULMAN, THOMAS	77
Brougham, Mary Anne, Lady	13	BULMER, SIR BARTRAM	2
Brougham, Lord	13	Bulmer, Sir Bertram	2
Broughton, —	8	Bulmer, Isabel	2
BROWELL, ELIZ.	65	BURDEN, ELIZABETH	63
Brown, Abigail	10	BURDESS, ANNAM	44
BROWN, ANN	73	BURDON, ANNE	56
BROWN, ELIZ.	73	BURDON, CATHARINAM	45
Brown, Elizabeth	10, 125	BURDON, JOHN	84
BROWN, ISABEL	67	BURDON, MARY	60
BROWN, ISABELLA	75	BURDON, RICHARD	56
Brown, Janam	44	BURDON, THOMAS	84
BROWN, JANE	72 : n. 10	BURELL, MARY	62
Brown, Jerrard	10	BURGESS, MARGERY	141

BURGESS, DR. THOMAS, BISHOP OF SALISBURY	141
Burgess, William	141
BURGESS, —	24
Burgess, Dr. —, Prebendary of Durham, Bishop of Salisbury	146
Burke, — 19, 20, 24, 26, 27, 61, 75, 81, 113, 125, 128, 136	
BURLETSON, BRYANUS	45
BURLETSON, DOROTHEAM	44
BURLETSON, JANE	53
BURLETSON, THOMAS	44
BURLETSON, THOMASINA'	45
Burletson, Thomasine	7
Burletson, William	7
BURLISON, MARY	62
BURNE, ELIZABETH	56
BURNE, ISABEL	59
BURNE, SAMUEL	56
BURNELL, GRACE GREIG	80
BURNELL, JOHN	80
BURNET, FRANCES	47
BURNET, JOHANNES	39
BURNET, MARIAM	39
BURNET, DR. ROB.	47
Burnet, Thomas	47
BURNOP, MARIAM	40
BURNOP, MICHAELL	40
BURNOPP, ELIZABETHAM	42
BURNOPP, MICHAEL	42
Burrell, Ann	136
BURRELL, ANNAM	36
Burrell, Barbara	18
BURRELL, CICILIAM	42
BURRELL, ELIZ.	116
Burrell, Elizabeth	118
BURRELL, JOH'ES	42
BURRELL, JOHN	116 : n. 136
Burrell, Margaret	117
BURRELL, MARGERY	77
BURRELL, MARY	52 : n. 118, 125
BURRELL, PETER 52, 77, 113, 116 : n. 18, 117, 118, 125	
BURRELL, REV. THOMAS	36
Burrell, —	118
BURROW, AN.	95
BURROW, JOHN	6, 94
BURROW, PEREGRINA	6, 94
BURROW, ROBERT	95
Burt, John William	155
Burt, Maria	155
Burt, Phyllis	155
Burt, William	155
Burton, Anne	17
Burton, Charlotte Belasyse	26
Burton, Deborah	55
BURTON, ELISABETH	61
BURTON, DAME ELIZ.	109
Burton, Elizabeth, Lady	7, 12, 99
Burton, Frances	109
Burton, Henry	109
Burton, Rev. Henry	26
BURTON, JANE	37
BURTON, JOHN	17, 61
Burton, Margaret	121
BURTON, MARTHA	18 : n. 49
Burton, Mary	109
BURTON, NICH.	17, 18
BURTON, REV. NICH.	49
Burton, Rev. Nicholas	109
Burton, Richard	109
Burton, Rev. Richard	109
Burton, Sir Thomas	109
BURTON, —	49
Burton, Archdeacon —	49
BURWELL, ANNA	92
BURWELL, ELIZABETH	120
Burwell, Francis	4
BURWELL, FRANCISCA	4
BURWELL, JOHANNA	4
Burwell, John	4
BURWELL, SETH	5
BURWELL, THO'A	5
BURWELL, THOMÆ	4, 92
BURWELL, THOMAS	5
Burwell, Rev. Thomas	36
Busbie, Henry	73
Busbie, Lively	73
BUSBY, ELIZ.	53
BUSBY, ELIZABETH	73
BUSBY, ISABELL	62
BUSBY, LIVELY	73
BUSBY, MARY	52 : n. 73
BUSBY, THO.	53
Busby, William	52, 73
Bussie, Jayne	84
Bussie, John	84
BUSSYE, EDWARD	84
Buston, Deborah	55
Buston, Elizabeth Jane	24
Butler, Hylton	43
BUTLER, CAPT. JAMES	52
BUTLER, MARG.	51
Butler, Margaret	51
BUTLER, MARIA	15
BUTLER, MARIAM	43
BUTLER, MARY	52
Butler, Samuel	149
BUTLER, THO.	15
BUTLER, THOMAS	43 : n. 51, 52
BUTTERWICK, ANN	72
BUTTLER, ANNAM	40
Buttler, Elizabeth	151
Buttler, Margaret Pearson	131
BUTTLER, RICHARD	131 : n. 151
Button, Jno.	63
Button, Margt.	63
BYERLY, MARG.	51
BYERS, DOROTHY	55
BYERS, HANNAH	69
BYERS, MARY	61
BYERS, ROBT.	55
BYERS, THOMAS	69
BYERS, WM.	15
Byng, Hon. Anna Maria Bridget	134
Byng, —, Viscount Torrington	134
Byrne, Katherine	133
Cadogan, Charles, Earl	145
CADOGAN, CHARLOTTE GEORGIANA MARY	29
CADOGAN, HON. EMILY FRANCES GERALDINE MATILDA	142
Cadogan, Lady Emily Mary	145
Cadogan, George Henry, Earl	79
CADOGAN, HENRY, VISCOUNT CHELSEA	29
Cadogan, Admiral Henry Charles, Earl	79
Cadogan, Henry Charles, Viscount Chelsea	79
CADOGAN, MARY SARAH, VISCOUNTESS CHELSEA	29 : n. 79
CADOGAN, —, VISCOUNT CHELSEA	142
CAFFIN, REV. BENJAMIN CHARLES	32, 33
Caffin, Bethia	32

CAFFIN, ERNEST GREGORY	33	CARTWRIGHT, ELIZABETH		151
Caffin, Admiral Sir James Crawford	32	CARTWRIGHT, REV. J.	138,	150
CAFFIN, MARGARET	32, 33	CARTWRIGHT, J., MINOR CANON OF DURHAM		146
Caffin, William	32			
Caldcleugh, John	90	Cartwright, John		151
Caldcleugh, Phyllis	27	CARTWRIGHT, REV. JOHN		141
Caldcleugh, William	27	Cartwright, Rev. John, Minor Canon of Durham		151
CALDWELL, SUSANNA	6			
Calverley, Anne, Lady	82	CARTWRIGHT, SARAH		102
Calverley, Isabel	87	CARTWRIGHT, THOMAS, PREBENDARY OF DURHAM	11,	98
Calverley, John	87			
CAMPBELL, GEORGE	105	Cartwright, Thomas		97
Camplin, Elizabeth	129	CARTWRIGHT, DR. THOMAS, DEAN OF RIPPON		102
Camplin, —	129			
Cane, Anne	20	CARTWRIGHT, WILL'US		98
Cane, Catherine Louisa	20	Casaubon, Florence		103
Cane, Col. —, M.P.	20	CASAUBON, ISA.		103
CARLETON, EDVARDI	15	Casaubon, Isaac		103
Carleton, Elizabeth	8	Casaubon, Dr. Meric, Prebendary of Canterbury		103
Carleton, Dr. Guy, Dean of Carlisle, Prebendary of Durham, Bishop of Bristol and Chichester	8	Castlecoote, Charles Henry, Lord		25
		CATCHESIDE, DOROTHY		60
Carleton, Hester	8	CATCHESIDE, JOHN		60
Carleton, Jane	8	CATHERICK, JANE		50
CARLETON, MARTHA	15	Cator, George Albemarle		149
Carleton, Prudence	8	Cator, Mary Susan		149
Carleton, —	8	CATTERICK, ANNA'		41
CARLISLE, ANN	58	CATTERICK, FRANCISCUS		41
Carlisle, Sir Anthony	23	Cavendish, Sir William, Duke of Newcastle		93
Carlisle, Barbara	23			
CARLISLE, GEO.	49	Cavendish, —, Lord Mansfield		93
CARLISLE, GEORGE	50	CAYLEY, GEORGE, M.D.		136
CARLISLE, JONATHAN	58	Cayley, John		136
CARLISLE, MARG.	50	Cayley, Sir William		136
CARLISLE, MARGERY	49	CHAIMBERS, ALICIAM		41
Carlisle, Thomas	23	Chambers, Eleanor		63
Carlton, Edward	14	CHAMBERS, ELIZ.		63
CARLTON, EDWARDI	14	CHAMBERS, GEORGIANA LAMBTON		33
CARLTON, GEORGIUS	14	CHAMBERS, JOHN		33
Carlton, Bishop Guy	8	Chambers, Richard		63
Carlton, —	82	Chambers, Sir Robert		63
Carlton. Lady —	8	CHAMBERS, SOPHIA LOUISA		33
CARNABY, HANNAH	46	Chandler, Joyce		19
CARNABY, RICH.	46	CHANDLER, WADHAM, PREBENDARY OF DURHAM		120
Carr, Anne	137			
CARR, BRIDGETTA'	40	Chandler, Dr., Bishop of Durham		19
CARR, CHARLES	137	Chantrey, —		19
CARR, ELIZABETH	54	CHAPMAN, ANN		70
CARR, ELLEN ELIZABETH	134	CHAPMAN, ANNÂ		3
CARR, ISABELLA	75 : n. 81	CHAPMAN, ANNAM		36
Carr, Jane	8	Chapman, Anne		3
CARR, JOHN	67, 134	CHAPMAN, BARBARY		96
CARR, REV. JOHN	136, 137	CHAPMAN, ELIZABETHAM		36
CARR, MARY	67, 72 : n. 128	Chapman, Grace		23
Carr, Ralph	75, 81	CHAPMAN, HANNAH		77
Carr, Robert	8	CHAPMAN, MARGARETAM		39
CARR, ROSETTA ANNE	134, 136 : n. 137	CHAPMAN, MARGT.		61
CARR, THOMAS	54 : n. 128	Chapman, Seth		36
Carr-Ellison, —	81	CHAPMAN, THO.		61
CARTER, ANNE	57	CHAPMAN, THOMAS		39
Carter, Dorothy	10	Chapman, —		36
CARTER, ELIZ.	65, 70	Charles I., King of England	47, 90, 93, 94,	95
CARTER, HENRY	57	Charles II., King of England	47,	97
Carter, Sir John	10	CHARLETON, FRANCES		62
CARTER, MARY	64	CHARLETON, THOMAS		62
CARTER, WILL	64	CHARLTON, ANN		73
Carteret, Bridget	15	CHARLTON, DOROTHY		72
Carteret, Edward, M.P.	15	CHARLTON, EDWARD		73
CARTHERET, THOMAS	97	CHARLTON, JOHN		9
CARTINGTON, JANE	57	CHARLTON, MARGARET		136
CARTWRIGHT, CAROLUS	11	CHARLTON, MARY		76

z

170   REGISTERS OF DURHAM CATHEDRAL.

CHARLTON, PRUDENCE	8	CLARK, THOS.	20
CHARLTON, W.	136	CLARKE, ABIGAIL	72
Charlton, William	136	CLARKE, ANN	118
CHAYTOR, ANN	135	CLARKE, ANNA	11
CHAYTOR, ANNE JANE	147	Clarke, Elizabeth	6, 93
CHAYTOR, ANNIE MARTHA	151	Clarke, Rev. Gabriel, D.D., Archdeacon of	
Chaytor, Caroline Mary Anne	28	Durham	2, 6, 93, 94, 106
CHAYTOR, GUSTAVUS ADOLPHUS, M.D.	142	CLARKE, DR. GABRIELE, PREBENDARY OF	
CHAYTOR, HARRIET	140	DURHAM	3
Chaytor, Henry	28	CLARKE, DR. GABRIELL, PREBENDARY OF	
Chaytor, Lieut.-Col. Henry	137, 142, 147, 150, 152	DURHAM, ARCHDEACON OF NORTH-	
CHAYTOR, REV. HENRY, PREBENDARY OF		UMBERLAND AND DURHAM	95
DURHAM	135, 140, 142 ; n. 145	CLARKE, GUALFRIDI	11
CHAYTOR, ISABELLA	142	CLARKE, JNO	28
Chaytor, Jane	137, 142, 150, 152	CLARKE, JNO, MINOR CANON OF DURHAM	130
CHAYTOR, JOHN	152	Clarke, John	95
Chaytor, Col. John	151	CLARKE, REV. JOHN	131
CHAYTOR, JULIANA	145	CLARKE, MARIA	11
CHAYTOR, MARY	135, 137	Clarke, Mildred	94, 95
Chaytor, Thomas	82	CLARKE, MILLE	94
CHAYTOR, WILLIAM CHARLES	150	CLARKE, RALPH	114
Chaytor, Sir William	28	CLARKE, RUTH	73
CHELSEA, HENRY, VISCOUNT	29	CLARKE, SAM.	117
CHELSEA, HENRY CHARLES, VISCOUNT	79	Clarke, Sibella	106
CHELSEA, MARY SARAH, VISCOUNTESS	29, 79	CLARKE, THOMAS	72, 73 ; n. 126
Cherry, Benjamin	27	CLARKE, WIL' FREDI	2 ; n. 126
Cherry, Charlotte Cassandra	27	CLARKE, —	
CHESTER, J. B.	30	CLARKE, DR.	5
Chesterfield, Lord	154	Clavering, John	124
CHESTERMAN, ELIZABETH	120	Clavering, Mary	124
CHESTERMAN, JOSEPH	120	CLAXTON, SARAH	65
CHEVALLIER, CANON	154, 155	CLAYPETH, ANN	47
CHILTON, JOH'ES	41	CLAYTON, ELIZ.	51
CHILTON, MARGARETAM	41	CLAYTON, FRANCISCAM	40, 41
CHIPCHACE, ELIZABETH	77	CLAYTON, ROB'TUS	41
CHIPCHACE, THOMAS	77	CLAYTON, WILL.	51
CHIPCHASE, ANNAM	44	CLEMENT, DOROTHY	108
CHIPCHASE, GULIELMUS	40	Clement, Elizabeth	113
CHIPCHASE, JANAM	40	CLEMENT, HAMMOND	18, 118, 119
CHIPCHASE, JANE	51, 102	CLEMENT, HAMOND	16
CHIPCHASE, JOH'ES	44	CLEMENT, JOHN	16, 17, 108, 113
CHIPCHASE, MARIA'	44	Clement, Margaret	18
CHRISHOP, JOHN	78	CLEMENT, MARGARETT	18, 118
CHRISHOP, MARTHA	78	CLEMENT, MARY	18
Christian, Sarah	110	CLEMENT, PRISCILLA	18, 120
Christian, —	110	Clennell, —	10
Christopher, Dorothy	138, 139, 148, 157	Clerk, Ann	101
Christopher, John Thomas	138, 139, 148, 157	CLERK, ANNAM	46
Christopher, William	157	Clerk, Dorothy	101
CHURCH, GULI'O	6	CLERK, HENRICUS	46
Church, Margaret	41	Clerk, John	101
CHURCH, MARIAM	41	Clerk, Maria	101
Church, Mary	36	Clerk, Mary	101
CHURCH, WILLIAM	7 ; n. 41	Clerk, Richard	101
CHURCH, —	7	CLERK, WILFRID	101
CHURNSIDE, DOROTHY	24	Clerk, William	101
CHURNSIDE, WILLIAM	24	CLERKE, HENRICUS	41
CLAPHAM, CIBELLE	63	CLERKE, JOANNEM	41
CLAPHAM, GEORGE	63	CLERKE, MARG'TAM	42
CLARK, ANN	49	Clerke, Mildred	2
CLARK, ANNE	20	CLERKE, RICHARD	100
CLARK, CATHERINE	20	CLERKE, RICHARDUS	11
CLARK, EDWARD	57	CLERKE, ROB'TUS	42
CLARK, ELIZ.	57, 72	CLERKE, SIBBY	7
CLARK, FRANCES	53	CLERKE, WILFRID	100
CLARK, JAMES	53	CLERKE, WILFRIDI	11
CLARK, JANE	66	CLERKE, DR.	2
CLARK, JOHN	49, 54	Clifton, Ann	65
CLARK, MARY	54	Clifton, Robert	65
CLARK, ROBERT	20	CLOSE, MARGT.	68
		CLUES, ANN	151

INDEX.

COALE, LADY	8
COATES, ANN	60
COATES, ELIZ.	70
COATES, MARGARETA	4
COATES, WILLIAM	60
COATESWORTH, ANNE	63
COCKANEY, JANE	71
COCKANEY, THO.	71
Cockayne, Charles, Viscount Cullen	48
Cockayne, Hon. Mary	48
Cockayne, Lady Mary, Viscountess Cullen	48
COCKERELL, JANE	53
COCKNIDGE, REV. GEORGIUS	92
Coghill, Jane	132
Coghill, Oliver	132
COLBERG, ANNE ELIZABETH	136
Colberg, Jane Charlotte Mary	29
Colberg, Mary	136
Colberg, Capt. Samuel	136
Colberg, Col. Samuel Thomas	39
COLE, ANNE	56
COLE, ELIZ.	72
Cole, Lady Margaret	9
Cole, Sir Nicholas	9
COLEPITT, RA.	102
COLLEDGE, JOSHUA	66
COLLEDGE, MARY	66
COLLIN, ANNAM	41
COLLIN, JOH'ES	41
COLLING, JANE	58
COLLINGWOOD, JOHN	70
COLLINGWOOD, SARAH	70
Collinson, Frances Sybel	157
Collinson, Rev. John	157
Collinson, Admiral	157
Collison, Mary Ann	153
Collison, William	153
COLMER, TYMOTHY	82
COLMER, DR., PREBENDARY OF DURHAM	82
Colmore, A.	84
COLMORE, CLEMENS, PREBENDARY OF DURHAM	83
Colmore, Rev. Clement, Prebendary of Durham	82
Colmore, Joan	83
Colmore, Mary	84
Colmore. William	83
COLSON, ANNAM	44
COLSON, JACOB	44
Coltpits, Ann	87
COMMIN, MARGARETA	3
COMMIN, TYMOTHEO	92
COMPTON, JANE	112
Comyn. Alice	92
Comyn, Elizabeth	92
Comyn, Francis	92
Comyn, Simon	92
Comyn, Timothy	4
Comyn, Tymotheo	92
Comyn, —	4
CONDUIT, MICHAEL	122
CONINSBY, JULIUS	64
CONINSBY, MARY	64
Conyers, Sir Baldwyn	61
Conyers, Sir Blakiston	61
CONYERS, GULIELMS	42
CONYERS, JANE	61
CONYERS, MARGARETT	38
Conyers, Mary	38
Conyers, Sir Nicholas	61
CONYERS, NICHOLAUS	8, 38
CONYERS, RALPH	62
CONYERS, SARAH	43
CONYERS, THOMAS	8 : n. 13
Conyers, Sir Thomas	61
Cooch, Alice	152
Cooch, Louisa	152
COOCH, MARIA	158
Cooch, Robert	152
COOK, ELIZA	3
COOK, ISABEL	59
COOK, MARY	71, 127
COOK, SARAH	70
Cooke, Margaret	4
COOKE, MARGARETA	5
COOKE, MARY	62
COOKE, THOMAS	4
COOKE, —	4
Cookeson, Dorothy	3
Cookeson, Frances	3
Cookeson, John	3
COOKESON, SUSANNA	3
COOKESON, XPOFER	3
COOLING, ELIZ.	64
Cooper, Alice	85
Cooper, Catherine	85
Cooper, Elizabeth	85
COOPER, ELIZABETHAM	39
Cooper, Francis	85
Cooper, Isaac	85
Cooper, John	85
Cooper, Katherine	85
Cooper, Margaret	85
COOPER, MARIAM	45
Cooper, Mary	36, 46
Cooper, Mathe	85
Cooper, Matthew	85
Cooper, Murial	105
Cooper, Philadelphia	36, 46
Cooper, Robert	85, 105
Cooper, Robin	85
Cooper, Thomas	85
COOPER, REV. V. K.	158, 159
Cooper, William	36, 46
COOPER, —	1, 101
Coote, Dr. Charles, Dean of Kilfenora	25
Coote, Charles Henry, Lord Castlecoote	25
Coote, Grace	25
COPAS, —	6
COPEMAN, FREDERICK JOHN	157
Copeman, James Robert	157
COPLIN, ANNAM	46
COPLIN, THOMAS	46
COQUO, MARGARETÂ	4
COQUO, THOMA	4
CORDERY, ANNE	124
CORK, DOROTHY	51
CORNEFORTH, ANN	68
CORNEFORTH, HANNAH	71
CORNEFORTH, JO.	62
CORNEFORTH, MARY	62
CORNER, ANNAM	44
Cornwallis, Earl, Dean of Durham, Bishop of Lichfield and Coventry	134
Cornwallis, —, Archbishop of Canterbury	21
Cosens, Catherine	120
Cosens, John	120, 121
Cosens, Sarah	120
Cosin, Anne	106
Cosin, Elizabeth	99, 109
Cosin, Frances	106, 114
Cosin, Giles	96

COSIN, JOANNES, BISHOP OF DURHAM	96	Cradock, John	85, 86
COSIN, JOHANNE	4	Cradock, Dr. John, Archdeacon of Northumberland	85, 93
COSIN, DR. JOHANNIS, BISHOP OF DURHAM	88	Cradock, Joseph	85
Cosin, Dr. John, Bishop of Durham	87, 90, 96, 97	Cradock, Sir Joseph	106
		Cradock, Margaret	1, 86, 93
Cosin, Mary	12, 43, 96	Cradock, Margery	85
COSIN, RICHARDUS	88	Cradock, Mary	85
Cosin, Dr., Bishop of Durham	9, 12, 43, 86, 95, 99, 106, 109, 111, 114, 128	Cradock, Rachel	85
		CRADOCK, RICHARDO	2
COSINS, BARBARA'	42	Cradock, Sibella	106
COSINS, GEORGE	3	CRADOCK, THOMAS	106
COSINS, DR. JOHN, PREBENDARY AND BISHOP OF DURHAM	3, 87	Cradock, Timothy	85
		Cradock, William	85
COSINS, RICHARD	87	Cradock, —	85
COSINS, SARAH	121	Cradock, Archdeacon	106
COSSIN, JOHANNE	3	Cradock, Dr.	2
Cosyn, Giles	96	CRADOCK, DR., PREBENDARY OF DURHAM	1 : n. 86
Cosyn, Dr. John, Bishop of Durham	96		
Cosyn, Mary	96	CRADOCKE, DOROTHE	1
COULSON, ANN	67	CRADOCKE, JANE	1
COULSON, CATHERINE	75	CRADOCKE, JO.	1
COULSON, CUTHBERT	100	CRADOCKE, JOHANNES, PREBENDARY OF DURHAM, ARCHDEACON OF NORTHUMBERLAND	86
COULSON, ELIZ.	42		
COULSON, ELIZABETH	100		
COULSON, ELIZADETHAM	42	Cradocke, Margaret	86
COULSON, ISABELL	54	CRADOCKE, RICHARD	86
COULSON, JOHN	75	CRADOCKE, DR.	2, 3
COULTAS, JOHN	62	CRAGGS, ANNE	61, 63
COULTAS, SARAH	62	CRAGGS, GEORGE	68
COULTMAN, ANNAM	40	CRAGGS, HANNAH	69
COULTMAN, RICHARDUS	40	CRAGGS, MARY	68
Courtiss, Anne	96	CRAGGS, THO.	69
Courtiss, Bridget	96	Crawford, Bethia	32
Courtiss, Elizabeth	96	Crawford, Lieut. George	32
Courtiss, Margery	96	CRAWFORD, MARGARETAM	45
Courtiss, Richard	96	CRAWFORTH, AN	38
COWENS, MARY	133	CRAWFORTH, CICILIAM	42
COWLE, DOROTHY	101	CRAWFORTH, MARIA'	41
COWLE, ELIZ.	63	CREED, CHRISTOPHER	23
COWLE, JANE	78	CREED, STEPHEN	23
COWLE, JOHN	101	Crespigny, see De Crespigny.	
Cowlemer, Clem.	84	CREW, DOROTHY, LADY	47
Cowlemer, Isabel	84	Crew, Jemima, Baroness	47
COWLIN, ANNE	56	Crew, John, Baron	47
COWLIN, GEO.	56	CREW, REV. NATHANIEL, LORD, D.D., DEAN OF CHICHESTER, BISHOP OF OXFORD AND DURHAM	47
Cowper, Dorothy	124		
Cowper, Elizabeth	85		
Cowper, Margaret	85	Crew, Penelope, Lady	47
Cowper, Mary, Countess	124	Crew, Sir Randolph	47
COWPER, ROBERT	85	Crew, Temperance	47, 114
COWPER, HON. REV. DR. SPENCER, DEAN OF DURHAM	124	Crew, Sir Thomas	47
		Crew, Thomas, Lord	114
Cowper, Sir William, Earl	124	Crew, —, Bishop of Durham	45
COXE, ARCHDEACON	152	CREW, LORD, BISHOP OF DURHAM	114
COXON, DOROTHY	55	Crewe, Jemima, Baroness Crew	47
COXON, ROBT.	55	Crewe, John, Baron Crew	47
CRACROFT, CAPT. JOHN	23	Crewe, Nathaniel	47
CRACROFT, PENELOPE ANN	23	Crewe, Rev. Nathaniel, Lord, D.D., Dean of Chichester, Bishop of Oxford and Durham	47, 48
CRACROFT, ROBERT	23		
Cradock, Ann	85		
Cradock, Anne	85, 86	Crewe, Penelope, Lady	47
CRADOCK, ANTHONIE	85	Crewe, Lord	18, 122, 126
Cradock, Anthony	85, 96	CREYTON, ALICE	62
Cradock, Catherine	85	CROFT, ELIZ.	41
Cradock, Cuthbert	85	CROFT, GULIELMUS	41
Cradock, Dorothy	86, 106	CROFT, HANNAM	43
Cradock, Elizabeth	85	CROFT, JAMES	55
Cradock, George	85	CROFT, MARY	55, 62
Cradock, Grace	85	Croft, Thomasine	121
CRADOCK, JOHANNE	2	Crofton, Ann	24

CROFTON, ANTHONY JAMES	27	D'Arcy, Margaret, Lady	117
CROFTON, ANTHONY MOWBRAY	24, 25, 26, 27	D'Arcy, Lady	18
Crofton, Dorothy Basto	24	D'AUTIN, SAM. DAV. JOSEPH DE MON-	
CROFTON, ELIZABETH	25	CEAUX	121
Crofton, Elizabeth Jane	24	D'Este, Mary	47
CROFTON, JANE	24, 25, 26, 27	Dagnia, Benjamin Clayton	78
Crofton, Mary Elizabeth	27	Dagnia, Christopher	78
CROFTON, RICHARD	26 ; n. 24	DAGNIA, EDWARD	78
Crofton, Thomas	24	DAGNIA, HANNAH	78
Crompton, —	10	Dagnia, Jane	78
Cromwell, —	7	Dagnia, John	78
Crosby, Ambrose	113	Dagnia, Margery	78
CROSBY, ANN	60 ; n. 113	Dagnia, Onesiphorus	78
CROSBY, EDWARD	49, 60	DALE, ELIZ.	57
CROSBY, ELIZ.	49	DALE, GEORGE	56
CROSBY, ELIZABETH	108	DALE, HANNAH	56
CROSBY, ELIZABETHA'	44	Dale, Jane	78
CROSBY, FRANCIS	110 ; n. 113	DALE, JOHN	78
Crosby, John	113	DALE, LYDIA	78
CROSBY, RICHARD	104 ; n. 113	DALE, MARTHAM	42
CROSBY, THO.	104, 110, 113	Dale, Mary	78
CROSBY, THOMAS	44, 108	DALL, ANDREW	80
Crosby, Watson	113	DALL, GRACE GREIG	80
Crosby, —	96	DALLIVALL, —	6
Crosyer, Eleanor	56	Dalton, Dulcibella	105
Crosyer, George	56	Dalton, Rev. Thomas	105
Crosyer, Jane	56	Danby, Elizabeth	90
CROW, ANN	52	DAND, ALCE	37
Cullen, Charles, Viscount	48	DAND, ROBERT	37
Cullen, Mary, Viscountess	48	Daniel, —	43
CUMMIN, ANN	78	DARBY, JOHN	107
CUMMIN, DO'IA	5	DARBYSHIRE, ANNE	105
CUMMIN, WM.	78	DARBYSHIRE, JOHN	105
CUMMINS, MARGARET	129	DARBYSHIRE, MARG'TAM	44
CUNNINGHAM, ELIZABETH	61	Darcy, Conyers, Lord	104
CUNNINGHAM, ROBERT	61	Darcy, Conyers, Earl of Holderness	45
Currie, Charlotte Georgiana Mary	29	Darcy, Margaret	104
Currie, Rev. Maynard Wodehouse	29	Darcy, Ursula	45
CURRY, AGNAS	126	DARNELL, ELIZ.	67
CURRY, ANN	72	DARNELL, ELIZABETH	29, 152 ; n. 157
CURRY, THOMAS	126	DARNELL, ELIZABETH JANE	29
Curry, William	72	DARNELL, FRANCES	30
CURRYE, ANNAM	39	DARNELL, JANE GRACE	29
CURSTT, ANN	70	DARNELL, LUCY ELIZABETH	30
CURSTT, WM.	70	DARNELL, PHILIP WHELER	29
Curteis, Mary	85	DARNELL, THOMAS CHARLES	29
Curteis, Richard	85	DARNELL, W. N.-	29
CURTIOUS, JOHN	2	DARNELL, REV. W. N.	131, 132, 133
CURTIOUS, RICHARD	2	DARNELL, W. N., PREBENDARY OF DUR-	
CURTISE, RICHARDUS	96	HAM	134, 135
CUTHBERT, CHARLES	110 ; n. 10	DARNELL, WILLIAM	157
Cuthbert, Dorothea	10	DARNELL, REV. WILLIAM	30 ; n. 157
Cuthbert, Dorothy	10, 110, 111, 123	DARNELL, REV. WILLIAM NICHOLAS, PRE-	
Cuthbert, George	10	BENDARY OF DURHAM	29, 153 ; n. 152, 157
Cuthbert, Jane	10	Darnell, Rev. —, Prebendary of Durham	153
CUTHBERT, JOHN	110 ; n. 10, 111	DARNETON, GULIELMUS	39
Cuthbert, John, M.D.	10	DARNETON, SUSANNAH	39
Cuthbert, Margaret	10	DARNTON, ELIZ.	69
Cuthbert, Philadelphia	10	DARWIN, MAJ. CHARLES WARING	80
Cuthbert, Ralph	10	DARWIN, FRANCIS	80
Cuthbert, Rev. Richard	10, 123	DARWIN, MARY DOROTHEA	80
Cuthbert, Robert	10	DAVIES, JOHN, MINOR CANON OF DUR-	
CUTHBERT, THEOPHILUS	111 ; n. 10	HAM	84
Cuthbert, William	10	DAVIES, MARGARET	84
CUTHBERT, REV. —	127	DAVISON, ANN	61, 77, 126
CUTHBERT, —	110, 111, 123, 127	DAVISON, ANNE	56, 63
CUTTER, BARBARA	63	DAVISON, ANNE CAROLINE	156 ; n. 154
CUTTER, JOHN	63	Davison, Caroline	146
		DAVISON, CHARLOTTE	146
D., J.	25	DAVISON, CUTHBERT	66
D'Arcy, James, Lord	117	DAVISON, DOROTHY	104

Davison, Dulcibella 13, 123
Davison, Rev. Edward 131, 151
DAVISON, ELIZABETH ...... 123, 143 : *n.* 7, 109
DAVISON, ELIZABETHAM 39
Davison, Jane 133
DAVISON, JOHANNA............................. 66
DAVISON, JOHANNES 39
DAVISON, JOSEPH .... 63, 143, 154 : *n.* 156
DAVISON, MARG'TAM 44
DAVISON, MARGARET PEARSON... 151 : *n.* 131
DAVISON, MARIAM 41
DAVISON, MARY ....37 : *n.* 112
Davison, Matthew 133
Davison, Samuel 109
DAVISON, SAMUELL 7
DAVISON, THOMAS .... 44 : *n.* 154
DAVISON, REV. THOMAS........................ 37
DAVISON, WILL................................ 61
Davison, William 13, 123, 126
Davison, — 112, 136, 154
DAVY, ANN................................... 72
DAVY, ELIZABETH 75
DAVY, THO.................................. 72
Dawnay, Dorothy............................ 119
Dawnay, Henry, Viscount Downe............ 119
Dawson, Anne 148
DAWSON, ELIZ................................. 52
DAWSON, ELIZABETH 55
DAWSON, JANE 51
DAWSON, JOHN............................ 51, 55
DAWSON, MARG. 65
DAWSON, SARAH 70
DAWSON, THO. 52
Dawson, Dr., Canon of Windsor ....
DAY, ELIZABETHAM 40
DAY, JOHANNES 40
De Crespigny, Caroline 25
De Crespigny, Rev. Heaton Champion..... 25
De Félice, Augusta 33
De Karp, Augusta............................ 33
De Karp, Eleanora 33
DE KARP, ELÉONORE 33
DE KARP, LOUIS BERNARD 33
DE KARP, MARIE LOUISE 33
De Karp, Maurice 33
DEANE, — 87
DEANHAM, CHRISTOPHER 41
DEANHAM, JANAM 41
DEAR, MARY 47
DEASON, J.................................... 27
DEASON, JAMES 124, 126
DEASON, —................................... 22
DEE, ANN 26
DEE, ELIZABETH 26
DEEMSTER, SUSANNA 48
DEERING, REV. HENEAGE, DEAN OF RIPON 127
DEERING, MARY 127
Delabene, Henry 23
Delabene, Martha 23
Delamere, Lady Elizabeth, Baroness 107
Delamere, Sir George, Baron 107
Delamere, Lord 107
Delaval, Elizabeth 6
Delaval, Thomas.......................... 6, 13
DELAVAL, —.................................. 73
DELAVALL, ROB. 13
Delavall, Robert 13
DELAVALL. ROBERTO 15
Denison, Isabel 69
DENNIS, S., MINOR CANON OF DURHAM 125
DENNIS, SAMUEL 20, 121

DENNIS, SAMUEL, MINOR CANON OF DURHAM 124
DENNIS, SARAH 123, 125
DENNIS, WILLIAM 124
DENNIS, REV. — 123
DENT, ISABEL 52
DENT, JANE 60
DENT, JOHANNES 40
DENT, MARGARETAM 40
DENT, MARY 78
DENTON. ALICE............................. 121
DENTON, ANNE 116
DENTON, JOHN .... 112, 119 : *n.* 116, 121
DENTON, ROBERT 119
DEVORAX, REV. — 94
DICKENS, GEORGE 23
Dickens, Henry John 22
DICKENS, MARGARET .... 21 : *n.* 22
DICKENS, MARY 23
DICKENS, RICHARD 23
DICKENS, CAPT. RICHARD 23
DICKENS, COL. RICHARD MARK ... 21 : *n.* 23
DICKENS, DR. SAMUEL, PREBENDARY AND ARCHDEACON OF DURHAM ...... 21 : *n.* 22
DICKENS, SAMUEL RICHARD................ 23
Dickens, —................................. 137
DICKENS, DR., PREBENDARY AND ARCHDEACON OF DURHAM 23
Dickenson, Ann.............................. 65
Dickenson, Edwd............................ 65
Dickins, Thomas 152
DICKINSON, ELEANOR 55
DICKINSON, HANNA 66
Dickinson, —................................ 85
DICKONS, JOHN RALPH 156
DICKONS, MARY ....144, 148 : *n.* 131, 141
DICKONS, SARAH 144
DICKONS, THOMAS ...... 148, 156 : *n.* 144, 152
Digby, Elizabeth 122
Digby, William, Dean of Durham........... 122
Digby, William, Lord 122
DIKES, ISABEL 57
DIKES, JEREMIAH 57
DIPPER, JOAN 56
Ditmas, Georgina 30
Ditmas, John................................ 30
DIXON, ANN 46, 110
DIXON, DAVID 44
DIXON, DOROTHY........................... 65
DIXON, ELIZ. 72, 113
Dixon, Elizabeth 44, 110, 120
DIXON, FORTUNE 67
DIXON, FRANCIS 114
DIXON, GEO. 110, 113, 114, 115
DIXON, GEORGE 112, 120 : *n.* 122, 123, 125, 126, 127, 128
DIXON, ISABELL 56
DIXON, JANAM 44
DIXON, JANE 73
DIXON, JOHN .... 67, 73, 123 : *n.* 126
DIXON, JOSEPH 46, 113, 114
DIXON, MARY .... 67, 115 : *n.* 128
DIXON, ROBERT 119
DIXON, SARAH .... 114, 123 : *n.* 120, 128
Dixon, Tabitha 122, 125, 126, 127, 128
DIXON, WILL. 112
Dixon, William 83
DIXON, — 114
DOBBINSON, MARY 62
DOBBINSON, MICHAEL...................... 62
DOBBISON, ALICE........................... 56

DOBINSON, ALICE	66	Douglas, Lord Drumlanrig and Earl	49
DOBSON, ANTHONY	77	Douglas-Gresley, Robert Archibald	151
DOBSON, CATH.	57	DOUGLASS, REV. JAMES, D.D., PREBENDARY OF DURHAM	125
DOBSON, DOROTHY	17		
DOBSON, ELISABETH	61	DOUGLASS, JANE	125
DOBSON, ELIZ.	13, 17, 57, 109	Douglass, Jean	125
Dobson, Elizabeth	13	DOUTHWAIT, DOROTHY	65
DOBSON, FITZ-HERBERT	18	DOUTHWAIT. JNO.	65
DOBSON, HEN., D.D.	18	DOUTHWAITE, JO.	104
Dobson, Rev. Henry, D.D., Prebendary of Durham	17	DOUTHWAITE, MARGARET	58
		Downe. Henry, Viscount	119
DOBSON, JAMES	68	DOWNES, ALICE	64
DOBSON, JENNETTAM	42	DOWNES, ELIZ.	43
DOBSON, MARGARET	77	DOWNES. ISABELL	55
DOBSON, MARGT.	68	DOWNES. MATTHEUS	43
DOBSON, MARY	63	DOWSON, MARY	54, 76
DOBSON, PENELOP	17	Dowson, Sarah	76
DOBSON, ROBERT	95	DOWTHWAITE, ELIZABETH	38
DOBSON, THOMAS	63	DRIZEDELL, ELIZ.	43
Dobson, Welbury	13	DRUMER, JANE	61
Dobson, Wheatley	13	Drumlanrig, Lady Isabel	49
DOBSON, DR.	17, 109	Drumlanrig, Lord	49
DODDESLY, ROBERT	123	Drummond, Susanna	33
DODDS	63	DRURY, ISABELL	94 : n. 7
DODDS, HANNAH	77	DRURY, JOHN	94
Dodds, Hylda	46	Drury. Rev. John	12, 113
DODDS, ISABEL	57	Drury, Joyce	113
DODDS, JNO.	63	Du Boulay, Rev. Francis	28
DODDS, MARY	46	Du Boulay. Sybella	28
Dodds, Tho.	46	Du Pin, J. de Grevelle	103
DODDS, THOMAS	46	DUCKETT, Ann	52
Dodshon, Anne	39	Dudley, Ambrose	36
Dodsly, Robert	123	Dudley, Anne	36
Dodsworth, Anthony	83	Dudley. Isabel	36
Dodsworth, Magdalen	93	DUEL, MARGARET	60
DODSWORTH, SARAM	36	Dugdale, —	10, 88, 92, 100, 105, 116
DOESHON. GULIELMUS	40	DUN, JO.	105
DOESHON, MARGARETAM	40	Duncan, Eleazer	93
Dolben, Elizabeth	122	Duncan, Dr. Eleazer, Prebendary of Durham	92
DOLBEN, SIR JNO., PREBENDARY OF DURHAM	122		
		Duncan, Phœbe	93
Dolben, Sir John	122	Duncan, —	4
Dolland, Anne	155	DUNCON, DR. ELEAZ., PREBENDARY OF DURHAM	92
Dolland, Peter	155		
Dongwith, Rev. Richard	125	DUNCON, FLORA	92
DONGWITH, REV. RICHD.	123	DUNCON, —	5
DONGWITH, —	125	Dungannon, Arthur, Viscount	145
DONGWORTH, CATHERINE	120	DUNKON, DO'IA	5
DONGWORTH, RICHARD	120	DUNN, ANNE	54
Dongworth, —	121	DUNN, ELIZ.	67
DORMA', ELIZABETH	9	DUNN, GEORGE	39
Dorrien, see Smith-Dorrien.		DUNN, JACOB	54
DOSSY, ISABELLAM	40	DUNN, JANAM	39
Douglas, Lieut.-Col. Archibald	138	DUNN, JAS.	70, 79
Douglas, Lieut.-Gen. Archibald	151	DUNN, MARTIN	79
Douglas, Eleanor	151	DUNN, MERRIELL	39
DOUGLAS, REV. HENRY, CANON OF DURHAM	150	DUNN, RALPH	67
		DUNNE, ANNAM	40
Douglas, Lady Isabel, Lady Drumlanrig and Countess	49	DURANT, ISABELLA	49
		DURANT, JOHN	49
Douglas, Rev. James, D.D., Prebendary of Durham	125	DURELL, ANNE	128
		DURELL, REV. D.	28
Douglas, Jane	138	Durell, David, D.D., Prebendary of Canterbury	128
Douglas, Lady Margaret	49		
DOUGLAS, MARY	51	DURELL, REV. DAVID, D.D., PREBENDARY OF DURHAM	128
Douglas, Mary Anne	150		
DOUGLAS, ROBT.	51	Durell, John	128
Douglas, Rev. Robert	150	DURELL, PHILIP VAVASOR	128
Douglas, Robert Archibald	151	Durell, Thomas Vavasour	128
Douglas, —	151	Durell, see also Vavasseur-dit-Durell.	
DOUGLAS, REV. CANON	144	Durham, Earl of	87

Durham, Lord	81
DURY, JOCOSAM	44
DURY, JOH'IS	12
Dury, Rev. John	113
Dury, Joyce	44, 113
DURY, ROBERTUS	12
DURYE, ISABELL	7
DURYE. JOHN	7
DUXBURY, MARIAM	41
DUXBURY, SAMUEL	41
DYKES, REV. J. B.	150, 151, 152
Dykes, John Bacchus	149
DYKES, REV. JOHN B.	148, 149, 156
DYKES, GEORGE LIONEL ANDREW	149
Dyllycote, Jane	82
EALES, DAVID	102
EARL, ANN	72
EARLE. ANN	58
EARLE, ROBERT	58
EASTER, SARAH	101
EASTERBY, ANN	46
EBDON, T.	132, 133, 134, 135, 136, 137, 138, 139, 140, 141, 142
EBDON, THOMAS	136, 142, 143, 144, 145
Ebdon, Rev. Thomas, Minor Canon of Durham	139
EBDON, THOS.	131, 132
Ebutts. Grace	4
Ebutts, Philip	4
EBUTTS. PHILIPPO	4
Eden, Catherine	13, 22
EDEN, CHRISTIAN FLORENCE	35
EDEN, DOROTHY	119
Eden, Elizabeth	73
EDEN, FLORENCE	35
Eden, Hannah	16
Eden, Henry, M.D.	53
Eden, Jane	53
Edeu, John	13
EDEN, LIEUT.-COL. JOHN HENRY	35
Eden, Rev. John Patrick, Canon of Durham	35
Eden, Margaret	122
Eden, Mary	53
Eden, Mary Anne	13
EDEN, ROBERT	36
Eden, Sir Robert	16, 22, 35, 73, 122
EDEN, REV. DR. THO., PREBENDARY OF DURHAM	119
EDEN. REV. DR. THOMAS, PREBENDARY OF DURHAM	122
Eden, Sir William	13
EDEN, —	36
EDEN, DR.	73 : n. 16
EDEN, LADY	126
Eden, Lord Auckland	22
Edmonds, Elizabeth Margaret Anne	31, 147
Edmonds, Elizabeth Nicholls	147
Edmonds, Rev. Richard	147
EDMUNDSON, ELISABETH	107
EDMUNDSON, ELIZAB.	112
EDMUNDSON, JOHN	112, 113
Edmundson, Mary	112
EDMUNDSON, WILLIAM	112 : n. 107, 113, 121
EDMUNDSON, —	121 : n. 113
Edward III., King of England	141
Edward IV., King of England	88
Edwards, Ambrose	69
EDWARDS, ANNE	69
Edwards, Rev. Edward	152
EDWARDS, FREDERICA LOUISA	31
EDWARDS. GEORGE	69
Edwards, Isabel	69
Edwards, Isabella	69
EDWARDS, REV. JOHN, CANON OF DURHAM	152
EDWARDS. REV. JOHN GEORGE	31
Edwards, Louisa	152
EDWARDS, LOUISA MARIA	31
Edwards, Sarah	152
Edwards, Canon	31
EEYLES, DAVIDIS	96
EEYLES, —	96
EGERTON, CATHERINE	24
EGERTON, REV. CHARLES	24
Egerton, Francis	24
Egerton, Francis, Earl of Bridgewater	24
EGERTON, HENRY	24
Egerton, John, Bishop of Durham	24
Egerton, John, Earl of Bridgewater	24
Egerton, Mary	24
Egerton, Bishop	20
Egglestone, Margaret	83
Ekins, Anne	148
Ekins, Rev. Frederick	148
Ekins, Dr. Jeffrey, Dean of Carlisle	148
Ekins, Sarah Janetta	148
ELDER, AUGUSTA	146
ELDER, EDITH	144
ELDER, REV. EDWARD	144, 146
ELDER, REV. EDWARD, D.D.	149
ELDER, EDWARD FARLEY	147
ELDER, JANE	66
ELDER, THOMAS	66
Eldon, Lord	27
ELDRIDG, JOHN	109
ELDRIDGE, JOHANNES	45
ELDRIDGE, JOHN	106
ELDRIDGE, MARGARETA'	45
ELDRIDGE, MARGARETT	106
ELLERAY, ELIZABETH	125
ELLERAY, GEORGE	122
ELLINGTON, JOHN	20
ELLINGTON, MARY	20
Elliot, Dorothy	155
Elliot, John	155
Elliot, Sarah	155
Ellison, Cuthbert, M.P.	81
Ellison, Henrietta	81
Ellison, Isabella Caroline	81
Ellison, Isabella Grace	81
Ellison, Laura Jane	81
Ellison, Louisa	81
Ellison, Sarah Caroline	81
Ellison, see also Carr-Ellison.	
ELLS, DAVID	40
ELLS, MARGARETAM	40
ELRINGTON, ELIZ.	48
ELSTOB, ALICIAM	45
ELSTOB, ANN	49
ELSTOB, EDVARDUS	45
ELSTOB, JANAM	40
ELSTOBB, GULIELMS.	43
ELSTOBB, JANAM	43
Elton, Ashley	131
Elton, R. W.	131
EMBLETON, ALCE	37
EMERSON, ANNA	38
EMERSON, ANNA'	43
Emerson, Anthony	52
EMERSON, ELIZ.	43

EMERSON, ELIZABETH	63	EYRE, SAMUEL, D.D., PREBENDARY OF DURHAM	107
Emerson, Frances	128		
EMERSON, GEORGE	63		
EMERSON, GEORGIUS	43	Faber, —	138
EMERSON, GULIELMS.	42	FAIRBARNES, ANNA'	43
EMERSON, HANNA	66	FAIRBARNES, ANNAM	46
EMERSON, ISABEL	59	FAIRBARNES, MARIAM	46
Emerson, Isabella	128	FAIRBARNES, THOMAS	43, 46
Emerson, Jane	52	FAIRBARNS, ISABEL	47
Emerson, Rev. John	128	Fairclas, Edward	92
EMERSON, MARGARETAM	45	Fairelas, Margaret	92
EMERSON, MARY	48	Fairelas, Richard	92
EMERSON, OBADIAH	66	Fairfax, —	141
EM'ERSON, ISABELLAM	39	FAIRLESSE, JANE	110
EMMERSON, ALICE	77	FAIRLESSE, JOHN	110
EMMERSON, ANNE	61	Falle, Rev. Philip, Prebendary of Durham	128
EMMERSON, CHRISTOPHER	64	Fanshaw, Lady	15
EMMERSON, DOROTHY	75	Farrah, Mark	68
EMMERSON, ELIZ.	64	Farrah, William	68
EMMERSON, GEO.	61	FARRAR, REV. CANON	158
EMMERSON, GEORGE	77	FARRER, AN	7
EMMERSON, GEORGIUS	40	FARRER, JOHN	7
EMMERSON, JOHN	83	Farrer, Mark	68
EMMERSON, MARGARET	77	Farrow, Anne	68
EMMERSON, MARY	77	FARROW, ELIZ.	65
EMMERSON, RALPH	75	Farrow, John	68
ERINGTON, JANE	52	FARROW, MARIAM	38
ERRINGTON, ANN	66	FARROW, MARK	68
ERRINGTON, BARBARA	63	FARROW, MARY	68
ERRINGTON, JOHN	66	FARROW, NICHOLAUS	38
ERRINGTON, MARY	68	Farrow, William	68
Errington, William	68	FAUCET, THOMAS	120
Este, see D'Este.		FAWCETT, REV. DR., PREBENDARY OF DURHAM	125
Estienne, Florence	103		
Eture, Alice	92	Fawcett, Elizabeth	125
Eture, James	92	Fawcett, John	125
Eture, Mary	92	Fawcett, —	81, 148
EUBANK, ALICIAM	43	FAWDON, ALICE	58
EUBANK, MILO	43	FAWDON, ELIZ.	53
EUBANKE, JOHANNE	3	FEA, PETER	74
Eure, Frances	87	FEA, SARAH	74
Eure, Sir Ralph	87	Feaster, Dorothy	102
Eure, Lord	87	FEATHERSTONE, ISABEL	117
EVANCE, MARY	131	Feilding, Anue	141
EVANCE, WILLIAM	131	FEILDING, ANNE MATILDA	133
EVANS, ARTHUR THOMAS FABIAN	155	Foilding, Charles Israel	147
EVANS, JOANE	94	Feilding, Charlotte	127
Evans, Rev. Robert	124	Fcilding, Charlotte Anne	147
EVANS, ROSAMOND	152 : n. 33, 156, 158	FEILDING, ELIZABETH ELEANOR	141
EVANS, THOMAS SAUNDERS, D.D., CANON OF DURHAM	53, 158 : n. 155	FEILDING, GEORGE	133 : n. 141
		Feilding, Israel	123, 127
Evans, Rev. T. S., Canon of Durham	156	Feilding, Margery	127
EVANS, CANON	154, 157	Feilding, Martha	123
EVENING, ANN	71	FEILDING, SOPHIA ELIZABETH	147
EVETT, ANN	150	Félice, see De Félice.	
EVETT, WILLIAM	152 : n. 150	FELLS, JANE	50
Ewbanck, Ann	59	FELLS, ROBERT	50
Ewbanke, Anne	89	Fenwick, Christopher Hardinge	153
Ewbanke, Elizabeth	82	FENWICK, DOROTHY	140
Ewbanke, Elsabeth	89	FENWICK, DR.	134
Ewbanke, Henry	98	FENWICK, ELIZ.	54
Ewbanke, Henry, Prebendary of Durham	89	FENWICK, ELIZABETH	23 : n. 4
		FENWICK, FRANCES	153
Ewbanke, Jana	98	FENWICK, J. R., M.D.	140
Ewbanke, Toby	82	FENWICK, JANE	51
EWBANKE, —	2 : n. 98	Fenwick, John, M.D.	136, 148
EXETER, H.	80	FENWICK, JOHN RALPH, M.D.	148 : n. 136
Exton, Bridget	15	FENWICK, LADY	49 : n. 50, 106
Exton, Sir Thomas	15	Fenwick, Margaret	136
EYLES, ANN	65	Fenwick, Mary	148
Eyles, Thomas	65	FENWICK, NICH.	54

A A

FENWICK, ROBERT	23	FORD, JOHN	79
Fenwick, Sir Robert	49	FOREMAN, MARIA'	42
FENWICK, THOMAS	153	FOREMAN, RAD'US	42
Fenwick, Tristram	4	FORREST, MARG'TAM	42
Fenwick, —	118	FORSAITH, ANDREW	65
Fenwick-Clennell, Frances	153	FORSAITH, DOROTHY	65
Fenwick-Clennell, Thomas	153	Forster, Abigail	66
Ferelesse, Jane	82	FORSTER, ANN	121
FERGUSON, JANE	68	FORSTER, ANN ESTHER	135
FERGUSON, SAMUEL	68	FORSTER, CATHERINA'	42
FERRABY, ISABEL	48	FORSTER, CUTHBERT	66
Ferrand, Ann	155	FORSTER, DOROTHY	47 : *n.* 48
Ferrand, Rev. Thomas	155	Forster, Elisab	45
FETHERSTENHAILGH, JANE	36	FORSTER, ELIZABETH	74 : *n.* 6, 7, 124
FETHERSTON, JANAM	44	Forster, Frances	7
FETHERSTON, JOH'ES	44	Forster, Francis	6, 45
Fetherston, Maria	146	Forster, Gabriel	7
FETHERSTON, MARY	51, 58	FORSTER, ISAB.	58
Fetherston, Sir Ralph	146	FORSTER, ISABEL	59
Fetherstonhalgh, Elizabeth	58	FORSTER, JOAN	63
Fetherstonhalgh, Mary	58	FORSTER, JOHN	78, 119 : *n.* 7, 41, 59
Fetherstonhalgh, William	58	FORSTER, JOSEPH	60, 74
FEWLER, MARY	67	FORSTER, MAGDALENAM	42
FEWSTER, DOROTHY	102	FORSTER, MARGT.	78
Fewster, Elizabeth	75	FORSTER, MARIA'	42
FEWSTER, JOH'ES	12	FORSTER, MARTINUS	42
FEWSTER, JOHN	102	FORSTER, MARY	60, 66
Fewster, Margrett	101	Forster, Matthew	7
FEWSTER, MARY	55	FORSTER, PHYLLIS	71
FEWSTER, REV. NICH'H	12	Forster, Thomas	6, 47
FEWSTER, NICHOLAS	102	FORSTER, REV. WILL., MINOR CANON OF DURHAM	63
Fewster, Rev. Nicholas	102	Forster, Sir William	48
FEWSTER, REV. NICHOLAS, MINOR CANON OF DURHAM	101	FOSTER, ABRAHAM	125
FIELDING, ANN	125	Foster, Ann	11
FIELDING, CHARLOTTE	127	FOSTER, CATHERINE	107
Fielding, Israel	125	FOSTER, CHRISTIAN	103
Fielding, Margery	125	FOSTER, CHRISTIANUS	9
FIELDING, MARTHA	123	FOSTER, ELISAB.	45
FILMOOR, JOAN	56	FOSTER, ELIZABETHA	98
FILMOOR, ROBT.	56	FOSTER, ELLENORA'	63
FINCH, CATHARINE	58	FOSTER, FRANCIS	6, 7, 94
FINCH, CATHERINE	75	FOSTER, GABRIELL	7
Finch, Lady	22	FOSTER, JACOBUS	37
FINCH, MARY	75	FOSTER, JANA'	37
FINCH, PHYLLIS	71	FOSTER, JOH'ES	98
FINCH, ROBERT	71	FOSTER, JOH'IS	98
FINCH, TOBIT	75	FOSTER, JOHANNIS	9
FINNEY, DR. JAMES, PREBENDARY OF DURHAM	112, 118	FOSTER, JOHN	7, 8, 94 : *n.* 16
FINNEY, MARY	112 : *n.* 118	FOSTER, JOSEPH	123
Finney, William	118	FOSTER, KATHERINE	108
FIRTH, EDMUND NELSON MAY	34	FOSTER, MARGARET	126
FIRTH, REV. G. W. ANSON	159	FOSTER, MARGARETT	7
FIRTH, GEORGE WILLIAM ANSON	34, 158	FOSTER, MARIAM	43
FIRTH, LOUISA CAROLINE	34	FOSTER, THOMAS	122
Fitch, Sarah	146	Foster, Thomasine	124
FLETCHER, ALICIAM	43	FOSTER, WILLIA'	8
FLINTOFF, BEATRICE	155 : *n.* 153	Fountayne-Wilson, —	26
FLINTOFF, DAVID	152 : *n.* 153, 156	FOWLER, AN	38
FLINTOFF, ELIZABETH	154	FOWLER, EDEN	40
Flintoff, James	153	FOWLER, ISABELL	38
Flintoff, Jane	153	FOWLER, J. T.	159
FLINTOFF, MARIANNE	156	FOWLER, JOHN	38
Flintoff, Mary Ann	153	FOWLER, MARIAM	41
FLINTOFF, SARAH	142	FOWLER, THOMAS	38
Flintoff, Thomas	153	FOX, SARAH	51
Follonsby, Henry	83	FRANCES, —	18
Follonsby, Jane	83	Freeman, Sarah	152
FORD, FANNY JOAN	79	Freeman, Col.	152
FORD, GERARD	79	FREWIN, FRANCIS	100
		FRICKLETON, PATIENCE	94

FRIEND, MARY	49
FRIZZELL, —	7
Frowde, Penelope	47
Frowde, Sir Philip	47
FULTHORP, MARIAM	43
Fulthorp, Timothy	43
FURBANK, CHRISTIAN	71
FURBANK, EDVARDUS	44
FURBANK, MARIA'	44
Fyler, Elizabeth	138
Fyler, Mary	138
Fyler, Samuel	138
FYNNEY, JAMES, D.D., PREBENDARY OF DURHAM	52
FYNNEY, JANE	52
Fynney, Mary	118
Fynney, William	118
G., SIR JOHN	7
GALLALY, ISABEL	59
GALLALY, WILLIAM	59
GALLOWLY, ANNA'	43
GAMESBY, HANNAH	69
GAMLEN, REV. S.	137
Gamlen, Rev. Samuel, Minor Canon of Durham	137
GARFOOT, ELIZABETH	57
GARFOOT, THO.	57
Garfoot, —	69
GARFOOTE, KATHERINAM	39
GARGETT, JANE	50
GARGRAVE, ELIZABETH	134
GARGRAVE, FRANCISCAM	39
GARGRAVE, JOHANNES	39
GARRET, ELIZ.	51
GARRET, LANCELOT	51
GARRY, ELIZ.	117
GARRY, GEO.	117
GARRY, GEORGE	117
GARTH, ANN	52
GARTH, ELIZ.	64
GARTH, JAMES	117
GARTH, JOHN	52, 117 : *n*. 116
Garth, Margaret	117
GARTH, WILL.	64
GARTHWAITE, ALICE	50
GARTHWAITE, JANE	48
GASCOIGNE, ALICE	77
GASCOIGNE, DOROTHY	62
GASCOIGNE, WILL.	62
Gascoyne, —	141
Gaydon, Agnes	4
GAYDON, JOHANNIS	4
Gaydon, John	4
GAYDON, MARGARETA	4
Gaynes, Anthony	2
Gaynes, Christopher	2
Gaynes, Eleanor	2
Gaynes, Francis	2
Gaynes, Jane	2
Gaynes, Margaret	2
Gaynes, Sarah	2
GEDLIN, MARY	71
Gee, Stephen	23
Gee, —	23
GEERES, ELIZABETH	4
GEERES, JOHN	91
GEERES, MATHEW	91
GEERES, —	4
GEERS, GULIELMUS	5
Geers, Isabel	92
Geers, Jo.	3
GEERS, JOHANNES	3, 92
GEERS, JOHANNIS	3, 5
Geers, John	88
GEERS, MARGARETT	88 : *n*. 3
GEERS, MATHEW	5
GEERS, —	5
GELDART, ANN	47
GELDERT, ANNAM	42
GELDERT, JOH'ES	42
GELSON, HANNAH	71
GELSON, RALPH	60
Gelson, Rev. Ralph, Minor Canon of Durham	60
GELSON, REBBECCA	60
GELSON, ROB.	71
GENT, MARY	74
George, *see* St. George.	
George III., King of England	154
George IV., King of England	154
Gerard, Charles	114
Gerard, Frances	114
Gerard, Sir Gilbert	12
Gerard, Mary	12
Gerrard, Charles	114
Gerrard, Frances	114
GERRARD, GILBERTO	12
GIBBIN, CATHERINE	57
GIBBON, ANN	24, 49
GIBBON, ELIZABETH	23
Gibbon, Grace	23
GIBBON, HANNAH	26
GIBBON, JANE	51, 78
GIBBON, JOHN	49
GIBBON, THOMAS	23, 24 : *n*. 26
Gibbons, Judith	87
Gibbons, Rev. Marmaduke	87
GIBSON, ANN	60, 70
GIBSON, ANNAM	42
GIBSON, ELIZ.	51
Gibson, Elizabeth.	51
GIBSON, FRANCISCAM	45
GIBSON, GEO.	70
GIBSON, GEORGE	62
GIBSON, GULIELMS.	42
GIBSON, HANNAH	46, 62
GIBSON, ISABEL	58
GIBSON, JANE	59
GIBSON, JOHN	59 : *n*. 58
GIBSON, JOSEPH	59
GIBSON, MARG'TAM	43
GIBSON, MARY	59
GIBSON, THOMASINE	62
GIBSON, WILL.	62
Gifford, Fredismund	82
Gifford, Ralph	82
GILKIN, MARY	51
GILL, ANNE	56
Gill, Eliza.	33, 158
GILL, JOHN	56
Gill, John Slater	33, 158
GILLY, ALICE ANNE	29
GILLY, CHARLES PUDSEY	30
GILLY, FREDERICK DAWSON	29
GILLY, JANE CHARLOTTE MARY	29, 30
GILLY, W. S., PREBENDARY OF DURHAM	135, 136, 139
GILLY, WILLIAM STEPHEN, D.D., PREBENDARY OF DURHAM	29, 30
GILPIN, JANAM	40
GLASSINGTON, MARY	73

GLOVER, ANTHONY	95
GLOVER, SARAH	95
GOLBOURN, ANN	66
GOLBOURN, THO.	66
GOODAYRE, ALICIAM	36
GOODCHILD, ANNE	57
GOODCHILD, GRACE	64
GOODCHILD, JOHN	64
GOODCHILD, RALPH	57
GORDON, ALEXANDRI	92
Gordon, Ann	110
GORDON, ANNA'	42
Gordon, Anne	110
GORDON, ELIZABETHA	92
Gordon, Isabella	110
Gordon, James	110
Gordon, John	110
Gordon-Hallyburton, Lady Catherine Louisa	20
Gordon-Hallyburton, Lord Douglas, M.P.	20
GOUERUEGER, ELIZABETH	38
GOWER, EVERS, ARCHDEACON OF DURHAM	6
Gowland, Robert	90
Grace, Ann	139
Grace, John	139
GRAHAM, ANN	67
GRAHAM, GEO.	112
Graham, Sir George	49, 105
GRAHAM, JANE	65
GRAHAM, JOHN	67
Graham, Lady Mary	49, 105
Graham, Richard	112
Graham, Richard, Viscount Preston	49, 105
GRAHAM, WILL., D.D.	112
Graham, William, D.D., Dean of Carlisle and Wells	105
Graham, —	49
Graham, Dr.	50
GRAHME, RICHARDUS	11
GRAHME, WMI, DEAN OF CARLISLE AND PREBENDARY OF DURHAM	11
GRAINGE, MARY	62
GRAINGER, ANN	67
GRAINGER, JOHN	68
GRAINGER, MARY	68
Grantley, Lord	69
GRANVILLE, ANNE	106
Granville, Sir Bevil	106, 117
Granville, Bridget	117
Granville, Dean	117
Granville, Dean and Archdeacon	107
GRANVILLE, DR. DENYS, DEAN OF DURHAM	106
Granville, Dr.	9
Granville, —	97
Granville, Earl of Bath	106
Granville, Lord	106
GRAVELLE, FRANCES	103
GRAVENER, —	113
GRAY, DR.	7, 132
Gray, Dr., Bishop of Bristol	147
GRAY, DR., PREBENDARY OF DURHAM	132
GRAY, EDMOND	129
Gray, Edward	7
GRAY, ELIZABETH	94, 129, 132
GRAY, ELIZABETHAM	39
GRAY, ELLENORAM	45
Gray, Hillary	95
GRAY, JOHANNES	39
GRAY, ROBERT	7, 94
GRAY, ROBERTO, PREBENDARY OF DURHAM	11
GRAY, REV. ROBT., D.D., PREBENDARY OF DURHAM	129
GRAY, THOMAS	7
GRAYE, AN.	7
GRAYE, DORITYE	95
GRAYE, HENRYE	95
GRAYHM, DR.	105
GRAYHM, RICHARD	105
Greatorex, Annie Martha	151
GREATOREX, ANNIE MAUDE	31
Greatorex, Anthony	154
GREATOREX, CECILIA	31
GREATOREX, CHARLES THORP	32, 153
GREATOREX, CONSTANCE MARY	32
Greatorex, Dan	154
GREATOREX, EDITHA MAUDE	148
GREATOREX, REV. E.	157
GREATOREX, REV. EDWARD	148, 153
GREATOREX, REV. EDWARD, MINOR CANON OF DURHAM	31, 32 : n. 154, 158
GREATOREX, REV. EDWARD HARCOURT	31
GREATOREX, EDWD.,	31, 32, 145, 146, 147, 148, 149, 150, 151
GREATOREX, ELIZABETH	31, 32, 154, 158
GREATOREX, ELIZABETH ANTONIA	31
GREATOREX, MARY CHRISTINE	31
Greatorex, Thomas	31, 151, 154
Greatorex, —	154
GREEN, ANNE	106
GREEN, BARBARA	72
Green, Christopher	96
GREEN, ELIZ.	72
Green, Elizabeth	4
GREEN, HELLENEN	38
Green, Margaret	96
GREEN, JACOBI, MINOR CANON OF DURHAM	4
GREEN, KATHERINA	4
GREEN, MARGARETA	4
GREEN, MARGARETT	53
GREEN, MURIEL	66
Green, Robert	53
GREEN, ROWLAND	72
GREEN, WM.	53
GREEN, —	106
GREENE, JAMES	6
GREENE, JAMES, MINOR CANON OF DURHAM	5, 94, 96
GREENE, JOANE	5
GREENE, MARGARETT	8
GREENE, MARYE	6, 94
GREENSIDE, MARY	50
Greenvile, Dionysio	12
GREENVILL, DENNIS, PREBENDARY AND ARCHDEACON OF DURHAM	9
GREENWELL, ELIZ.	60
GREENWELL, JANAM	38
GREENWELL, THOMAS	38, 60
Greenwill, Alan	139
Greenwood, Agnes	154
Greenwood, Agnes Harrison	154, 159
Greenwood, John	154, 159
GREGGS, GEORGE	16
Greggs, Jo.	16
GREGGS, WILLIAM	16
GREGORY, REV. EDWARD	119
GREGORY, ELIZ.	71
GREGORY, JAMES	71
GREGORY, MARY	119

Gregson, Ann	62
Gregson, Deborah	55
Gregson, George	55
Gregson, Hannah	55
Gregson, Thomas	55, 62
Gregson, William	55, 62
Gregson, Wm.	55
Grenville, Isabel	36
Grenville, Richard	36
Grosley, *see* Douglas-Grosley.	
Grey, Hon. Rev. A., Prebendary of Durham	130
Grey, Ann	113
Grey, Eliz.	113
Grey, Elizabeth	110, 120, 147
Grey, Sir Henry	147
Grey, Lord	7, 25
Grey, Mad.	40
Grey, Margaret	75
Grey, Rob.	14
Grey, Robert	110, 113, 120
Grey, Dr. Robert, Prebendary of Durham	7
Grey, Thomas	75
Grey, —	7
Greye, —	95
Grice, William Henry	159
Griffith, Edward	130
Griffith, Elleanor	155
Griffith, Frances	155
Griffith, George	147
Griffith, Henry	140
Griffith, John	130, 140, 143 : *n.* 145, 147, 155, 157
Griffith, Mary	130, 157 : *n.* 143, 145, 147, 155
Griffith, Thomas	155
Grim, Isabellam	40
Grim, Thomas	40
Grinwell, Elizabeth	86
Grinwell, John	86
Grinwell, Robert	86
Grinwell, Margaret	86
Grossier, Margt.	68
Grundy, Ellenr.	53
Grundy, Tho.	53
Guidon, Agnes	4
Guidon, John	4
Guorden, Ann	110
Guorden, —	110
Guy, Anna'	44
Guy, Charles	70
Guy, Margt.	70
Gyll, Thos.	77
Hackworth, Elizabeth	90
Haggitt, Catherine	25
Haggitt, Christina	25
Haggitt, Rev. F.	132
Haggitt, Rev. Francis, D.D., Prebendary of Durham	25
Haggitt, Lucy	25
Hale, Rev. Edward	80
Hale, Dr. Geoffrey Edward	80
Hale, Mary	80
Halhead, Margery	127
Halhead, Nicholas	127
Halifax, Carolus, Baron	45
Hall, Agnes	4
Hall, An	38
Hall, Ann	66, 130 : *n.* 131, 132, 134, 139
Hall, Hon. Anna Maria Bridget	134
Hall, Annam	43, 44

Hall, Anne	131, 134
Hall, Anthony	74
Hall, Barbara	111
Hall, Charles, Dean of Bocking	134
Hall, Rev. Charles Henry, D.D., Dean of Durham	134
Hall, Cuth.	109
Hall, Dorothea'	41
Hall, Eleanor	2
Hall, Eliz.	63
Hall, Elizabeth	54, 130, 131, 146
Hall, Frances	153
Hall, Franciscam	45
Hall, Hester	46
Hall, Isabella	135
Hall, Isabella'	37
Hall, Isabellam	44
Hall, Jana'	37
Hall, Jane	72, 130 : *n.* 127
Hall, John	54, 66, 130, 131, 140 ; *n.* 74, 135, 138, 146, 151
Hall, Jonathan, Prebendary of Durham	120
Hall, Josephus	45
Hall, Margt.	67
Hall, Mary	74, 75, 156
Hall, Matthæus	37
Hall. Ovington	138
Hall, Philip	63
Hall, Robert	130, 131, 138, 144 : *n.* 139
Hall, Sarah	55
Hall, Thomas	44, 55, 75
Halliburton, Ann	58
Hallifax, Georgiana	27
Hallifax, Rev. R. F.	27
Hallifax, Samuel, Bishop of St. Asaph	27
Hallyburton, James	120
Hallyburton, Mary	120
Hallyburton, *see* Gordon-Hallyburton.	
Hallyman, Elisabeth	62
Hallyman, Will.	62
Halyburton, Jean	125
Halyburton, —	125
Hamilton, Eliza Arabella Sarah	79
Hamilton, G. H., Archdeacon of Northumberland	158
Hamilton, George Hans, D.D., Archdeacon of Northumberland, Canon of Durham	79
Hamilton, Rev. Archdeacon, Canon of Durham	158
Ham'on, Lady	93
Hammon, Dominâ Elizabethâ	6
Ham'ond, Lady	6
Hammond, Sir William	37
Hammond, Lady	6, 37, 93
Hanby, Dorothy	52, 71
Hanby, Elizabetha	16
Hanby, Frances	13
Hanby, Francis	13 : *n.* 52
Hanby, Francisci	16
Hanby, Isabella	13
Hanby, Jonathan	60
Hanby, Mary	60 : *n.* 13
Hanby, Thomas	52
Hanby, William	13
Hanby, —	13
Handy, John	130
Harding, Isabell	55
Hardinge, Frances	153
Hardinge, Frederick	153

Hardinge, Viscount	153	HASLEWOOD, REV. DICKENS	133
HARDY, JANE	77	HASLEWOOD, REV. DICKENS, MINOR	
HAREBOTTLE, JANE	55	CANON OF DURHAM	126
HAREBOTTLE, WM.	55	HASLEWOOD, ELIZA	126
HARGRAVE, REV. —	94	HASLEWOOD, ELIZABETH	130, 133, 134
Harington, Frances	21	HASLEWOOD, HENRY	126
HARISON, ANN	37	HASLEWOOD, SARAH	130
HARISON, JOH'IS	38	HASLEWOOD, THOMAS	127
HARISON, JOHN	37	Hastings, Edmund	145
HARISON, MARGARETAM	38	HASWELL, MARY	54
HARKER, MARGARET	69	Haswell, Sarah	135
HARKER, MARY	68	Hauxley, Catherine	52
HARLAND, ANNE	141 : n. 137	HAUXLEY, ELLINOR	49
Harland, Charles	137	Hauxley, John	52
HARLAND. SARAH	70	HAUXLY, ANNAM	44
HARLAND, WILLIAM	137, 141 : n. 23	HAWDON, ANNAM	40
Harland, William Charles	137	HAWDON, CHRISTOPH.	40
HARLE, JACOBUS	44	HAWDON, JANAM.	40
HARLE, MARGARETT	53	HAWDON. RICHARDUS	40
HARLE, MARY	76	HAWKINS, ESTHER	120
HARLE, RACHEL	44	Hawkins, Sir John Cæsar	27
HARPER, CIBELLE	63	HAWKINS, WILL.	109
HARPERLEY, FRANCISCAM	40	HAWKSWORTH, MARGARETT	74
HARPERLY, MARIAM	41	HAWKSWORTH, MARGT.	66
HARPERLY, THOMAS	41	HAWKSWORTH, ROBERT	74
Harrison, Agnes	154	HAWKSWORTH, ROBT.	66
HARRISON, ANNA'	41, 45	HAYES, JAMES	119
Harrison, Anne	86	Hays, Eleanor	143, 145
HARRISON, ANTHONY	57	Hays, John	130, 143, 145, 155, 157
HARRISON, ANTONIUS	39	Hays, Mary	130, 143, 145, 147, 155, 157
HARRISON, CICILIAM	41	HAYTON, ELEANOR	75
HARRISON, EDVARDS	41	HAYTON, RICHARD	75
HARRISON, ELEANOR	65	HAZARD, JNO.	64
HARRISON, ELIZ.	53, 67, 70	HAZARD, REBEC'	64
HARRISON, ELIZABETHAM	39, 40	Hazlewood, Rev. Dickins	159
HARRISON, ELLENORA'	43	Hazlewood, Rev. Dickins, Minor Canon of	
HARRISON, ELLENORAM	39	Durham	134
HARRISON, FRANCISCA'	41	Hazlewood, Elizabeth	134, 159
Harrison, Isabel	92	HEADLAM, AURELIUS	49
HARRISON, JACOBUS	39	Headlam, Frances	128
HARRISON, JANE	57, 63	HEADLAM, MARY	49
HARRISON, JOHANNES	39, 40	Headlam, Thomas Emerson	128
HARRISON, JOHN	65, 67, 70 : n. 86	Headlam, Archdeacon	128
HARRISON. MARGARET	60 : n. 55, 104	HEADLEY, KATHERINA	96
HARRISON, MARGARETT	74	HEADLEY, ROBERTI	96
HARRISON, MARIA'	41	HEADS, ANN	68
HARRISON, MARIAM	39, 40	HEARD, MARY	54
HARRISON, MARY	67 : n. 104	HEARDE, IS.	69
HARRISON, RICHARD	60	Heath, Dorothy	86, 106
HARRISON, ROBT.	53	HEATH, ELIZABETH	2 : n. 8
HARRISON, THOMAS	43	HEATH. JANE	65
Harrison, Sir Thomas	104	HEATH, JOHAN'E	5
Hartfell, James, Earl of	105	HEATH, JOHANNE	4, 5
Hartfell, Lady Margaret, Countess of	49	Heath, John	8, 88
Hartfell, Earl of	49	Heath, Margaret	88
HARTLEY, PHILLIS	154	HEATH, MARGARETA	5
HARTLEY, WILLIAM	156	HEATH, NICHOLAS	2 : n. 106
Hartwell, Dr.	106	HEATH, ROBT.	65
Hartwell, Frances	117	Heath, Thomas	86
HARTWELL, DR. WILLIAM, PREBENDARY		HEAVISIDE, HENRY	65
OF DURHAM	117	HEAVISIDE, ISABEL	65
Harvey, Mary	152	HEAWOOD, CHRISTIANA	34, 79
Harvey, —	152	HEAWOOD, GEOFFREY LEONARD	34
Harwood, Margaretta	10	HEAWOOD, REV. JOHN RICHARD	79
Harwood, Stephen	10	HEAWOOD, PERCY JOHN	34, 79
HASLEWOOD, BOULBY	127	HECCLES, ANNA'	45
HASLEWOOD, D.	28, 130, 131	HECKLES, GERARD	67
HASLEWOOD, REV. D.	134	HECKLES, ISABEL	67
HASLEWOOD, DICK., MINOR CANON OF		Hedlam, Ann	49
DURHAM	127	Hedlam, George	49
HASLEWOOD, DICKENS	130, 131	Hedlam, Hannah	49

Hedlam, Phœbe	49	Hetherington, Mary	139, 150
Hedlam, Ralph	49	Hetherington, Hon. Richard	139, 150
Hedlam, William	49	HETT, MARGARETAM	41
Hedley, Sarah	156	HEWISON, GEO	66
HEDLY, CAROLUS	43	HEWISON, MARY	66
HEDLY, MARG'TAM	43	HEWITSON, CATHERINE	65
Hedworth, Alice	95	Heyden, Katherine	133
Hedworth, Christopher	95	Heyden, Samuel	133
HEDWORTH, RALPH	95	HICKERONGILL, ANNA'	42
Hedworth, Richard	95	HICKERONGILL, TIMOTHEUS	42
Heethe, John	86	HICKSON, ELIZ	51
Hegg, Ann	87	Higgons, Bridget	117
Hegg, Anna	84	Higgons, Sir Thomas	117
Hegg, Anne	87	Hildesley, Margaret	21
Hegg, Elizabeth	82, 87	Hildesley, Dr. Mark, Bishop of Sodor and Man	21
Hegg, Frances	87	Hill, Annabella	89
Hegg, Isabel	87	Hill, Anne	145
Hegg, John	87	Hill, Arthur, Viscount Dungannon	145
Hegg, Judith	87	Hill, John	89
Hegg, Richard	87	Hill, Martha	138
Hegg, Robert	87, 89	HILLARY, MARY	63
Hegg, Stephen	82, 84, 87	HILLS, ANN	78
Hegg, Rev. Stephen	87	HILLS, GEORGIUS	41
HEGG, STEVEN	87	HILLS, MARGERIA'	41
HEGGE, ANNA	84	HILTON, ANNAM	42
Hegge, Anne	84	HILTON, BARBARA	11 : n. 6, 92, 121
Hegge, John	87	Hilton, Catherine	91
Hegge, Ralph	87	HILTON, CUTH	102, 117
Hegge, Richard	87	HILTON, CUTHBERT	9, 59, 104, 117 : n. 121
HEGGE, STEPHANI	84	HILTON, CUTHBERTI	11, 12, 98
Hegge, Stephen	87, 89	HILTON, DOROTHEA	97
Hegge, Rev. Stephen	87	HILTON, DOROTHEAM	46
HEIGHINGTON, AMBROSII	14	Hilton, Dorothy	46
Heighington, Catherine	14	HILTON, ELIANOR	104
HEIGHINGTON, DEBORAH	46	Hilton, Elizabeth	78, 116, 118
Heighington, Frances	14	HILTON, ELLENOR	38
Heighington, Gartrett	14	HILTON, FRANCES	78
HEIGHINGTON, MARIA	14	HILTON, JAMES	91 : n. 6, 92
Heighington, Richard	14	HILTON, JANE	59, 117, 119
Heighington, William	14	HILTON, LANCELOT	104 : n. 46, 91, 116, 118
HEIGHLEY, RICHARDUS	40	HILTON, LANCELOTI	97
HEIGHLEY, THOMASINAM	40	HILTON, LANCELOTT	9
HELESTINE, FRANCES	73	HILTON, MARGARET	120
HELESTINE, JAMES	73	HILTON, MARGARETA	12
HEMING, THOMAS	141	HILTON, MARIA	98
HENDERSON, ISAB.	53	HILTON, MARTHA	12, 102
HENDERSON, JANE	64	HILTON, MARY	104, 114
HENDERSON, MARY	55, 66	HILTON, ROB.	104
HENDERSON, MATTHEW	55	HILTON, ROBERT	9, 103
HENDERSON, RICH.	53	HILTON, ROBT.	117
Henderson, William	81	Hilyard, Francis	86
HENEKAR, ELIZABETH	93	Hinde, see Archer-Hinde, and also Hodgson-Hinde.	
Henshaw, Anne	137		
HENSHAW, CAROLINE	138	HINDMARSH, CHARLES	70
Henshaw, Emily	137	HINDMARSH, SARAH	70
HENSHAW, EMILY CHARLOTTE	137	HINMERS, ELEANOR	71
Henshaw, Joseph	137	HINMERS, WM.	71
HENSHAW, W.	137	HINSON, ISABELLA	34
HENSHAW, WILLIAM	139: n. 137	HINSON, JAMES	34
HERNE, —	74	HINSON, JAMES-ARTHUR	34
HERON, FRANCES	38	HIRZEL, —	121
Heron, Mary	93	HIXON, ELIZ.	71 ; n. 51
Herries, Sir John Maxwell, Lord	50	HIXON, ELLINOR	51
HESELTINE, FRANCES	119	HIXON, JOHN	71
HESELTINE, JAMES	119, 123	HIXON, MARG'TAM	41
HESLOP, SARAH	56	HIXON, ROBERT	51
HESLOPP, ANN	49	HIXON. THO.	41
HESLOPP, DINAH	54	Hoar, Anne	141
HESLOPP, JOHN	49	Hoar, Charles	137
HESTER, MIRRIAMA'	41	Hoar, Frances	23, 137
Hester, Sarah	101		

Hoar, George	23, 137
Hoar, Mary	23
Hoar, William	23, 137, 141
HOBMAN, FRANCISCA'	44
HOBSON, ANNAM	40
HOBSON, ELEANOR	65
HOBSON, ELIZ.	70
HOBSON, JEREMIAH	40
HOBSON, MARGARETT	73
HODGHSON, JANE	59
HODGSHON, JANE	48
HODGSHON, MARY	72
HODGSHON, RALPH	48
HODGSHON, SUSANNA	59
HODGSON, DOROTHY	74
HODGSON, FORTUNE	67
HODGSON, HILDA	72
HODGSON, JOHN	71, 74 : n. 150
HODGSON, MARY	71
HODGSON, NICHOLAS	103
HODGSON, RALPH	67
HODGSON, SARAH	103 : n. 150
Hodgson-Hinde, —	150
HODSHON, ANNA'	41
HODSHON, CATHERINE	57
HODSHON, ELIZ.	51
HODSHON, GEO	57
HODSHON, MICHAEL	41
HOGG, ANNE	21, 22
Hogg, Christopher	43
HOGG, DOROTHY	23
Hogg, Eleanor	43
HOGG, ELIZABETH	22
HOGG, ISABEL	21
HOGG, JANE	22
HOGG, JOHN	21
HOGG, THOMAS	21, 22, 23, 123, 124
HOGG, THOS.	21, 22
HOGG, URSULA	43
HOGG, WILLIAM	22
HOGG, WM.	123
HOLDEN, BEATRICE BLANDINA	31
HOLDEN, ELIZABETH MARGARET ANNE	31, 147
HOLDEN, FLORENCE TOVEY	32
HOLDEN, GEORGIANA	32
HOLDEN, GEORGIANA BAILEY	31, 32, 33
HOLDEN, REV. HENRY	147
HOLDEN, REV. HENRY, D.D., CANON OF DURHAM	31, 32, 33
HOLDEN, HENRY EDMONDS	31
HOLDEN, HYLA	32
HOLDEN, JOSEPHINE FANNY	32
HOLDEN, RACHEL BELASYSE	33
HOLDEN, ROSE	32
HOLDEN, VERE	32, 153
Holder, Ashley	131
HOLDER, HENRY EVANS, M.D.	131
Holderness, Conyers Darcy, Earl of	45
HOLLAND, DOROTHY	58
HOLLAND, ELEANOR MARY	34
HOLLAND, MARY GERTRUDE	34
HOLLAND, STEPHEN	58
HOLLAND, REV. WILLIAM LYALL	34
Hollingbery, Charlotte Charlton	149
Hollingbery, J.	149
Hollingbery, Thomas, D.D., Prebendary of St. Paul's	149
HOOD, MARGT.	62
Hopper, Anne	137
HOPPER, ANTHONY	132
Hopper, Barbara	84
Hopper, Rev. Edmund Hector	73, 104
HOPPER, ELIZ.	49
HOPPER, ELIZABETH	126, 129 : n. 3, 73
HOPPER, ELIZABETHAM	139
HOPPER, HENDRY	129 : n. 73
HOPPER, JANE	54
Hopper, Jarard	84
HOPPER, JOHN	49 : n. 73
Hopper, John Thomas Hendry	10, 137
Hopper, Margaret	54
HOPPER, MARY	118
Hopper, Philadelphia	10
HOPPER, THO.	118
Hopper, Ralph	10
Hopper, Rosetta Anne	137
HOPPER, WM.	54
Hopper, —	81
HOPPER, REV. —	126
Hopper-Williamson, —	73
Horne, Elizabeth	85
Horne, John	85
HORNESBY, ELISABETHAM	45
HORNESBY, NICOLAUS	45
HORNSBY, CATHERINE	76
HORNSBY, ELIZ.	62
Hornsby, Elizabeth	76
HORNSBY, MARY	73
HORNSBY, THOMASIN	124
HORNSBY, THOS.	124
HORNSBY, —	124
HORSELEY, BARBARA	48
HORSELEY, ELEANOR	71
HORSELEY, THO.	48
HORSEMAN, ANN	75
HORSEMAN, BRIGIDA	15
HORSEMAN, ELEANOR	120
HORSEMAN, ELISABETH	16, 108
HORSEMAN, GULIELMI	15
HORSEMAN, MARY	18, 71 : n. 107
HORSEMAN, ROBERT	18
HORSEMAN, THOMASIN	102
HORSEMAN, TIMOTHY	107 : n. 12
HORSEMAN, WILLIAM	18 : n. 12, 107, 114
HORSEMAN, WM.	16, 71, 108, 117
Horseman, —	100
HORSMAN, HORATIUS	111
HORSMAN, JOHN	101
HORSMAN, KATHERINE	114
HORSMAN, MAGDALENA'	40
HORSMAN, MARY	109
HORSMAN, THO.	111, 114
HORSMAN, WILL.	109
Horsman, WILL'M	12
HORSMAN, —	12
HOW, CATH.	57
HOW, FRANCIS	57
HOW, ISABEL	64
HOW, PHILIP	64
How, see Walsham-How.	
HOWARD, HENRY	127
HOWELL, ELLENORAM	46
HOWELL, MARY	54
HOWELL, WM.	54
Howley, Dr. William, Archbishop of Canterbury	32
Howson, Elizabeth	90
Howson, Elsabeth	90
Howson, John, Bishop of Durham	90
Howson, —, Bishop of Durham	92
Hubback, Barbara	23
Hubback, Jane	23

Hubback, John	23
HUBBOCK, KATHERINE	103
HUBBOCKE, MARY	37
HUBRUCK, KATTERN	8
HUCHINSON, JAMES	1 : n. 95
HUCHINSON, RICHARD	1
HUCK, HANNAH	69
HUCK, JONATHAN	69
HUDD, JANAM	44
Huddleston, Elizabeth	110
Huddleston, Ferdinando	110
HUDDLESTON, MARG.	110
Huddleston, Sarah	110
Huddleston, —	112
Hudson, Anne	124
HUDSON, ELIZ.	70
HUDSON, ISABEL	51
HUDSON, JANE	75
HUDSON, MARGARET	54
HUDSON, MARGARETT	73
Hudson, Matthew	70
HUDSON, NEWARK	70
Hudson, Peter	124
HUDSON, THOMAS	73 : n. 70
Hudson, Ursula	124
HUDSPETH, ELLEN.	46
HUDSPETH, ISABELL	54
HUDSPETH, JOHN	46, 54
HUGALL, MARY	53
HUGALL, WM.	53
Hughes, Anne	140
Hughes, Philip	140
HUGHES, WILLIAM	140
Hugonin, Charlotte	69
Hugonin, Isabella	69
Hugonin, Gen.	69
HULL, CATHERINA'	43
HULL, ELIZABETH	53
HULL, JANE	75 : n. 61
HULL, MARY	56
HULL, RICH'US	43
HULL, ROBERT	75 : n. 61
HULL, THOMAS	100
HUMBLE, ALICE	51
HUMBLE, ANNE	69
HUMBLE, ELISABETHAM	45
HUMBLE, JANE	58
Humble, Joseph	69
HUMBLE, MARGARET	59
HUMBLE, THO.	51, 85
Humble, —	69
HUME, GULIELMS.	43
HUME, JANAM	43
HUMES, ELIZ.	64
HUMES, JNO.	64
Hunt, Alfred William	150
HUNT, ELISABETHÂ	4
HUNT, HENRY	83
HUNT, JOAN	83
Hunt, Margaret	150
HUNT, DR. RICH., DEAN OF DURHAM	1
Hunt, Dr. Richard, Dean	36
HUNT, RICHARDO, DEAN OF DURHAM	3
HUNT, RICHARDUS, DEAN OF DURHAM	91
HUNT, —	5 : n. 36
HUNTER, ANN	49, 120
HUNTER, ANNE	103
HUNTER, ANTHONY	72
HUNTER, BENJAMIN	78
Hunter, Burnett	135
HUNTER, CHRISTOPHER	48

HUNTER, ELIZ.	48, 72. 78
HUNTER, ELIZABETH	121
HUNTER, JANE	78
Hunter, John	135
HUNTER, MARGARET	77
HUNTER, MARY	129
HUNTER, THO.	78
HUNTLEY, CATHERINE	76
HUNTLEY, DOROTHEAM	38
HUNTLEY, JANE	53
HUNTLEY, JOH'IS	38
HUNTLEY, JOHN	76
HUNTLEY, RICH.	53
Huntly, Charles, Marquess of	20
HUNTLY, JANE	60
HUNTLY, ROBT.	60
HUSON, —	75
Hutchin, Anne	117
Hutchin, John	117
HUTCHINGS, DORA EMILY	80
HUTCHINGS, REV. HENRY REGINALD	79
HUTCHINGS, REV. WILLIAM HENRY	80
HUTCHINSON, ALICIA'	42
HUTCHINSON, ANDREW	63
HUTCHINSON, ANN	52, 75
HUTCHINSON, ANNA'	41, 44
HUTCHINSON, ANNAM	44
HUTCHINSON, ANNE	54
Hutchinson, Barnabas	109
Hutchinson, Barnaby	82
HUTCHINSON, CATH.	63
Hutchinson, Christopher	74
HUTCHINSON, ELIZABETH	60, 128 : n. 10
HUTCHINSON, FRANCES	62
HUTCHINSON, FRANCIS	93
HUTCHINSON, GRACIA	98
HUTCHINSON, HENRICUS	44
HUTCHINSON, ISABELLA	74
HUTCHINSON, ISABELLAM	40
HUTCHINSON, JAMES	62
HUTCHINSON, JANE	50, 73, 102, 105 : n. 10, 74, 108, 109
HUTCHINSON, JNO.	62, 63
HUTCHINSON, JOHN	54, 63, 73, 74, 101 : n. 50
HUTCHINSON, LUKE	93
Hutchinson, Margaret	93
HUTCHINSON, MARGT.	63
HUTCHINSON, MARY	54, 63, 64, 72 : n. 74
HUTCHINSON, RICHARD	95 : n. 10
HUTCHINSON, ROB'TUS	42
HUTCHINSON, ROBT.	52
HUTCHINSON, SARAH	72
HUTCHINSON, THOMAS	44, 99
HUTCHINSON, THOMASINE	62
HUTCHISON, ELIZABETHAM	40
HUTON, ANNE	83
HUTON, EDWARDE	83
HUTTON, ANNAM	41
Hutton, Anne	82, 83
HUTTON, CATHERINE	54
Hutton, Edward	82, 83
HUTTON, ELISABETHAM	44
Hutton, Elizabeth	99, 109
Hutton, Frances	109
Hutton, Francisca	99
HUTTON, FRANCISCAM	41
HUTTON, GEORGE	54
Hutton, Grace	4
HUTTON, GRATIA	89
Hutton, Henry	99, 109
HUTTON, JANE	91 : n. 4, 83, 86, 88, 89

B B

Hutton, John	83
HUTTON, MARGERIA'	41
Hutton, Matthew, Bishop of Durham, Archbishop of York	89
HUTTON, RALPH	116
Hutton, Sir Richard	109
Hutton, Dr. Robert	4
Hutton, Robert, D.D., Prebendary of Durham	89
HUTTON, ROBERTI, D.D., PREBENDARY OF DURHAM	89
Hutton, Sir Timothy	82
Hutton, —	84
Hutton. —, Bishop of Durham	82, 92
I'Anson, John	138
I'Anson, Mary	138
I'Anson, Sir Thomas Bankes	138
Ibbetson, Grace Ord	81
Ibbetson, Henry	75, 81
Ibbetson, Sir Henry	81
Ibbetson, Isabella	81
Ibbetson, Isabella Grace	81
Ibbetson, —	75
IBBOTSON, SIR HENRY	75
IBBOTSON, ISABELLA	75
Iley, Elizabeth	91
ILEY, ISABELLAM	38
Iley, William	91
INGAH, DOROTHY	68
Ingledew, —	86
INGO, MARY	63
INGOE, DOROTHY	73
INGRAM, ANN	59
INGRAM, MATTHEW	70
INGRAM, REBECCA	70
INGRAM, RICHARD	59
Inman, Charles	125
INMAN, ELIZABETH	143
Inman, Mary	125
INNMAN, MARY	125
Irby, Sir Anthony	45
Irby, Elizabeth	45
Ironside, Mary	48
IRONSIDE, RAD'US	43
IRONSIDE, URSULA'	43
Ironside, William	48
Ironside, see also Bax-Ironside.	
IVESON, ELIZ.	42
Jackson, Ann	131, 141
JACKSON, ANNA'	44
JACKSON, BENJAMIN	115
Jackson, Charles	43
Jackson, Dorothy	68
Jackson, Elizabeth	90
JACKSON, GEORGE	141 : n. 148
JACKSON, JANE	90, 141
JACKSON, JOHN	102
Jackson, Lawrence	21
JACKSON, MARY	8, 55 : n. 21, 141, 148
Jackson, Ralph	131, 148
JACKSON, RICHARD	104
Jackson, Rev. Richard	90
Jackson, Sarah	131, 148
JACKSON, SUSANNA'	42
Jackson, Thomas George	141
Jackson, Wm.	68
JACQUES, MARGT.	61
JAMES, ANN	6
JAMES, ANNA	6
JAMES, ANNE	2
James, Catherine	83
James, David	133
JAMES, EDWARD	2
James, Elenor	83
JAMES, ELIZAB.	6
JAMES, ELIZABETH	3, 87 : n. 6
JAMES, ELIZABETHA	6
JAMES, ELSABETH	89
James, Francis	6
JAMES, GULIELMI, PREBENDARY OF DURHAM	3, 4, 89
JAMES, GULIELMO, PREBENDARY OF DURHAM	5
JAMES, GULIELMUS	3, 89
JAMES, HARRIE	2
James, Henrietta	133
JAMES, JANE	56
James, John	83
JAMES, MARIA	4
JAMES, MARYE	37
JAMES, RICHARD	2
JAMES, RICHERD	85
JAMES, WILL'M, PREBENDARY OF DURHAM	2
JAMES, WILLIA', PREBENDARY OF DURHAM	94
JAMES, WILLIAM	3, 6, 7 : n. 83
James, William, Bishop of Durham	94
JAMES, WILLIAM, PREBENDARY OF DURHAM	83, 87 : n. 37
James, Prebendary	98
JAMES, —	3
James, —, Bishop of Durham	2, 91
JAMES, —, PREBENDARY OF DURHAM	2, 5, 85
James I., King of England	83
James II., King of England	47, 107
Jaunsen, Cornelius	90
JECKELL, ELIZABETHAM	39
JECKELL, JOHANNES	39
JEFFERSON, ANN	67
JEFFERSON, ELIANOR	59
JEFFERSON, ELIZABETH	10
JEFFERSON, JOHN	59
JEFFERSON, NICHOLAS	67
JEFFREYSON, JENNETTAM	42
JEFFREYSON, JOH'ES	42
JEFFRYSON, GRACE	71
JEFFRYSON, ISRAEL	71
JENKINSON, REV. J. B., DEAN OF DURHAM	138
Jenkinson, John Bankes, Bishop of St. David's, Dean of Durham	129
JENKYNS, REV. H., D.D., CANON OF DURHAM	150
Jenkyns, Harriet	154
Jenkyns, Rev. Henry, D.D., Canon of Durham	154
Joby, Elizab.	54
John, Bishop of Durham	9
JOHNSON, AGNES HARRISON	154 : n. 159
JOHNSON, ALICE	59 : n. 50
JOHNSON, ALICIA'	41
JOHNSON, ANN	52, 71, 75, 77
JOUNSON, ANNA ELIZABETH	150
JOHNSON, ANNAM	39
JOHNSON, ANNE	57 : n. 86, 92
JOHNSON, ANTH.	40
JOHNSON, ANTHONY	49
JOHNSON, BARBAIRE	36
JOHNSON, CHRIST.	122

Johnson, Christopher 125, 126, 127. 128 : n. 122, 139
Johnson, Dorotheam 39
Johnson, Dorothy 74
Johnson, Edward 78
Johnson, Eleanor 123
Johnson, Eliz. 71
Johnson, Elizabeth 78
Johnson, Elizabetham 41
Johnson, Frances 56
Johnson, Francis 139 : n. 114, 120, 123, 146, 150
Johnson, Francis Dixon .... 159 : n. 154
Johnson, Geo. 122
Johnson, Georgius 39. 40
Johnson, Gulielmus 40
Johnson, Hannah 49. 78
Johnson, Isabel 148
Johnson, James 75
Johnson, Janam 40
Johnson, Jo................................... 36
Johnson, John .... 52, 56 : n. 78
Johnson, Marg................................. 49
Johnson, Marg'tam 40
Johnson, Margeriam 40
Johnson, Mary 49, 58, 74, 139 : n. 139, 146, 150
Johnson, Mary Ann........................... 146
Johnson, Ralph 8, 49
Johnson, Rebecca 78
Johnson, Richard......................... 86, 92
Johnson, Rob................................... 48
Johnson, Robert......................... 74, 119
Johnson, Sarah 114, 120, 123
Johnson, Tabitha 125, 127 : n. 122, 126, 128
Johnson. Tho.................................. 71
Johnson, Thomas 77
Johnson, Trotham 40
Johnston, Arthur 131
Johnstone, James, Earl of Hartfell 105
Johnstone, Lady Margaret, Countess of Hartfell 49
Johnstone, Lady Mary 49, 105
Johnstone, —, Earl of Annandale 105
Johnstone, —, Earl of Hartfell............. 49
Johnstone, —, Marquess of Annandale ... 49
Jon, Henry 33
Jon, Rebecca 33
Jon, Robert 33
Jon, Susanna 59
Jon, Thomas 59
Jones, Frances Henrietta 33, 158
Jones, Francis 158
Jones, Rev. Francis 33
Jones, Mary 158
Jones, Mary Anne Georgiana................. 33
Jones, Thomas 147
Jones, William .... 147 : n. 158
Joplin, Isabell 62
Joplin, Will. 62
Jopling, Anna' 44
Jopling, Elizabeth 52, 54
Jopling, Mariam 46
Jopling, Thomas 44
Jordan, Willia'................................. 8
Jurdison, Annam 38
Jurdison, Eliz. 62
Jurdison, Elizabetham 41
Jurdison, Gulielms 41
Jurdison, Jane 38
Jurdison, Rebecca 70

Karnabye, Hellen 7
Karp, see De Karp.
Kay, Margaret 53
Kaye, Thomas 154
Kearsly, Francisca' 44
Kearsly, Oliverus 44
Kell, Ann...................................... 73
Kell, Mary 37
Kell, Rowland 37
Kelly, Hannah 62
Kemble, Charles 132
Kemble, Elizabeth 140
Kemble, John 132
Kemble, Roger 131
Kemble, S. G. 132
Kemble, Sarah 131
Kemble, Stephen 131, 132
Kemble, Stephen George............. 131, 140
Kendall, Annam 39
Kendall, Nicolaus 39
Kennebye, David 67
Kennebye, Eleanor 67
Kensington, Lady Laura Jane 81
Keppel, Lady Caroline....................... 26
Keppel, —, Earl of Albemarle 26
Ker, Claud Buchanan, M.D. 158
Ker, Francis Allan........................... 158
Kerr, Lady Isabel............................. 49
Kerr, Margaret, Countess of Lothian 49
Kerr, Mark, Earl of Lothian 49
Key, Mary 39
Kilburn, Anne 77
Kilburn, Tho.................................. 77
King, Alice Jane 150
King, Rev. Charles William 150
King, Harry 159
King, John 125
King, Mary Anne............................. 150
King, Sarah 150, 159
King, Rev. William Clark, Canon of Durham 150
King Charles I. of England... 47, 90, 93, 94, 95
King Charles II. of England............. 47, 97
King Edward III. of England 141
King Edward IV. of England 88
King George III. of England 154
King George IV. of England............... 154
King James I. of England 83
King James II. of England 47, 107
Kinge, Gen. 93
Kipling, Alicia'............................... 38
Kipling, Georgius 38, 96
Kipling, Hannah 143, 157
Kirbie, Kathrine 87
Kirby, Elizabeth 8
Kirby, George 8, 104
Kirbye, Roger 7
Kirkby, Edvardus 100
Kirkby, Edvardus, Minor Canon of Durham....................................... 40
Kirkby, Edward 105
Kirkby, Eliz. 15, 40
Kirkby, Elizabetham 42
Kirkby, George............................... 107
Kirkby, Mary................................. 107
Kirkby, — 116
Kirkham, Elianoram 44
Kirkham, Johan'es 44
Kirkley, Eliz. 49
Kirtley, Mariam 39
Kirtly, Dorotheam 44

Kirton, Rev. —	105
Kitchin, Christopher	68
Kitchin, Margt.	68
Kitching, Elizabetham	39
Kitching, Gulielmus	39
Knaggs, Isabellam	38
Knaggs, Thomas	38
Knatchbull, Alice	123
Knatchbull, Catharine Maria	20
Knatchbull, Catherine	20
Knatchbull, Sir Edward	20, 123
Knatchbull, Harriett	123
Knatchbull, Harriot	20
Knatchbull, Wadham	19
Knatchbull, Rev. Dr. Wadham	123
Knatchbull, Rev. Dr. Wadham, Prebendary of Durham	19, 20
Knatchbull, Windham	20
Knewstob, Sarah	52
Knight, Catherine	20
Knight, Thomas	20
Kynaston, Eleanor Charlotte	80
Kynaston, Herbert, Canon of Durham	80
Kynaston, Mary	80
Kyrby, Alice	85
Lackenby, Dorotheam	44
Lackenby, Ellen.	46
Lackenby, Janam	40
Lake, Rev. W. C., Dean of Durham	155, 157, 158
Lamb, Elizabeth	115
Lamb, Jane	58
Lamb, Joh'es	42
Lamb, John	58 : n. 39
Lamb, Joseph	69
Lamb, Margaret	56
Lamb, Mariam	42
Lamb, Mary	50 : n. 112
Lamb, —	75, 76 : n. 69
Lambe, Elizabeth	95
Lambe, Franciscam	39
Lambe, Kattern	95
Lambe, Robertus	39
Lambe, Trotham	40
Lambe, Willia'	95
Lambert, Ann	159
Lambert, David	156
Lambert, James	156 : n. 158, 159
Lambert, Jane	135
Lambton, Alice	87
Lambton, Catherina	92
Lambton, Frances	87
Lambton, Henrietta	81
Lambton, Henry Ralph	81
Lambton, Isabel	87
Lambton, James	88
Lambton, Jane	61, 103
Lambton, John	87, 88, 92, 122
Lambton, Kathrine	87
Lambton, Margaret	122
Lambton, Robert	87, 103
Lambton, William Henry	81
Lambton, —, Lord Durham	81
Lampton, John	87
Lampton, —	86
Lancaster, Peter	15
Lane, A.	84
Langley, Bishop	84, 88, 101, 102
Langstaff, Jane	114
Langstaffe, Anne	54
Langstaffe, Eliz	54, 69
Langstaffe, Elizabetham	39
Langstaffe, George	77
Langstaffe, Henry	54
Langstaffe, Jeremiah	54
Langstaffe, Mary	77
Lansdowne, Lord	106
Lascelles, Anne	83
Lascelles, Francis	83
Latimer, Jane	59
Latus, Anne	85
Latus, Anthony	85
Law, Aaron	61
Law, Elisabeth	61
Lawrence, Robert	83
Lawrence, Thomas	83
Lawrence, Thomazine	83
Laws, Ann	67
Laws, Geo.	67
Lawson, Alice	51
Lawson, Is.	69
Lawson, Jane	59
Lawson, Ric.	69
Lawson, William	59
Lax, Eliz.	70
Lax, Ralph	70
Laxe, Jane	75
Lay, Isabel	60
Lay, Thomas	60
Layburne, Ann	71
Laye, Thamar	116
Laye, Will.	116
Layne, Mary	68
Lazenby, Catherina'	38
Le Neve	117, 119
Le Vavasseur-dit-Durell, Anne	128
Le Vavasseur-dit-Durell, John	128
Le Vavasseur-dit-Durell, Mary	128
Le Vavasseur-dit-Durell, Thomas	128
Le : pla, Jane	79
Leake, Catherine	24
Leake, —.	24
Learmouth, Elizabeth	24
Learmouth, Thomas	24
Lechmere, Caroline Amelia	30
Lechmere, Vice-Admiral William	30
Lee, Anne	57
Lee, Cuthbert	58
Lee, Isabel	58
Lee, Marg'tam	42
Lee, Wm.	57
Leek, —	57
Leeke, Robert	53, 114
Leeke, Rev. Robt.	18
Leighton, Frances	58
Leivers, Anne	65
Lem'an, Isabellam	44
Lem'an, Joh'es	44
Lesley, Anne	20
Lesley, Barbara	19
Lesley, Catherine Elizabeth	20
Lesley, Sir Edward, M.P.	20
Lesley, Elizabeth	20
Lesley, Rev. Dr. James, Prebendary of Durham, Bishop of Limerick	19, 20
Lesley, Joyce	19, 20
Lesley, Martha	20
Lesley, Mary Ann	19
Lesley, Rev. Richard	20

Leslie, Barbara	21
Leslie, Rev. Dr. James, D.D., Prebendary of Durham, Bishop of Limerick	19, 20
Lever, Anna	101
Lever, Anne	84
Lever, Rev. Christopher	83
LEVER, ELLINOR	51
Lever, Margarett	83
Lever, Ralph	83
Lever, Rev. Ralph	83
Lever, Samson	83
Lever, Thomas	101
Lever, Rev. Thomas	84
LEVETT, —, PREBENDARY OF DURHAM	5
LEWEN, RICHARD	101
LEWIN, CATHERINE	68
LEWINS, ELLENOR	108
Ley, Elizabeth	91
Leybourne, Ann	139
LEYBOURNE, JOHN	139 : n. 143, 157
Lichfield, Earl of	81
LIDDEL, ANN	46
LIDDEL, GEORG.	46
LIDDEL, JANE	51
LIDDEL, THO.	51
Liddell, Elizabeth	23
LIDDELL, ELIZABETHAM	45
Liddell, Emily Ann Charlotte	142
Liddell, Frances	12
LIDDELL, FRANCIS AUGUSTUS	142
Liddell, George	23
Liddell, George William	23
Liddell, Jane	23
LIDDELL, HON. REV. ROBT.	142
LIDDELL, THOMAS	45
Liddell, Sir Thomas	12
Liddell, Thomas Henry, Lord Ravensworth	142
Liddell, —	23
LIDDLE, ANN	58
LIDDLE, ROBERT KIRKUP	158
LIGHTFOOT, ANNAM.	42
Lightfoote, Elizabeth	83
LIGHTFOOTE, GEORGE	82 : n. 83
Lightfoote, James	83
Lightfoote, John	83
Lightfoote, Margaret	88
Lightfoote, Simon	82, 83, 88
LIMEY, ISABELLA	79
LIMEY, MARIAN	79
LIMEY, RALPH	79
Lindsell, Dr. Augustus, Dean of Lichfield	88
LINDSEY, GEORGIUS	100
LINDSEY, CAPT. JAMES	93
LINDSLEY, BARBARA	53
LINDSLEY, ISABEL	51
LINDSLEY, ROBERT	51
LINDSLY, ISABEL	60
LINN, DOROTHY	77
LINSEL, AUGUSTINO, DEAN OF LICHFIELD, BISHOP OF PETERBOROUGH AND HEREFORD	3
LINSKILL, HANNAH	69
LINSLAY, JONATHAN	132
Lisle, Catherine	113
LISLE, EDWARD	107
LISLE, HENRY	17, 107 : n. 16
LISLE, JOHN	106
LISLE, REV. JOHN	106, 107
LISLE, JOHN, MINOR CANON OF DURHAM	16
Lisle, Maurice	16
LISLE, SAMUEL	16
LISLE, —, MINOR CANON OF DURHAM	17
LISTER, MARGT.	63
LITSTER, AN	38
LITSTER, JOHN	38
Lively, Edward	2
LIVELY, JOHN	3
Lively, Rev. John	52, 73
LIVELY, KATHERINE	3
Lively, Mary	52, 73
LOADMAN, ANN	126
LOANESDALL, MARG'TAM	43
LOCK, GEORGE	63
LOCK, MARGT.	63
LODGE, ANTHO.	105
LODGE, ANTHONY	8, 9, 102
Lodge, Catherine	18
Lodge, Christopher	105
LODGE, ELIZABETH	8
LODGE, FRANCES	9
LODGE, JANE	46, 67
LODGE, JOANNAM	41
Lodge, John	18
LODGE, MARGARET	57
LODGE, MARIAM	41
LODGE, MERIELL	102
Lodge, —	79
LOFTHOUSE, GRACE	6, 119
LOFTHOUSE, WILLIAM	119
LOFTUS, GRACE	67
Logan, Alexander	133
LOGAN, ALEXR.	133
LOGAN, JANE	133
LOGAN, JOHN	51
LOGAN, MARG.	51
Londonderry, Frances Anne Emily, Marchioness of	22
Londonderry, Marquess of	22, 88
LONGFIELD, —	109
Longstaffe, William Hylton Dyer	91
Longstaffe, —	9, 69, 76, 135
Loraine, Sir William	156
LORRAINE, WM.	97
LORRAINE, —	97
Lothian, Margaret, Countess of	49
Lothian, Mark, Earl of	49
Louth, Dr., Bishop of Oxford	124
Low, Canon	106, 139
Low, —	3, 7, 97, 114, 138, 139
Lowdon, Catherine	121
LOWDON, FRANCES	78
Lowdon, Richard	121
LOWE, J. C.	32, 33, 152, 153, 154, 155
LOWE, REV. J. C., MINOR CANON OF DURHAM	156, 158
LOWE, J. CONRAN	152
LOWE, JULIUS CONRAN	153, 158
Lowe, Rev. Julius Conran, Minor Canon of Durham	153
Lowe, Rev. Richard	158
Lowrie, Henrietta Marian	30
Lowrie, Capt. William Frederick	30
Lowry, Rev. James	20
Lowry, Martha	20
LOWTH, CHARLOTTE	22
Lowth, Frances	21
LOWTH, MARGARET	21
Lowth, Maria	21
LOWTH, MARTHA	20 : n. 21
LOWTH, MARY	20, 21
LOWTH, REV. ROBERT	21

LOWTH, REV. DR. ROBERT, D.D., PREBENDARY OF DURHAM, ARCHDEACON OF WINCHESTER, BISHOP OF ST. DAVID'S, OXFORD, AND LONDON	20, 21, 22	MALTBY, REV. HENRY JOSEPH, CANON OF DURHAM	152
Lowth, Rev. William, Prebendary of Winchester	20	MALTBY, HERCY ELIZA CECILIA	34
		Maltby, Julia Katherina	152
		Maltby, Mary	152
Lowth, Archdeacon, Bishop of London	19	MALTBY, RALPH HOWARD	153
Lowther. Dorothy	100	Maltby, Sophia	156
LOWTHER, JANE	46	Maltby, Bishop	156, 157
LOWTHER, LANCELOT	46, 112	Maltby, Canon	153
LOWTHER, LANCELOTUS	12	MAN, DOROTHY	55
LOWTHER, MARGARET	38	MAN, JANE	55
LOWTHER, MARGARETA'	45	MAN, MARY	50
LOWTHER, THOM.E	12	MAN, RICH.	50
LOWTHER, THOMAS	38 ; n. 46	Manchester, Anne, Countess Dowager of	45
Lowthian, Barbara	151	Manchester, Henry, Earl of	45
Lowthian, Rev. George	151	Mangey, Dorothy	122
LOWTHIAN, MARG.	51	MANGEY, REV. DR. THO., PREBENDARY OF DURHAM	122
LOWTHIAN. MATH.	51	MANGEY, DR.	71
Lowthian, Richard	151	MANSFIELD, RT. HON. LORD	93
LOWTHROP, GULIELMUS	89	MARCH, ANN	49
LOYSELURE, FRANCES	61	MARCH, HUMPH.	49
LUPTON, FRANCIS	79	Markendale, Evers	45
LUPTON, HUGH	79	MARKENDALE, MARGARETA'	45
LUPTON, ISABELLA	79	MARKUP, ANN	57
LUPTON, MARY	50	MARKUP, JOHN	57
LYDDEL, HENRY	72	MARLAY, MARY	49
LYDDEL, MARY	72	Marlborough, Duchess of	141
LYN, ELIZABETH	60	MARLEY, ANN	68, 69
LYNN, JANE	63	MARLEY, DR. CURTO.	6 : n. 5
LYNN, MARIAM	40	MARLEY, CUB'US	92
LYNN, THO.	63	MARLEY, DOROTHY	76
Lyster, Anthony	19	MARLEY, ELIZ.	42
Lyster, Elizabeth	19	MARLEY, ELIZABETHAM	42
Lyster, Joyce	19	Marley, Frances	117
LYVELEY, SARAH	2	MARLEY, GULIELMS.	42
LYVELEY, REV. —	2	Marley, Henry	117
		MARLEY, MARG'TAM	43
MAC PEN, DONALD	125	MARLEY, MARY	50
MACHALL, —	5	MARLEY, THOMAS	68
Machell, —	5	MARLEY, WILL.	50
MACHON. ANN	50, 66	Marriott, Jane	137, 142, 150, 152
MACHON, DEBORAH	70	Marriott, William	137, 142, 150, 152
Machon, Gilbert	50, 66, 71	MARSDEN, CHARLES SURTEES	138
Machon, —	5	MARSDEN, DOROTHY	138, 157 : n. 139, 148
MADDISON, JANE	72	MARSDEN, ELIZABETH	126, 144
MADDISON. MARGARETAM	39	Marsden, Georgiana Lambton	33
MADDISON, MARIAM	41	MARSDEN, PHILLIS GEORGIANA	139
MAIRE, JACOB	41	MARSDEN, T.	138
MAIRE, MARG'TAM	41, 42	MARSDEN. THOMAS	144, 148 : n. 33, 126, 138, 139, 157
MAITLAND, ANNE	61	Marsh, Barbara	146
MAITLAND, JAMES	61	Marsh, Mary	146
MAJOR, MARY	68	Marsh, Dr., Bishop of Limerick and Kilmore	146
MAJOR, ROBERT	68		
MAKEPEACE. HANNAH	70	MARSHALL, ALICE	50
MAKEPEACE, JOSHUA	70	Marshall, Eliza	131
MAKEPEACE, MARGT.	66	MARSHALL, REV. J. M.	159
MAKEPEACE, ROBT.	66	MARSHALL, JANE	78
MAKINS, ELIZABETHAM	40	MARSHALL, MARIAM	40
MALCHIN, THOMAS	93	MARSHALL, MARY	78
Malkin, Dr. Benjamin Heath	156	MARSHALL, RD.	78
MALL, DOROTHY	64	MARSHALL, RICHARDUS	40
MALL, JNO.	64	MARSHALL, ROB.	50
Maltby, Rev. Edward, Bishop of Durham	34, 152	MARTIAL, REV. WILLIAM, MINOR CANON OF DURHAM	107
Maltby, Elizabeth Mary	152		
Maltby, Frances Sybel	157	Martin, Anne	56
Maltby, George	156	MARTIN, DOROTHEA	98
MALTBY, GERALD EDWARD	34	Martin, Dorothy	53, 102
MALTBY, GERALD RIVERS	34	MARTIN, ELIZAB.	8
MALTBY, HENRY CHARLES BRADFORD	153	MARTIN, ELIZABETH	108
Maltby, Rev. Henry, Canon of Durham	34		

Martin, Ellinor	56	
Martin, Jo., Minor Canon of Durham	108	
Martin, John	111 : n. 53, 56, 102	
Martin, Joseph	56	
Martin, Samuel	98	
Martin, Rev. Samuelis, Prebendary of Durham	98	
Martin, Samuell, Minor Canon of Durham	102	
Martin, Rear-Admiral Thomas Hutchinson	74	
Martin. Wm. James	156	
Martin. --	7, 9	
Martindale, Mary	66	
Martindill. Isabel	56	
Martindill. James	56	
Martyn, Joh'is	15	
Martyn, —	15	
Martyne, —	2	
Marwood, Anne	45	
Marwood. Sir George	45	
Mason, Ann	53	
Mason, Annam	44	
Mason, Gulielmus	39	
Mason, Janam	39, 40	
Mason, Jane	46	
Mason, John	46, 60	
Mason, Mary	60	
Massam, Alice	119	
Massam, Ellinor	97	
Massam, John	110 : n. 97, 119	
Massam. Mary	95, 105 : n. 110	
Massam, Thomas	95	
Massam. —	116	
Massom, Gulielmus	96	
Massom, Thom.e	96	
Massom, Thomas	97	
Maston, Jane	71	
Maston, Wm.	71	
Mathew, Margeria	97	
Mathew, Toby, Bishop of Durham	84	
Mathew, Wmi.	97	
Mathewes, Rebecca	103	
Mathewes. Richard	103	
Mattaire, Michael	103	
Matthews, Isabell	105	
Maud, Mary	78	
Maude, Lydia	78	
Maugham, Eliz.	51	
Maugham, Elizabeth	60	
Maugham, Peter	60	
Maugham, Annam	40	
Maughan, Lancelotus	40	
Mawker, Margery	85	
Maxson, Anne	36	
Maxson, Rev. Anthonius	36	
Maxson, Jane	36	
Maxston, Anthonio, Prebendary of Durham	4	
Maxton, Anne	50	
Maxton, Anthony	83	
Maxton, Anthony, Prebendary of Durham	50	
Maxton, Jane	6	
Maxton, —	7	
Maxton, —, Prebendary of Durham	5	
Maxwell, Sir John, Lord Herries	50	
Maxwell. Margaret	49	
Maxwell, Marg'tam	41	
McDonnell, Anne Katherine, Countess of Antrim	22	
Meek, Ann	59	
Meek, Simon	59	
Meggison, Joyce	97	
Meggison, Saram	39	
Melbanke, Ellenoram	39	
Melbanke, Robertus	39	
Mensforth. Anne	57	
Merley, Eliz.	54	
Merrington, Eliz.	70	
Merrington, Richard	70	
Merry, Eleanor Charlotte	80	
Merry, Dr. William Joseph Collings	80	
Merry, William Walter, M.D.	80	
Messenger, Christopher	39	
Messenger, Elizabetha'	39	
Messervy, Anne	128	
Metcalf, Alice	69	
Metcalf, Catherine	72	
Metcalf, Margt.	72	
Metcalfe, Ann	71	
Metcalfe, John	71	
Mewburn. Elizabeth	76	
Mewburn, Francis	76	
Mewburn, James	76	
Mewburn, Margaret	76	
Mewburn, Thomas	76	
Michelmore. Henry	79	
Michelmore, Henry William	79	
Michelmore, Marian	79	
Mickleton. Abigail	117	
Mickleton, Ann	114	
Mickleton, Anna	12	
Mickleton, Annam	39	
Mickleton. Anne	39	
Mickleton, Christopher	8, 115, 116 : n. 9, 39, 123	
Mickleton, Christopherus	96	
Mickleton, Dorothy	123	
Mickleton, Elisabetham	45	
Mickleton, Eliz.	112	
Mickleton, Elizabeth	123	
Mickleton, Hannah	16	
Mickleton, Jacobus	16	
Mickleton, James	107 : n. 16	
Mickleton, Johan'is	12	
Mickleton, John	103, 113, 114, 116, 117	
Mickleton, Margareta'	44	
Mickleton, Margt.	116	
Mickleton. Mich.	108, 112	
Mickleton, Michael	45, 112, 114	
Mickleton, Michaele	108	
Mickleton, Michaelis	16	
Mickleton, Richard	108	
Mickleton, Robert	103, 112	
Mickleton, —	9 : n. 13, 44, 98	
Middleton, Ann	49	
Middleton, Annam	38	
Middleton, Barbara	57	
Middleton, Barbariam	38	
Middleton, Carolus	38	
Middleton, Frances	120, 123	
Middleton, Francis	124	
Middleton, George	64	
Middleton, Grace	124	
Middleton, Hannan	40	
Middleton, Margt.	64	
Middleton, Mary	48	
Middleton, Radulphus	40	
Middleton, Richard	120	
Middleton, Sarah	76	
Middleton, Thomasine	60	
Middleton, William	76	
Midford, Anne	3 : n. 1	

MIDFORD, BULMER .... 2 : n. 1	MITFORD, ROBERT .... 100 : n. 103, 112
MIDFORD, DOROTHEAM 39	MITFORD, ROB'TUS 12
MIDFORD, DOROTHIE 1	Mitford, Swinburne 103
MIDFORD, JANE 116	Mitford, Thomas 109
MIDFORD, JOHANNES 39	MITFORD, WILLIA' 95
MIDFORD, JOHN 1, 3, 112	Mitford, William 103
MIDFORD, — 2	Mitford, — 96
MIDLETON, ANNA' 45	MOFFETT, ELIZ. 67
MIDLETON, JOHAN'ES 45	MOFIT, JANE... 78
MIDLETON, JOHN 101	Mole, John 89
MIDLETON, RALPH 101	MONKHOUSE, ANN 69, 77
MILBORN, CATH. 63	MONKHOUSE, THOMAS........................ 69
MILBORNE, ELIZ. 63	Montagu, Anne, Countess Dowager of Man-
MILBOURN, ELIZ. 65	chester.. 45
MILBOURN, ROBT. 65	MONTAGU, CAROLUS, BARON HALIFAX ... 45
MILBOURNE, ANN........................ 68	MONTAGU, ELISAB. 45
MILBOURNE, EDWARD 68	Montagu, Elizabeth 45
MILBURNE, MARGT........................ 65	Montagu, Hon. George 45
MILBURNE, WM. 65	Montagu, Henry, Earl of Manchester 45
Mildert, see Van Mildert.	Montagu, — 26
Miller, Burnett 135	MOON, FRANCISCAM. 40
MILLER, DORITYE 9	MOON, RADULPHUS 40
Miller, Elizabeth 135	MOOR, CATHERINE 22
MILLER, ELLENOR 48	MOOR, CHARLES 22
MILLER, GEORGE JAMES 136	MOOR, ELEANOR 67
MILLER, GRACE HUNTER 136	MOOR, REV. GEORGE, CANON OF CANTER-
Miller, Henrietta B. 135	BURY 22
MILLER, ISABELL 8, 95	Moor, Harriet Mary 22
MILLER, REV. J. 136	MOOR, JAMES 143
MILLER, REV. J., MINOR CANON OF DUR-	MOOR, JANE 143
HAM........................ 135	MOOR, JOHN .... 143, 156 : n. 140
MILLER, JAMES 135	MOOR, REV. DR. JOHN, PREBENDARY OF
MILLER, JOHN 8, 9, 95	DURHAM AND ARCHBISHOP OF CAN-
Miller, John Burnett 135	TERBURY.................................... 22
MILLER, MARG'TAM........................ 44	MOOR, SARAH 140
Millet, — 36	Moor, Thomas 143
MILLS, ANN 58	MOOR, — 112
Mills, Elizabeth 23	Moorcroft, Katherne 6
Mills, Henry 23	MOORE, ANNAM 89
Mills, Isabella 23	Moore, Anne 150
MILLS, JOHN 58	Moore, Catherine 13
MILNER, JANE 104	MOORE, DO'IA 13
MILNER, JO. 113	Moore, Elizabeth 108, 112
MILNER, JOANNA 118	Moore, George 13
MILNER, JOANNAM 41	Moore, Jane Catherine 156
MILNER, JOHANNES 101	Moore, John 156
MILNER, JOHANNES, MINOR CANON OF	Moore, Dr. John, Archbishop of Canter-
DURHAM.. 41	bury.. 13
MILNER, JOHN .... 112 : n. 105	Moore, Marg............................... 110
MILNER, THO. 113	Moore, Sarah 156
MINGAY, JOHN 144	Moore, Thomas............... 108, 110, 112, 156
MITCHEL, RICHARD........................ 107	Moore, William 150
MITCHELL, ANNAM 41	Moorcroft, Edward 90
MITCHELL, JOH'ES 41	MOORECROFT, FRANCISCAM 37
MITCHELL, MARY 102	Moorcroft, Rev. Ferdinand 90
MITCHINSON, FRANCES 66	MOORECROFT, REV. JACOBUS............... 37
MITCHINSON, MARY........................ 67	Moorcroft, James 90
MITCHINSON, ROBERT..................... 67	Moorcroft, Jane 90
MITCHINSON, RODT........................ 66	Moorcroft, Sarah.......................... 90
MITFORD, ANTHONY 95	MOHCROFT, — 5
MITFORD, BARBARA 101	MORCROFTE, FERDINAND 5
MITFORD, CHRISTOPHER 103	MORE, ELIZ. 72
MITFORD, DOROTHY .... 104 : n. 112	MORE, PETER.............................. 72
MITFORD, ELIZABETH .... 103 : n. 112	Morecroft, Anne 6
Mitford, Frances 109	Morecroft, Barbara 6, 92
MITFORD, REV. GEORGE.................. 115	MORECROFT, ELIZABETHA 6
Mitford, Jane 112	MORECROFT, FARDINANDI, PREBENDARY
MITFORD, JO. 104	OF DURHAM 36
MITFORD, JOH'IS 12	MORECROFT, FARDINANDO 2
MITFORD, JOHN...... 100, 101 : n. 103, 116, 119	Morecroft, Rev. Ferdinand, Prebendary of
MITFORD, MARY 119	Durham 36

MORECROFT, FERDINANDI, PREBENDARY OF DURHAM	37	MORTON, DR.	17, 108
MORECROFT, FRANCISCAM	36	MORTON, DR., PREBENDARY OF DURHAM	116
Morecroft, George	6	Morton, —	75
MORECROFT, GEORGIUS	92	Morton, —, Bishop of Durham	5, 89, 90, 91
MORECROFT, HENRICI	6, 92	Moss, Elizabeth	113
Morecroft, Henry	6, 92	MOUBRAY, MARGARET	123
Morecroft, Joanna'	36	MOUNTAGU, DEAN	115
MORECROFT, MARGARETT	6	Mowbray, Ann	70 : n. 24, 139
MORECROFT, SARAH	2	MOWBRAY, ELIZ.	51
Morecroft, Dr.	4	MOWBRAY, ELIZABETH	132
MORECROFT, —	4	Mowbray, Elizabeth Gray	132
Morecroft, —, Prebendary of Durham	6	Mowbray, George	132
MORECROFTE, ANN	6	MOWBRAY, GEORGE ISAAC	132
MORECROFTE, HENRYE	6	MOWBRAY, JANE	122 : n. 132
MORGAN, ANN	67	Mowbray, Rt. Hon. Sir John Robert	132
MORGAN, CICILIA	59	MOWBRAY, WILL	51
MORGAN, ELIZ.	72	Mowbray, —	129
MORGAN, ISABEL	59	MOWBREY, ANNAM	40
MORGAN, JOHN	59	MUDD, THOMES	96
Morgan, John Pilkington	59	MUDD, —	6, 7
MORGAN, WILLIAM	67	MUDSPETH, ANNAM	39
MORGAN, WM.	72	MUDSPETH, JOHANNES	39
MORISBY, CATH.	66	MUNDAY, JANA'	40
MORLAND, CAPT. CUTHBERT	56	MUNDAY, WILL'US	40
MORLAND, MARGARET	56	Murchison, Charlotte	69
MORLEY, ELIZABETH	105	Murchison, Sir Roderick Impey	69
Mornington, Anne, Countess of	145	Murray, Anne Elizabeth	148
Mornington, Garret or Garrett, Earl of	145	MURRAY, GEORGE	147
Morrell, Jane	143	Murray, John Dalrymple	147
Morrell, Robert	143	Murrey, Barbara	84
MORRESBYE, ANNE	54	Murrey, Elizabeth	84
Morrice, Mary	90	MURREY, ROBERT, MINOR CANON OF DURHAM	84
Morrice, William	90	Murrey, William	84
Morrice, —	90	MURTON, ISABELLAM	39
MORRIS, FRANCIS	144	Musgrave, Catherine	14
Morris, Susannah	149	MUSGRAVE, MARGARET	75 : n. 104
MORRISON, ANNA'	44	Musgrave, Mary	104
MORRISON, GULIELMUS	44	Musgrave, Sir Philip, Baron	104
MORROW, JANE	51	MUSGRAVE, THO., D.D., CANON AND ARCHDEACON OF CARLISLE, CANON OF DURHAM AND CHICHESTER, DEAN OF CARLISLE	104
MORROW, MATH.	51		
Mortimer, —	141		
Morton, Andrew	81		
MORTON, ANNA	15	Musgrave, Dr. Thomas, Prebendary of Durham, Dean of Carlisle	14
MORTON, ANNE	104		
MORTON, DULCIBELLA	13, 105 : n. 5, 17, 104, 117, 123	MUSGRAVE, —	14
		MYARS, AMBROSE	7, 94
MORTON, ELISABETHA	16	MYARS, STEVEN	94
MORTON, ELIZABETH	108	MYDDLETON, FRANCIS	77
MORTON, FRANCES	78	MYDDLETON, GRACE	77
MORTON, GEO.	78	Mydforth, —	86
MORTON, GEORGE	106	MYERS, AMBROSE	96 : n. 7, 8
MORTON, GEORGIUS	14	MYERS, DORITYE	95
Morton, Grace Ord	81	MYERS, ELIZABETH	8
MORTON, JO., PREBENDARY OF DURHAM	104, 117	MYRES, ELIZABETH	104
MORTON, REV. JO., D.D.	111	MYRES, ELIZABETHA'	44
MORTON, JOH'IS, PREBENDARY OF DURHAM	13, 14, 16	MYRES, REBECCA	101
MORTON, JOHAN'IS, PREBENDARY OF DURHAM	15	NAILOR, CHAR.	65
		NAILOR, JOHN	7
MORTON, JOHN, PREBENDARY OF DURHAM	106	NAILOR, JOSEPH	5
		NAILOR, MARG	65
Morton, Rev. John, Prebendary of Durham, Archdeacon of Northumberland	13	NAILOR, MARY	37
		NAILOR, THOMAS	5
MORTON, OSITHA	17, 111	NAILOR, DR., PREBENDARY OF DURHAM	5
MORTON, OSSYTHA	111	NAILOR, —	4, 5
MORTON, PSYCHE	111	NATEBY, HENRY	39
Morton, Sarah	81	NATEBY, MARY	39
MORTON, THOMAS	17, 116	NATTRESS, MARY	59
Morton, Dr. Thomas, Prebendary of Durham	105	NATTRESS, SARAH	54
		Naylor, Dulcibella	5, 13, 105

C C

NAYLOR, DULCIBELLÂ 13
Naylor, Joseph, D.D., Archdeacon of Northumberland 5
Naylor, Rev. Joseph, Prebendary 37
Naylor, Josephi 105
Naylor, Mary 5, 37
Naylor, — 4
Naylor, —, Prebendary of Durham 4
NEDBY, MARY 58
NEDBY, WILLIAM 58
NEELE, ELIZABETH 10
NEELE, ELIZABETHA 93
NEELE, FRANCISCA 6, 92
NEELE, HURR. 86
NEELE, PAULI 6, 92, 93
NEELE, RICHARD 10
Neile, Catherine 97
Neile, Elizabeth 6, 93
Neile, Elizabetha 93
NEILE, FRANCES 11
NEILE, VEN. DR. JOH'ES, D.D., PREBENDARY OF DURHAM, ARCHDEACON OF CLEVELAND, PREBENDARY OF YORK, DEAN OF RIPON 97
NEILE, MARGARETTA 10
Neile, Mildred 94, 95
NEILE, PAUL 11
Neile, Sir Paul 6, 93
NEILE, RICH'DI 11
NEILE, RICHARDI 10, 11
Neile, William 94, 95, 97
Neile, —, Bishop of Durham 2, 3, 86, 88, 92, 94, 95
NELSON, ANN .... 49 : n. 116
NELSON, MATHEW 111
NELSON, PETER .... 102, 111 : n. 116
NELSON, THOMAS 102
NELSON, — 99, 116
NESHAM, DOROTHY 58
Neve, see Le Neve.
NEVILL, JOHN 25
Newby, Ann 63
NEWBY, JOAN 63
NEWHOUSE, BARD. 5
Newhouse, Gabriel 9
NEWHOUSE, JANE 52
NEWHOUSE, RICHARDO 5
NEWHOUSE, — 73
NEWTON, ALICE 64
NEWTON, ANNE 54
NEWTON, CUTH. 50
NEWTON, ELIZ. 51, 69
NEWTON, JNO. 64
NEWTON, JOHN 69
NEWTON, JONATHAN 58
NEWTON, MARG. 50
NEWTON, MARGARET 58
NEWTON, MARGT. 65
NEWTON, THOMAS 98
Nichol, — 21
Nicholls, Hester 101
NICHOLLS, JOHN .... 7, 101 : n. 45
Nicholls, Samuel 7
NICHOLLS, SAMUELL 7
Nicholls, Thomasina' 45
Nicholls, Thomasine 7
Nichols, Cuthbert, Minor Canon of Durham 101
NICHOLS, HESTER 109
NICHOLS, THOMASINA' 45
NICHOLSON, ANN 66
NICHOLSON, CATHERINE 76

NICHOLSON, ELIZABETH 56
NICHOLSON, ELIZABETHAM 40
NICHOLSON, GEORGIUS 40
NICHOLSON, GRACE 64
NICHOLSON, JAMES 77
NICHOLSON, JANE 51, 77
NICHOLSON, MARG. 52
NICHOLSON, MARIA' 44
NICHOLSON, MARIAM 41
NICHOLSON, MARTHA 62
NICHOLSON, RICH'US 41
NICHOLSON, ROBT. 52, 62
NICHOLSON, SUSANNA 74
NICHOLSON, THOMAS 44, 74
Nixon, Mary Ann 153
Nixon, Thomas 153
NIXON, WILLIAM 153
Nixon, William Yates 153
NOBLE, MARGARETT 74
Norcliffe, Stephen 7
Norcliffe, — 7
Norfolk, — 43
Norris, Jane 25
Norris, Rev. Roger 25
Northbourne, Lady Sarah Caroline 81
Northbourne. Lady 75
NORTON, ANN 65
Norton, Anne 69
Norton, Catherine 65
NORTON, HUMPHREY 65
Norton, Roger 65
Norton, Thomas 69

O'Brien, Henry, Earl of Thomond 48
O'Brien, Lady Mary 48
OAKELEY, CAROLINE HOWLEY TURNER 32, 34
OAKELEY, HENRY EVELYN 32, 34
Oakeley, Rev. Sir Herbert, Prebendary of St. Paul's 32
OAKELEY, HILDA DIANA 32
OAKELEY, MARION ADELA 34
OGLE, ANNE 29
Ogle, Annie Charlotte 29
OGLE, MAJ. ARTHUR 30
OGLE, BERTRAM SAVILE 30
OGLE, CAROLINE AMELIA 30
Ogle, Catherine Hannah 29, 133
OGLE, DOROTHY 64
Ogle, Edith 30
Ogle, Edward Challoner 29
OGLE, EDWARD CHALONER 29
Ogle, George 64
OGLE, J. S., PREBENDARY OF DURHAM ... 139
Ogle, Dr. J. S. 146
OGLE, REV. J. S., PREBENDARY OF DURHAM 133
Ogle, Rev. John Savile, D.D. 29, 133
OGLE, REV. NEWTON, D.D., DEAN OF WINCHESTER, PREBENDARY OF DURHAM 128 : n. 133
OGLE, SARAH 52
OGLE, SOPHIA 29
OGLE, SUSANNAH 133
OGLE, THO. 52
OLIVER, ANNAM 40
OLIVER, JANE 38
OLIVER, WILL' 38
OLLIVER, MARGARET 57
ORD, ANN 65
ORD, ELISABETH 62
Ord, Elizabeth 84

ORD, JANE	59
ORD, LUCIE	43
ORD, RUTH	46
ORFEUR, MARY	73
ORFEUR, WILLIAM	73
Ornsby, Anne	69
Ornsby, —	69
Orton, Humphrey	76
Orton, Sarah	76
OVINGTON, FRANCES	62
OVINGTON, JOHN	72
OVINGTON, MARGT.	72
Owen, Anna Maria	127
OWEN, MARY	57
OWEN, WILLIAM	57
PADMAN, MARGARETT	74
Padman, Richard	74
Page, Alice	2
PALLACER, JANA'	40
PALLACER, JOH'ES	42
PALLACER, MARG'TAM	42
PALLASTER, ANN	49
PALMAR, HENRICI	90
PALMAR, JOHANIS	90
PALMER, ANNAM	44
Palmer, Anne	140
PALMER, CATHARINE	58
PALMER, ELIZABETH	53 : n. 18
PALMER, GULIELMUS	5
PALMER, HENRICI	4, 5
PALMER, HENRY	3, 91
PALMER, JOHANNES	4
PALMER, KATERNE	91
PALMER, NICHOLAS	58
PALMER, RICHARD	3, 91
PALMER, SARAH	55
PALMER, THOMAS	44
Palmer, William	18
PALMERLY, ANN	53
PALMERLY, THO.	53
PARKER, JANE	53
Parker, Mary	33
Parker, Vice-Admiral Sir William	33
Parker, Rev. Dr.	132
PARKIN, ELEANOR	55
PARKIN, JOSEPH	55
PARKIN, MARY	68
PARKIN, THOMAS	68
PARKINS, THOMASINAM	40
PARKINSON, ELISABETHAM	44
PARKINSON, MARG'TAM	42
PARKINSON, THOMAS	44
Parry, Charles	123
Parry, Harriett	123
Parry, Lucy	25
Parry, William	25
PARTIS, ANN	61
PARTIS, FLETCHER	61
PARTIS, THO.	61
PATE, ELIZ.	64
PATERSON, JOSEPH	53
PATERSON, MARGARET	53
PATTESON, ANN	37
PATTINSON, ISABEL	67
PATTISON, ANN	72 : n. 99
PATTISON, ANNAM	40
PATTISON, FRANCES	56
PATTISON, ISABEL	47
PATTISON, JOHN	54
PATTISON, MARG.	50
PATTISON, MARGARET	54
PATTISON, MERRIELL	39
PATTISON, PETER	72
PATTISON, SIMONUS	40
PAUL, JANE	68
PAUL, RICHARD	68
PAXTON, BARBARA	57
PAXTON, BARBARIAM	39
PAXTON, CATHERINA'	42
PAXTON, CHRISTOPHERUS	39
PAXTON, DOROTHY	53, 55, 122
PAXTON, ELIZ.	51
PAXTON, FRANCISCAM	41
PAXTON, GULIELMUS	39
PAXTON, JANAM	39
PAXTON, JOHN	57
PAXTON, RICH'US	42
PAXTON, THOMAS	123 : n. 53
PEACOCK, ANN	61
PEACOCK, ANNE	78
Peacock, Bridgett	142
PEACOCK, GEO.	72
Peacock, Rev. George, Dean of Ely	150
Peacock, Margaret	150
PEACOCK, MARY	72
Peacock, Simon	8
Peacock, Rev. Thomas	150
PEACOCKE. —	8
PEARCE, MARY	76
PEARETH, ANN	60
PEARSON, ANN	127, 129, 133
PEARSON, ANTHONY	8, 126 : n. 129
PEARSON, ELIZAB.	124
PEARSON, ELIZABETH	123, 135 : n. 131, 143
PEARSON, JAMES	128 : n. 125, 134, 135, 143
PEARSON, JANE	127
PEARSON, JOHN	125, 127, 134
PEARSON, MARY	140
Pearson, Hon. Mary	48
PEARSON, MICHAEL	143, 146
Pearson, Robert	48
PEARSON, THOMAS	54
PEARSON, WALTER	120, 122
PEARSON, WILLIAM	129, 134 : n. 128, 133
PEARSON, WILLM.	129
Peart, Elizabeth	92
Peart, George	92
PEART MARG'TAM	42
PEART, STEPHANUS	42
PEARTE, ANNAM	41
PEARTE, GEORGIUS	41
PEDDER, ALICE	154
Pedder, Harriet	154
Pedder, Rev. John	154
PEERS, JANE	71
PEIRSON, ELIZ.	43
PEIRSON, ELLENORAM	45
PEIRSON, FRANCISA'	42
PEIRSON, HENRY	102
PEIRSON, JACOBUS	45
PEIRSON, JOH'ES	43
Pell, Elizabeth Nicholls	147
Pell, Robert	147
Pemberton, Anne	43
PEMBERTON, JOHN	51
Pemberton, Mary	43
Pemberton, Michael	43
PEMBERTON. THOMASIN	51
PENIMAN, JACOBO	6
PENNIMAN, LADY	6 : n. 7
PENNIMAN, —	5

Pennyman, Elizabeth	147	PICKERING, GEO.	77
Pennyman, Frances Harriett	147	PICKERING, GEORGE	47
Pennyman, James	7	PICKERING, ISABEL	47
Pennyman, Sir James	7	PICKERING, JANE	77
Pennyman, Thomas	7	PICKERING, JOH'ES	40
Pennyman, Sir William	147	PICKERING, MARIA'	42
Pennyman, Lady	6	PIERSON, MARG.	48
PENSON, REV. P.	131	Pierson, Hon. Mary	48
PENYMAN, LADY	7	Pierson, Robert	48
Percy, —	141	Pigot, Charles	19
PERKINS, ISABELLAM	46	Pigot, Edward	19
PEVERELL, ALICIAM	39	Pigot, Edward Loyd	19
PEVERELL, ANNAM	40	Pigot, Elizabeth	19
PEVERELL, ELLENORAM	40	PIGOT, HENRY	19
PEVERELL, GULIELMUS	40	Pigot, Hollis	19
PEVERELL, ROBERTUS	40	Pigot, Richard	19
PEVERLEY, ANNE	56	Pigot, Robert	19
PEVERLEY, THOMAS	56	PIGOT, REV. ROBERT, MINOR CANON OF	
Phelps, Anne Katherine, Countess of Antrim	22	DURHAM	19
		PIGOT, ROBT.	18, 72, 117
Phelps, Edmund	22	Pigot, Thomas	19
PHENICKE, ELIZABETH	4	Pigot, William	19
PHILIPS, JANE	108	Pilkington, Anne	84
PHILIPS, MARY	102	Pilkington, Grace	4
PHILIPSON, CUTHBERTUS	44	Pilkington, Gratia	89
PHILIPSON, MARG'TAM	44	PILKINGTON, ISABELLAM	44
PHILLIPPS, ARTHUR	101 : n. 108	Pilkington, James, Bishop of Durham	84, 89
PHILLIPS, ABRA.	47	Pilkington, Jane	82
Phillips, Alexander	132	PILKINGTON, JOSEPH	84
PHILLIPS, ANN	47, 132	Pilkington, Leonard, D.D., Prebendary of	
PHILLIPS, ARTHUR	9 : n. 101	Durham	84
PHILLIPS, CATHERINE	142	Pilkington, Dr. Leonard	82, 89
PHILLIPS, CHRISTIAN	9	PILKINGTON, RICHARDUS	44
Phillips, Mary Ann	132	Pilkington, Bishop	82
PHILLIPS, MARY JANE	133	Pilkington, —	82
Phillips, —	139	Pin, see Du Pin.	
PRILLIPSON, GODFREY	51	PINKNEY, MARGARET	57
PHILLIPSON, JANAM	43	PINKNEY, MARY	55
PHILLIPSON, JOH'ES	43	PINKNEY, WAISTELL	55
PHILLIPSON, SARAH	54	PITCHFORD, REV. JOHN	129
PHILLPOTTS, MAJ.-GEN. ARTHUR THOMAS	28	PITCHFORD, MARGARET	129
PHILLPOTTS, CHARLOTTE CASSANDRA	27	PITT, ALICIA'	41
PHILLPOTTS, DEBORAH MARIA	27, 28, 129	PITT, BALDWYNUS	41
PHILLPOTTS, EDWARD COPLESTON	27	Pius IX., Pope	149
PHILLPOTTS, GEORGE	28	Place, Alice	86
PHILLPOTTS, GEORGIANA	27	Place, Robert	86
PHILLPOTTS, H.	28	Place, —	86
PHILLPOTTS, HARRIET SIBYLLA	27, 129	Pleasance, Anne	90
PHILLPOTTS, REV. HENRY, PREBENDARY OF DURHAM	28, 129	Pleasance, Foster	90
		Pleasance, Grace	90
PHILLPOTTS, REV. HENRY, PREBENDARY OF DURHAM, BISHOP OF EXETER	27	Pleasance, Grizell	90
		Pleasance, Jane	90
PHILLPOTTS, JOHN SCOTT	28	Pleasance, Johu	90
PHILLPOTTS, JULIA	28	Pleasance, Mary	90
PHILLPOTTS, SIBELLA	28	Pleasance, Richard	90
Phillpotts, Bishop	29	PLEASANCE, RICHERD	86
Phillpotts, Dr., Bishop	153	PLEASANCE, ROBERT	86
Phillpotts, Dr., Bishop of Exeter	151	Pleasance, Rev. Robert	90
Phillpotts, Dr., Bishop of Exeter, Prebendary of Durham	149	PLEASANCE, —	86
		PLEASANT, ROBERT	3
PHILPOT, HENRYE	82	Pleasant, —	4, 7
PHILPOT, JAMES	83	PLEASANTS, JANE	7
PHILPOT, JOHN, MINOR CANON OF DURHAM	82	Pleasaunce, Elizabeth	90
		Pleasaunce, Forster	90
Philpott, Jane	82	Plesant, Jane	90
PHILPOTT, JOHN, MINOR CANON OF DURHAM	83	PLESANT, ROBERTUS	90
		PLESENCE, JANA	98
Philpott, Sir John	82	PLESUNST, JANE	4
Phylpott, Jane	82	POLLETT, FRANCISCA'	42
Phylpott, John	82	POLLETT, RICH'US	42
PICKERING, BRIDGETTA'	40	Ponton, Elizabetham	136

Name	Page
POOLE, JOHN	122
Pope Pius IX.	149
Porter, Elizabeth	103, 112
PORTER, MARG'TAM	42
PORTER, RICH'US	42
PORTESSE, MARGARETT	38
POTTER, ANN	73
POTTER, ELIZABETH	53
POTTER, JOHN	53
POTTER, MARY	64
POTTER, THOMAS	73
POTTER, WILL.	64
POTTS, ELIZABETH	20
POTTS, GILBERTUS	44
POTTS, JANAM	44
POTTS, JNO.	20
POTTS, JOHN	73
POTTS, MARY	73
POTTS, WILLIAM	20
Poulson, —	124
POWEL, SARAH	125
POWEL, —, MINOR CANON OF DURHAM...	125
POWELL, JOHN	57, 115
POWELL, JOHN, MINOR CANON OF DURHAM	116
Powles, Frederica Louisa	31
Powles, John Diston	31
Powles, Thomas Octavius	31
PRAT, JANE	51
PRAT, MAT.	51
Pratt, Ann	87
Pratt, William	87
PREST, EDWARD, ARCHDEACON OF DURHAM	156
PREST, —, ARCHDEACON OF DURHAM ...	33
Preston, Richard, Viscount	49, 105
PRICE, COL. BARRINGTON	24
Price, Caroline	28
PRICE, LADY MARIA	24
Price, Lady Mary	24
PRICE, MARY ANN	127
Price, Robert	24
PRICE, REV. ROBERT, PREBENDARY OF DURHAM	127
Price, Hon. Sarah	24
PRICE, UVEDALE ROBERT	127
PRICE, WILLIAM	24
PRICE, DR.	129, 130
PRICE, DR., PREBENDARY OF DURHAM	132 : n. 28
PRIESTLY, ELIZ.	65
PRIESTLY, GEORGE	65
PRINGOR, ISABEL	64
PROCKTER, DOROTHY	65
PROCTER, AMBROSE	52
PROCTER, ELIZABETH	148
PROCTER, JANE	52
PROCTER, MARY	65
Procter, Robert	148
PROSSER, REV. R., D.D., ARCHDEACON AND PREBENDARY OF DURHAM	132
Prosser, Dr. Richard	132
PROSSER, RICHARD SAMUEL	129
PROSSER, SARAH	132
Prosser, Archdeacon	135
PROSSER, DR., PREBENDARY AND ARCHDEACON OF DURHAM	129
PROSSER, —	129
Prosser, see also Wegg-Prosser.	
PROUD, ANNE	16
PROUD, CATHERINE	54
PROUD, CICILIA	59
PROUD, FRANCES	17
PROUD, JANE	64
PROUD, JOH'IS	16
PROUD, JOHAN'ES	16, 45
PROUD, JOHN	16, 17, 54
PROUD, MARG'TAM	45
PROUD, ROBERT	59
PROUD, THOMAS	16
PRUDDUS, ANN	60
Pulteney, —	125
PURVIS, GEO.	67
PURVIS, MARGT.	67
Pye, Margaret	121
Pye, Mary	122
PYE, WM.	122
Queen Anne of England	106
Quin, —	131
RACE, ANN	58
RADDON, MARGERIAM	40
Radnor, Lord	146
RAIN, GILES	50
RAIN, MARY	50
Raine, Alice	50
RAINE, ANNAM	39
Raine, Anne	150
Raine, Elizabeth	50
Raine, James	150
RAINE, REV. JAMES	134, 150
Raine, Rev. Canon James	150
Raine, John	50
Raine, Margaret	150
RAINE, MARY	64
Raine, Dr.	96
Raine, —	6
RAINSFORD, ELIZ.	122
RAISBECK, ISABELLAM	46
RAMSAY, ANN	58
RAMSAY, THOMAS	58
RAMSEY, CATH.	66
RAMSEY, ROBT.	66
Randall, —	88
RANDOLPH, —	75
RANGALL, ELIZABETH	2
RANGALL, JO.	84
Rangall, John	2, 84, 90
RANGHALL, GEORGE	90
RANSOM, ALICIA'	42
RANSON, ELLENR.	53
RANSON, HANNAH	70
RASHELL, CHRISTOPHER	101
RASHELLS, MARGARET	76
RAULIN, NICOLAI	4
RAULIN, THOMAS	4
RAW, ANNE	61
RAW, CATHERINE	104
RAW, GEORGE	55
RAW, JANAM	43
RAW, JO.	103, 104
Raw, John	104, 116, 124
RAW, MARGARET	55
RAW, MARIA	42
RAW, RICHARD	103
Raw, —	100
RAWE, CATHERINE	113
RAWE, JOHN	113
RAWE, RICHARD	100
Rawe, —	100
Rawlin, Barbara	4

RAWLIN, ELIZ.	78, 122	RENWICK, MATTHEW	24
Rawlin, Elizabeth	4	REVELY, DAVID	59
Rawlin, Mary	4	REVELY, MARY	59
Rawlin, Nicholas	4	RICABY, ANNAM	46
Rawling, Sir Benjamin	123	RICHARBY, JANE	72
RAWLING, ELIZ.	48	RICHARBY, JOHN	72
Rawling, Elizabeth	123	RICHARDSON, ALICE	50
RAWLING, MAGDALENAM	42	Richardson, Ann	92, 113
RAWLING, MARTHAM	42	RICHARDSON, ANNE	54, 86 : n. 3, 92
RAWLING, MICHAEL	48	Richardson, Anthony	2
RAWLING, SAMUEL	42	Richardson, Bryan	92
RAWLING, THOMAS	42	Richardson, Christopher	3
Raynsforth, Elizabeth	122	RICHARDSON, DOROTHEA'	41
Raynsforth, John Nicholls	122	RICHARDSON, ELEANOR	121
Read, George	105	RICHARDSON, ELIZABETH	55, 94 : n. 3, 92
Rend, —	117	RICHARDSON, FRANCES	47
READHEAD, MARY	65	RICHARDSON, FRANCIS	3
READSHAW, CHRISTOPHER	122	Richardson, Helene	92
READSHAW, GEORGE	118	Richardson, Helme	92
READSHAW, ISABEL	118	RICHARDSON, JAMES	51
READSHAW, JACOB	118, 120 : n. 121	RICHARDSON, JANAM	43
READSHAW, JAMES	64	RICHARDSON, JANE	51, 54, 69 : n. 3
READSHAW, JANE	53	RICHARDSON, JOHANNES	91
READSHAW, MARY	121	RICHARDSON, JOHN	54, 86 : n. 3, 92, 113
READSHAW, ROBERT	53	Richardson, Margaret	3, 46
READSHAW, SARAH	64	RICHARDSON, MARGAR'TAM	46
REAH, ANN	77	RICHARDSON, MARIAM	46
REAH. MARY	75	RICHARDSON, MARY	50, 55 : n. 3
REAVELEY, ADAM	71	Richardson, Michael	92
REAVELEY, DOROTHY	71	RICHARDSON, NICHOLAUS	94
REAY, ANNE	56	Richardson, Ralph	2
Reay, Hannah	134	RICHARDSON, RICH'US	41
Reay. Joseph	10	Richardson, Sarah	2
Reay, Margaret	10	Richardson, Thomas	92
REAY, MARY	69	Richardson, William	3, 92
REAY, ROBT.	56	RICHARDSON, WM.	69
Reay, Utrick	134	RICHARDSON, XPOFER	3
REDDISH, WINIFRED	74	RICHED, BISHOP OF DURHAM	84
REDHEAD, IS.	65	RICHESON, JOHN	1
REDHEAD, ROBT.	65	RICHMOND, BARBARA	48
REDSHAW, JANE	64	Richmond, Christopher	74
REDSHAW, JNO.	64	Richmond, Elizabeth	74
REED, ANNAM	40	RICHMOND, ISABELLA	74
Reed, Eleanor	43	RICHMOND, ROBERT	72
REED, GULIELMI	99	RICHMOND, SARAH	72
REED, HANNAH	134	RICHMOND, WILLIAM	48
Reed, Hannah Jane	134	Ricknby, Catherine	121
REED, ISABELLA	99	RIDLEY, CATHERINE	57
REED, JANAM	39, 41	RIDLEY, ELIZ.	71
REED, JOANNA	57	RIDLEY, ISABELLA	75
REED, MARGARET	54 : n. 134	RIDLEY, JOHN	75
REED, MARY	63, 71	RIDLEY, MARGARET	69, 76
Reed, Michael	43	RIDLEY, THOMAS	69
REED, THO.	71	RIDLEY, WM.	57
REED, WILL.	63	Rigby, Ellen	143
Reed, William	134	Rigby, William	143
REED, —	111	RIPPON, ALICIAM	45
REEDE, ANN	75	RIPPON, ELIZ.	52
REEDSHAW, BARBAIRE	36	RIPPON, JOHN	52
REID, MARY	50	RIPPON, SUSANNA	67
Relph, Mary	136	Risby, Catherine	83
RELTON, HENRY RENNET	145	Risby, William	83
Relton, Henry Rennett	145	ROANTREE, JANE	58
Relton, Rev. John Rudge	145	ROANTREE, WILLIAM	58
Relton, Sophia	145	ROBERTS, MIRRIANA'	41
RENISON, ROBERT	120	ROBERTS, RICH'US, MINOR CANON OF DURHAM	41
Rennison, Elizabeth	76		
RENNY, ANN	57	ROBERTSON, ARCHIBALD HARVEY	34
RENTON, MARGARETAM	40	Robertson, Eliza	33, 158
RENWICK, BENJAMIN	24	ROBERTSON, FRANCES HENRIETTA	33, 34 : n. 158
RENWICK, JANE	24		

Robertson, Capt. George 30
ROBERTSON, HILDA 34
Robertson, Marianne 30
Robertson, Mary 33
Robertson, Mary Anne Georgiana 33
ROBERTSON, NORMAN 33
Robertson, Lieut.-Col. Peter Taylor 33
ROBERTSON, W. H. 33, 34, 155, 156, 157
ROBERTSON, REV. W. H 157
ROBERTSON, WILLIAM HENRY 158
Robertson, William Henry, M.D. 33, 158
ROBERTSON, REV. WILLIAM HENRY,
 MINOR CANON OF DURHAM 33, 34
Robin, Anne 128
Robin, Philip 128
Robinson, Alice 95
Robinson, Ann 135
Robinson, Anne Caroline 154, 156
ROBINSON, BARBARA 72
ROBINSON, CATHERINE 54
Robinson, Charles 135
ROBINSON, DOROTH 52
ROBINSON, DOROTHY .... 48 : n. 10
ROBINSON, ELIZABETH .... 58, 74 : n. 10
ROBINSON, ELIZABETHAM 45
ROBINSON, ELIZABTH. 122
ROBINSON, FRANCES HARRIETT 147
ROBINSON, FRANCISCAM 40
ROBINSON, GEORGE 59
ROBINSON, GEORGIUS 43, 44
ROBINSON, HANNAM 43
ROBINSON, ISABEL 69
Robinson, J. C. W. 154
ROBINSON, JANAM 44
ROBINSON, JANE 58, 59
ROBINSON, JOH'ES 43
ROBINSON, JOHN 69
Robinson, John Christopher Wall 147
ROBINSON, LEONARDS 42
ROBINSON, MARG'TAM 43
Robinson, Margaret 86
ROBINSON, MARIA' 42
ROBINSON, MARIAM 44
ROBINSON, MARY 60
ROBINSON, MICHAEL 74
ROBINSON, NATHANIEL 40
Robinson, Ositha 117
ROBINSON, THOMAS 58
ROBINSON, WILLIAM 58
ROBINSON, — .... 116 : n. 10, 86, 156
Robson, Alice 92
ROBSON, ALICE MAUDE 146
ROBSON, ANN .... 49 : n. 141, 153
ROBSON, ANNA' 42
ROBSON, EDWARD 71
ROBSON, ELIANOR 64
ROBSON, ELIONOR 78
ROBSON, ELIZ. 50, 65, 71
ROBSON, ELIZABETH ANN 151
Robson, Frances 153
ROBSON, JOHANNE, PREBENDARY OF DUR-
 HAM 3
ROBSON, JOHANNES 2
ROBSON, REV. JOHANNIS 2
ROBSON, JOHN .... 2, 49, 153 : n. 92, 93, 140
ROBSON, JOHN, PREBENDARY OF DURHAM   93
ROBSON, REV. JOHN 1
ROBSON, JOSEPH 93
Robson, Margaret 93
ROBSON, MARGARETA 3
ROBSON, MARGARETÂ 4

ROBSON, MARIA 96
Robson, Mary 140
ROBSON, RICHARD .... 1, 93 : n. 2
Robson, Robert Naisbitt 154
ROBSON, SARAH .... 97 : n. 148
Robson, Simon, Dean of Bristol 92
Robson, Thomas 153
ROBSON, WILL. 64
ROBSON, WILLIA' 95
ROBSON, WILLIAM 50
RODDAM, JANE 129
RODDAM, JOHN 129
ROGERS, REV. TH. 156
ROOKBY, RAD'US 42
ROOKBY, SUSANNA' 42
ROOKSBY, ELIZ. 64
ROOKSBY, MARTHA 78
ROSBY, ANN 70
ROSBY, EDW. 70
ROSDEN, ISABELLAM 39
ROSDEN, JOSEPHUS 39
Ross, Elizabeth 42
Ross, Patrick 42
Rothwell, Anne. 2
Rowe, Annabella 116
ROWE, JANE 109, 122
ROWE, JOHN .... 116 : n. 104, 124
ROWE, RICH. 109
ROWE, REV. RICHARD 124
Rowe. — 16
ROWEL, REBBECCA 60
ROWELL, ELIZ. 53
Rowell, John 115
ROWELL, — .... 8 : n. 115
Rowland, John 154
Rowland, Phillis 154
ROWLANDSON, ANNIE SARAH 147
ROWLANDSON, CHARLES 143
Rowlandson, Christopher 143, 157
ROWLANDSON, HANNAH .... 157 : n. 143
ROWLANDSON, KATE MARION 147
ROWLANDSON, SAMUEL .... 145, 157 : n. 143
ROWLANDSON, SARAH .... 153 : n. 143, 157
ROXBY, ELIZ. 49
Rubridge, Emma 28
Rubridge, James 28
Rud, Rev. Tho. 17
Rud, Rev. Thomas 119
RUDD, JOHN 17
Rudd, Joseph 92
RUDD, THO. 17
RUDD, THOMAS 17
Rudd, Rev. Thomas 111
Rudd, Wilbraham 17
Rush, Mary 96
Rush, Samuel 96
RUSH, SAMUELL 96
RUSSEL, CATHERINE 124
RUSSEL, ISABEL 56
RUSSELL, ELIZABETH 132
RUSSELLS, JANAM 40
RUTLIDGE, MARIAM 42
RUTLIS, GRACE. 71
RUTTER, CUTHBERT 69
RUTTER, ELIZ. 69
Rydale, — 83
RYDER, ELIZABETH 38
RYDER, OTTIWELL 38
RYDLEY, ANNE 116
RYE, JOHN 121
RYMER, ELIZABETH 18, 118

Rymer, Rev. Jo.	18
Rymer, Rev. John	118, 119, 121
Rymer, Michal	121
St. George, —	85, 88, 92, 115
Salkeild, Jane	64
Salkeld, Frances	62
Salmon, Catherine	159
Salmon, Thomas	159
Salt, George	137, 144
Salt, Mary	137
Salvin, Ann	50
Salvin, Anthony	14, 50, 137, 141, 147, 148
Salvin, Caroline Sophia	146
Salvin, Eleanora Elizabeth	137, 141, 147, 148
Salvin, Gerard	50
Salvin, Henry	146
Sampson, Alicia'	40
Sampson, Anne	89
Sampson, Dr. Thomas, Dean of Christ Church	89
Sanders, Christopher	130
Sanderson, Eliz.	52
Sanderson, Ellenora'	41
Sanderson, Francisca'	43
Sanderson, Joh'es	41, 43
Sanderson, Joshua	43
Sanderson, Lucy	134
Sanderson, Mariam	43
Sanderson, Mary	76
Sanderson, Patrick	76
Sands, Margarett	38
Sands, William	38
Sandwich, Earl of	154
Sandys, Edwin, Archbishop of York	37
Sandys, Margaret	37
Satchell, Elizabeth	140
Saunders, Catherine	84
Savage, Elizabetham	39
Savill, Thomas	95
Saxton, John	113
Sayer, Ann	72
Sayer, Catherine	119
Sayer, Exton	119
Sayer, Rev. George	24
Sayer, James	60
Sayer, Mary	24
Sayer, Tho.	72
Sayer, Thomasine	60
Sayre, Catharinam	45
Sayre, Laurentius	45
Schepper, Frances	119
Schneeberger, John	121
Scisson, Isabella	4
Scorer, Jane	63
Scorer, Will.	63
Scott, Adam	125
Scott, Ann	128
Scott, Catherine Elizabeth	20
Scott, James	20
Scott, John	60
Scott, Mary	60
Scott, Thomas	60
Scourfield, Anne	107
Scroggs, Ann	69
Scroggs, Samuel	69
Scruton, Doritye	9
Scruton, Dorotheam	39
Scruton, Dorothy	9
Scruton, Margarett	117
Scurfeild, Alicia'	41
Seamer, Ann	60
Seamer, Edward	60
Seddon, Hannah	69
Seddon, John	69
Sedgewick, Mary	75
Sedgwick, Eliz.	54
Selby, Christopher	50
Selby, Jane	68
Selby, Rebecca	50
Serpell, Jane	140
Setton, Frances	11
Setton, John	11
Sexton, Elioner	122
Seymour, Caroline Mary Anne	28
Seymour, John C. G.	28
Shaclock, Francisca'	44
Shaclock, Johan'es	44
Shadforth, Marg.	51
Shadforth, Margarett	74
Shadforth, Mary	74
Shadforth, Robert	74
Shadforth, Thomas	74
Shadforth, Thomasin	51
Shaffield, Elizabeth	59
Shafto, Dorothy	116
Shafto, Jannam	40
Shafto, Mary	66
Shafto, Robert	119
Shafto, Robert Ingram	136
Shafto, Sarah	136
Shaftoe, Mary	52
Shaklock, Marg'tam	45
Sharp. Rev. Andrew	19
Sharp, Ann	19, 120
Sharp, Ann Jemima	130
Sharp, Sir C.	4
Sharp, Catherine	18
Sharp, Sir Cuthbert	84, 113
Sharp, Dorothy	122
Sharp, Elizabeth	18
Sharp, Frances	18
Sharp, Granville	19 : n. 122
Sharp, James	18 : n. 19
Sharp, Jane	73
Sharp, John, Archbishop of York	122
Sharp, Rev. John, D.D., Archdeacon of Northumberland, Prebendary of Durham	126
Sharp, Judith	19, 122, 129 : n. 18
Sharp, Dr. Tho.	75
Sharp, Rev. Dr. Thomas, Prebendary of Durham	19, 120
Sharp, Rev. Dr. Thomas, D.D., Prebendary of Durham, Archdeacon of Northumberland	18, 122
Sharp, Archbishop	18
Sharp, Archdeacon	122
Sharp, Dr.	75, 77
Sharp, Dr., Prebendary of Durham	125, 129
Sharpe, Annam	43
Sharpe, Anthonius	43
Sharpe, Beatrice	155
Sharpe, James	155
Shaw, Alexander	41, 110
Shaw, Alice	64
Shaw, Barbara	11, 121
Shaw, Catherine	121
Shaw, Ellenor	110
Shaw, Ellenora'	41
Shaw, Ellenoram	40

Shaw, Geoffrey	11, 121	SIMPSON, JO.	104 : n. 113
SHAW, GULIELMO	3	SIMPSON, JOH'ES	43
SHAW, HILTON	121	SIMPSON, JOH'IS	12
SHAW, MURIEL	66	SIMPSON, JOHAN'IS	14
SHAW, SARAM	41	SIMPSON, JOHANNES	39
SHAW, WM.	66	SIMPSON, JOHN	105, 113
SHAWE, ALEXANDR	8	SIMPSON, JOSEPH	76
SHAWE, CICILIAM	41	SIMPSON, MARGARET	121
SHAWE, HENRICUS	41	SIMPSON, MARIA	12
SHAWTER, ANNAM	39	SIMPSON, MARY	76, 107
SHAWTER, LANCELOTUS	41	SIMPSON, THO.	113
SHAWTER, MARIAM	41	SIMPSON, THOMAS	105, 113
SHEFFEILD, ANNE	36	SIMPSON, WM.	78
SHEFFEILD, NICHOLAS	84	SISSON, CUTH.	99
Sheffield, Ann	87	SISSON, CUTHBERTUS	97
Sheffield, Jane	94	SISSON, ESTHER	65
SHEILD, MARY	54	SISSON. FRANCISCA	99
SHEILD, RALPH	54	SISSON, JOS.	65
SHEPHEARDSON, ELIZABETHAM	39	SISSON, MURIAL	105
SHEPHEARDSON, JOHAN'ES	39	SISSONS, CAPT. JOHN	95
SHEPHERD, AGRETEM	43	SISSONS, MATTHEW	95
SHEPHERD, GEORGIUS	43	SISSONS, MERRILL	8
SHEPPARD, ANN	52	SKELTON, JANE	72
SHEPPARD, JAMES	61	SKELTON, ROBT.	72
SHEPPARD, JANE	61	SKENE, A. P.	135
SHERATON, ELIZABETHAM	40	SKENE, ANDREW PHILIP	133
SHERMAN, THO., MINOR CANON OF DURHAM	110	SKENE, HENRIETTA	135 : n. 133
		Skene, Katherine	133
SHETHUM, DAVID	49	Skene, Capt. Philip (Wharton)	133
SHETHUM, ELIZ.	49	Skepper, Christopher	115
SHEVILL, ELIZ.	69	SKEPPER, JANE	104
SHEVILL, GEO.	69	Skepper, Moses	115
SHIPLEY, ANNA'	44	SKEPPER, THOMAS	104, 115
SHIPLEY, BARBARA	70	SKINNER, GEORGIUS	43
SHIPLEY, EDWARD	55	SKINNER, MARIAM	43
SHIPLEY, JANE	69	Skinner, Mary	43
SHIPLEY, MARY	55	Skinner, William	43
Shipley, Michael	55	Skinner, —	43
Shipperdson, Rev. Edmund Hector	73, 104	SKURFEILD, WM.	105
Shipperdson, Margaret	104	SKURREY, BARBARA'	42
Shipperdson, Ralph	104	SKURREY, GULIELMS.	42
Shipperdson, —	81	SLATER, ELIZABETH	53
SHORT, MARGERY	49	Sleigh, Frances	23, 137
SHOTTON, MARY	77	Sleigh, William	23, 137
Shrewsbury and Talbot, Earl of	119	SMAILES, JANE	77
SHUTE, ANN	71	Smallpage. Dan.	46
SHUTTLEWORTH, ELIZABETH	108 : n. 112	Smallpage. Ruth	46
Shuttleworth, Nicholas	108, 112	SMART, JAMES	108
SHUTTLEWORTH, RICHARD	112	SMART, JANE	121
Shuttleworth, Sir Richard	112	SMART, MARGARET	55
Shuttleworth, —	112	Smart, Peter. Prebendary of Durham	3
Siddons, —	132	SMART, SUSANNA	3
SIDGEWICK, ELIZ.	53	SMELT, MARGARETAM	42
SIDGEWICK, GERRARD	53	Smelt, Richard	4, 112
SIDGWICK, MARY	55	SMELT, RICHARDO	4
SIDWICK, JANE	38	SMILES, ELIONOR	78
SIMEY, ISABELLA	79	SMILES, JOHN	78
SIMEY, MARIAN	79	SMIRK, GEORGE	57
SIMEY, RALPH	79	SMIRK, JOANNA	57
SIMON, —	73	SMITH, ALICE	59
SIMPSON, ALICIAM	39	SMITH, AN	38
SIMPSON, ANNE	78 : n. 43	SMITH, ANN	69, 75, 111
SIMPSON, BOLTON, MINOR CANON	142, 144	SMITH, ANNE	54, 56, 102 : n. 110
SIMPSON, REV. BOLTON	145, 147	SMITH, BARBARA	53
SIMPSON, DOROTHY	60, 68	SMITH, BETTY	129
SIMPSON, ELIZABETH	104 : n. 43	SMITH, DAVID	59
SIMPSON, ELIZABETHA	14	SMITH, DULCEBELLA	5
SIMPSON, GEORGE	60	SMITH, DULCIBELLA	91
SIMPSON, ISABEL	114	SMITH, EDWARD	1
SIMPSON, ISABELL	107	Smith, Eleanor	56
SIMPSON, JANA'	43	SMITH, ELI.	37

D D

SMITH, ELI., MINOR CANON OF DURHAM 97
SMITH, ELIÆ, MINOR CANON OF DUR-
HAM 4, 5, 6, 90, 91
SMITH, ELIAS .... 3, 8 : n. 13
SMITH, REV. ELIAS, MINOR CANON OF
DURHAM .... 37, 94, 98 : n. 115
SMITH, ELISABETH 107
SMITH, ELISABETHA 4
SMITH, ELIZ.......................... 18, 65
SMITH, ELIZAB'A 5
SMITH, ELIZABETH .... 94, 140 : n. 17, 45
SMITH, ELIZABETHAM 36, 39
SMITH, ELLINOR 56
SMITH, FAITH 130
SMITH, FRANCES 78
Smith, Francis 88
Smith, Rev. George 46
SMITH, GOLIBRIGHT 107
SMITH, GRACE 77
SMITH, GRATIÁ 4
SMITH, GULIELMI 88
SMITH, GULIELMUS 88
SMITH, HENR'O 5
SMITH, HENRICUS 36
SMITH, HENRY .... 107, 110 : n. 88
SMITH, REV. HENRY 100, 104, 108
SMITH, ISABEL 47
SMITH, ISABELL........................... 8, 56
SMITH, ISABELLA' 37
SMITH, JAMES .... 66 : n. 82, 88
SMITH, JANA 98
SMITH. JANE 46, 61
SMITH, JO. 110
SMITH, JOAN 61
SMITH, JOHN 17, 56, 105, 119, 121, 128, 130, 136 :
n. 46
SMITH, JOHN, D.D. 17, 18
Smith, Dr. John, Prebendary 36
SMITH, REV. JOHN, PREBENDARY OF DUR-
HAM....................................... 111
SMITH, JOH'NES, MINOR CANON AND PRE-
BENDARY OF DURHAM 45
SMITH, JOSEPH .... 17, 75, 104 : n. 46
SMITH, MARGARET............... 60 : n. 14, 88
SMITH, MARGARETA 5
SMITH, MARGARETÂ 14
SMITH, MARGARETA' 44
SMITH, MARGARETAM 41
SMITH, MARGARETT 74
SMITH, MARIA 4
SMITH, MARIAM .... 45 : n. 43
SMITH, MARY 17, 62, 64, 66, 71, 75, 109, 118,
128 : n. 18, 36, 46, 107
SMITH. MARY ANN 136
SMITH, MARYE............................. 93
Smith, Peter 43
Smith, Philadelphia 36, 46
SMITH, POSTHUMUS 116, 117
SMITH. RICARDUS 90
SMITH, RICHARD 3, 56
SMITH, ROB. 13, 14
SMITH, ROBERT 1, 64, 74, 88, 102, 111 : n. 12, 14
SMITH, ROBT. 53, 62
SMITH, SARAH 6, 7, 37
SMITH, SUSANNA 6, 7, 97, 100, 115
SMITH, TAMAR 108
SMITH, THO. 78
SMITH, THOMAS .... 44 : n. 88
Smith, Dr. Thomas, Prebendary of Dur-
ham, Bishop of Carlisle 13
SMITH, WILLIA' 38

SMITH, WILLIAM 1, 18, 47, 93, 111, 118 : n. 17,
46, 82, 90, 94
Smith, Rev. William 45
SMITH, WM. 18, 117
SMITH, ZADOCK 111
SMITH, DR. 17, 109
Smith, Dr., Bishop of Carlisle 105
SMITH, DR., DEAN OF CARLISLE 13
SMITH, DR., PREBENDARY OF DURHAM ... 118
SMITH, — .... 17, 109, 116 : n. 107
SMITH-DORRIEN, REV. W. M., MINOR
CANON OF DURHAM 158
SMITHSON, DEBORAH 46
SMITHSON, GEO. 46
SMURFOOT. THO. 114
SMURTHWAITE, MARGERIAM 40
SMYTH, ELIÆ, MINOR CANON OF DUR-
HAM 6
SMYTH, HENRICUS 6
SMYTH, MARGARETA 3
SMYTH, — 2
SMYTHE, EDWARDE......................... 82
SNAITH, ELIZ. 65
SNAITH. ISABELL 55
SNAITH, PETER 55
SNAITH, ROBT. 65
SNAWDON, BARBARA 106
SNAWDON, BARBARA' 42
SNAWDON, ELIZABETH 53
SNAWDON. GEORGIUS 14
SNAWDON, GULIELMS. 42
SNAWDON, JACOBUS 40
SNAWDON, JOHN 48
SNAWDON, MAGDALENA' 40
SNAWDON, MARGARETA 12
SNAWDON, MARIAM....................... 42
SNAWDON, SUSANNA 48
SNAWDON, WILLIAM 102, 106, 107
SNAWDON, WILMI. 14
SNAWDON, WMI. 12
Sneyd, Barbara 146
Sneyd, Catherine Hannah 29, 133
Sneyd, Edward 29, 133, 146
SNEYD, REV. EDWARD... 29, 139, 146, 148, 151
Sneyd, Rev. Edward, Minor Canon of Dur-
ham 133
Sneyd, Maria............................. 146
Sneyd, Nathaniel 146
Sneyd, Archdeacon Wettenhall............ 146
Sneyd, Rev. William 146
SNOWDEN, ELIZABETH 120
SNOWDEN, GEORGE 118
SNOWDEN, SARAH 51
SNOWDEN, WILLIAM 51
SOFLEY, ISABEL 70
Somerset, Lord Arthur 30
Somerset, Arthur Edward 30
Somerset, Edith 30
Somerset, Henry, Duke of Beaufort 30
SOMMERS, MARY 76
SOMMERS, RICHARD 76
Sonkey, Ann 98
Sonkey, Dorothea......................... 98
Sonkey, Thomas 98
Southeron, Eliz. 63
Southeron, Robt. 63
SOWERBY, ANN 60
SOWERBY, HANNAH 56
SOWERBY, ISABELLAM 44
SPARK, ANN 73
SPARK, ELIZ. 51

Spark, Janam	43	Steadman, Maria'	42
Spark, John	51, 73	Steele, Ann	126
Sparke, Annam	39	Steele, Elizabeth	44, 126
Sparke, Johannes	39	Steele, Ralph	44
Sparke, Mary	60	Steele, William	126
Speare, Elisabetham	44	Stell, Eleanor	65
Spearman, Anne	11	Stell, Wm.	65
Spearman, Dorothea	10	Stephanus, Florence	103
Spearman, Dorothea	9	Stephen, Florence	103
Spearman, Dorothy	115 : n. 11, 110, 111, 123, 137, 140	Stephenson, Ann	50
		Stephenson, Anne	63
Spearman, Elisabetham	45	Stephenson, Conon	63
Spearman, Eliz.	112	Stephenson, Doroth.	52
Spearman, Elizab.	15	Stephenson, Eliz.	67
Spearman, Elizabeth	8, 108 : n. 11	Stephenson, Henry	67
Spearman, Elizabetha	9	Stephenson, Jane	67
Spearman, Franciscus	10, 99	Stephenson, John	50
Spearman, George	8, 95	Stephenson, Margaret	57
Spearman, Gilbert	48, 109, 110, 111, 113, 115	Stephenson, Will.	52
Spearman, Gilbertus	11	Stephenson, Wm.	57
Spearman, Han.	48	Stevenson, Elizabeth	53
Spearman, Hannah	120	Stevenson, Jane	10
Spearman, Isabella	11	Stevenson, John	10
Spearman, Jo.	111	Stevenson, Mary	59
Spearman, Joh'is	11, 99	Stevenson, Thomas	53
Spearman, Johannes	11	Steward, Col.	9
Spearman, Johannis	9, 10, 11	Stewart, Jana'	42
Spearman, John	8, 95, 108, 109, 111 : n. 11, 112, 118	Stobbert, Eliz.	60
		Stobert, Anne	82
Spearman, Marg.	48	Stobert, Elizabeth	82, 87
Spearman, Mary	110, 115	Stobert, Richard	82 : n. 87
Spearman, Michael	104 : n. 11	Stockdell, Joh'nes	45
Spearman, Phillis	11	Stockdell, Margaretam	45
Spearman, Rob.	48	Stoddert, Christopher	38
Spearman, Robert	109, 118 : n. 48, 111, 140	Stoddert, Frances	38
Spearman, Robt.	115	Stoddert, Jane	38
Spearman, Theophilus	113	Stoddert, Thomas	38
Spearman, —	16	Stokeld, Ann	153
Speck, Mary	60	Stokeld, Elianoram	44
Spencelay, Isabellam	46	Stokeld, Eliz.	50
Spencelay, Robertus	46	Stokeld, Elizabeth	50
Spenceley, Alicia'	38	Stokeld, John	50
Spenceley, John	38	Stoker, Jane	24
Spencer, George	57	Stoker, William	24
Spencer, Margaret	57	Stoker, Dr. William	24
Spooner, Mary	105	Stone, Mary	55
Spoor, Hannah	132	Stone, Peter	55
Spoor, Margaret	60	Stonehewer, Elizabeth	127 : n. 125
Spoor, Robert	60	Stonehewer, Mary	120
Stagg, Alicia'	41	Stonehewer, Rich.	117
Stagg, Elizabeth	119	Stonehewer, Richard	120 : n. 125
Stagg, Gulielmi	12	Stonehewer, Tho.	117
Stagg, Gulielms	12, 41	Stonehewer, Dr.	117
Stagg, William	107	Stones, Christopher	8, 96 : n. 41
Stagge, Alice	116	Stones, Joannam	41
Stainesby, Anne	56	Stones, Margaret	96
Stainesby, Henry	56	Stones, Margarett	8
Stainsby, Janam	42	Stoney, Andrew Robinson	24
Stainsby, Thomas	42	Stopes, Catherine	97
Stanhope, Anthony	89	Storey, Jonathan	120
Stanhope, Arthur	89	Stormont, Viscountess Louisa	81
Stanhope, Elizabeth	89	Story, Doroth.	52
Stanhope, Thomas	89	Story, Eliz.	52
Stanhope, Dr.	89	Story, Elizabetha'	39
Stapleton, Elizabeth	10	Story, Hen.	52
Stapylton, Miles	104 : n. 43, 114	Story, Marg.	50
Stapylton, —	10	Story, Robt.	52
Starkin, Garret	55	Stot, Anne	61
Starkin, Mary	55	Stothard, Barbara	38
Stawart, Jane	52	Stothard, Christopher	38
Stawart, John	52	Stothard, Frances	38

Stothard, Margaret	38
STOTHART, ANNE	65
STOTHART, THO.	65
STOTT, GEORGE	75
STOTT, JANE	76
STOTT, JOSEPH	68
STOTT, MARGARET	105
STOTT, MARY	68, 75
STOTT, TIMOTHY	105
Stott, —	67
STOUT, ABRAHAM	67
STOUT, ANN	67, 71
STOUT, JO.	71
STRAKER, FRANCES	70
STRAKER, NICHOLAS	70
Strathmore, John, Earl of	24
STUBBS, MARY	55
STUKELEY, JOHANNA	66
SUDALL, —	13
Sudbury, Anne	15
Sudbury, Bridget	15
Sudbury, Elizabeth	13, 14, 15
SUDBURY, JO., DEAN OF DURHAM	104
SUDBURY, JOH'E	15
Sudbury, John	15
Sudbury, Sir John	104
Sudbury, Dean	13, 14, 15
Sudbury, Lady	16
SUDDICK, CIPRIAN	1
SUDDICK, DR. GEORGE	1
Suddick, Michael	37
Suddick, Philip	1
Suddick, Richard	1
SUDDICKE, FRANCISCAM	37
SUGAR, ALICE	36
SUM'ERSIDE, JANE	64
SUMNER, GEORGE	87
Sumner, Dr. John Bird, Prebendary of Durham, Bishop of Chester, Archbishop of Canterbury	140
Sumner, Maria	30
Sumner, Marianne	30
SURAT, MARY	75
SURETIES, ANN	52, 61
SURETIES, HAUXLEY	52
Suretyes, Marian	39
Surtees, Catherine	52
Surtees, Crosier	157
Surtees, Deborah Maria	27
Surtees, Dorothy	157
Surtees, Edward	56
Surtees, Elizabeth	126
Surtees, Hauxley	52, 126
Surtees, Jane	56
Surtees, Robert	52, 56
Surtees, William	27
Surtees, —	2, 4, 8, 9, 11, 13, 15, 16, 17, 43, 44, 46, 50, 63, 74, 75, 82, 83, 85, 87, 88, 90, 92, 93, 96, 97, 103, 107, 111, 115, 116, 126, 127, 135, 140, 150.
SWAINESTON, EDEN	40
SWAINESTON, ROBERTUS	40
SWAINSTON, ALICE	62
Swainston, Frances	118
SWAINSTON, MARGARET	57
SWAINSTON, MARY	61
Swainston, Nicholas	118
SWAINSTON, ROBT.	61
SWAINSTON, THO.	62
SWALWELL, ELIZ.	65
SWALWELL, JANE	51

SWALWELL, ROBT.	65
Swift, Anne	87
SWINBORNE, TOBIAS	5
Swinburne, Elizabeth	8
SWINBURNE, MARG'TAM	41
Swinburne, Thomas	8
SWINSED, ELIZABETH	55
Swyft, Anna	84, 101
Swyft, Robert	84
Swyft, —	101
Symson, Eliz.	50
Talbot, Catherine	119
TALBOT, ELLENORAM	46
TALBOT, THO.	46
Talbot, William, Bishop of Durham	119
Talbot, Earl	119
Talbot, see also Shrewsbury and Talbot.	
TALENTINE, HANNAH	69
TALER, MARGARETT	95
TALER, WILLIAM	95
TARN, ALICE	58
Tarn, John	58
Tatam, Ann	110
Tatam, Robert	110
TAYLER, ELIZ.	71
TAYLER, MATHEW	96
TAYLER, MICH.	71
TAYLER, WILL	96
TAYLOR, ALICE	77
TAYLOR, ANN	67
TAYLOR, ANNE	61
TAYLOR, ANTHONY	69
Taylor, Barbara	109
TAYLOR, BARBARIAM	39
TAYLOR, CATHERINE	68
TAYLOR, ELIZ.	69, 70
Taylor, Frances Anne	22
Taylor, George	85
TAYLOR, GULIELMUS	39
TAYLOR, JANAM	40
Taylor, Bishop Jeremy	146
TAYLOR, JOCOSAM	44
TAYLOR, JOHAN'ES	44
TAYLOR, JOHANNES	14
TAYLOR, JOHANNIS	14
TAYLOR, JOHN	103 : n. 109
TAYLOR, JOYCE	113
TAYLOR, KATHERINE	114
Taylor, Margaret	58, 61, 70, 85
TAYLOR, MARGARETAM	39
TAYLOR, MARY	47, 67 : n. 109, 146
Taylor, Rt. Hon. Michael Angelo	22
TAYLOR, PETRUS	40
TAYLOR, RALPH	77
Taylor, Sir Robert	22
TAYLOR, RUTHAM	45
TAYLOR, SARAH	106
TAYLOR, THO.	47
TAYLOR, THOMAS	68 : n. 109
TAYLOR, WM.	61, 70
TAYLOR, WRIGHTINGTON	45
TAYLOUR, ISABELLA	49
TEASDAILE, ALICE	58
TEASDAILE, SARAH	50
Tempest, Bridget	15
Tempest, Elizabeth	8, 13, 14, 15
TEMPEST, ELIZABETHA	14
Tempest, Fitz-Herbert	18
Tempest, Frances	22
TEMPEST, FRANCIS	93

TEMPEST, GULIELMI	14
TEMPEST, GULIELMO	15
TEMPEST, GULIELMUS	13
Tempest, Isabel	2
TEMPEST, JOHN	8, 95 : n. 7, 22
Tempest, Margaret	7
TEMPEST, MARGARETT	7, 38
Tempest, Sir Nich.	2
Tempest, Sir Nicholas	93
TEMPEST, ROBERT	94, 95
Tempest, Rowland	93
TEMPEST, SIR THO.	93
Tempest, Thomas	93
TEMPEST, WILLIA'	95
Tempest, Col. William	8, 13, 14, 15, 18
TEMPEST, WMO.	14
TEMPEST, COL.	8
Tempest, see also Vane-Tempest.	
TEMPLE, REV. W. S.	133
THIN, STUARTA	6
THIN, THOM.E	6
Thistlethwayte, Tryphena	25
THOMAS, FREDERICK JOHN	30
THOMAS, REV. JOHN, CANON OF CANTERBURY	30
THOMAS, MARIA	30
Thomas, Thomas	30
THOMLINSON, ELIZ.	62
THOMLINSON, JANE.	78
THOMLINSON, JOSEPH.	78
THOMLINSON, RICHD.	62
Thomond, Henry, Earl of	48
Thompson, Agnes	27
THOMPSON, ALICIAM	36
THOMPSON, AN	38
THOMPSON, ANN	49, 60, 67 : n. 63
THOMPSON, ANNA'	41
THOMPSON, ANNE.	56
THOMPSON, ANTHONIUS	36
Thompson, Anthony	41
THOMPSON, BARBARA	48
THOMPSON, CATHERINE	144
Thompson, Rev. Christopher	63
THOMPSON, CUTHBERTUS	43
THOMPSON, ELIANOR	59
THOMPSON, ELIZ.	40, 43, 48
THOMPSON, ELLENORAM	45
THOMPSON, ELLINOR	97
THOMPSON, EZEKIEL	52
THOMPSON, FRANCES	58
THOMPSON, GEORGE	58
THOMPSON, GRACE	67
THOMPSON, GULIELMS.	43
THOMPSON, GULIELMUS	45
THOMPSON, HANNAH	55
THOMPSON, HENRY	72
THOMPSON, JANAM	44
THOMPSON, JANE	67
THOMPSON, JOHN	38, 67
THOMPSON, REV. JOHN	144
THOMPSON, LUCIE	43
THOMPSON, MARGARET	122 : n. 41, 46
THOMPSON, MARGAR'TAM	46
THOMPSON, MARGT.	72
THOMPSON, MARY	67
THOMPSON, MICHAEL	60
THOMPSON, RICHARD	70
THOMPSON, ROB.	67
Thompson, Robert	46
THOMPSON, ROBERTUS	46
THOMPSON, SARAH	52, 70

THOMPSON, SUSAN	47
THOMPSON, THOMAS	101
Thompson, William	27
Thompson, —	36
THOMSON, ANN	77
THOMSON, ANNAM	39
THOMSON, THOMAS	77
Thomson, —	86
THORNEWILL, ELIZA ARABELLA SARAH	79
THORNEWILL, ROBERT	79
THORNTON, HANNAH	55
Thornton, John	148
Thornton, Margaret	55
Thornton, Mary	148
THORNTON, REV. ROBERT	107
Thornton, Roger	55
Thorp, Ann	116
THORP, C., PREBENDARY OF DURHAM	140
THORP, CHARLES, ARCHDEACON OF DURHAM	144
Thorp, Charles, Archdeacon and Prebendary of Durham	30, 31
THORP, CHARLES, PREBENDARY OF DURHAM	136
Thorp, Charles, D.D., Archdeacon and Canon of Durham	158
Thorp, Elizabeth	31, 158
Thorp, Frances	30
THORP, ARCHDEACON	141
Thorpe, Archdeacon	157
THUMBLE, BARBARA	70
Thwaites, —	134, 155
THWING, ELIZABETH	95
Thynne, Maria	37
THYNNE, STEWARTAM	37
Thynne, Thomas	37
THYNNE, SIR THOMAS	37
Thynne, —, Marquess of Bath	37
Tilly, Ann	135
Tilly, Anthony	135
Tilly, Elizabeth	135
Tilly, Sarah	135
Tilson, Grace	25
Tilson, Thomas	25
TINDALL, MARIAM	44
Tinkler, Barbara	151
Tinkler, Elizabeth	151
Tinkler, James	151
TINKLER, JOHN	96 : n. 151
Tinkler, Mary	151
TIPLADY, JANE.	49
TIPLADY, JO.	49
TODD, ANN	62
TODD, ANTHONY	52
TODD, BARBARA	70
TODD, CHRISTIAN.	71
TODD, DOROTH.	52
TODD, DOROTHY	73
TODD, ELIZ.	50
TODD, ELLENORA'	42
TODD, ISABEL	52
TODD, ISABELL	62
TODD, JANA'	42
TODD, JANE	68
TODD, JOH'ES	42
TODD, JOHN	70
TODD, REV. JOHN, MINOR CANON OF DURHAM	88
TODD, MARK	8
TODD, ROBERT	73
TODD, THO.	62

Todd, Thomas	71	Tristram, Thomas Barrington	28
Todd, Timosin	88	Trotter, Anne	84
Todd, William	8	Trotter, Catherine	84
Todde, Barbariam	38	Trotter, Ellenora'	43
Todde, Richardus	38	Trotter, Hannah	55
Toe, Joh'es	42	Trotter, Henrietta	133
Toe, Mariam	42	Trotter, Jane	62
Toft, Thomas	88	Trotter, Thomas	55
Toft, Timosin	88	Trotter, William	84, 133
Tomlins, Anne	137	Trowlop, Elizabeth	74
Tomlins, Emily	137	Tuart, Dorothy	51
Tomlins, James	137	Tuart, Lamerick	51
Tomlins, Thomas	137	Tucker, Annam	41
Tompson, Jane	90	Tucker, Thomas	41
Tonge, Ezechell	94	Tuke, Edith Mary	158
Tonge, Ezerell	7	Tuke, Kate	158
Tonge, Jane	7, 94	Tunstall, Francis	82
Toong, Sir George	3	Turnbull, Andrew	71
Topham, Dorothy	77	Turnbull, Ann	71
Topham, Wm.	77	Turner, Ann	126
Torrington, Viscount	134	Turner, Bryan	71, 74, 120 : *n.* 124, 129
Touchet, George, Earl Audley	37	Turner, Rev. Bryan	120 : *n.* 126
Touchet, Maria	37	Turner, Eliz.	69
Toward, Anne	62	Turner, Elizabeth	120, 124 : *n.* 51
Toward, Eliz.	72	Turner, Jane	129
Toward, Geo.	72	Turner, John	51
Toward, Jo.	62	Turner, Joseph	68
Toward, Mary	62	Turner, Marg.	51
Townsend, Charles John Henry Fyler	30	Turner, Margaret	114
Townsend. Charlotte Charlton	149	Turner, Mary	63
Townsend, Charlotte Constance Spenser	30	Turner, Rutham	45
Townsend, Elizabeth	138	Turner, Theophila	51
Townsend, G., Prebendary of Durham	137, 139, 142	Turner, Will.	51
		Turner. William	114 : *n.* 51
Townsend, Rev. G.	29	Turner, Rev. Dr. William	51
Townsend, Rev. G., Canon of Durham	142	Turner, William Parthericke	51
Townsend, Rev. G., Prebendary of Durham	138, 140, 141	Turner, Rev. William Parthericke, Minor Canon of Durham	114
Townsend, Geo.	147	Turner, Rev. Wm.	114
Townsend, Rev. George	149	Turner, Wm. Parthericke	65, 116
Townsend, Rev. George, Prebendary of Durham	79	Turvey, Martha	121
		Turvill, Andrew	9
Townsend, Rev. George, D.D., Canon of Durham	30, 149	Turvill, Elias	9
		Tweddell, Joh'es	41
Townsend, George Charlton Leugers Barnard	30	Tweddell, Margaretam	41
		Tyler, Agnes	27
Townsend, Rev. George Fyler	30 : *n.* 149	Tyler, Anne	36
Townsend, Georgina	30	Tyler, Anthony	27, 28, 145
Townsend, Georgina Elizabeth Frances	30	Tyler, Anthy.	27
Townsend, Henrietta Marian	30	Tyler, Charles	28
Townsend, James Frederick	30	Tyler, Edwin	27, 155
Townsend, Rev. James Frederick	142 : *n.* 149	Tyler, Elizabeth	27, 28, 151 : *n.* 145
		Tyler, Emma	28
Townsend, John	149	Tyler, Phyllis	27
Townsend, Mabel Surtees	30	Tyler, Susannah	27
Townsend, Mary Susan	149	Tyler, Tho.	36
Townsend, Stephen Chapman	30	Tyler, Thomas	86
Townsend, Susannah	149	Tyler, William	28, 133
Townsend, Dr.	152	Tyndall, Janam	42
Townshend, Viscount Charles	124	Tynte, Sir Hugh	47
Trear, Anne	57	Tynte, Penelope	47
Trear, John	57		
Trevor, Bishop	21	Ubanke, Philadelphia	4
Tristram, Caroline	28	Ushaw, Anne	56
Tristram, Christina	79	Usher, Mary	71
Tristram, Frances Eliza	34		
Tristram, Rev. H. B., Canon of Durham	34, 156, 157, 158, 159	Van Mildert, Cornelins	138
		Van Mildert, Jane	139 : *n.* 138
Tristram, Rev. Henry Baker, Canon of Durham	79 : *n.* 34	Van Mildert, Martha	138
		Van Mildert, William, D.D., Bishop of Durham	138, 139
Tristram, Mary Gertrude	34		

Van Mildert, Bishop	149
VANE, ANN.	66
VANE, FRANCES	22
Vane, Lady Frances	12
VANE, FRANCES ANNE	22
VANE, GEO.	66
Vane, George	8
VANE, HENRY	22
VANE, REV. DR. SIR HENRY, PREBENDARY OF DURHAM	22
Vane, Rev. Sir Henry	66
Vane, Hester	8
Vane, Lionel	66
Vane, Thomas	12
Vane, D'na	12
Vane-Tempest, Anne Katherine, Countess of Antrim	22
Vane-Tempest, Frances Anne Emily	22
Vane-Tempest, Sir Henry	22
Vasey, Ann.	71
Vasey, Joan	36
Vasey, John	36
Vasie, Aurelius	49
Vasie, Mary	49
Vasie, Phœbe	49
Vasie, Thomas	49
VASIUS, FRANCISCAM	36
VASIUS, JOHANNES	36
Vavasseur-dit-Durell, see Le Vavasseur-dit-Durell.	
Vernon, Caroline Maria	81
Vernon. Hon. George John, Lord	81
Vernon, Isabella Caroline	81
VINER, —	5
VIPONT, JANAM	44
VIPONT, REBEC'	64
Vipont, Thomas	44
Vipont, William	44
W., E. A. 2, 6, 10, 11, 19, 23, 30, 31, 39, 58, 61, 65, 71, 72, 76, 78, 93, 97, 110, 112, 113, 114, 118, 120, 122, 123, 125, 126, 127, 128, 130, 134, 137, 138, 139, 140, 141, 143, 144, 145, 146, 147, 148, 149, 150, 151, 152, 153, 154, 155, 156, 157, 159.	
Waddell, Archibald	2
Waddell, Elizabeth	2
Waddington, Ann	155
Waddington, Anne	155
Waddington, Rev. George	155
WADDINGTON, REV. GEORGE, D.D., DEAN OF DURHAM 30, 140, 142, 145, 149, 151, 152, 155	
Waddington, Rt. Hon. Horatio	155
Waddington, Rev. Joshua	155
Waddington, M.	155
Waddington, William	155
Waddington, Dean	154
Waddington, Dr., Dean of Durham	1
Waiklinge, Jane	94
Waiklinge, Rev. Richard	94
WAINWRIGHT, ANN.	52
WAINWRIGHT, THO.	52
WAISTELL, ALICE	50
WAISTELL, CHRISTOPHER	56
WAISTELL, JOHN	50
WAISTELL, MARG'TAM	43
WAISTELL, SARAH	56
WAITE, ARTHUR	33
WAITE, JOHN HUMBLE	144
WAITE, REV. JOSEPH	33 ; n. 144
Waite, Rev. Joseph, D.D., Canon of Newcastle	144, 156
WAITE, ROSAMOND	33, 157 ; n. 156
WAITE, WILLOUGHBY	156
WAKE, ELLENOR	48
WAKE, JANE	52
WAKE, MARY	66
WAKE, THO.	66
WAKE, THOMAS	48
WAKELIN, RICH.	109
Waldegrave, Edward	47
Waldegrave, Jemima	47
WALES, JACOBUS	43
WALES, MARG'TAM	43
WALKER, AN.	38
WALKER, ANN	126
WALKER, CHRISTOPHER	124
WALKER, ELIZ.	70
WALKER, FRANCIS	118, 121
WALKER, JAMES	70
WALKER, MARG.	51
WALKER, MARY	57, 130
WALKER, THOMAS	118
WALKER, WILLM.	126
WALL, ELIZ.	49
Wall, Elizabeth	51
WALL, GEO.	56
WALL, MARIAM	46
WALL, MARY	56
WALL, RICHARDUS	46
Wallace, Ambrose	130
WALLACE, ANN	130, 139, 140 ; n. 132, 134
WALLACE, ELIZABETH	130 ; n. 139
Wallace, Jabez	144
WALLACE, JAMES	130, 142, 144 ; n. 132, 139
WALLACE, JANE	145
Wallace, Lucy	134
Wallace, Mary Ann	132
WALLACE, ROBERT	134
Wallace, —	131
WALLASS, MARG.	52
Waller, Gartrett	14
WALLICE, AMBROSE	128
WALLICE, ANN	128
WALLIS, DOROTHY	76
WALLIS, JOSEPH	76
Walpole, Sir Robert	124
Walpole, —	124
Walsh, Barbara	72
WALSH, REBECCAM	42
Walsham-How, Dr. William, Bishop of Wakefield	151
Walsham-How, —	151
WALTER, MARGARETT	83
WALTER, THOMAS	83
WALTON, ANN	72
WALTON, ANNE	53 ; n. 92
WALTON, BARBARA	48
WALTON, ELIANOR	71
WALTON, ELIZ.	64
WALTON, FRANCIS	88
WALTON, GEO.	2
Walton, George	92
Walton, Hugh	37, 88
WALTON, ISABELL	55, 62
WALTON, JANE	48
WALTON, JO.	62
WALTON, JOHN	7, 37
WALTON, MARY	71
WALTON, MARYE	37
WALTON, MICHAEL	71

Walton, Nicholas	112	WATSON, JO.	48
WALTON, REV. NICHOLAS	88	WATSON, JOHN	106 : n. 48
WALTON, WILLIAM	71	WATSON, MARG'TAM	40
WALTON, WM.	55	WATSON, MARGT.	66
WALTON, —	96	WATSON, MARIAM	41
Wandless, Edward	102	WATSON, MARY	48, 52, 53, 59, 66
Wandless, Thomas	102	WATSON, RUTH	73
WANLESS, JANE	62	WATSON, SARAH	52 : n. 110
WANLESSE, JANE	55	WATSON, SARAM	42
WANLESSE, WILLIAM	55	WATSON, SUZANNA	50
Warburton, —	155	WATSON, THO.	62
WARCUP, JANE	59	WATSON, THOMAS	39, 59
WARD, ANN	59	WATSON, WILLIAM	52, 76
WARD, ANNAM	41	WATSON, WINIFRED	74
WARD, CATHERINA'	38	WATSON, WM.	66
WARD, CHRISTOPHERUS	38	WATT, JANE	75
WARD, FRANCISCA'	43	WATT, PETER	75
Ward, Sarah	131	WATTS, CATHERINE	54
WARD, THOMAS	41	WATTS, MARY	121
Ward, —	131	WATTS, DR. WILLIAM, PREBENDARY OF DURHAM	119
Wardell, Christopher	123	
Wardell, Elizabeth	123	WATTS, REV. DR., PREBENDARY OF DURHAM	121
WARDLE, ELIZABETH	123	
WARING, BARBARA	18	WAUGH, ANN	46, 70
WARING, JNO.	18	WAUGH, ANNA'	41
WARING, JO.	62, 116	WAUGH, ELIZABETH	118
WARING, JOHN	18, 116	WAUGH, RICH'US	41
Waring, Rev. John	118	WEAMS, ANN	73
WARING, REV. JOHN, MINOR CANON OF DURHAM	18	Wearmouth, Mary	61
		WEBSTER, HAN.	48
WARING, MARGARETT	118	WEBSTER, JANE	64
WARING, —	71, 72, 73, 74	WEBSTER, JOHN	64, 66
Warren, Elizabeth	19	WEBSTER, MARG'TAM	42
WARREN, ISABEL	67	WEBSTER, ROB'TUS	42
Warren, Joyce	19	WEBSTER, SUSANNA	66
WARREN, RICHARD	67 : n. 19	Webster, William	48
WASCOE, ELIZ.	67	WEDDELL, JANE	73
WASCOE, JOHN	67	WEEMS, JANE	57
Watkin, Anna Maria	127	WEERES, JANE	101
WATKIN, REV. JOSEPH, MINOR CANON OF DURHAM	127	WEERES, THO.	101
		WEGG, SAMUEL	132
WATKIN, MARTHA	127	WEGG, SARAH	132
Watkin, Mary	72	Wegg-Prosser, Francis Richard	129
Watkin, Samuel	72	Welbury, Elizabeth	13
WATKINS, DOROTHY KATE GWYLLYAM	34	WELFOOT, FRANCISCAM	43
WATKINS, GWENDOLEN EDITH GWYLLYAM	35	WELFOOT, ROB'TUS	43
		WELFOOTE, GEORGE	50
WATKINS, HELEN MARGARET GWYLLYAM	34	WELFOOTE, JANE	50
		Wellesley, Anne, Countess of Mornington	145
WATKINS, HENRY WILLIAM, ARCHDEACON OF DURHAM	34, 35	Wellesley, Emily Ann Charlotte	142
		Wellesley, Lady Emily Mary	145
WATKINS, KATE MARY MARGARET	34, 35	Wellesley, Garret or Garrett, Earl of Mornington	145
Wats, Dr. William, Prebendary of Durham	119	
		WELLESLEY, HON. REV. GERALD VALERIAN, D.D., CANON OF DURHAM	29, 145
WATSON, ALICE	66 : n. 92	
WATSON, ANN	52 : n. 48	Wellesley, Mary Sarah	79
WATSON, ANTHONIUS	41	WELLESLEY, DR., PREBENDARY OF DURHAM	142
WATSON, DOROTHY	52, 74	
WATSON, ELIANOR	64	WELLESLEY, HON. REV. DR.	79
WATSON, ELIZABETH	58	Wellington, Duke of	145
WATSON, ELIZABETHAM	40	Wells, Alice	152
Watson, George	90	WELLS, MARIAM	43
WATSON, GULIELMUS	40	Wells, Samuel	152
WATSON, HANNAH	76	WELSFORD, MARY	64
WATSON, HESTER	46	WELSH, ANNAM	39
WATSON, HUGH	46	WELSH, MICHAEL	39
WATSON, ISABELLA	42	WENNINGTON, ANNE	56
WATSON, ISABELLAM	39	WERDON, JANE	105
WATSON, JAMES	74	WERDON, MARY	105
WATSON, JANE	59, 62 : n. 46	WERDON, WILLIAM	111
Watson, Jayne	83	WERDON, WM.	105

INDEX. 209

WERE, THOMAS	107
WEST, ANTHONY	95
WEST, GEORGE	57
WEST, MARGARET	57
WEST, WILLIA'	95
WESTGARTH, SARAM	39
WESTGARTH, THOMAS	39
WESTMORELAND, MARIA'	44
Weston, Arabella	22
Weston, Charles, Prebendary of Durham	124
WESTON, CHARLES, PREBENDARY OF DURHAM, ARCHDEACON OF WILTS	22, 23
Weston, Prebendary Charles	26
Weston, Charlotte	124
WESTON, CHL.	124
WESTON, EDWARD	22
Weston, John	126
WESTON, PENELOPE ANN	23
WESTON, DR. PHIPPS, PREBENDARY OF DURHAM	126 ; n. 124
Weston, Rev. Phipps	126
WESTON, REV. —, PREBENDARY OF DURHAM	124
Weston, —	124
WETHERELL, ALICE	63
Wetherell, Anne	45
Wetherell, Cornelius	76, 78
Wetherell, Eleanor	143, 145
Wetherell, Elizabeth	45
Wetherell, Giles	45
WETHERELL, HENRY	76
Wetherell, Margaret	76
WETHERELL, MARGT.	78
WETHERELL, MARY	76
WETHERELL, NATHAN, DEAN OF HEREFORD	78
Wetherell, Richard	145
Wetherell, Richard, Dean of Hereford	143
Wetherell, Dean	96
WEYBRIDGE, JOHN	76
WEYBRIDGE, MARGARET	76
WHARRAM, ELLENORA'	42
WHARRAM, GULIELM'S	42
WHARTON, JOHN LLOYD, M.P.	80
WHARTON, MARY DOROTHEA	80
WHATELY, ARCHBISHOP	146
WHEAT, CATHERINE	65
WHEAT, ROBT.	65
WHEATHEY, JANAM	40
WHEATLEY, ANN	68
WHEATLEY, DOROTHY	60
WHEATLEY, GEORGE	73
WHEATLEY, MARTHA	62
WHEATLEY, MARY	73
WHEATLEY, THOMAS	68
WHEATLY, ANN	60
WHEATLY, MARGT.	64
WHEELRIGHT, JANE	59
WHEELRIGHT, JOSEPH	59
WHEERS, ELIZABETHA	3
WHEERS, JOHANNIS	3
WHELDELL, EMMETTAM	42
WHELDELL, PARCIVALLUS	42
WHELDON, ELIZABETHAM	40
WHELDON, HENRICUS	40
Wheler, Anne	117
WHELER, BRAEMS	75
Wheler, Col ·Charles	117
WHELER, FRANCES	73
WHELER, SIR GEO.	112
WHELER, SIR GEO., PREBENDARY OF DURHAM	117
WHELER, SIR GEORGE	115
Wheler, Rev. Sir George, Prebendary of Durham	18, 122
Wheler, Grace	117
WHELER, HIGGONS	112
WHELER, JANE	115
Wheler, Judith	18, 122
WHELER, MARY	75
WHETHERELL, ALICE	63
WHETHERELL, ROBT.	63
WHIGHT, JOAN	64
WHITAKER, CHARLES	120
WHITAKER, ELIZABETH	120
WHITAKER, GRACE	122
WHITE, ANN	75
White, Anne	90
WHITE, FRANCISCAM	39
WHITE, ISABELLAM	46
WHITE, JOHANNES	46
WHITE, MARGARET	38
WHITE, MARY	156 ; n. 90, 140
WHITE, ROBERT	75
WHITE, THOMAS	75, 98, 157 ; n. 140
White, —	90
WHITFEILD, ELIZABETH	49
WHITFEILD, OSYTHA	73
WHITFEILD, ROBERT	73
WHITFIELD, ELIANOR	71
Whitfield, Elizabeth	73
WHITFIELD, MARY	69
Whitfield, Matthew	73
Whitfield, Osith	73
Whitfield, Robert	59
WHITFIELD, WM.	69
WHITHEAD, MARGT.	63
WICKLIFFE, FRANCIS	100
Widdifield, John	26
Widdifield, Matthew	26
Wikelin, Ann	94
Wikelin, Barbara	94
Wikelin, Elizabeth	94
Wikelin, Jane	94
Wikelin, Richard	94
WIKELIN, REV. RICHARD, MINOR CANON OF DURHAM	94 : n. 109
Wikelin, Thomas	94
WILD, ELISABETH	61
Wildbore, Franciscam	37
Wildbore, Rev. Gilbert	37
Wildbore, Robert	124
Wildbore, Ursula	124
WILDE, ANTHONY	48
WILDE, DOROTHY	48
Wilde, Mary	48
WILKIN, ABIGAIL	72
WILKINSON, ALICE	58
WILKINSON, ANDREÆ	14
WILKINSON, ANDREAS	44
WILKINSON, ANN	76
WILKINSON, ANNAM	44
Wilkinson, Anne	141
WILKINSON, ANTHONY	70 : n. 132
WILKINSON, CATHERINA'	43
WILKINSON, CATHERINE	72
WILKINSON, DEBORAH	70
WILKINSON, DOROTHEAM	46
WILKINSON, DOROTHY	68, 113
WILKINSON, ELIZ.	72
WILKINSON, ELIZABETH	73 : n. 76, 123, 132

E E

WILKINSON, ELLENORAM	45
WILKINSON, FRANCES	61 : n. 87
WILKINSON, ISABEL	69
WILKINSON, JANE	53, 61 ; n. 90
WILKINSON, JO.	61
WILKINSON, JOHAN'ES	14
WILKINSON, JOHN	68, 72, 74 : n. 141
WILKINSON, MARGARET	54 : n. 58, 61, 70
WILKINSON, MARGT.	66
Wilkinson, Martin	76
WILKINSON, MARY	58, 63, 68, 74, 76
WILKINSON, RADULP.	46
WILKINSON, RALPH	113
Wilkinson, Richard	123
WILKINSON, ROBERT	50, 76
WILKINSON, ROWLAND	53
WILKINSON, SUZANNA	50
WILKINSON, THO.	61
WILKINSON, THOMAS	54, 58
WILKINSON, WILL.	72
Wilkinson, William	58, 61, 70
WILLANS, JOHN	67
WILLANS, MARY	67
WILLCOCKS, ELIZ.	49
WILLCOCKS, JOHN	49
WILLIAMS, ALYN ARTHUR	34
WILLIAMS, CATHERINE	34
WILLIAMS, MARY ELIZABETH	34
WILLIAMS, RICHARD HOWARD	34
WILLIAMS, REV. SAMUEL BLACKWELL GUEST	34
WILLIAMS, WARREN KIRKHAM	34
WILLIAMS, WYNNE AUSTIN	34
Williamson, Ann	85
WILLIAMSON, CATHERINE	76
WILLIAMSON, FRANCES	70
WILLIAMSON, JOSEPH	47
WILLIAMSON, MARGARETAM	39
WILLIAMSON, MARY	47 : n. 58
WILLIAMSON, REV. WILLIAM, MINOR CANON OF DURHAM	76
Williamson, Sir William	58
WILLIAMSON, —	76
Williamson, *see also* Hopper-Williamson.	
WILLIAMSTONE, JOSEPH	40
WILLIAMSTONE, MARGARETAM	40
Willis, Browne	83, 89
WILLIS, EDWARD	53
WILLIS, ELIZABETH	53, 77
WILLOWS, ELIZ.	72
WILLSON, ANN	76
WILLSON, DOROTHY	72
WILLSON, MARY	76
WILLSON, ROBT.	72
WILLSON, SUSANNA	74
WILSBY, HANNAH	49
WILSBY, JAMES	49
Wilsher, Dorothy	15
Wilshere, Mary	15
WILSON, AGNAS	26
WILSON, ALICE	56
WILSON, ALLAN AYLMER	34
WILSON, ANN	49
WILSON, ANNAM	41, 45 ; n. 39
WILSON, ANNE LOUISA	34
WILSON, BARBARA'	42
Wilson, Bridget	15, 16
WILSON, BRIGIDA	16
Wilson, Caroline	136
WILSON, CATH.	116
WILSON, DOROTHEAM	38

WILSON, ELIZ.	55, 65
WILSON, ELIZABETH	57 : n. 15
WILSON, GULIELMI	15, 16
WILSON, GULIELMS	42
WILSON, HENRY	59
WILSON, IS.	65
WILSON, JANAM	40
WILSON, JANE	49, 56, 58, 73
WILSON, JOHAN'ES	15
Wilson, John	104
WILSON, JOHN GEORGE	34
WILSON, MARGARET	59
WILSON, MARGARETAM	40
WILSON, MARIA	42
WILSON, MARIA'	42
WILSON, MARY	50, 52, 60, 106 : n. 15
WILSON, REBECCA	50
WILSON, RICH'US	42
WILSON, RICHARD	26 : n. 15
WILSON, RICHARDUS	40
WILSON, ROBERTUS	39
WILSON, ROGER	49, 57
WILSON, SUDBURY	110 : n. 15
WILSON, THO.	65
WILSON, TIMOTHEUS	96
WILSON, WILL.	50
WILSON, WILLIAM	73, 106 : n. 110
WILSON, WM.	106
Wilson, *see also* Fountayne-Wilson.	
WILTON, JOHN	132
Winship, William	57
WINSHIPP, ELIZ.	67
WINSHIPP, MARY	57, 68
WINSHIPP, WELBERY	67
Woldrige, James	86
Woldrige, Rev. —	86
Wolfe, Caroline	136
WOLFE, ELIZABETH	143 : n. 131, 148, 151
Wolfe, John	136, 143 : n. 77, 131, 148, 151
WOLFE, MARGARET	77
Wolfe, Margaret Pearson	131, 151
WOLFE, ROBERT	77 : n. 136
Wolfe, —	134, 135
WOOD, ANDREW	68
Wood, Ann	24
WOOD, ELIZ.	54
WOOD, ELIZABETH	38, 49 : n. 146
WOOD, ELIZABETHAM	39
WOOD, FRANCIS	54
WOOD, HANNAH	76
WOOD, ISABEL	118
WOOD, JANE	68
WOOD, JOH'IS	16
WOOD, JOHAN'ES	16
WOOD, JOHAN'IS	15
Wood, John	24, 118
WOOD, MARG'TAM	42
WOOD, ROBERTUS	15
WOOD, THO.	49
WOOD, WILLIA'	38
Wood, —	87
Woodger, Elizabeth	17
WOODIFIELD, ANN	26
WOODIFIELD, ELIZABETH	26, 135
WOODIFIELD, HANNAH	26
WOODIFIELD, JAMES	26
WOODIFIELD, MATTHEW	26, 135, 146
Woodifield, Robert	26
WOODIFIELD, SARAH	146
Woodifield, —	129, 130, 132 : n. 136
WOODMAS, ELIZABETH	59

INDEX.

WOODMAS, FRANCISCUS	108	Wyndham, John	123
WOODMAS, JOSEPH	59	Wyndham, Sir Wadham	123
Wooler, Anthony	59	Wytham, Doritye	95
Wooler, Elizabeth	59	Wytham, George	95
WOOLER, ISABEL	59	Wyvill, Sir Christopher	45
Wooler, Jane	127	WYVILL, MARGARETA'	45
WOOLER, JONATHAN	59	Wyvill, Ursula	45
Wooler, Joseph Snaith	127	WYVILL, XPOFERUS, D.D., DEAN OF	
Worley, John	86	RIPPON	45
Worley, Timothy	86		
Worlich, George	86		
WORLICH, JAMES	86	YAP, ABRA.	47, 108
Worlich, John	86	YAP, ABRAHAM	108
WORLICH, REV. —	86	YAP, ANN	47
Wrangham, Jane	82	YAP, JANE	108
WRAY, ANN	59	YAPE, JOHANNIS	11
WRAY, JACOB	59	YAPE, MARIA	11
WREN, ANN	72	YAPP, ABRA.	48, 49, 111, 113
WREN, BARBARA	6	YAPP. REV. ABRA.	109, 119
Wren, Charles	87	YAPP, ABRAHAM, MINOR CANON OF DUR-	
Wren, Peregrina	87	HAM	118
Wren, Thomas	72	Yapp, Rev. Abraham	107
WRENCH, AN	37	YAPP, REV. ABM.	117
WRENCH, RICHARD, PREBENDARY OF		YAPP, ANN	117, 119
DURHAM	37	YAPP, BARBARA	109
WRENCH, RICHARDUS, PREBENDARY OF		YAPP, ELIZABETH	74
DURHAM	97	YAPP, ELLENOR	111, 112, 116
WRIGHT, ALICIAM	40	YAPP, JACOBUS	13
WRIGHT, ANN	66	YAPP, JANA	11, 97
Wright, Dorothy	46	YAPP, JOH'ES	97
WRIGHT, ELIZ.	57	YAPP, JOH'IS	11, 13, 97
Wright, Elizabeth	91	YAPP, JOHN	111, 113 : n. 107
WRIGHT, ELIZABETHAM	39	YAPP, MARY	47, 112 : n. 109
WRIGHT, GULIELMUS	39	YAPP, THOMAS	111
WRIGHT, ISABELLA	125	YAPP, WILLIAM	113
WRIGHT, JANE	91 : n. 4, 86, 88, 89	YAPPE, ELLENOR	38
WRIGHT, JOHANNES	36, 40	YAPPE, JOHN	38, 107
WRIGHT, JOHANNIS	89	YARROW, GIBSON	129
WRIGHT, JOHN	142 : n. 91	YARROW, ANN	59
WRIGHT, MARG.	51	YARROW, PERCIVAL	59
WRIGHT, MARGARET	125	Yelverton, Anne	45
Wright, Margrett	101	Yelverton, Sir Christopher	45
Wright, Mary	91	York, Mary, Duchess of	47
WRIGHT, OSYTHA	73	York, Duke of	47
WRIGHT, RICHARDUS	88	YOUNG, AGNETEM	43
WRIGHT, S.	125	YOUNG, JOHN	55
WRIGHT, SARAM	36	YOUNG, LUCYE	55
WRIGHT, THO.	57	YOUNG, MARY	46, 55, 59
WRIGHT, THOMA	4	YOUNG, ROBT.	55
WRIGHT, THOMÆ	88, 89	Young, Admiral Sir William	131
WRIGHT, THOMAS	91 : n. 86, 88	Younghusband, Edward	78
WRIGHT, WILL.	51	Younghusband, Hannah	78
Wright, —	73	Younghusband, Susannah	78
WRIGHTE, JANE	86		
WRIGHTE, THOMAS	86		
WYCKLIFFE, ANN	58	Zouch, Isabella	128
Wykeham, William of	21	ZOUCH, DR.	128
Wyndham, Alice	123	Zouch, —	128

London: Mitchell and Hughes, Printers, 140 Wardour Street, W.

www.ingramcontent.com/pod-product-compliance
Lightning Source LLC
Chambersburg PA
CBHW031830230426
43669CB00009B/1299